Constructions of Neoliberal Reason

Constructions of Neoliberal Reason

Jamie Peck

OXFORD
UNIVERSITY PRESS

OXFORD
UNIVERSITY PRESS

Great Clarendon Street, Oxford OX2 6DP

Oxford University Press is a department of the University of Oxford.
It furthers the University's objective of excellence in research, scholarship,
and education by publishing worldwide in

Oxford New York

Auckland Cape Town Dar es Salaam Hong Kong Karachi
Kuala Lumpur Madrid Melbourne Mexico City Nairobi
New Delhi Shanghai Taipei Toronto

With offices in

Argentina Austria Brazil Chile Czech Republic France Greece
Guatemala Hungary Italy Japan Poland Portugal Singapore
South Korea Switzerland Thailand Turkey Ukraine Vietnam

Oxford is a registered trade mark of Oxford University Press
in the UK and in certain other countries

Published in the United States
by Oxford University Press Inc., New York

© Jamie Peck 2010

The moral rights of the author have been asserted
Database right Oxford University Press (maker)

First published 2010

British Library Cataloguing in Publication Data

Data available

Library of Congress Cataloging in Publication Data

Data available

Typeset by SPI Publisher Services, Pondicherry, India
Printed in Great Britain
on acid-free paper by
MPG Books Group, Bodmin and King's Lynn

ISBN 978–0–19–958057–6

1 3 5 7 9 10 8 6 4 2

For Bryony, Holly, and Hannah

Contents

Tables

Figures

Boxes

Preface

The form of market fundamentalism that we have come to know as *neoliberalism* has been the work of many hands, a lot of them hidden. A half-century in the making, the free-market revolution gained traction as a political project during the macroeconomic crisis years of the 1970s and 1980s, before establishing an increasingly stubborn global grip. Its ideology of pro-market governance has, in subsequent decades, become increasingly normalized, even as it has faced escalating crises of its own making. In the aftermath of the made-in-Wall-Street crisis of 2008 and the period of global economic turbulence that followed, the project of deregulation and liberalization was again brought starkly into question, only to be reconsolidated, almost by default, through a series of pragmatic accommodations. Business as almost-usual is apparently being restored, albeit with Washington and Wall Street sutured together as never before, and with Beijing, of all places, being amongst the new capitals calling the shots on global market integration.

It might be said about dominant policy paradigms like neoliberalism that it can be difficult to think *about* them when it has become so commonplace to think *with* them. The conventional wisdom can seem ubiquitous, inevitable, natural, and all-encompassing. To many, neoliberalism has become practically indistinguishable from the alleged "logic" of globalization—it seems to be everywhere, and it seems to be all that there is. *Constructions of Neoliberal Reason* proposes a fresh way of looking at the free-market revolution, asking where it came from and where it continues to come from. It does so by bringing neoliberalism to earth, countering the (prevalent) understanding of neoliberalism as a shorthand term for the ideological atmosphere. Instead, a sustained focus is placed on some of the diverse ways that the project has been made and remade, through the twentieth century and into the twenty-first, in ideational, ideological, and institutional terms. This means tracking the project's uneven and uncertain progress, from its inauspicious beginnings as a reactionary cult, through its moments of vanguardist advance, to its effective mainstreaming as a restructuring ethos and as an adaptive form of regulatory practice.

This is not, then, a broad-brush account of neoliberalism as a global regulatory architecture, imposed from above, or as a metaphor for the ideological air that we all (must) breathe. Neither does it invoke neoliberalism as a summary label, to be applied to particular politicians, policy techniques, or parts of the world. Rather, it is a story of the never-inevitable ascendancy of neoliberal*ization,* as an open-ended and contradictory process of politically assisted market rule. This is no bloodless, semi-automatic process, but the work of situated social actors, who along the way displayed just about every human flaw, coupled with a share of vision and determination. The book's goal is to convey some sense of the neoliberal project as a lived phenomenon, with an insistent focus on some of its central protagonists, while also documenting some of its out-of-character moments and more banal manifestations. It sets out to denaturalize neoliberalism by calling attention to its socially produced form, tracking the project to some of its "natural" settings but also into sites where it is "out of place." The concern here is not merely to reiterate the big picture (or big N) story of neoliberalism,[1] in broad political-economic strokes, nor to propose some contingent or "bottom up" alternative, but to elaborate an explanation complementary to more structural accounts, one that keep agents and agency in sight. This is not a vision of a neoliberal world from 30,000 feet, but one located much closer to the ground—close enough to see the whites of the protagonists' eyes, if you will. The purpose is not merely to add "color," or dramatized subjects, to extant accounts, but to shed light on some of the spaces in which neoliberalism has been made and remade, as a *constructed* project.

If neoliberalization were simply a matter of imposing a Hayekian blueprint, or stepping back to enable markets to work their magic, there would be no need for a book like this. Far from being predestined, the free-market revolution looks in retrospect to have been a rather improbable achievement. Its pioneers were initially guided only by their shared distaste for what they saw as the totalizing tendencies of the Leviathan state. This was associated with a near-paranoid worldview: the wide-eyed advocates of the market often had an almost phobic reaction to the state and stat*ism.* As Alvin Hansen wrote in his rebuttal of Friedrich von Hayek's *Road to Serfdom,* one of the movement's foundational scripts, in 1945, "This . . . is not scholarship. It is seeing hobgoblins under every bed."[2] The flipside of this fear and denigration of the state, however, was the pursuit of liberty. This was neoliberalism's "positive" project, its creative face, and one that has too often been "misunderestimated," to borrow an apposite Bushian malapropism. This was Hayek the "Boy Scout Leader" (Hansen's term), armed with an essentially utopian vision of the minimally regulated free market. Ironically, the very unavailability of this imagined destination—the space of pure freedoms—would only reinforce the determination to move always-onward, in the futile pursuit of the free-market nirvana, removing whenever and wherever possible obstacles along the way (like labor unions and other collective institutions, systems of economic planning and social redistribution, and so on). Once neoliberals themselves had their hands on the levers of power, so they were to find—repeatedly—that markets would fail, that bubbles would burst, that deregulation would descend into overreach, that privatization would make monopolies. They were thus drawn into the murky worlds of market-oriented "governance," the purgatory in which they have been destined to dwell ever since. If there is an enduring logic to neoliberalization, it does not follow the pristine path of rolling market liberalization and competitive convergence; it is one of repeated, prosaic, and often botched efforts to *fix* markets, to build quasi-markets, and to repair market failures. Neoliberalization, in this sense, is not the antithesis of regulation, it is a self-contradictory form of regulation-in-denial. It does not glide forward along some teleological track, it tends to lurch three steps forward and two steps back, in the form of an adaptive, mutating, and contradictory mode of governance.

Developing an adequate account of neoliberalism consequently means paying due attention to these twists and turns, contradictions and compromises. Certainly, it cannot be reduced to the high-church pronouncements of Hayek and his followers, or to the parsimonious logic of Chicago School economics. In fact there was never a pristine moment of mountain top clarity or blackboard proof; neoliberalism never represented a singular vision free of doubt and dispute. It follows that there is no beeline trajectory from the complicated present back to some foundational eureka moment. The process of *constructing* neoliberalism has been a continuous one. So the neoliberal idea, its conceptual moment, did not "come first"—to be followed by a series of translations, all the way down to the prosaic practices and mundane manifestations of market governance "on the ground." The ideational, ideological, and institutional moments of neoliberalization have always been mixed up, mutually constituted. "Finding neoliberalism" is therefore not about locating some essential center from which all else flows; it is about following flows, backflows, and undercurrents across and between these ideational, ideological, and institutional moments, over time and between places.

Hayek's long-range vision from the mountain top at Mont Pelerin, where he assembled that nucleus of the free-market "thought collective" after the Second World War,[3] may have established some of the critical ideational preconditions for the program of neoliberalization, but the *realization* of this program would not only depart from, but repeatedly rewrite, the playbook. Critical analysis of the program must therefore also descend from the mountain top, moving beyond the interpretation of Hayekian encyclicals, and deep into the weeds of everyday market governance, routine regulatory failure, and unprincipled political accommodation. *Constructions of Neoliberal Reason* retains a singular focus on the articulation and realization of the free-market project, but it does so by tracking the project through some of its diverse settings—from the backrooms of think tanks to the seminar rooms at the University of Chicago, from the op-ed pages to guru performance spaces, from the brightly lit stages of presidential politics to the shady world of political advice. What follows is a non-reductionist reading of neoliberalization, which takes due account of (but tries not to get lost in) the project's sociological complexity. It looks at some of the ways in which the scripts of neoliberalism have been repeatedly rewritten, the roles of lead actors and bit-part players, the stages and backstages of several notable performances, and the reactions of audiences and critics. Although this is not a work of prediction, there are nevertheless implications for how—and how long—this play might continue to run.

Tangling with Maggie

I confess, I have never much cared for neoliberalism—even before I knew it had a name. I grew up in the English coalfields, and was one of that generation of school children to be denied free school milk by a particularly hard-nosed education minister called Margaret Thatcher. It is surely a recovered memory that the chant "Maggie Thatcher, milk snatcher" reverberated around our schoolyard, though an abiding, visceral distaste for the Tories and all their works certainly formed around this time. Yet it was my next arm's-length encounter with Mrs. T that was in retrospect a more consequential one. I graduated from college in the middle of the monetarist recession of the early 1980s, and what I like to think of as structural causes for my subsequent unemployment were also the proximate reasons for my accidental entry into graduate school. Maybe it was an attempt at catharsis, but my doctoral work tackled the package of labor-market programs that the Conservatives were introducing at the time. Their objective was not simply to mop up unemployment, but to foster more "flexible" attitudes amongst the workless, to lower reservation wages, to redefine skills (down), and to build the foundations for a more competitive job market. While this was being done in the name of "helping markets work better," in no sense was it a textbook form of deregulation. "Mrs. Thatcher's employment prescription," as David Robertson correctly pointed out, was "an *active* neo-liberal labor market policy."[4] This was not about "rolling back the frontiers of the state," as Thatcher once characterized her program, but about restructuring and retasking the state, about new forms of intervention and regulation based on new strategic goals.

The point of this reminiscence is to indicate where this reading of neo-liberalism comes from, literally and metaphorically, practically and politically. These first encounters with neoliberalism were a far cry from the global abstraction that is often invoked in contemporary discourse. They were up-close confrontations with a politically constructed project, forcefully advanced yet nevertheless flawed in execution. The epitome of the conviction politician, Thatcher once interrupted a policy discussion by flamboyantly slamming Hayek's *Constitution of Liberty* on the table while declaring "*This* is what we believe."[5] Meanwhile, out at the nether regions of the Thatcherite project, nothing seemed quite as certain. To take a mundane example, the Young Workers Scheme (YWS) had offered employers a government subsidy if they would *reduce* the wages of young employees, on the impeccably logical grounds that falling wages would stimulate job creation, enabling the market to clear. In the early 1980s, figuring out how this arch-neoliberal policy actually worked was my job for a while. Moonlighting as a policy-evaluation grunt, in the hope of understanding how such programs were actually realized, I found myself talking to scores of employers in the towns around Manchester, to whom the policy made almost no practical sense. Low-paying employers, if they could put up with the paperwork, would sometimes shrug, take the subsidy and continue hiring just as before. The more "respectable" firms were more likely to be bemused by the scheme, or to dismiss the idea as rather sordid. The program continued for a few years, unloved and underutilized, before eventually folding.[6]

Yet there were other areas where neoliberalism's bite was every bit as bad as its bark. At the same time as the YWS was floundering, an epic confrontation with unions in the (nationalized) coal industry was grinding towards a fateful conclusion, following a year-long strike. The defeat of the National Union of Mineworkers in 1985 presaged not only the breakup and privatization of the coal industry, but a historic-tipping point for both the labor movement and the Labour Party. In the fullness of time, this would pave the way for Tony Blair's reconstruction of *New* Labour, and the soft neoliberalism of the third way—or at least its British variant. But while there may have been a sense that Tony Blair was, in Eric Hobsbawm's memorable phrase, "Thatcher in trousers,"[7] it is debatable whether Thatcher*ism* even outlived the Thatcher administrations. By the end of the 1980s, Thatcher and Thatcherism had both lost their way; a period of ideological drift preceding and following the Iron Lady's unceremonious exit from office. At the end of the next decade, it seemed to some that Blair's New Labour project, as a smoothly presented hybrid of neoliberalism and a recalibrated form of social democracy, might constitute not only a governing ideology for the UK but perhaps even the "best shell" for globalizing capitalism.[8] Before long, however, that project, too, was in tatters. Blair's misadventures in Iraq, and his deadly "coalition" with George W. Bush's regime, signaled perhaps the most egregious moment of overreach for that transatlantic ideological alliance that had been (re)born amid the free-market fervor of the early 1980s. And then, almost on cue, came the global financial crisis—surely the last, squalid act of what some were retrospectively calling the "neoliberal era"? On the face of it, this represented a frontal challenge to what Joseph Stiglitz calls "market fundamentalism":

For a quarter-century, certain free-market doctrines have prevailed: Free and unfettered markets are efficient; if they make mistakes, they quickly correct them. The best government is a small government, and regulation only impedes innovation [...] When the world economy went into freefall during 2008, so too did our beliefs.[9]

Stiglitz goes on to observe that it might have been expected that the global crash would seal the fate of neoliberalism—and "the debate over market fundamentalism would be over"—but apparently not; at least not yet. This was the world-historical moment, of course, that Barack Obama inherited. Would the election of this self-described transformative president mark a turning point, the advent of some sort of new, center-left compromise. Or, would the neoliberal project be exhumed once more, to live on in (yet) another form?

Histories do not repeat themselves. So the governing circumstances inherited by Obama were quite different from those of his vanguardist neoliberal forebears, Reagan and Thatcher, not to mention Clinton and Blair. And if there is a spatial analogy to this historical aphorism, geographies are never replicated, either. There is no "master transition" to neoliberalism, against which all others can be measured, just as there are no varieties of Thatcherism.[10] Each pathway toward market rule is fashioned under a unique set of conjunctural conditions (and often in the face of "domestic" crises of one kind or another), even as over time these "local" neoliberalizations have become cumulatively intertwined and mutually referential. In the process, new historical geographies are, in effect, constantly in the making. And this uneven and uncertain terrain across which the project of neoliberalism has been projected, prosecuted, and peripatetically reconstructed. Tracing threads of connection across the polymorphic phenomenon of neoliberalism—the approach adopted here—consequently means finding echoes and connections across these uneven geographical terrains and through zigzagging histories.

Between Ordoliberalism and Obamanomics

How to do this? The following chapters could never constitute a comprehensive historical geography of neoliberalism. Instead they are offered as explorations of a series of vectors, moments, and oscillations in the protracted process of neoliberalization, arranged in a loose historical sequence from the early twentieth century to the first decade of the twenty-first, more of less from Ordoliberalism in interwar Germany to Obamanomics in the contemporary United States. The focus is on generative sites and moments of neoliberalization, mainly located in the global North. By no means has neoliberalism been confined to these regions, of course—the project has checkered and complex histories in Latin America, Eastern Europe, Africa, and Asia, all of which deserve parallel treatments. The field of vision here is "less global" for a number of reasons . . . in part because the ideational origins of the project, a particular focus here, were transatlantic, in part due to my own positionality as a researcher, and in part reflecting a desire to expose the workings of neoliberalism in some of its supposedly "natural" settings.

The conceptual, methodological, and definitional terms for the subsequent analysis are outlined in Chapter One, which presents a first sketch of the etymology of neoliberalism, commenting on its various translations and mistranslations. This includes a provisional definition of neoliberalism, the meaning of which tends not only to be in the eye of the beholder, but also to vary with the *location* of the beholder. This should not be taken as an invitation to relativism, however. Rather, it calls for the development of a *working* definition of neoliberalism, one that works not only in different contexts but across those contexts—in many respects, the central challenge of the book.

Chapter Two begins to tell the story proper, examining neoliberalism's polycentric formation, in the half century bisected by the inaugural Mont Pelerin Society gathering of 1947. This was the period in which neoliberalism was negotiated and refined, largely as an ideational project, in the problem space between strands of continental European liberalism on the one hand and the upstart Chicago School on the other. Although it never secured a monopoly position, Chicago would eventually emerge as the dominant pole in the ideational universe of neoliberalism, the preconditions and consequences of which are examined in Chapter Three. Here, the distinctive character of neoliberalization as a locally situated but nevertheless interconnected process—from Chicago but not really of Chicago—is drawn out, in part through a commentary on the restless travels of Milton Friedman. If this chapter ends with the intersection of Chicago theory and state power, Chapter Four takes the nexus of ideational innovation and adaptive practice as its point of departure, concentrating on the role of conservative think tanks in the real-time construction of neoliberal projects in New York City, Washington, DC, and New Orleans. New York City's fiscal crisis in the mid-1970s and Hurricane Katrina thirty years later both served as cradles of neoliberal reinvention, but if Gotham's bankruptcy preceded the maturation of think-tank networks, the crisis in the Gulf of Mexico stretched their formidable capacities to the limit.

The reinvention of neoliberal practices often occurs, in fact, at the limits of the process of neoliberalization. Neoliberalism's destructively creative dynamic is reflected in the ways in which these limits have been reworked and extended. Very often, this is a crisis-driven or crisis-animated process, though not inevitably so. Illustrating this point, Chapter Five retains a focus on the urban scale, but moves from two of the hard centers of neoliberal reinvention, New York and New Orleans, to its soft edges, in the form of the creative cities movement. By way of a critique of the recently popularized concepts of the "creative class" and "creative cities," the chapter suggests that geographic reach and policy salience of these discourses cannot be explained in terms of their intrinsic merits, which can be challenged on a number of grounds, but should be understood as by-products of the profoundly neoliberalized urban landscapes across which they have been traveling. For all their performative display of liberal cultural innovation, creativity strategies barely disrupt now-extant urban-policy orthodoxies, based on interlocal competition, place marketing, property- and market-led development, gentrification, and normalized sociospatial inequality. But more than this, creativity discourses provide an entrée into some of the (imagined and real) everyday spaces of neoliberalization. The much-celebrated hipster subjects of the creative class are not only self-absorbed but self-*managing* individuals, trading on innate talent in a world of cosmopolitan competitiveness. A far cry from the tweedy intellectuals who met at Mont Pelerin, they are new-age neoliberals, dressed in black.

Moving back from the frivolous fringes to what many would consider to be the pressurized epicenter of the neoliberal project, the book closes with a discussion of the promise and practice of Obamanomics. Washington, DC was clearly one of the epicenters of first-wave neoliberalization, in the Reagan era. It would become a pre-eminent site of third-way triangulation during the 1990s, and reckless overextension during the George W. Bush regime. But how might the age of Obama be correspondingly characterized—as a rerun of the pragmatic centrism of the Clinton years, or as a path-changing presidency a la Reagan? Deconstructing Barack Obama's economic philosophy and assessing his first year in office, the chapter asks whether this represents the beginning of the end of neoliberalism, or yet another rhetorical do-over and midcourse adjustment. Obama has been presented with the challenge, and the opportunity, of governing through a historic crisis, interpreted by many as a potentially paradigm-busting event. The very real risk, however, is that the crisis will ultimately define his presidency, not the other way around. Hope and change, the keywords of Obama's campaign, seem already to be losing their original meaning.

Debts

So much of my own work on neoliberalism has been developed in collaboration and conversation with others that merely acknowledging the advice and assistance provided by friends and colleagues seems entirely inadequate. With increasing intensity over the last decade, many of us have been grappling with the meaning and consequences of "neoliberalism," such that elements of a shared (critical) understanding can often be found between texts as well as within them. Although I must accept the ultimate responsibility for the limits of the analysis presented here, it has benefited enormously from the collaborative efforts, constructive advice, and corrective interventions of a great many fellow travelers and occasional interlocutors. In particular, my understanding of neoliberalism has been shaped (and reshaped) through collaborations with Neil Brenner, Bob Jessop, Helga Leitner, Eric Sheppard, Nik Theodore, and Adam Tickell. Thanks are also due, for all kinds of reasons, to Trevor Barnes, Noel Castree, Jane Collins, Rob Fairbanks, Jim Glassman, David Harvey, Nik Heynen, Martin Jones, Roger Keil, Bob Lake, Wendy Larner, Roger Lee, Andrew Leyshon, Gordon MacLeod, Rianne Mahon, Margit Mayer, Eugene McCann, Philip Mirowski, Katharyne Mitchell, Anette Nyqvist, Phil O'Neill, Neil Smith, Matt Sparke, Anthony Vigor, Kevin Ward, Loic Wacquant, Erik Wright, and Elvin Wyly.

More formally, the support of the John Simon Guggenheim Memorial Foundation and the Social Sciences and Humanities Research Council of Canada is gratefully acknowledged. Chapter Two is a revised version of the paper, "Remaking laissez-faire," *Progress in Human Geography,* 32(1): 3–43 (2008), with permission from Sage Publications. Chapter Four is a revised and expanded version of the paper, "Liberating the city: between New York and New Orleans," *Urban Geography,* 27(8): 681–713 (2006), with permission from Bellwether Publishing.[11] Chapter Five is a revised version of "Struggling with the creative class," *International Journal of Urban and Regional Research* 24(4): 740–770 (2005), with permission from Wiley-Blackwell.

The book is dedicated to Bryony and the girls—all of them this time. Not only have they had to endure neoliberalism, actually existing, neo-*lib*-eralism has also for some time been an unwelcome presence at (or on) the dinner table. Thanks for the space, and the quiet. Neoliberalism may not yet be over, but at least the book is.

Vancouver
February 2010

Notes

1. See Gill (1995), Harvey (2005); cf. Ong (2007); Brenner *et al.* (2010).
2. Hansen (1945). See also Hayek (1944).
3. The provocative term belongs to Mirowski and Plehwe (2009), from their authoritative account of the Mont Pelerin Society.
4. Robertson, D. B. (1986) Mrs. Thatcher's employment prescription: an active neo-liberal labor market policy, *Journal of Public Policy,* 6/3: 275–296, emphasis added.

5. Margaret Thatcher, quoted in Ranelagh, J. (1992) *Thatcher's People.* London: Fontana, ix, emphasis added; Hayek (1960).

6. See Deakin, B. M. (1996) *The Youth Labour Market in Britain: The Role of Intervention.* Cambridge: Cambridge University Press.

7. See Anderson, P. (2002) The age of EJH, *London Review of Books,* October 3: 3–7.

8. See Hall (2003: 20).

9. Stiglitz (2010: xi–xii, xvi).

10. For further discussion, see Peck (2004), Peck and Theodore (2007), and Brenner *et al.* (2010).

11. ©Bellwether Publishing, Ltd., 8640 Guilford Road, Suite 200, Columbia, MD 21046. All rights reserved.

1

Neoliberal Worlds

Followers of the "Notes and Queries" page of the left-tilting *Guardian Weekly* are accustomed to the exchange of witty and occasionally factual answers to questions submitted by curious readers, concerning everything from garden gnomes to papal dress codes and the movements of the planets. Definitive replies are, it must be said, relatively rare, as most questions are formulated in a manner designed to invite diverging responses. "What's the difference," enquired an Estonian reader in the Spring of 2009, "between a neoliberal and a neocon?" Responses came in for several weeks, picking over the legacy and etymology of neoliberalism, but few were more pithy and direct than that of Jordan Bishop from Ottawa, who simply replied: "The Atlantic Ocean."[1] In the absence of a correct answer, this can at least be considered to be provocative, and in its own way perhaps, profound. And like all good answers, it raises new questions. While, for many, the capitals of neoconservatism are unambiguously located the United States, somewhere around the nexus of the Bush doctrine, the Project for a New American Century, and the political philosophy of Leo Strauss,[2] the same cannot be said of the elusive and promiscuous concept of neoliberalism. Many would also loosely equate neoliberalism with "Americanization," though the term is scarcely recognized in the United States, in part due to long-established associations between the word "liberal" and left-interventionism. But is our Ottawan correspondent suggesting that neoliberal is therefore a European construction, or that it is simply more often found in popular circulation there? And while we are on the subject, where did neoliberalism come from? Where does it belong?

In large parts of the world, *neoliberalism* is practically synonymous with the market-oriented philosophy of the "Washington consensus" agencies, including the World Bank and the International Monetary Fund (IMF), a usually pejorative signifier for a distinctly American form of "free-market" capitalism, propagating globally. As such, it has entered the lexicon of protest, in Venezuela, France, South Africa, and most places in between. Curiously, though, the term conspicuously lacks purchase in the United States itself—outside graduate-school seminar rooms and the organs of the left intelligentsia, anyway. Significantly, another notable deaf zone for the supposedly potent signifier is the US economics profession, where many (neo)liberal propositions are effectively taken for granted, while the term itself is rarely used.[3] In North America, neoliberalism has largely remained a subterranean, critics' word. Normalized neoliberalism, it seems, can fade into invisibility.

Maybe the term makes more sense on the other side of the Atlantic, outside its allegedly "domestic" sphere? In a grumpy leader on the ambiguous meanings of liberal and neoliberal on each side of the Atlantic, *The Economist* once demanded that the term be handed back to its "original owners," those with roots in English and Scottish liberal philosophies of the eighteenth century who defend "individual rights and freedoms [while challenging] over-mighty government and other forms of power." In popular discourse, the editors complained, the term neoliberal had been shorn of this original meaning, being perverted into a signifier for a new breed of "market-worshipping, nihilistic sociopaths" bent on the destruction of not only the state but perhaps even society itself.[4] In fact, neoliberalism may have resonance in Europe in part because it is *understood to be* both "out there" and "in here." Its out-there meaning is as a byword for a distinctly American form of deregulated capitalism, most often portrayed as an off-shore threat to European traditions of social solidarity and the accompanying "social model" of organized capitalism.[5] But as such critical evocations of neoliberalism imply, this viral ideology is disconcertingly in-here as well; it has entered the European bloodstream.[6] The United Kingdom, of course, has helped write the book on neoliberalism as a modern political phenomenon, with its dramatic shift from Keynesian crisis management in the 1970s to the no-turning-back conviction politics of Thatcherism. Thatcher herself became the personification of the more market/less state project. And Thatcherism, in this sense, was Europe's enemy within. Subsequently, the "transition economies" of Central and Eastern Europe would define an entirely different neoliberal pathway, with their wrenching experience of large-scale privatization and "shock treatment" during the 1990s, but again these neoliberal nostrums were often portrayed as imported projects, borne by Washington technocrats and American economists. In here, but from over there?

Even though most Europeans would point West when asked to identify the origins of neoliberalism—identifying London, Washington, DC, and Chicago, in particular as germinal sites of the free-market project, and the United States as the locus of deregulated capitalism—most would also acknowledge that there are now distinctively European strains of the virus too. At the very least, then, neoliberalism exists on both sides of the Atlantic. And on closer inspection, the process of neoliberalization turns out to have been more of a transatlantic *dialogue* than one of unidirectional, Eastward diffusion. Identifiable (and even explicitly self-identifying) forms of *neolib*eral thinking have existed on both sides of the Atlantic at least since the 1920s, with Ordoliberalism in Germany, the reconstruction of Austrian economics, and the "first Chicago School" around Henry Simons.[7] These disparate elements were later organized into a transnational conversation, first at the "Colloque Lippmann" in Paris in 1938, and in a more sustained manner through the meetings of the Mont Pelerin Society (MPS) from 1947. These contrarian moves, it must be remembered, occurred against the backdrop of an almost implacably hostile ideological terrain. As the MPS's founding statement dramatically put it, "Over large stretches of the earth's surface the essential conditions of human dignity and freedom have already disappeared," aggravated forms of statism being seen to represent a "constant menace" to (neo)liberal values.[8]

Writing in 1951, Milton Friedman had sensed that, while the embattled network of free-market intellectuals would surely have to "live through a long era of collectivism," there was hope that the tides of intellectual opinion would eventually turn. A free-market project fit for the purpose of countering mid-twentieth-century collectivism could not, however, be simply recovered from the founding texts of philosophical liberalism. It would have to be constructed:

[The] fundamental error in the foundations of 19th century liberalism [was that it] gave the state hardly any other task other than to maintain peace, and to foresee that contracts were kept. It was a naïve ideology. It held that the state could only do harm [and that] laissez-faire must be the rule ... A new ideology must ... give high priority to limiting the state's ability to intervene in the activities of the individual. At the same time, it is absolutely clear that there are truly positive functions allotted the state. The doctrine that, on and off, has been called neoliberalism and that has developed, more or less simultaneously, in many parts of the world ... is precisely such a doctrine ... [I]n place of the nineteenth century understanding that laissez-faire is the means to achieve [the goal of individual freedom], neoliberalism proposes that it is *competition* that will lead the way ... The state will police the system, it will establish the conditions favorable to competition and prevent monopoly, it will provide a stable monetary framework, and relieve acute poverty and distress. Citizens will be protected against the state, since there exists a free private market, and the competition will protect them from one another.[9]

This is a positive form of neoliberalism as a tentative, counterhegemonic project, articulated at a time when the vanguardist conviction politics of the 1980s and the hubristic swagger of the 1990s must have been almost unimaginable. As the young Friedman confessed, "No one can tell if this doctrine will become victorious."

The neoliberal ascendancy was never a sure thing. It was a remarkable ascendancy, not an inevitable one—remarkable in the sense that its journey from the margins to the mainstream was not guided by some secret formula or determinant blueprint; its zigzagging course was improvised, and more often than not enabled by crisis. Perplexingly, its success as an ideological project reflects its deeply contradictory nature, as a combination of dogmatism and adaptability, strategic intent and opportunistic exploitation, programmatic vision and tactical smarts, principle and hypocrisy. Exhibit A: capturing and transforming the state was always a fundamental neoliberal objective. Only at its wildest, anarcho-capitalist fringe did the neoliberal project venture to imagine life without the state. Notwithstanding its trademark antistatist rhetoric, neoliberalism was always concerned—at its philosophical, political, and practical core—with the challenge of first seizing and then retasking the state.

Milton Friedman's own more-than-modest efforts in this regard, as Chapter Three will explore in greater detail, included several decades in and around the orbit of state power, including a prominent role in Senator Barry Goldwater's ill-fated (but nevertheless catalytic) presidential campaign of 1964, an infamous association with General Pinochet's regime in Chile, and a distinctly purple patch as Ronald Reagan's favorite economist. It was the stark contrast between the first and the last of these assignments that surely convinced Friedman that battles over ideas were more often settled on the murky terrain of politics. The role of the intellectual, he reflected, was

to keep options open until circumstances make change necessary. There is enormous inertia—a tyranny of the status quo—in private and especially governmental arrangements. Only a crisis—actual or perceived—produces real change. When that crisis occurs, the actions that are taken depend on the ideas that are lying around. That, I believe, is our basic function: to develop alternatives to existing policies, to keep them alive and available until the politically impossible becomes politically inevitable.[10]

Under the leadership of Friedrich von Hayek, the Mont Pelerin Society had assiduously pursued the mission, from the late 1940s onward, of "develop [ing] alternatives to existing policies," and not so much keeping them alive as bringing them to life. They were never just "lying around." Ironically, the Mont Pelerinians first "policy victory" tends to be almost forgotten in received histories of the neoliberal counter-revolution—maybe because it occurred out of place and out of time. It came in the form of West Germany's radical monetary makeover, in 1948, when Mont Pelerinian Ludwig Erhard launched a daring plan for the Deutschemark, along with a pre-emptive deregulation of the wartime economy. The subsequent mutation of the German "social model," which by the 1980s would be understood as an institutionalized *alternative* to neoliberalism, may explain the Mont Pelerinians' ambivalence, but it also serves as a reminder that neoliberal pathways are not preordained, of which more later.

In contrast, accounts of neoliberalism as a hegemonic wave tend, for understandable reasons, to begin in the 1970s, airbrushing out many of the tangled prehistories. It was the 1970s, of course, when the dominoes began to fall in the direction of market-oriented reform, even though again history delivered something of a false start. As Naomi Klein and others have recounted, the Chilean coup of 1973 provided a now-notorious opportunity for a (barely) controlled experiment in neoliberal shock treatment, with Chicago boys already on the ground.[11] And then China began gradually to "open up" its economy after 1978. But it was the extended macroeconomic travails of the 1970s, especially in the United States and the United Kingdom, which represented the historical opening for which the neoliberal script had been painstakingly constructed. Stagflation broke the back of the Keynesian orthodoxy—as both a generative theory and as a system of government—the long-anticipated crisis for which Friedman's style of monetarist economics provided readily presentable, if ultimately flawed, "solutions." It was no mere coincidence that neoliberal ideas filled the attendant vacuum. Of course, it is absurd to suggest that they were passively "lying around," as Friedman would have it. They had been scrupulously formulated for this very eventuality, as a total critique of Keynesian rationality and welfare-state government, and they had been peddled relentlessly through free-market think tanks, through the financial community and business organizations, and through the elite and mainstream media, not least by Friedman himself.

The demonstrated reach and penetration of Chicago School networks— the subject of meticulous empirical investigation, and so no longer the preserve of conspiracy theorists—is such as to confer at least a degree of credibility on centrifugal theories of the diffusion of neoliberalism.[12] The best-known account is Naomi Klein's *Shock Doctrine,* in which the neoliberal virus is cooked up at the University of Chicago, in anticipation of its journey into the "live laboratories" of Pinochet's Chile, and beyond. Powered by the proselytizing genius of Milton Friedman, the tenacity of monetarist economics, and the enabling power of the greenback, the neoliberal tsunami eventually overwhelmed much of the world. This is a powerful story, but a one-way diffusion model of neoliberalism will not do.

As Bockman and Eyal have perceptively demonstrated in the case of Eastern Europe, the production of neoliberalism has been "dialogic."[13] In some senses, Eastern Europe during the 1990s, rather like Chile a generation earlier, did indeed become for a while the pre-eminent "laboratory" of neoliberal practice. But it would be a mistake to take such "frontier" manifestations of neoliberalism as indicators of its most "advanced" form. Even in Iraq, which in the shock-and-awe invasion of 2003 was pulverized into something close to a socio-institutional tabula rasa, conditions were still barely accommodating to the neoliberal treatment. This included the unilateral imposition of a flat tax, a long-frustrated goal of the Republican right in the United States, along with a host of other reforms designed to liberalize what had been one of the most state-managed economies in the world.[14] Enforced at gunpoint, many of these reforms also failed. The sociospatial "frontiers" of neoliberalism may therefore be zones *both* of audacious experimentation and catastrophic failure. And just the same can be said of experimental reforms in the "heartland," as the hapless domestic policy record of the second Bush presidency illustrates.

There are unique and contextually specific features of every such experiment, each of which reshapes the contradictory "whole" of actually existing neoliberalism. Certainly, there is no neoliberal replicating machine. Rather, each experiment should be seen as a form of reconstruction, representing a conjunctural episode or moment in the contradictory *evolution* of neoliberal practice. The analytical—not to say political—challenge is to figure out how these have chained together over time, how they have become interwoven, how the project has achieved a form of evolutionary consolidation. It is both an indictment of neoliberalism and testament to its dogged dynamism, of course, that the laboratory experiments do not "work." They have nevertheless tended to "fail forward," in that their manifest inadequacies have—so far anyway—repeatedly animated further rounds of neoliberal invention. Devolved governance, public–private partnership, management by audit, neopaternalism...all can be seen as examples of institutional reinvention spawned as much by the *limits* of earlier forms of neoliberalization as by some advancing "logic."

Neoliberalism, it will be argued here, has only ever existed in "impure" form, indeed *can* only exist in messy hybrids. Its utopian vision of a free society and free economy is ultimately unrealizable. Yet the pristine clarity of its ideological apparition, the *free market*, coupled with the endless frustrations borne of the inevitable failure to arrive at this elusive destination, nevertheless confer a significant degree of forward momentum on the neoliberal project. Ironically, neoliberalism possesses a progressive, forward-leaning dynamic by virtue of the very *unattainability* of its idealized destination. In practice, neoliberalism has never been about a once-and-for-all liberalization, an evacuation of the state. Instead, it has been associated with rolling programs of market-oriented reform, a kind of permanent revolution which cannot simply be judged according to its own fantasies of free-market liberation. Hence the concern here with *neoliberalization* as an open-ended and contradictory process of regulatory restructuring. Beneath the mythology of market progress lies a turgid reality of neoliberalism variously failing and flailing forward—for example, as the initial forays into privatization and deregulation triggered quasi-market failures, and then further rounds of (mis)intervention in the form of market-friendly governance. Neoliberalism's curse, then, is that it cannot help itself but to be a kind of interventionist project, which confers on the project a certain dynamic directionality, if not a destination. To the extent that neoliberalism has been, since the 1970s, "victorious" in the war of ideas, its victories have always been Pyrrhic and partial ones. Yet the project ploughs forward, never arriving at its stated destination, and never knowing where to stop. The neoliberal lemmings, in this sense, are always prone to throw themselves (not to mention others) off the cliffs of deregulation.

Neoliberalism's burden—as a resilient, responsive and deeply reactionary credo—is that it can never remake the world in its own image. As a result, it is doomed to coexist with its unloved others, be these the residues of state socialism, developmental statism, authoritarianism, or social democracy. Like the idealized market to which it defers, neoliberalism is destined to remain a frustrated presence in an impure world, a condition with profound consequences for the righteousness and dogged momentum that have become long-run characteristics of the market revolution. The residues of these discrepant formations provide an array of convenient scapegoats for neoliberal policy failures. Even after decades of neoliberal reconstruction, it is remarkable how many present-day policy failures are still being tagged to intransigent unions, to invasive regulations, to inept bureaucrats, and to scaremongering advocacy groups. Again and again, the task of market-modeled reconstruction has proved to be an intractable one, even if in other ways it has been an unstoppable one.

"Neoliberalism," Dieter Plehwe has remarked, "is anything but a succinct, clearly defined political philosophy."[15] Crisply unambiguous, essentialist definitions of neoliberalism have proved to be incredibly elusive. The word has become the bane of many a political lexicographer. It would be a wrongheaded endeavor, in fact, to attempt to reduce neoliberalism to some singular essence—say, as a condensate of Hayek's personal philosophy, or Chicago School theory, or hard-boiled Thatcherism—and not only because these, too, have been movable objects. By its nature, as an oxymoronic form of "market rule," neoliberalism is contradictory and polymorphic. It will not be fixed. Perhaps, instead, the closest one can get to understanding the nature of neoliberalism is to follow its *movements,* and to triangulate between its ideological, ideational, and institutional currents, between philosophy, politics, and practice. This is necessarily an exercise, moreover, in historical geography, as any such effort must be attentive to the spaces in and through which the neoliberal project has been (re)constructed. There is no ground-zero location—at Mont Pelerin, in the White House, or in the Chilean Treasury—from which to evaluate all subsequent "versions" of neoliberalism. There are only unruly historical geographies of an evolving, interconnected project.

Death and definitions

Neoliberalism lost another one of its nine lives in the financial crash of 2008. This prompted mainstream political leaders like France's Nicolas Sarkozy to announce, as flamboyantly as possible, the end of the laissez-faire affair. In the thick of the financial crisis, repudiations of neoliberalism—belatedly named for what it supposedly *was*—suddenly became commonplace. The sound bite version was that regulation, intervention, and the state were now back, and therefore that the "era" of neoliberalism, which began with the joint ascendancy of Thatcher and Reagan, was officially over. Political elites, everywhere from Japan to Australia, and France to Iceland, were busily declaring that the infatuation with market fundamentalism had passed.[16] These claims found a willing echo on parts of the left, not least because they appeared to ratify the long-held (but often rescheduled) belief that neoliberalism was always destined to collapse under the weight of its own contradictions.[17] As Greg Albo has observed, it has long been "taken for granted in most quarters of the Left that [neoliberalism] was neither politically nor economically sustainable."[18] The crash therefore represented what Joseph Stiglitz, Eric Hobsbawm, Naomi Klein, and others portrayed as a "Berlin Wall moment" for neoliberalism.[19]

Declarations of the death of neoliberalism, however, are surely premature—for all the vincibility of the project. There is something faintly Orwellian about the claims of political elites and media commentators that the end of the free-market period has been marked by a "return of the state" . . . as if it ever went away. Neoliberalism, in its various guises, has always been about the capture and reuse of the state, in the interests of shaping a pro-corporate, freer-trading "market order," even though this has never been a process of cookie-cutter replication of an unproblematic strategy. Thatcherism, for example, represented a particular way of (re)connecting, in Andrew Gamble's felicitous phrase, "the free market and the strong state";[20] contemporary China represents a radically different combination of state power and market forces, but a combination nevertheless;[21] and yes, Estonia has its own configuration too, as the *Guardian Weekly*'s correspondent no doubt suspected all along.[22] Moreover, these variably neoliberalized state/social formations proved to be differently susceptible to the financial crisis, and to the broader economic downturn that followed, revealing this as a processes of global *restructuring*, rather than (simply) a world recession. Witness, for example, the diverging fortunes of Iceland, Canada, Brazil, Ireland, Singapore, and Hungary. Although it is still early to make a conclusive call on this, the global crisis seems to have been associated with a geographical uneven reformatting and reconstruction of neoliberal rule, not its wholesale collapse.[23]

Adequate approaches to neoliberalization consequently need to take account not only of its ideational "essence," but to the shifting topographies of what Neil Brenner and Nik Theodore have called "actually existing neoliberalism."[24] The critical literature on neoliberalism has its origins, in fact, in a series of studies of *national* transformation, including situated and contextually rich accounts of the United Kingdom's path, first to Thatcherism and then into New Labour's embrace of the "Third Way,"[25] Mexico's wrenching experience of structural adjustment and technocratic "modernization,"[26] and, more recently, comparative analyses of these and other country cases.[27] What is especially striking, in a context in which there is now a sprawling literature on "national neoliberalisms," from Argentina to Zimbabwe,[28] and most countries in between, is the paucity of comparable analysis of the United States, the elephant-in-the-room case and the supposed "home" of neoliberalism.[29]

Notwithstanding such anomalies of analytical coverage, it is important to underline the folly of attempting to construct some encyclopedic map of the postKeynesian world, shaded according to measures of the "degree" of neoliberalization. At root, this is because neoliberalization refers to a qualitatively differentiated process, rather than to a developmental stage or quantitative threshold; it denotes the *form* of state/economy relations, not a linear path towards a purely free-market state. Neoliberal statecraft, in fact, can often be both extensive and expensive, but more fundamentally it varies *in kind*.[30] So a stage model will not do, but neither will a taxonomic classification of varieties of neoliberalism. In fact, national and local forms of neoliberalization are becoming increasingly interdependent. For example, the unsustainable reliance on debt and credit in the American form of deeply financialized neoliberalism, in the decade before the crash of 2008, was clearly predicated not only on a particular configuration of international economic and geopolitical relations, it also actively enabled a *distinctive* path of neoliberal development in China, such that the American and Chinese forms of neoliberalization were effectively coproduced.[31] They were not (indeed could not have been) free-standing "models." Neoliberalism, in this sense, does not connote some universal, singular pathway, with the United States at the end of the path, and other countries lined up behind, shuffling in the same direction.

Curiously, perhaps, just about the only place where crude, quantitative measures of market modernization have any credibility is in the very heart of the neoliberal project itself, amongst the free-market think tanks, though venturing into this world inevitably means wading through a morass of euphemistic statistics. Even if these assessments should be taken with a large dose of salt, they can be seen as a rough guide to the actually existing neoliberal world, as seen by its true believers—while also revealing something of the neoliberal worldview itself. The Heritage Foundation in Washington, DC produces an annual "Index of Economic Freedom" in association with the *Wall Street Journal* since 1995, calculating movements along some imaginary free-market slide rule according to a ten-point methodology. Their latest assessment of the state of the world is summarized at Table 1.1. Hong Kong comes closet to achieving "pure" freedom, though still falls ten points short of a Hayekian nirvana on Heritage's "freedom score"; meanwhile, North Korea is barely two points clear of *absolute* repression.[32] The more libertarian wing of the think tank community, appropriately perhaps, has been producing a competing measure over a longer time period, boasting an intellectual lineage directly back to the Nobel trio of Milton Friedman, Douglass North, and Gary Becker. The Fraser

Institute's "Economic Freedom of the World Index" is compiled with the support of more than seventy free-market think tanks around the world, including the Cato Institute in the United States. Even though, tactically speaking, such organizations have little to gain from declaring deregulatory "victories," and indeed typically refrain from publicly doing so, their data nevertheless indicate an uneven drift in the direction of neoliberal policy principles since the 1970s—including access to "sound money," security in property rights, flexibility in labor markets, reduced rates of taxation and social transfers, corporate-sector deregulation, and trade liberalization. These are summarized in Figures 1.1 and 1.2, which provide snapshots of the neoliberal worldview, circa 1970 and 2007, respectively. Amongst the most conspicuous transformations, on these measures, came Chile, which surged from the most repressive regime on earth in 1970 to a secure top-ten position by the mid-2000s, and the neoliberal "success stories" of Central and Eastern Europe, like Estonia and the Slovak Republic, which were literally blank spaces on the map until the mid-1990s, subsequently rising into the Fraser Institute's top twenty.

At # 11 in the neoliberal charts of 2007, Estonia was singled out as "one of the freest economies in the world," several places ahead of Iceland, which at the time was (still) the Fraser Institute's poster child for the deregulation of banking and credit.[33] These were the very conditions, of course, that would shortly lead Iceland into bankruptcy, as its currency collapsed and debt spiraled to 850 percent of gross domestic product (GDP); the subsequent run on the nation's overextended banks resulted in their nationalization and the collapse of the country's government. As a

Table 1.1. Economic freedom and repression, ranked

World rank	Ten most "free"	Freedom score	World rank	Ten most "repressed"	Freedom score
1	Hong Kong	90.0	170	São Tomé and Príncipe	43.8
2	Singapore	87.1	171	Libya	43.5
3	Australia	82.6	172	Comoros	43.3
4	Ireland	82.2	173	D. R. Congo	42.8
5	New Zealand	82.0	174	Venezuela	39.9
6	United States	80.7	175	Eritrea	38.5
7	Canada	80.5	176	Burma	37.7
8	Denmark	79.6	177	Cuba	27.9
9	Switzerland	79.4	178	Zimbabwe	22.7
10	United Kingdom	79.0	179	North Korea	2.0

Source: Derived from Miller, T. and Holmes, K. R. (2009) *2009 Index of Economic Freedom*. Washington, DC: Heritage Foundation.

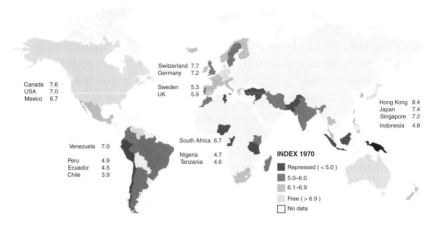

Figure 1.1. A neoliberal view of the Keynesian world: the economic freedom index for 1970

Source: Compiled from data in Gwartney, J. and Lawson, R. (2009) *Economic Freedom of the World*. Vancouver: Fraser Institute.

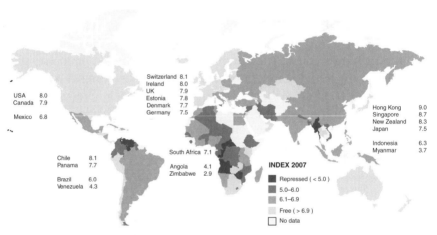

Figure 1.2. A neoliberal view of a neoliberalizing world: the economic freedom index for 2007

Source: Compiled from data in Gwartney, J. and Lawson, R. (2009) *Economic Freedom of the World*. Vancouver: Fraser Institute.

representative of the International Monetary Fund brought in to assess the crisis belatedly recognized, "Iceland is no longer a country. It is a hedge fund."[34] (The free-market lemmings had not seen this one coming either, apparently.) Iceland's new prime minister, Social Democrat Johanna Sigurdardottir, declared after the 2009 election that, "The people of Iceland are

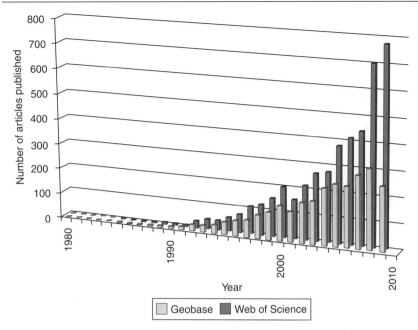

Figure 1.3. Neoliberalism as social-science keyword, 1980–2009: academic articles on neoliberalism by publication year

Source: Web of Science; Geobase.

settling the score with the past, with the neo-liberalism that has been in power here for too long."[35] The explicit *naming* of neoliberalism in mainstream political discourse is, however, both a rare and a recent event. And it is nearly always seen in the rearview mirror, or someplace else.

In contrast to these fleeting representations of neoliberalism in the wild, deployment of the term neoliberalism in academic discourse has become commonplace, especially in the critical social sciences during the past decade. As Figure 1.3 demonstrates, neoliberalism is very much a post-globalization keyword in the social sciences; it was barely used at all in the decade of Reagan and Thatcher. And notwithstanding the upturn in scholarly currency after the mid-1990s, the *manner* of this usage remains confusing and inconsistent. In their content analysis of the term *neoliberalism* in the political-science literature, for example, Boas and Gans-Morse find it to be almost indiscriminately applied to a wide range of phenomena by critics, while being virtually absent, if not a taboo word, amongst advocates of market reform.[36] Again, practically all uses of the term seem to be situational.

The originator of perhaps the best-known synonym for neoliberalism, John Williamson, carefully seeks to distinguish the "Washington Consensus," as a set of policy prescriptions, from the minefield that discussions of free-market ideologies had become:

Right from the start, the term "Washington Consensus" evoked controversy...Had my intention been to make propaganda for reform in Latin America, the last city that I would have associated with the cause of reform is Washington [...] The reason is obvious: This was a godsend to all those unreconstructed opponents of reform who yearned for socialism or import-substituting industrialization or a state in which they could play a leading role. The term fed the desire to believe that the reforms were designed by the United States in its own interests and imposed by Washington-based international financial institutions under its thumb...Anyone with a smidgen of anti-Americanism could be persuaded to foam at the mouth with indignation at the idea that Washington was seeking to impose its interests, and they could, it was hoped, be easy to recruit to the anti-reform cause. Before long, the term had escaped from its original meaning of a list of 10 specific reforms that most influential people in a certain city agreed would be good for a specific region of the world at a certain date in history, to mean an ideological agenda valid for all time that was supposedly being imposed on all countries.

That ideology was...neoliberalism, meaning the set of ideas emanating from the Mont Pelerin Society and developed primarily by Milton Friedman and Friedrich von Hayek, and then to some extend implemented by Ronald Reagan and Margaret Thatcher...[The term was subsequently used to denote] the full conservative agenda of the Reagan and Thatcher administrations, rather than distinguishing between those things that had outlasted Reagan and Thatcher (like globalization and privatization) and those that were unceremoniously ditched when their rule ended (like monetarism and supply-side economics and belief in minimalist government), as I had intended.[37]

The apparent toxicity of neoliberalism as a signifier amongst mainstream politicians and policy reformers, who will often only be caught using the word when somehow distancing themselves from it, stands in stark contrast, then, to the term's accelerating circulation in the critical social sciences. Here, John Clarke finds academic deployment of the term notable not only for its ubiquity, but also for its apparent omnipotence, as an alleged first (or ultimate) cause of a bewildering array of contemporary developments. In effect, *neoliberalism* seems often to be used as a sort of stand-in term for the political–economic zeitgeist, as a no-more-than approximate proxy for a specific analysis of mechanisms or relations of social power, domination, exploitation, or alienation. The forms and registers of the phenomenon can seem almost without limit. On Clarke's count, the adjectival promiscuity of neoliberalism extends at least as far as the following sites, situations, practices, and processes: "states, spaces, logics, techniques, technologies, discourses, discursive framework, ideologies, ways of thinking, projects, agendas, programs, governmentality, measures, regimes, development, ethno-development, development imaginaries, global forms of control...."[38]

For their part, although they continue to find value in the concept, Boas and Gans-Morse conclude that "neoliberalism has become a conceptual trash heap capable of accommodating multiple distasteful phenomena without much argument as to whether one or the other component really belongs."[39] In some respects, the term's troubled life reflects the fraught and polarized ideological fields that it has controversially occupied, while its sprawling and yet uneven reach may also signify something perplexingly "real," if methodologically inconvenient, about the diverse and tentacular manifestations of market rule. Just because neoliberalism is not a universal and ubiquitous phenomenon; just because it is not monolithic, unilogical, and free of contradiction; just because it is not teleologically trained on a history-ending form of global convergence; just because it is not an unstoppable, self-replicating system, utterly impervious to outside influences and immune from effective contestation... just because neoliberalism does not, indeed cannot, satisfy these absolutist, hyperbolic criteria, this does not mean that it is a figment of the (critical) imagination.[40] From a slightly different perspective, the contested and unstable character of the signifier itself might actually reveal something about the nature of the signified processes, phenomena, and practices. The tangled mess that is the modern usage of neoliberalism may be telling us something about the tangled mess of neoliberalism itself.

What does seem to be indefensible, however, is "flying blind," continuing to invoke neoliberalism—however obliquely, ambivalently, or ironically—in the absence even of a working definition. But as Boas and Gans-Morse document, this is precisely how much of the literature "on" neoliberalism does indeed proceed: it is not just that neoliberalism is a contested concept, the problem is that its meaning is often only implicitly understood, such that "we are faced not with too many definitions but with too few."[41] This is not to say that any attempt to define neoliberalism must descend into hair-splitting between this and that hybrid assemblage or contingent formation, that there are as many varieties of neoliberalism as there are social formations to neoliberalize. But it does surely mean that attempts to transcendentally "fix" neoliberalism are destined to be frustrated, and for good reason. It has been argued here that, for all its doctrinal certainty, the neoliberal project is paradoxically defined by the very *unattainability* of its fundamental goal—frictionless market rule. Rather than the goal itself, it is the oscillations and vacillations around frustrated attempts to reach it that shape the revealed form of neoliberalism as a contradictory mode of market governance. Pristine definitions of neoliberalization are therefore simply unavailable; instead, concretely grounded accounts of the process must be chiseled out of the interstices of state/market configurations.

Adversarial geographical imaginaries

These analytical challenges have a real-world political analogue in the impossibility of pristine "zero-state" solutions, which dooms market reformers, however zealous, to the netherworlds of compromise, cohabitation, and "governance." The attendant, frustrated insecurity of the neoliberal id is, in turn, reflected in the long-established tendency to ostentatiously act out in the face of others. As Foucault noted, one of the decisive challenges confronting the pioneering neoliberals, in the years between the World Wars, was how to frame their emergent project, relative to its various contenders, enemies, and alternatives, in other words, how to "constitute [the] field of adversity"?[42] In essence, the position that they developed was that most of the contemporaneous alternatives, while they have may looked quite distinctive from one another, would in fact all lead down the same "road to serfdom," to use Hayek's provocative term. For example, Wilhelm Röpke, one of the moderate members of the German *Ordo* school of neoliberalism,[43] and an exile during the Second World War, attacked Britain's Beveridge Report of 1942 on the grounds that its vision of the British welfare state was a step in the direction of Nazism, no less. The Ordoliberal strategy at the time, Foucault argued, was

to pinpoint a sort of economic-political invariant that could be found in political regimes as different as Nazism and parliamentary England, the Soviet Union and America of the New Deal. They tried to identify this relational invariant in these different regimes and they laid down the principle that the important difference was no longer between this or that constitutional structure. The real [choice] was between a liberal politics and *any other form whatsoever* of economic interventionism, whether this takes the mild form of Keynesianism or the drastic form of an autarchic plan like that of Germany. So we have an invariant that could be called . . . the anti-liberal invariant, which possesses its own logic and internal necessity. This is what the ordoliberals deciphered in the experience of Nazism.[44]

The Ordoliberal project, centering on a diasporic network of German intellectuals and pivoting on the "German question," was the dominant manifestation of neoliberal thinking between the two World Wars. At the time, its Chicago School cousin was at a much earlier, and more fragile, stage in its evolution. In important respects, though, these were separate intellectual projects, in style as well as in substance. It was only with the inauguration of the Mont Pelerin meetings in 1947 that they were unevenly conjoined into a transnational project—with Hayek working as the primarily interlocutor between the two camps. By contemporary standards, the Ordoliberals were relatively moderate and pragmatic, espousing a humanist form of market economics. This was rooted in the understanding that the full capacities of markets could only be realized through their embedding in a robust legal and social order, including preemptive, "market conforming" interventions on the part of the state. The foil for these arguments, which defined the Ordo group as *neo*liberals, was provided by the demonstrable limits of nineteenth-century laissez-faire, Austrianism, and Manchesterism, against which the Ordoliberals maintained a critical, if not antagonistic, relationship.[45] The Chicagoans, in contrast, retained a more idealistic affinity to their nineteenth-century predecessors, while developing a position that endowed the market with vigorously autonomous capacities. In its earlier manifestations, through the work of Henry Simons,[46] the proto-Chicago School had acknowledged a range of "positive" functions for the state, but under the more partisan leadership of Milton Friedman, after 1946, the Chicago line would become doctrinally anti-state. It was this position that Foucault later characterized as "anarcho-liberalism," and which leading Ordoliberals had previously portrayed as "liberal anarchism" or *paleoliberalism*.[47]

It is the problem space *between* the Chicago and Ordoliberal positions—between, respectively, the free-economy-and-minimalist state on the one hand, and the socially embedded market order on the other—that really defined the nexus of the neoliberal project between the 1930s and the 1960s. The transatlantic joint venture that was constructed over this period was held together, in part, by a shared embrace of certain strands of market utopianism, but much more consequentially by mutual antipathy towards a crude agglomeration of those invariant ideological others, Keynesianism, socialism, and development economics. It was Keynes who came to symbolize what Foucault called the "main doctrinal enemy," notwithstanding the marked absence of an unambiguous "economic-political invariant" across the neoliberal thought coalition itself.[48] With occasional strains and defections, however, this group of intellectual and ideological outsiders forged the foundations of a common position during the lonely decades of the Keynesian ascendancy, animated by their shared sense of marginalization and exclusion.

But if the Ordoliberals represented the conservative establishment of this neoliberal project during the middle decades of the twentieth century, the upstart Chicagoans were on their way to seizing the limelight. The historical inflection point eventually arrived in the late 1960s, around the time when Milton Friedman delivered his monetarist critique of the Keynesian orthodoxy from the president's podium of the American Economic Association. In the turbulent decade that followed, this would find a much wider audience. This was, as Andrew Gamble recalls, nothing less than

a great convulsion in world capitalism—at once economic, political and ideological—a period of major restructuring, the contours of which were often hard to discern at the time, and frequently misunderstood. This was particularly true of the role played by new forms of ideology in the crisis, and in particular of neo-liberalism. The revival of doctrines of the free market, both as ideology and as political economy, was a significant feature of the period, but there was little agreement at first as to what it meant, and whether it indicated any deeper change of substance. The strong temptation in the West was to see neo-liberalism as trying to put the clock back to a kind of capitalism which no longer existed. It took some time to appreciate that neo-liberalism did have some new features as the prefix "neo" implied, and was an integral part of [a wider] re-organisation of capitalist relations.[49]

Although they were rarely caught in moments of public uncertainty, few of the free-market revolutionaries would have been so bold has to predict the ideological sea change of the 1970s. If the Mont Pelerinians and their small band of fellow travelers in the economics profession, the financial press, and the fledgling network of conservative think tanks had figured out the first moves, the project would have to be constantly renewed and recalibrated once it entered the wild as a governing strategy. In truth, Hayek had always envisaged that the new liberalism would have to be "flexible credo"; as a part-improvised "art of governing," it would have to be even more adaptive. Nevertheless, Hayek himself mainly worked in broad brush strokes; as one of his contemporary critics pointed out, "at the moment he becomes concrete and specific, he finds his task pretty difficult."[50]

If neoliberalism's encounter with state power in the 1970s—notably in Chile, New Zealand, and the UK—represented another moment of inflection in the project, it also marked something of an axial adjustment in its "internal" constitution. The long-established transatlantic dialogue, with

Chicago as its Western node, would be complemented, from the 1970s, with a hemispheric dialogue, with Chicago as its Northern node. What started out as a set of abstractions in Chicago would take on dramatically concrete form in Chile. The Pinochet regime's pact with the Chicago Boys represented the first international flashpoint for an emergent *politics* of neoliberalism. Already, the meaning of this inconsistently used ideological keyword was beginning to shift. "Only once the term had migrated to Latin America, and Chilean intellectuals starting using it to refer to radical economic reforms under the Pinochet dictatorship," Boas and Gans-Morse observe, "did neoliberalism acquire negative normative connotations and cease to be used by market proponents."[51] When Milton Friedman sat down with General Pinochet, in 1975, it was the immediate postwar German model that he cited as a real-world example of the radical program that he was advocating. The Ordo current was, however, on the wane.[52] Chile's Chicago Boys, while drawing their inspiration from Friedman and Hayek, were soon to be actively engaged in *making up neoliberalism,* as a yet-more radical regulatory project. As such, it would take on many of the characteristics of a "home-grown" program, for all its Windy City inspirations. As Silva writes, "in Chile, the 'paternity' of the model has never been in dispute . . . supporters and adversaries agree that neo-liberalism has mainly been 'made in Chile.'"[53] In subsequent decades, the Chilean path towards free-market governance would itself be variously adjusted, consolidated, and normalized, a process that has involved the cumulative depoliticization of economic policy, the deepening of technocratic forms governance, and the almost complete "disappearance" of *neoliberalism* from the political lexicon, which had mutated into a critics' term by the 1980s, before losing its mainstream currency.[54]

The Thatcher–Reagan decade of the 1980s, coupled with the neoliberal turns of the international financial institutions, effectively secured the position of Chicago, both as the metaphorical capital of free-market thinking and as the premier source of the new economic expertise. The Ordo contribution, in effect, became part of neoliberalism's lost history, at least until the quite recent wave of historiographical work.[55] Foreshortened conceptions of neoliberalism, that begin in the 1970s and which pay insufficient attention to this long trajectory of ideational evolution, run the risk of underestimating the market/order dialectic which lies at the contradictory heart of the neoliberalization process.

For this reason, moreover, processual definitions of neoliberal*ization* are preferable to static and taxonomic renderings of neoliberal*ism,* since the latter tend to rely too heavily on regime-like conceptions, bracketed in time and space. Neoliberalism defies explanation in terms of fixed coordinates. Rather, it denotes a problem space, together with an accompanying ethos of market-complementing regulation. In the most abstract of terms, one can say that neoliberalization refers to a contradictory process of market-like rule, principally negotiated at the boundaries of the state, and occupying the ideological space defined by a (broadly) sympathetic critique of nineteenth-century laissez-faire and deep antipathies to collectivist, planned, and socialized modes of government, especially those associated with Keynesianism and developmentalism. "Neo," in this formulation, can be taken to refer to the project's historical and ideological positioning *after* nineteenth-century liberalism, an instructive counterpoint for the Ordoliberals and an idealized past for the Chicagoans. In a more processual sense, "neo" also denotes the repeated (necessity for) renewal and reinvention of a project that could never be fixed as a stable formula, and which has lurched through moments innovation, overreach, correction, and crisis. Much of this dynamism, in turn, can be related back to the aforementioned market/order problematic, and to the awkward reality that neoliberals have never been able to live with, or without, the state. They are repeatedly drawn to rhetorical denigrations of the state, yet they literally do not know where to stop. Small-state idealists, they have always argued over where to "draw the line" on positive state roles, or on appropriate limits to spending or intervention. If neoliberalization describes a pattern of (incomplete, contradictory, and crisis-prone) restructuring, one that has been historically dominant since the 1970s but which has always been associated with uneven sociospatial development, then one should not anticipate some unidirectional convergence on small, more-or-less identical state forms. Uneven sociospatial development is not a transitional stage on the path to blanket neoliberalism. It is for this reason that recognition of the complex historical geographies of neoliberalization is not just a matter of calling contingent exceptions, it is key to understanding the process itself.

Market politics, doubled up: $N_2 \ldots N_3$

Neoliberalism has always come in varieties. In its long ideological gestation, between the 1920s and the 1960s, neoliberalism was for the most part a bipolar project—as the initial dialogue between Vienna and Freiberg gave way to an increasingly asymmetrical exchange between the Ordoliberals and the Chicagoans. Following the project's consummation with state power, during the 1970s and 1980s, the landscape of neoliberalism was destined to become not only more complex but also more restless. Domestic politics, of course, played a constitutive role in each "transition," but cumulatively, these were soon adding up to more than the sum of their parts. The diffusion of neoliberalism has not been a lateral, additive, and sequential process of country-by-country conversion. Neither was it simply imposed from above, by Washington agencies. Its progression, instead, has been geometric.

The Chilean experiment under Pinochet was formative, but on its own would no doubt have been judged to be an idiosyncrasy of authoritarian politics. When the United States and the United Kingdom made their parallel transitions to an especially assertive form of neoliberal politics, however, the balance of power began to shift. Both key players in international (not to say imperial) politics, and in the multilateral agencies, the US and the UK exerted cross-border influence through a variety of channels, mobilizing both hard and soft power. Together, these two countries accounted for almost one third of world GDP in the early 1980s, which was now being (mis)managed according to monetarist principles. And the attendant high-interest rate regime directly contributed to the global debt crisis that followed, delivering developing nations around the world into the hands of the structural adjusters in the multilateral banks. "Policy-based lending" would add external impetus to a series of subsequent, often violent neoliberal transitions, especially across Latin America, as more and more economies were folded painfully into the common matrix of neoliberalization. And next came the fall of the Berlin Wall, and the redesignation of Russia and Eastern Europe as transition economies—another new space of experimentation in neoliberal shock treatment.

Certainly, there were recurring themes in many of these transitions, not least of which were prior conditions of macroeconomic stress and the concomitant delegitimation of extant forms of macroeconomic management.[56] Yet no two transitions were the same. The kind of crisis-driven paradigm shift experienced in Britain, for example, was quite different to the "long transitions" of countries like Sweden, Singapore, and China, even though archetypal echoes of "classic" forms of neoliberalization can be found among all of these cases. Neither is this simply a matter of timing, of deciding when to slide a particular country from the social-democratic or state-socialist to the neoliberal side of the ideological abacus. Rather, there are common processes of regulatory transformation across all of these cases, with consequences not only for their internal constitution, but for their interrelation and interconnectivity. This is not simply a matter, then, of arithmetically adding actually existing neoliberalisms, once they have traversed some bright-line transition point, for not only does each "case" reveal a conjuncturally unique relationship with the evolving and globalizing neoliberal "whole," the distinctive integration of each regulatory formation also contributes to the remaking of transnational neoliberalism. John Clarke has aptly called this process of part–whole multiplication "doubling."[57]

This doubling metaphor provides a way to think about the mutation of neoliberalism through time and space, since it hints not only at potentially exponential processes of deepening and complexification, but also episodes of "redoubling" and occasionally "doubling back." First, and with respect to the temporal dynamics of neoliberalization, a preliminary distinction can be drawn between the "roll-back" and "roll-out" faces of neoliberalism.[58] Roll-back processes tend to be predominant with the initial onset of neoliberalization, when restructuring projects are typically focused on dismantling alien institutions, disorganizing alternate centers of power, deregulating zones of bureaucratic control, and disciplining potentially unruly (collective) subjects. Often prosecuted in the name of deregulation, devolution, and even democratization, this offensive is typically associated with attacks on labor unions, planning agencies, entitlement systems, and public bureaucracies, by way of the now familiar repertoire of funding cuts, organizational downsizing, market testing, and privatization. These maneuvers are animated not only by the prosaic concerns of governmental control and political self-preservation, they also reflect the Chicago mentality, that spontaneously organizing social and market forces will somehow automatically fill the vacuums created by the retrenched state institutions and disorganized collective spaces. However, this first front in the free-market counterrevolution tends quite quickly to encounter predictable limits—neoliberalism's own object lessons in market failure. Responses to these serve further to entrench a contextually specific medium-term politics of restructuring within each neoliberalizing social formation, the residues of which can be long-lasting, not only for the union movement, across the voluntary, nongovernmental organization (NGO) or "third" sector, and in the public bureaucracies, but for neoliberalizing formations themselves. Pathways of neoliberalization, in other words, are never constructed on some tabula rasa; they are very much defined by the *particular* terrains of struggle that free-market reformers confront "domestically."

With time, the rising costs of deregulatory overreach, public austerity, market failure, and social abandonment typically force neoliberals to engage with a range of unsavory challenges of intervention, amelioration, and reregulation. This protracted phase of "roll-out" neoliberalism differs substantially from the preceding politics of retrenchment, even as it is largely predicated on the limits and contradictions of the roll-back moment. It is typically associated with an explosion of "market conforming" regulatory incursions—from the selective empowerment of community organizations and NGOs as (flexible, low-cost, non-state) service providers, through management by audit and devolved governance, to the embrace of public–private partnership—in the form of an on-the-hoof rediscovery and reinvention of an Ordoliberal ethic. These can be classified amongst the "flanking mechanisms" of mutating neoliberal rule, though the metaphor of flanking suggests a secondary or supporting role for such devices, when in fact they may be more fundamentally implicated in the periodic reconstruction of neoliberal governance.[59] There is consequently both an internal-integral logic to roll-out neoliberalism (triggered by the failures of simple deregulation) and an extrinsic-contextual dynamic (derived from the increased reliance on various institutional supports, flanking mechanisms, and policy adjustments). By way of illustration, examples of these roll-back/roll-out dialectics in particular policy fields have included: labor-market flexibility and deregulation policies, coupled with welfare cutbacks, leading to the downstream imperative to develop "in work" support systems for the working poor; privatization of public utilities, like water and communications, leading to a need to extend regulatory oversight, in the face of system failures, private monopoly abuses, and legitimacy problems; social-service cutbacks in fields such as public housing and subsidized food being partially backfilled through new non-entitlement services, delivered by nonprofit or private providers; overreach in trade liberalization or financial deregulation, in cases of marked economic dislocation or market failure, being followed by exceptions-to-the-rule "deals" and reregulatory "corrections." These are, simultaneously, examples of neoliberal policy failure *and* neoliberal policy adaption, again underlining the sense in which neoliberal restructuring resembles not so much a triumphal, forward march as a series of prosaic "forward failures."

The repertoire of political projects and institutional experiments, under the tendentially dominant roll-out moment of neoliberalization, has been likewise proliferative and variegated, demonstrating again that late or deep forms of neoliberalization are associated not with simple convergence, but with the complex "cutting" of market and nonmarket modes of governance and with new forms of uneven sociospatial development. The wide range of roll-out maneuvers encompasses so-called post-Washington consensus initiatives in poverty alleviation and community empowerment, under the aegis of the multilateral and international donor agencies; the marriage of social interventionism and deference to economic globalization under the rubric of the Third Way; right-leaning accommodations in the form of compassionate conservatism and faith-based partnerships; and so on.[60] It should go without saying that none of these adaptations represents a "purely" neoliberal logic, nor to they resolve the failures and contradictions that are their impetus; rather, as messy hybrids, forged through practice, they reflect the radical non-achievability of such purity. If neoliberalism is a market-utopian ideal, rendered as a political destination, then the process of neoliberalization, while it may take many forms, can never mean simple movement along some path towards deregulated freedom. On the contrary, in as far as neoliberalism "survives," it does so through continued mongrelization.

If neoliberalism obviously existed with its mongrel others during the roll-back phase, when the geographies of the market revolution were being constructed across enemy territories, it has since been embroiled in a quite different array of cohabitative arrangements. Roll-out neoliberalization, then, represents more than an attempt to remake the world in the image of markets, most actually existing alternatives having been weakened. Instead, it represents a series of far-from-perfect attempts to wrestle with the challenges and contradictions of governance in a malmarketized world. One metageography of neoliberalism—deriving from efforts to support, flank, and consolidate roll-out forms of market governance—is therefore layered upon another—based on the landscapes of struggle and contestation that characterized the roll-back phase. It could be the case, as Cerny has suggested, that a discernible array of "varieties of neoliberalism" has been crystallizing during more recent experiences of late-neoliberal adjustment.[61] There may be some heuristic value in such analytical maneuvers, though they remain vulnerable to the critique that the search for taxonomic symmetry across a fixed grid of nation-states does little to expose the relational interpenetration of neoliberal regimes, and the corresponding ways in which the qualitative *form* of uneven spatial development has itself been evolving.[62] This is not simply a question of whether the neoliberalization process has passed some hegemonic tipping point, nationally or globally. Again, the transnational deepening of neoliberalization tendencies will not imply convergence on a singular model.

As Roger Keil has argued, a third phase of neoliberalization, defined in terms of *rolling with* an unstable, but normalized market order, might even be taking shape: the "double dynamics" of three decades of neoliberalization have, he has suggested, resulted in a consolidated form of neoliberal governmentality, around which most social actors (both progressive and conservative) now formulate their strategies.[63] An alliterative alternative here might be *roiling* neoliberalism, as a still-dominant but deeply flawed "settlement," increasingly buffeted by crises.[64] Certainly, there is evidence that various facets of neoliberal rule have been consolidated, quite often through crises. In the terms sketched out here, this entails a shift toward yet-more contradictory and reactive forms of roll-out neoliberalism, coupled with a deepening of the degree of interdependency between neoliberalizing regimes. Schematically, these conditions are summarized in Table 1.2.

This first form of doubling, then, refers to the spatiotemporal dynamics immanent within the process of neoliberalization itself, the "internal" dialectic of deregulation and reregulation, which in some respects represent real-world re-enactments of the Chicago–Ordo debates of the 1940s. Of course, these are social processes, not automatic mechanisms, and at best they tend to be associated with the rescheduling, displacement or temporary containment of crisis tendencies—variously triggered by marketization, commodification, and privatization—rather than their resolution.[65] This calls attention to a second important source of doubling, redoubling and doubling-back dynamics: active resistance to, and contestation of, neoliberalization. Neoliberal incursions have at times, and in certain places, been met by concerted resistance, while (actual and anticipated) forms of resistance have clearly shaped both the content and timing of market reform efforts. The epic confrontation between the Thatcher government and the coalmining unions, for example, had long-term consequences for both protagonists, and continues to be seen by many as a decisive tipping point in British political–economic history.[66] The mobilization in Chiapas, Mexico in the early 1990s, along with countless other struggles against structural adjustment and privatization across Latin America, and the Battle of Seattle at the end of that decade, likewise reshaped the terrains across which neoliberal strategies were formulated, (re)politicizing some of the most technocratic and anti-democratic forms of policymaking, and prompting amelioration and accommodation in some cases, evasion and intransigence in others.[67]

Less easily measurable, but arguably no less significant in shaping the politics and pathways of neoliberalization is that notional landscape of battles *not* fought. The anticipation of robust resistance or popular back-lashes, the presence of entrenched special interests, and the sheer intractability of some institutional or social problems effectively defines no-go areas, or zones of softly-softly incursion, for would-be market reformers: agricultural subsidies, disability benefits, and middle-class pensions are

Table 1.2. Relational spaces of neoliberalization

		SPATIAL RELATIONS ⇒	
		Shallow neoliberalization . . . pursuit of locally specific strategies	**Deep neoliberalization** . . . inter-local connectivities and reflexive relations
R E G U L A T O R	**Roll-back neoliberalism** . . . the destructive and deregulatory moment	*Attacks on inherited Keynesian-welfarist structures, coupled with primitive deregulation of markets,* including: ■ monetarist macroeconomic management ■ primitive marketization: dogmatic deregulation and privatization ■ place-specific assaults on institutional and spatial strongholds of welfare statism and social collectivism (e.g. social service cuts, deunionization)	*Extension of neoliberal strategies to the international domain,* including: ■ reductions in overseas aid ■ imposition of structural adjustment programs ■ initial liberalization of financial markets and trading relations ■ external imposition of neoliberal strategies ■ intensification of coercive pressures emanating from international markets
Y F O R M S ⇓	**Roll-out neoliberalism** . . . the creative and proactive moment	*Proactive statecraft and institution-building in service of neoliberal goals,* including: ■ invasive moral re-regulation of the urban poor ■ expansion of penal state apparatus and social control policies ■ continued crisis-management of deregulated and privatized sectors ■ extension of, and experimentation with, market-complementing forms of regulation ■ technocratic economic regulation within neoliberal parameters	*Normalization of neoliberal logics and premises in inter-local relations,* including: ■ "fast policy" development through inter-local transfer, learning, and emulation ■ appropriation of networking forms of governance and policy development ■ institutionalization of competitive globalism (e.g. through multilateral trade policies and public debt ceilings) ■ posture of permanent adaptability and reflexivity in fields like urban governance and social/penal policy

Source: Adapted from Tickell and Peck (2003).

among those fields where even neoliberal firebrands tend to tread carefully, or not at all; projects like tax and welfare reform, and the restructuring of health and education systems, often display nonlinear trajectories that span several administrations. Even some of the most formidable bastions of the neoliberal project, such as the largest of the free-market think tanks in Washington, DC, will candidly confess that they are confronted by an enduring challenge of "lots of targets, not many bullets."[68] For a complex range of reasons, some reform projects may be quickly stifled; some fail to gain early traction; others never get off the drawing board.

In addition to this history of non-events, there is a growing list of situated and specific responses to neoliberal policies (such as privatization and deunionization) which have evolved into active networks, social movements or multi-locale projects, such as the living-wage movement.[69] In this case, what began as a rather particularistic, if not defensive, struggle against wage exploitation and the outsourcing of municipal contracts in cities like Baltimore subsequently spawned not only imitative efforts in other cities (across the United States and beyond), it also generated a mutating network of "lateral" alliances with parallel movements, such as those around immigrants' rights, fair housing, social unionism, service-sector organizing, and so on. It should be acknowledged, of course, that notwithstanding these progressive achievements, the starting point for such efforts reflected labor's weakened bargaining position—not least with respect to the capacity for holding the line, nationally, on labor standards and minimum wages.[70] Nevertheless, resistance to neoliberalism does not always conform to the David-and-Goliath metaphor of plucky, local resistance to a metastasizing global project,[71] alternative politics may take radically different, unanticipated forms, cutting a very different course and, by the same token, (re)shaping the market offensive.

Social responses to neoliberalization that do not merely delay or displace the effects of free-market projects, but challenge their rationale, force changes to their form, or even stop them in their tracks, have been increasingly explained by reference to another doubling metaphor, that of the "double movement." Indeed, it might be said that the widespread rediscovery of Polanyi's classic text, *The Great Transformation*, owes a great deal not only to its prescient critique of free-market utopianism, haute finance, and liberal globalism, but its historical diagnosis of the tendency for reflexive countermovements to form in the wake of such unsustainable advances.[72] Polanyi's was not, of course, a predictive model, and he died believing that the historical errors of nineteenth-century laissez-faire would never be repeated. Furthermore, he left us with no guarantee that contemporary double movements will necessarily take a progressive form—authoritarian and conservative responses to the excesses of marketization, deregulation, and commodification might be just as likely.[73] Yet systematic vulnerability to failure in the "markets" for finance, labor, and for natural resources undoubtedly raises the persistent prospect of Polanyian reflexes—albeit of many kinds—and again calls attention to the zigzagging character of the neoliberalization process. It may be going too far to forecast that late-neoliberalism will fulfill Marx's dictum that capitalism will eventually produce its own gravediggers, say in the form of a unified class of contingent workers or a revolutionary "multitude,"[74] but there are nevertheless social (as well as ecological) limits to the globalization of market rule. This is another reason, then, why the "necessitarian" rhetoric of neoliberalism should not be confused with some bulletproof condition of inexorability.[75]

If there are grounds for optimism, at least of the will, in this regard, the third arena of doubling dynamics tends to be associated with more sobering messages regarding the reproductive doggedness of neoliberal rule. What might be called the relational spatialities of neoliberalization are embedded in a range of extra-local, transnational, and cross-scalar dynamics, which while never automatically securing market-oriented governance "from above" or "from offshore," have nevertheless played constitutive roles in its rise and reproduction. As Andrew Gamble has argued, if neoliberalism has been dependent

for its dissemination on the internal politics of each individual capitalist state, its spread might have been slower and its influence less profound. But the end of the fixed exchange rate mechanism in 1971 centered on the dollar and the floating of all the major currencies gave an enormous boost to monetarist ideas as the means for containing inflation from the mid-1970s onwards [...] In sense which is true but rather unenlightening all governments throughout the global economy are now neo-liberal governments, because they are obliged to operate within a set of structures in the global economy which reflect, however imperfectly, neo-liberal principles. What is important to grasp, however, is that neo-liberalism—like globalization—is not monolithic or proceeding in a single direction. It has different aspects and many contradictions, which create different political spaces and possible outcomes.[76]

These conditions, it must be reiterated, do not amount to a perfectly integrated and contradiction-free system of neoliberal globalism, even if they do establish broadly pro-market "rules of the game," feedback loops, default forms of regulatory politics, incentives, and sanctions that are tendentially favorable to the propagation of market rule, while never determining them. As Andrew Gamble, Phil Cerny, and others have noted, there remains considerable variability (and more than a little volatility) across the global political economy. Indeed, the degree of variety within the neoliberal "family" itself may be increasing, even as the trajectories of regulatory transformation continue to be framed in neoliberal terms.[77] According to Jessop's influential formulation, these conditions reflect the heightened "ecological dominance" of neoliberal globalization, which asymmetrically imposes its developmental logic (and contradictions) on other socioeconomic systems, while falling short of absolute dominance. Neoliberalism's expansionist dynamic is rooted in a recursive relationship with short-term, financialized, profit- and market-oriented forms of capital accumulation, the persistence of which has the potential to sustain the adaptive rule regimes, ecological dominance, and path-shaping capacities of neoliberalism, even after its moment of hegemony has passed. This environment exhibits, for want of a better term, jungle law-like properties, as the dull compulsion of financialized competition drives both ad hoc and strategic forms of neoliberal reinvention on an ongoing basis.[78]

Neoliberalism has achieved this (ecologically) dominant position by variously exploiting, reflecting, and intensifying conditions of globalizing economic turbulence since the 1970s, particularly with respect to co-constitutive trends like increased capital mobility and exposure to international trade; structural reorientations in favor of shareholder value and financialization; the generalized intensification of competitive pressures, speculation, and short-termism; widespread evasion and externalization of the costs of social and ecological reproduction; the development of various forms of state outsourcing, devolved governance, and lean bureaucracy, locking in competitive austerity; and the weakening of specific national government capacities, especially with respect to sociospatial redistribution and long-term (public, social) investment. According to Cerny, these circumstances have helped to secure a global regime of "embedded neoliberalism," enabled by and realized through a complementary reconfiguration of socioeconomic governance systems, which have become increasingly porous and interdependent.[79] This regime is certainly not stable, but neither is it likely to be readily "reversible" in any meaningful sense. Instead, embedded neoliberalism radically reconstitutes the playing field upon which political and economic strategies are being calculated and prosecuted—even under conditions of global economic crisis. It represents, in Phil Cerny's words, "a new 'bottom line' for the politics of both left and right":

Embedded neoliberalism involves first of all an acceptance that we live in a multi-level, more open and market-like globalizing world in which informal and nego-tiated policy processes do not merely complement relations among nation-states but constitute a complex, fungible, pluralized political game that is drawing in ever more actors. Furthermore, globalization has generated a range of multilevel, inter-locking playing fields on which actors have increasing scope to experiment and innovate policy approaches in practical situations ... [N]eoliberalism, with its mix-ture of free-market liberalism, arms'-length regulation, institutional flexibility and international openness, has proven to be a relatively manipulable and fungible platform for actors to use to reconstitute their strategies and tactics.[80]

Neoliberalization, according to this formulation, is characterized not only by serious constraints and limitations, but also by new registers of political opportunity, drawing on an increasingly wide range of (often co-opted) social actors. Echoing Jessop's vision of post-hegemonic entrenchment, embedded neoliberalism is seen to have become "overdetermined" in an increasingly transnationalized political–economic sphere. Cerny charac-terizes it as a "fusion project," with its own spatiality, since "neoliberalism [now] reaches the parts—the places and spaces—other discourses and polit-ical projects no longer reach."[81]

But even if neoliberalism sometimes travels alone, as a mobile technology of governance, it must always cohabit with others. The project is destined to remain incomplete, even as it aspires to remake the world in its own image. In political terms, "[n]eoliberalism needs coalition partners, allies and sup-porters"; in system-theoretic terms, it must coexist with others, even in circumstances of ecologically dominant market rule, spawning a range of hybrid species under conditions of contingent and conjunctural specifici-ty.[82] In this sense, it can be seen as a parasitic form of political practice, albeit an especially aggressive one.[83] There may therefore be a certain degree of truth in what otherwise might seem to be a sloppy and unprincipled claim, that neoliberalism has become omnipresent, but it is a complex, mediated, and heterogeneous kind of omnipresence, not a state of blanket conformity. Neoliberalism has not simply diffused as a (self-)replicating system. Pino-chet's authoritarian market revolution was never repeated; there are no doubles of Reaganomics. Rather, neoliberalism has evolved in a shape-shift-ing manner, through an uneven process of open-ended mutation and cross-referential development. It is therefore inescapable that neoliberalism is associated with institutional promiscuity and ideological sprawl, as it has been relationally reshaped as a multipolar project. It has always been so. There were even signs of bipolar disorder in its intellectual origins, which are nowhere near as pure as the Chicago School's revisionist scientism would suggest. The actually existing worlds of neoliberalism are not pristine spaces of market rationality and constitutional order; they are institutionally cluttered places marked by experimental-but-flawed systems of governance, cumulative problems of social fallout, and serial market failure.

"It all depends what you mean..."

Neoliberalism, Susan Watkins has observed, "is a dismal epithet...imprecise and over-used," while conceding that in a practical sense "some term is needed to describe the macro-economic paradigm that has predominated from the end of the 1970s."[84] This has, however, to be more than a placeholder term. The word must have content. Yet in practice, neoliberalism seems to be an unstable signifier, maybe an increasingly unstable one. Even in its earliest stages of ideational development, it denoted more a space of conversation and dispute than some transcendental essence. Once released into the world, it has evolved in a reeling, crisis-prone manner, apparently becoming even-more plastic, porous, and promiscuous. And not only is "neoliberalism increasingly what actors make of it," as Cerny has argued;[85] it has always been what (situated) actors make of it. But the project's potential for plasticity has only truly been revealed in the real-time context of its own roll out. So, when David Harvey was asked, in the midst of the global financial unraveling of 2009, whether the world was witnessing the death of neoliberalism, he felt it necessary to respond, "it depends what you mean by neo-liberalism."[86] He was not being evasive, for there is almost no other way to approach the question. (And his answer was basically "no," at least if *neoliberalism* is taken to denote a historically specific configuration of class relations, dispossessive accumulation, and regressive redistribution, backed by the combined powers of the state and capital.) Again, it all depends what you mean by neoliberalism.

Harvey can be credited with elaborating one of the more singular and unambiguous accounts of neoliberalization, as a class project, primarily animated by (national) states, in search of politically sustainable means of profit restoration, following the accumulation crises of the 1970s. Aiwa Ong, amongst others, has bridled at this "big N" formulation, alleging that its system-centricity and totalizing logic yields a conception of Neoliberalism as "an all-encompassing condition under the hegemony of unfettered markets," together with metaphorical rendering of the neoliberalization process "as an economic tsunami that attacks national space, represented by an inert space of market-driven forces and effects."[87]

Harvey's *Brief History* certainly does not skirt around the question of the incipient logic of the project, and it could only really sketch the broad contours of the "moving map" of neoliberalization, though the analysis is not nearly as mechanistic–militaristic as Ong suggests. Harvey explains, for example, that

The capitalist world stumbled towards neoliberalization...through a series of gyrations and chaotic experiments that really only emerged as a new orthodoxy with the articulation of what became known as the "Washington Consensus" in the 1990s. By then, both Clinton and Blair could easily have reversed Nixon's earlier statement and simply said "We are all neoliberals now." The uneven geographical development of neoliberalism, its frequently lop-sided and partial application from one state and social formation to another, testifies to the tentativeness of neoliberal solutions and the complex ways in which political forces, historical traditions, and existing institutional arrangements all shaped why and how the process of neoliberalization actually occurred.[88]

The crystallization of neoliberalism as a hegemonic ideological fix depicted here overlaps with Jessop's recent reconstruction of the historical geography of neoliberalism, which effectively hits both a high point and a tipping point in the mid-1990s, after which the accumulation of neoliberal state failures, coupled with a growing reliance on extra-neoliberal "flanking" institutions, yields increasingly incoherent forms of development—even as the "ecological dominance" of neoliberal globalism retains its dogged hold.[89] Amongst the global concatenation of circumstances that have been driving these contradictions to the surface, as Jessop and Harvey have both maintained, is the unsustainable, structural coupling of overproduction in China and overconsumption in the United States. China's pathway to neoliberalization has likewise been conjuncturally unique, predicated on a particular configuration of global political and economic conditions and entailing the complex "incorporat[ion of] neoliberal elements interdigitated with authoritarian central control."[90]

However, this is a yet-more egregious overextension of "big N" analysis, in Ong's view: "China is deviant because neoliberal policies are combined with state authoritarianism."[91] Yet as Harvey and others have pointed out, there is nothing *exceptional*, either in principle or in practice, in the construction of accommodations between neoliberalism and authoritarianism—witness Chile, Singapore, or indeed Stuart Hall's analysis of "authoritarian populism" in Britain. To style these configurations as deviant has the effect, moreover, of naturalizing neoliberalism in supposedly "normal" or non-deviant settings, such as the United States. If, as has been argued here, neoliberalism not only has, but *must,* parasitically coexist with (or off) other state forms and social formations, then manifestations of neoliberalization in the United States are neither more, nor less, "hybrid" than those found in China—indeed, the conditions of existence of each of these hybrids are, in this instance, also relationally interdependent.[92] Neoliberalization must be exposed to critical scrutiny *both* where it superficially appears to be out of place ("neoliberalism with Chinese characteristics") *and* where it is apparently normalized ("neoliberalism with American characteristics"). Making sense of these manifestations is not a matter of measuring degrees of deviation from a supposedly paradigmatic norm; or naming states of exception or varieties of neoliberalism in relation, implicitly or explicitly, to some ideal-typical "original" or perfect form; it calls for a qualitative analysis of conjunctures and connections.

Constructions of Neoliberal Reason seeks to make a contribution to this effort, methodologically speaking, by bringing neoliberalism to ground in various ways. This means approaching neoliberalization not as some automatic system, but as an earthly process, realized through political action and institutional reinvention. It means closely engaging with neoliberal programs and programmers in word and in deed. It means confronting actors in the flesh—literally if possible—engaging with those at the sharp and blunt ends of processes of socioregulatory transformation. Here, "neoliberalism" is not some disembodied artifact of political theory; it has a pulse and sometimes a stutter. These often prosaic and occasionally surprising encounters with neoliberalism—sometimes with its dander up, sometimes with its pants down—can be useful in exposing the seamy undersides of "the project," its daily dynamics and underlying frailties. There would be no "project" of course, absent these routine acts of reproduction, but the political economy of neoliberalization is more than just the sum of these parts; it is also a product of their articulation and interrelation. The explanatory and indeed political challenge, then, is constantly to track back and forth across cases and moments, between the (moving) "parts" and the (evolving) "whole"—whether these parts are antipoverty programs, the daily work of blue-chip think tanks, or the travels of vernacular theorists and policy entrepreneurs.

There would be little gained from such work if it presumed system-functionality, treating each element or actor as a cog in some smoothly functioning machine. The corresponding methodological challenge—of finding neoliberalism in its various moments of actualization, failure, normalization, and adaptation—is an intrinsically geographical one. It is a matter of determining the relational location of specific events, actors, and claims on the broader terrain of socioregulatory restructuring. The outcome is not so much a map of neoliberalization, more a series of traverses and triangulated readings across a shifting landscape. This is not a search for typical cases but for flashpoints and crossroads. It will be necessary, in this context, to take local specificities seriously, but this must also involve the sustained probing "extra-local" logics and illogics—in the spirit of open and critical investigation rather than premature explanatory closure.

The ontology of neoliberalism is consequently imagined here as an evolving web of relays, routines, and relations. The attendant methodological strategy, involves exposing and exploring some of the "connective tissues" of the neoliberalization process, their contingent textures and creative tensions. This will not, then, be an account of neoliberalism as some extraterrestrial force, reorganizing political–economic history in its own image and predetermining outcomes on the ground. Rather, the following chapters will trace some of the ways that neoliberalization works in a range of settings, across the ideational, institutional, and ideological registers. In particular, they will call attention to the "hidden hands" of the market revolution, placing actors back on the stage and studying their various scripts and improvisations, while also asking where some of their best lines and improvisations have come from. Complementing studies of "actually existing neoliberalism," the book will take account of the ebb and flow of market rule, of the ways in which projects and practices of neoliberalization are made and remade. The shape-shifting character neoliberalism is itself the focus of concern, in an analysis that seeks to *travel with* the neoliberalization process. The journey begins, appropriately some would say, in Vienna. But before it is over, it will have included stops—some brief, some more extended—in New York and New Orleans, London and Detroit, Chicago and Santiago, Washington, DC and Paris, and quite a few places in between. Such are the travels of neoliberalism.

Notes

1. Quoted in *Guardian Weekly,* May 22, 2009: 42.
2. See Dorrien, G. (1993) *The Neoconservative Mind.* Philadelphia: Temple University Press; Kristol, I. (1999) *Neo-conservatism.* New York: Free Press.
3. As Auerbach (2007: 27) observes, "economists never in any significant way used the term economic liberalism, let alone neoliberalism. The main reason for this is that mainstream economists fall so squarely within the paradigm of economic

liberalism that there is no need to ever think or talk about it as a shared mental model."

4. *Economist* (2004) There's a word for that, *Economist,* November 6: 14.
5. See Albert, M. (1993) *Capitalism Against Capitalism.* London: Whurr.
6. See, especially, Bourdieu (1998).
7. See Chapters 2 and 3 for further discussion; plus Foucault (2008) and Mirowski and Plehwe (2009).
8. Mont Pelerin Society statement of aims, reproduced in Hartwell (1995: 41).
9. Friedman, M. (1951) Nyliberalismen Og Dens Muligheter [Neoliberalism and its prospects], *Farmand,* February 17: 91–3; translated by Anette Nyqvist and Jamie Peck.
10. Friedman (1982: viii–ix).
11. See Klein (2007), Harvey (2005), and Valdes (1995).
12. See, especially, Kogut and Macpherson (2008).
13. See Bockman and Eyal (2002).
14. Grover Norquist of Americans for Tax Reform mused at the time that tax reform via military occupation might hold lessons for flat-tax advocates elsewhere, "Somehow, it's easier when you start from scratch" (quoted in *Washington Post,* November 2, 2003: A1). See also Peck (2004).
15. Plehwe (2009: 1).
16. See the commentary in *The Economist* (2009) Market fatigue, *The Economist,* October 3: S21–S24.
17. See Peck *et al.* (2010) and Peck and Tickell (1994b).
18. Albo, G. (2007) Neoliberalism and the discontented. In L. Panitch and C. Leys, eds., *Global Flashpoints.* London: Merlin Press, 354.
19. See Stiglitz (2010) and Peck *et al.* (2010).
20. See Gamble (1994); see also Hall (1988) and Jessop *et al.* (1988).
21. See Harvey (2005); Wang, H. (2003) *China's New Order.* Cambridge, MA: Harvard University Press.
22. See Bohle, D. and Greskovits, B. (2007) Neoliberalism, embedded neoliberalism, and neocorporatism: paths towards transnational capitalism in Central-Eastern Europe, *West European Politics,* 30/3: 443–66; Kostadinova, P. (2007) Neo-liberal supraterritoriality? The impact of economic liberalization on globalization in Central and Eastern Europe, *Contemporary Studies in Economic and Financial Analysis,* 89: 65–93.
23. See the discussion in Peck *et al.* (2010) and Watkins (2010).
24. Brenner and Theodore (2002a); on the "essence" neoliberalism, see Bourdieu and Wacquant (2001).
25. See Hall (1988); Jessop *et al.* (1988); and Gamble (1994).
26. See Otero, G. (1996) *Neoliberalism Revisited.* Boulder: Westview; Centeno, M. A. (1994) *Democracy Within Reason.* University Park, PA: Pennsylvania State University Press.

27. See Fourcade-Gourinchas and Babb (2002); Prasad (2005); and Weyland, K. G. (2002) *The Politics of Market Reform in Fragile Democracies*. Princeton: Princeton University Press.

28. Cooney, P. (2007) Argentina's quarter century experiment with neoliberalism: from dictatorship to depression, *Revista de Economia Contemporânea*, 11/1: 7–37; Bond, P. and Manyanya, M. (2003) *Zimbabwe's Plunge: Exhausted Nationalism, Neoliberalism and the Search for Social Justice*. Harare: Weaver Press.

29. See Peck (2004) and Peck and Theodore (2007). Amongst the notable exceptions to this general rule, see Davis, M. (1986) *Prisoners of the American Dream*. London: Verso; Moody, K. (1997) *Workers in a Lean World*. London: Verso; Blyth (2002); and Pollin (2003).

30. See Peck (2001) and Wacquant (2009).

31. See Arrighi, G. (2007) *Adam Smith in Beijing*. London: Verso; Harvey (2005); and Peck and Theodore (2007).

32. Miller, T. and Holmes, K. R. (2009) *2009 Index of Economic Freedom*. Washington, DC: Heritage Foundation.

33. Gwartney, J. and Lawson, R. (2009) *Economic Freedom of the World*. Vancouver: Fraser Institute, 15. Iceland was ranked #1 in the world, on the Fraser Institute's regulation measure up until 2006, on the basis of its highly privatized and "open" banking system.

34. Quoted in Lewis, M. (2009) Wall Street on the tundra, *Vanity Fair*, April: 140.

35. Quoted in *EUObserver*, April 27, 2009, accessed at <http://euobserver.com/15/28011>.

36. Boas and Gans-Morse (2009).

37. Williamson (2003: 325–326).

38. Clarke (2008: 138).

39. Boas and Gans-Morse (2009: 156).

40. On this theme, see Larner (2003); Peck (2004), and Mirowski (2009).

41. Boas and Gans-Morse (2009: 156).

42. Foucault (2008: 107).

43. See Ptak (2009) and Peacock and Willgerodt (1989). For further discussion, see Chapter Two.

44. Foucault (2008: 111, emphasis added).

45. See Boarman, Patrick M. (1964) *Germany's Economic Dilemma*. New Haven, CT: Yale University Press.

46. See Simons' (1934) pamphlet, and the further discussion in Chapter Three.

47. See Foucault (2008: 161). Röpke, the erudite Ordoliberal, insisted that in practical and intellectual terms economics must entail "moving beyond supply and demand." See Boarman, P. M. (2000). Apostle of a humane economy: Wilhelm Röpke, *Humanitas*, 13/1: 31–67.

48. Foucault (2008: 79). See also Mirowski and Plehwe (2009).

49. Gamble (2006: 21).

50. The critique of Hayek (1944) is in Hansen, A. (1945) The new crusade against planning, *New Republic*, 112/1: 9–12.

51. Boas and Gans-Morse (2009: 139).

52. See Valdes (1995: 236). Pre-1973 discussions of neoliberalism in Chile also typically hewed to the Ordo definition of the term, and to German scholars and cases (Boas and Gans-Morse, 2009).

53. Silva (2006: 44).

54. See Silva (2006: 39), Boas and Gans-Morse (2009), and Pollack, M. (1997) *The New Right in Chile*. New York: St. Martin's Press.

55. See, especially, Gamble (2006), Jayasuriya (2006), Mudge (2008), Turner (2009), and Mirowski and Plehwe (2009).

56. Fourcade-Gourinchas and Babb (2002).

57. See Clarke (2008) and Peck (2004).

58. For a discussion of these issues, see Peck and Tickell (2002).

59. For discussions of flanking, see Jessop (2003) and Graefe (2006).

60. For different takes on these issues, see Naím (2000); Cammack, P. (2004) What the World Bank means by poverty reduction, and why it matters, *New Political Economy*, 9/2: 189–211; Porter, D. and Craig, D. (2004) The third way and the third world: poverty reduction and social inclusion in the rise of "inclusive" liberalism, *Review of International Political Economy*, 11/2, 387–423; Graefe (2006).

61. Cerny (2008).

62. Rhetorically, "varieties" approaches tend to emphasize their differences with simple convergence arguments. More germane is the comparison between this form of static institutionalism and relational forms of political economy (see Peck and Theodore, 2007; Brenner *et al.*, 2010).

63. Keil, R. (2009) The urban politics of roll-with-it neoliberalization, *City*, 13/2–3: 231–245.

64. See Peck (2010) and Peck *et al.* (2010).

65. It may be possible to periodize national or local experiences of neoliberalism according the dominance of roll-back/roll-out dynamics, though these should not be reified as fixed analytical categories or regime types, since they are defined in relation to the neoliberalization *process* (see Peck *et al.*, 2009, 2010).

66. See Milne, S. (2004) *The Enemy Within*. London: Verso, and Beckett, F. and Hencke, D. (2009) *Marching to the Fault Line*. London: Constable and Robinson.

67. See, respectively, Harvey, N. (1998) *The Chiapas Rebellion*. Durham, NC: Duke University Press; Cockburn, A. and St. Clair, J. (2000) *Five Days That Shook the World*. London: Verso.

68. Strategist, free-market think tank, interviewed by Jamie Peck, September 2005, quoted in Peck, J. (2007) Response: countering neoliberalism, *Urban Geography*, 27/8: 729–733.

69. See Pollin, R. and Luce, S. (2000) *The Living Wage*. New York: New Press; Luce, S. (2004) *Fighting for a Living Wage*. Ithaca: Cornell University Press.

70. See Freeman, R. B. (2005) Fighting for other folks' wages: the logic and illogic of living wage campaigns, *Industrial Relations*, 44/1: 14–31.
71. See Leitner *et al.* (2007).
72. See Block, F. (2001) Introduction. In K. Polanyi, *The Great Transformation*, Boston: Beacon, xviii–xxxviii, and Silver and Arrighi (2003).
73. See Panitch, L. and Gindin, S. (2008) The current crisis: a socialist perspective, *The Bullet*, 142, September 30; Peck *et al.* (2010).
74. See Hardt, M. and Negri, A. (2000) *Empire*. Cambridge: Harvard University Press; Hardt, M. and Negri, A. (2004) *Multitude*. New York: Penguin; Prashad (2003), cf. Wacquant (2009) and Peck (2010).
75. See Munck, R. (2003) Neoliberalism, necessitarianism and alternatives in Latin America: there is no alternative (TINA)? *Third World Quarterly*, 24/3: 495–511.
76. Gamble (2006: 24, 34–35).
77. See Gamble (2006), Cerny (2008, 2009), Jessop (2000), and Brenner *et al.* (2010).
78. See Peck and Tickell (1994a, 1994b, 2002).
79. See also Gill (1995), for a parallel, Gramscian account.
80. Cerny (2008: 27, 39).
81. Cerny (2009: 33).
82. See Cerny (2008: 34) and Jessop (2000: 329).
83. See Peck (2004).
84. Watkins (2010: 7), emphasis added.
85. Cerny (2008: 4).
86. Harvey, D. (2009) The crisis and the consolidation of class power: is this *really* the end of neoliberalism? *Counterpunch*, March 13–15, accessed at www.counterpunch.org/harvey03132009.html.
87. Ong (2007: 4).
88. Harvey (2005: 13).
89. See Jessop, B. (2010) The continuing ecological dominance of neoliberalism in the crisis. In A. Saad-Filho and G. Yalman, eds., *Economic Transitions to Neoliberalism in Middle-Income Countries*. London: Routledge, 24–38.
90. Harvey (2005: 120).
91. Ong (2007: 4).
92. See Peck (2004), Peck and Theodore (2007), and Brenner *et al.* (2010) for elaborations of these arguments.

2

Freedom, rebooted

It would be convenient if the circuitous prehistories of neoliberalism could be traced to an immaculate ideational flashpoint—like some revelation in Hayek's bathtub at Mont Pelerin's Hotel du Parc—but the past is rarely organized in this way. Instead, this chapter will elaborate the claim that neoliberalism was a transnational, reactionary, and messy hybrid right from the start. Neoliberalism has many authors, many birthplaces. Its multiple lineages intersect and interact in ways that reveal a great deal about how this "free-market" project, from its beginnings, was a somewhat plural and socially produced project—the hybrid outcome of a protracted conversation between a series of (only partly complementary) "local" protoneoliberalisms. It was never simply *Manchesterism 2.0,* because as Polanyi rightly observed, that experiment could never be repeated.[1] But neoliberalism's explicit attempt to *remake* laissez-faire for twentieth-century conditions remains one of its definitive features. For this reason, *neoliberalism* is both philosophically and historically distinctive.

Neoliberalism has always been on the move. And even Hayek's *Road to Serfdom* represents just one of several beginnings of the creation story. "There is nothing in the basic assumptions of liberalism to make it a stationary creed; there are no hard-and-fast rules fixed once and for all," he claimed; reflecting that "nothing has done as much harm to the liberal cause as the wooden insistence on certain rough rules of thumb, above all the principle of laissez faire."[2] Constructing a flexible creed of neoliberalism would be a *creative* process, entailing the conscious production of new ideational and institutional networks, connecting islands of free-market thinking, and animating common threads of emergent thought-practice. Hayek's lifetime search for a political-economic credo not only outside socialism and fascism, but also *beyond* laissez-faire, would carry him back and forth between the generative sites of the twentieth-century liberal revival—Vienna, London, Freiburg, and Chicago. But these were difficult journeys, in all kinds of ways. International travel and communication, slow and expensive at the best of times back then, had been disrupted by two world wars, and might well have been impossible without the help of a handful of eccentric corporate benefactors. Moreover, these prophets of the market were the square pegs of their time, often embattled and lonely, even at home. All around them, peak institutions were invariably controlled by enemy forces, like Austromarxists, Nazis, and Keynesians. For many, even secure employment proved hard to come by.

But neoliberalism's minoritarian status was also generative: it bred a sect-like mentality, and a capacity to manage internal differences in the shadow of larger, external threats; it impelled an insistent search for intellectual amity at a distance, and the production of new channels of communication. The small band of self-styled "intellectual pilgrims" who gathered at Mont Pelerin in 1947 created what would become the preeminent space for calculation, exchange, and compromise—and a transnational intellectual project from the start.[3] The liminal existence of the often-untenured neoliberal intelligentsia may have been a constructively precarious one, but for half a century these fellow travelers could only envisage utopian, rather than real, destinations. They shared the same philosophical compass, but lost in the ideological wilderness, often disagreed about which steps to take. Back at base camp, their fringe ideas were carefully cultivated, albeit at the risk of irrelevance and ridicule. Struggling and inchoate, yet determined, the Mont Pelern Society was for many years a club of losers.

With the benefit of political-economic hindsight, the Nobel Committee's paradigm-busting elevation of Hayek in 1974 looks like a portentous sign of the coming neoliberal ascendancy. But as his friend Milton Friedman recalled, the award came out of the blue for the retired philosopher, who had become "extremely depressed, withdrawn, and unproductive."[4] Contemporary associations between Hayek and the Chicago School of economics, the rise of which would be affirmed in the subsequent trajectory of the Prize, were not always so clear-cut either: the iconoclastic philosopher had lived and worked in Chicago, but was never entirely "at home" there, either intellectually or socially. Hayek's intellectual biographer pointedly notes the decades of "seclusion and isolation" that preceded the Prize, during which Hayek had been "punished and shunned" for the heterodox adventurism of *Serfdom*.[5] The book may have sold well, but it was practically an act of self-immolation for Hayek-the-economist. Back in 1944, three decades prior to Hayek's glorification by the Nobel Committee, the climate was deeply inhospitable to the free-market project. Hayek's turn to popular philosophy during the second World War awkwardly coincided with the birth of positive economics, Chicago-style. Already, the "neoliberal" project was a multilingual one, and a lot was being lost in translation, even amongst the small cult of Mont Pelerinians. The Austrianism of Hayek's underemployed mentor, Mises, was on the way to becoming a parody of itself. His old friends from Freiburg were just barely keeping the candle of liberalism smoldering under the Third Reich, some of them fashioning their own questionable compromises along the way. And in pre-Chicago School Chicago, Hayek's closest ally had already been branded old school by the Young Turk quantifiers, and was beginning his descent into suicide. Meanwhile, Hayek's old rival, Keynes, was on the cusp of eponymously inheriting the earth.

The Road to Serfdom may have been a surprise bestseller, but it was Karl Polanyi's *Great Transformation,* published in the same year and something of a flop, that in retrospect said more about the historical moment. Humanity's historic encounter with laissez-faire had reaped its devastating consequences; the fiction of the self-regulating market, foisted on the world as if it represented some kind of natural order, had been exposed in the starkly utopian form of world war and financial crisis. "Freedom's utter frustration in fascism" was, Polanyi believed, the "inevitable result" of nineteenth-century liberalism's antisocial vision.[6] The "market mentality," Polanyi later concluded, had been rendered "obsolete" by these historical developments. Ironically, the posthumous rediscovery of Polanyi's seminal work, more than four decades later, would be prompted by the rise of neoliberal globalism, his failings as a forecaster paling into insignificance alongside the prescience of his historical insights. Ostensibly back from the dead, newly-constructed fables of the self-sustaining market were actively remaking the world in their own image, with an even greater geographical and social reach, in the autumnal moment of Pax Americana.[7]

Polanyi's own journey, also lonely in its own way, periodically intersected with those of neoliberalism's intellectual pilgrims, though he did not live long enough to witness their rise to power. This chapter samples some of these intellectual journeys, not simply to complicate the prehistory of neoliberalism, but to call attention to some of the distinctive *and dogged* qualities of this dissipated, experimental, and nonlinear project of ideational production. The essence of neoliberalism was not extracted, like pure mountain spring water, by Hayek and his fellow pilgrims at Mont Pelerin, only later to be blended, cut, and adulterated by less-principled governmental distributors; it was a volatile cocktail from the beginning. Neoliberalism was a mix of prejudice, practice, and principle from the get-go. It did not rest on a set of immutable laws, but a matrix of overlapping convictions, orientations, and aversions, draped in the unifying rhetoric of market liberalism.

The liberal revival had to be planned, but it did not yield a plan. Rather, as the previous chapter suggested, it established an institutional problem space and a zone of ideational struggle, framed by the distinctively post-laissez-faire question of appropriate forms and fields of state intervention in the socioeconomic sphere. The absentee state may have been an enduring rhetorical trope, but the *neo*liberal project was from the beginning pre-occupied with the necessary evils of governmental rule. What Friedman once called the "doctrine of neoliberalism" expressly sought to transcend the "naïve ideology" of laissez-faire, in favor of a "positive" conception of the state as the guarantor of a competitive order.[8] This order could not be exhumed from the nineteenth century, since in the preferred form it never existed there. Neoliberalism was never retroliberalism; it had to be constructed anew. Its meandering ideational journey, on the path to power, consequently represents rather more than historical curiosity.

From Vienna to London

In July 1919, a 32-year-old Karl Polanyi, gravely ill from injuries sustained during the Great War, was transferred from a hospital in Budapest to Vienna, where he would undergo a serious operation. A former cavalry officer in the Austro-Hungarian army, Polanyi, had been active in socialist politics and workers' education in Hungary before the war. He had arrived in Vienna at an extraordinarily propitious time. In the midst of Vienna's experiment with municipal socialism, the slowly recovering Polanyi committed himself to the challenge of developing a positive and practical theory of the socialist economy. Skeptical, on both political and practical grounds, of the feasibility of centralized economic planning, and increasingly wary of dogmatic strains of Marxism, he spent his long convalescence contemplating alternative ways to bridge the theory and practice of socialism. Drawing inspiration from the "guild socialism" of G. D. H. Cole and Robert Owen, and from the effervescent political and intellectual life of "Red Vienna," the 1920s were for Polanyi amongst the happiest and most productive of his life, a time when his "ideas about social issues . . . found passionate expression."[9]

The Vienna of the 1920s was Polanyi's intellectual "apprenticeship," the place where the lineages of *The Great Transformation* were first conceived.[10]

But the lessons came as much from practice as from theory. In the early 1920s, Polanyi learned the craft of newspaper journalism, later being appointed to the editorship of the influential weekly, *Der Oesterreichische Volkswirt*. And, in accordance with the fashion of the time, he hosted a regular *Privatseminar* at his home, focused on the vexing problem of "socialist accountancy." This ostensibly arcane, but challenging, zone of socialist practice had been a hotly disputed one for some years, not least following the blunt intervention from the finance director of the Vienna Chamber of Commerce, Handicrafts, and Industry, one Ludwig von Mises. Like Polanyi, Mises was both a practical and a theoretical economist, but there the similarities ended. Mises' 1920 paper on the alleged "impossibility" of central planning and socialized pricing, "Economic calculation in the socialist commonwealth," represented an unapologetic reassertion of liberal economic reason. The Chamber's philosopher-in-residence, railed against the socialist utopians that surrounded him, not least for their feeble grasp of economic principles:

Economics, as such, figures all too sparsely in the glamorous pictures painted by the Utopians. They invariably explain how, in the cloud-cuckoo lands of their fancy, roast pigeons will in some way fly into the mouths of the comrades, but they omit to show how this will take place ... When Marxism solemnly forbids its adherents to concern themselves with economic problems, beyond the expropriation of the expropriators, it adopts no new principle, since the Utopians throughout their descriptions have also neglected all economic considerations, and concentrated attention solely upon painting lurid pictures of existing conditions and glowing pictures of that golden age which is the natural consequence of the New Dispensation.[11]

Despite his reputation both as a formidable economic theorist and "expert on money and banking," Mises was unable to secure a full-time academic position in Vienna, since "the universities were searching for interventionists and socialists"; while he declined to work for any of the major banks because "they refused to give assurance that my advice would be followed," even as they teetered on the brink of insolvency. But Mises' "self-created" position at the Chamber of Commerce nevertheless afforded him some influence in economic policy debates, if not power: "The fact that in the winter of 1918–1919 Bolshevism did not take over and that the collapse of industry and banks did not occur in 1921, but in 1931, was in large part the result of my efforts," he later disclosed.[12]

Mises own *Privatseminar,* which gathered in the evenings at his office in the Chamber of Commerce, was renowned as a bastion of classical liberalism and "sound money" thinking in Red Vienna. The discussions, while focused on "the problems of economics," also embraced sociology, social psychology, logic, and epistemology: "in this circle," Mises recalled, "the Viennese culture produced one of its last blossoms."[13] The formidable economist generally gave little credit to his interlocutors, characterizing all of the Austromarxists (with the exception of Otto Bauer himself) as intellectually sub-par. But he took seriously Polanyi's interventions on the critical question of socialist calculation—which were distinctive for their emphasis on decentralized solutions, including instrumental roles for certain *kinds* of markets—later writing a specific rebuke to Polanyi's guild-socialist blueprint.[14] Yet Mises' strand of "intransigent liberalism," Hayek later recalled, was not only "unique," it also left him "almost completely isolated."[15]

Mises, who was remembered even by friends as temperamental, acerbic, and sometimes "personally obnoxious," would chair the meetings from behind his desk, having granted invitations to only "a select few of the most gifted."[16] One of those who had initially failed to make the grade was a newly-recruited economist from the Chamber, who later reflected that his exclusion had more to do with his intellectual immaturity than his mildly Fabian leanings.[17] The young Hayek, who would finally be granted admission to the Mises seminar in 1924, filled the intervening years by convening his own monthly discussion group, *Geistkreis*—translated as "circle or spirits," or more colloquially, "soul brothers"—which brought together a precociously talented group of young economists and philosophers, most of whom would subsequently relocate to the United States.[18] *Geistkreis* celebrated intellectual freedom as much as economic freedom, straying far and wide into the arts and culture, and inviting participants to select topics deliberately outside their specialist interests.

Under the influence of Mises, Hayek would later renounce socialism, his mentor's sustained attack on socialist calculation and central planning providing what he aptly characterized as the necessary "shock treatment."[19] But this was not simply a matter of succumbing to Mises' emphatic arguments, Hayek would have "a ringside seat for the crushing monetary disaster of the era [together with] the ear of one of its most astute economic analysts."[20] These experiences may have been formative, but they were certainly not comfortable. The "conditions of the 1920s," Hayek later recalled, left him feeling "somewhat estranged" from Austria.[21] Mises, too, had become intellectually and politically alienated. He regarded himself, somewhat immodestly, as the "economic conscience" of Austria, yet "[o]nly a few helped me and all political parties distrusted me."[22] In this reddest of cities, Mises and Hayek were "misfits," Polanyi-Levitt and Mendell have observed, "the remnants of old Vienna's privileged urban elites whose security had been shattered, whose savings had been decimated by wartime and postwar inflation, and whose taxes were financing the pioneering housing programs of Vienna's socialist municipal administration."[23]

If Mises' and Hayek's convictions were bolstered by their shared intellectual estrangement from the Viennese political culture of the time, Polanyi, in marked contrast, felt much more at home:

Vienna achieved one of the most spectacular cultural triumphs of Western history... 1918 initiated an...unexampled moral and intellectual rise in the condition of a highly developed industrial working class which, protected by the Vienna system, withstood the degrading effects of grave economic dislocation and achieved a level never surpassed by the masses of the people in any industrial society.[24]

In the historical arc the great transformation, Polanyi positioned these real-world innovations in municipal socialism as "paradigms and portents of a democratic socialism already evolving."[25] Likewise, his arguments for decentralized forms of "functional socialism," which were the flipside of his reservations concerning centralized planning, were very much "rooted in the reality of socialist Vienna."[26] For Mises and Hayek, on the other hand, these developments were localized aberrations or, worse still, premonitions of "council-house bolshevism."[27]

Mises and Hayek each made study and lecture tours of the United States during the 1920s, the latter returning with the conviction that new American techniques of monitoring and quantifying economic phenomena should be emulated in Austria. A staunch opponent of empiricism, Mises had at first been skeptical, but was eventually persuaded. He later assisted in the establishment, in 1926, of the Austrian Institute for Business Cycle Research, with Hayek installed as the founding director. This work would propel Hayek to the University of Vienna in 1929, and then to the Tooke Chair in Economics and Statistics at the London School of Economics (LSE) in 1931, the same year that Britain left the Gold Standard. At the LSE, Hayek continued to teach his "Austrian" theories of the business cycle, arguing along with Lionel Robbins that the causes of the Great Depression lay with the credit expansion (and "forced savings") of the preceding period, the economy's "natural" adjustment subsequently being impeded by price-fixing and wage controls. The slump was, in effect, "nature's cure."[28] This, however, was a minority position, to put it mildly. The Keynesian revolution was already taking shape. The preceding debate between Keynes and Hayek around the causes of the Depression, for all its later historical resonance, had occurred largely at cross purposes. Their private correspondence—while never less than polite—became mired in mutual incomprehension. Keynes described the exchange to Sraffa in the following way: "What is the next move? I feel that the abyss yawns—and so do I."[29]

By the end of the 1930s, Hayek had apparently lost everyone's attention. His support, even within the LSE, had dwindled.[30] He was continuing to elaborate his own position, including a further foray into the socialist calculation debate, ostensibly triggered by the flirtation, amongst left intellectuals in Britain, with Soviet economics. An outsider again, Hayek's *Collective Economic Planning,* which also singled out Polanyi's earlier contribution in the Vienna debate, was published in the same year as the Webbs' celebration of Soviet Communism.[31] The intellectual tides were continuing to move in the opposite direction. More worrying for Hayek, these radical forms of socialist revisionism were not only circulating amongst elites, they were also filtering down to the lumpen classes: adult education programs across the country were adopting the "tutorial version of history," emphasizing the "deterioration of the working classes under capitalism."[32]

Quite coincidentally, and no doubt affirming Hayek's fears, the Workers' Education Association (WEA) was about to recruit a new lecturer, to teach night-school classes on English social and economic history in Kent and Sussex. The impressive letters of recommendation, from G. D. H. Cole and R. H. Tawney, explained that while the subject was quite new to him, Karl Polanyi could be relied upon to rise to the challenge. Confronted by the ascendancy of Austrian fascism, Polanyi had reluctantly left Vienna in 1933, living a hand-to-mouth existence in Britain for several years before securing the WEA appointment. Both the rich historical subject matter and the immediate social context were to have a huge effect on Polanyi, since he could not help but contrast "the inferior status of the English working class in the richest country in Europe with the social and cultural achievements of the workers of socialist Red Vienna."[33] Experiencing at first hand the "trauma" of the British class system, Polanyi's wife recalled, "He was teaching and he was learning."[34] Polanyi's voluminous lecture notes formed the working draft of *The Great Transformation.*

The book's low-profile publication, in 1944, coincided with the Bretton Woods conference, which effectively institutionalized the Keynesian order. The negotiators at the conference, not least Keynes himself, were preoccupied with many of the same issues that animated Polanyi's treatise—the causes of the Great Depression and the destabilizing consequences of liberalized regimes of international finance. If *The Great Transformation* was, in the final analysis, an optimistic book, this found validation in the Bretton Woods settlement,[35] an institutional re-embedding of international economic relations. Recognizing the historical drift of these developments, Polanyi believed that, "In retrospect our age will be credited with having seen the end of the self-regulating market."[36] Capital controls and restrictions on currency convertibility would allow countries to balance the objectives of economic development with some degree of "co-operation between nations," together with a measure of "liberty to organize national life at will."[37] But when Keynes had boarded the ship on the way to Bretton Woods, he had a different book in his briefcase—*The Road to Serfdom*.

Between Chicago and Mont Pelerin

Hayek had grown tired of the debates around economics during the 1930s, which in the eyes of most he had conspicuously lost. During the wartime bombing of London, Keynes arranged for him to relocate to Cambridge, "a generous gesture," Yergin and Stanislaw comment, since "Keynes was the leading economist of his time, and Hayek, his rather obscure critic."[38] Volunteering for fire duty, Hayek spent his evenings sitting on the roof of Peterhouse College looking out for German bombers, while contemplating the manner in which the rise of Nazism had been preceded by developments now "equally familiar in America and England . . . increasing veneration for the state, the fatalist acceptance of 'inevitable trends,' the enthusiasm for 'organization' of everything."[39] *The Road to Serfdom* had been conceived in such a way as to maximize its contemporary relevance, in the closing months of the Second World War. Had it not been for wartime paper rationing, it would almost certainly have become a bestseller in Britain. It found a voracious audience in the United States, however, turning Hayek into something approaching a "celebrity."[40] *Reader's Digest* synopsized the book in April 1945 and speaking tours of the United States beckoned.

Essentially a work of moral and political critique, *Serfdom* asserted that socialism and central planning represented but the first steps on an inexorable path to tyranny and totalitarianism. It had been motivated by Hayek's visceral sense of apparently "twice living through the same period—or at least twice watching the same evolution of ideas"—the socialist ascendancy in Austria after the First World War, then its British variant, leading up to the Second World War. Recognizing the impossibility of going "back to the reality of the nineteenth century," Hayek implored his readers, instead, to seize any opportunity to "realize its ideals"—if the "first attempt to create a world of free men . . . failed, we must try again." He went on to insist that,

It is important not to confuse opposition to . . . planning with a dogmatic *laissez-faire* attitude. The liberal argument does not advocate leaving things just as they are; it favours making the best possible use of the forces of competition as a means of coordinating human efforts. It is based on the conviction that, where effective competition can be created, it is a better way of guiding individual efforts than any other. It emphasizes that in order to make competition work beneficially a carefully thought-out legal framework is required . . . [However there is no] "middle way" between competition and central direction . . . Planning and competition can be combined only by planning *for* competition, not by planning *against* competition. The planning against which all our criticism is directed is solely the planning against competition.[41]

Perhaps surprisingly, Keynes was to write of his "deeply moved agreement" with large parts of the book, while demurring on the question of Hayek's dismissal of both the feasibility and desirability of "middle ways." Keynes found the critique of centralized planning overdrawn, arguing that by alternately invoking the magic of markets and the austere power of the rule of law, Hayek had failed to specify "where to draw the line" in terms of the appropriate role and form of the state: "You agree that the line has to be drawn somewhere, and that the logical extreme is not possible. But you give us no guidance whatever as to where to draw it."[42]

Perversely affirming Polanyi's now-famous aphorism, "*Laissez-faire* was planned; planning was not,"[43] Hayek had since before the war been contemplating ways to rejuvenate the liberal project. *Serfdom* had provided the answer in at least one respect: it opened up access to organizational and financial resources in the United States that would prove critical for the revivalist effort. A member of the audience at the Detroit stop on Hayek's 1945 book tour was one Harold Luhnow, a strident business conservative and president of the Kansas-based Volker Fund. Luhnow sought to engage Hayek in the task of producing a distinctly American version of *The Road to Serfdom*. Even though the plan was ultimately unfulfilled, it triggered a sequence of events that would be decisive both in the development of the Chicago School of Economics and in the establishment of the Mont Pelerin Society.[44] If Hayek had originally moved to London "to fight Keynes," largely on the terrain of economic theory, he would eventually have to leave London, and shift tactics, to continue the effort.[45]

Hayek had always loved the Alps, and it was a fortuitous combination of American funding and Swiss organization that enabled him to bring together a hand-picked group of prominent liberal thinkers for an exploratory meeting at the resort of Mont Pelerin sur Vevey in 1947. In his welcoming address to the group, Hayek emphasized the need to "reconstruct a liberal philosophy" for the circumstances of the age, seeking to embolden the members of the fledgling network by insisting that "it is not sufficient [to have] 'sound views.' The old liberal who adheres to a traditional creed *merely* out of tradition . . . is not much use for our purpose. What we need are people who have faced the arguments from the other side."[46] The Mont Pelerinians' "great intellectual project" would involve both "purging traditional theory of certain accidental accretions," while confronting some of the intractable problems that "over-simplified liberalism has shirked." This called for an explicit engagement with real-world problems, from third-world development to tax and trade policy, forging critical alternatives to Keynesian orthodoxies. Consciously, this process was a geographically situated one, the evolving ideational project of neoliberalism gaining traction, and creative momentum, from the uneven landscape of the "collectivist consensus."

[T]he farther one moves to the West, to the countries where liberal institutions are still comparatively firm, and people professing liberal convictions still comparatively numerous, the less are these people prepared really to re-examine their own convictions and the more they are inclined to compromise, and to take the accidental historical form of a liberal society which they have known as the ultimate standard. I found on the other hand that in those countries which either had directly experienced a totalitarian regime, or had closely approached it, a few men from this experience had gained a clearer conception of the conditions and value of a free society.[47]

For Hayek, the task for what became the Mont Pelerin Society (MPS) was not compatible with anything other than an invitation-only "private organization." Such "contacts beyond national borders" were inherently vulnerable to monopolization by those "who were in one way or another tied up in the existing governmental or political machinery," and could therefore be expected to "serve dominating ideologies."[48] Moreover, the new Society's commitment to a long-run *war of position* in the "battle of ideas" was hardly compatible with the issue of frequent press releases. Privatized, strategic, elite deliberation was therefore established as the modus operandi.

Inadvertently channeling a distorted reading of Polanyi—whose concern had been to deconstruct the "stark utopia" of the unfettered market, and the wake of institutional and social reform that had been enacted in its chimerical image—Hayek insisted, in a paper circulated to MPS members just after their first meeting, that liberal intellectuals needed to *regain* the courage of their utopian convictions. Socialism, he insisted, was after all no more than a "construction of theorists," which began life as an elite intellectual project before being sold to the working classes on the way to becoming "the governing force of politics."[49] It was *deliberative* intellectual and unapologetically utopian projects, like Fabianism, that had set the stage for the subsequent establishment of socialism as a governing program. Achieving dominance amongst the active intelligentsia was therefore an initial and necessary stage in the process of hegemonic succession: foreshadowing contemporary conceptions of neoliberalism's *pensée unique,* Hayek characterized the consequences of socialist utopianism in terms of an effective monopolization of the political agenda, in which "actual developments in society...were determined, not by a battle of conflicting ideals, but by the contrast between an existing state of affairs and that one ideal of a possible future society which the socialists alone held up before the public." In his estimation, Germany had reached this hegemonic tipping point by the late nineteenth century; England and France together arrived around the time of the First World War; and the United States became functionally socialist by the end of the Second World War. It was in this context that, "there seemed to exist only one direction in which we could move," toward an increasingly planned and governmentalized society, "and the only question seemed to be how far the movement should proceed."[50]

The ideational climate surrounding the early MPS meetings, according to the Society's official historian, was one in which "socialist interventionist views were in the ascendant," its founding members being "drawn together by a common sense of crisis."[51] They also "shared the same basic philosophy," Hayek noted, their enlarged "circle of spirits" resembling a transnational version of Mises–Hayek *Privatseminars* of the 1920s.[52] Once this intellectual groundwork had been completed, there would be important tasks for sundry intermediaries, translators, and "secondhand dealers in ideas" in the transformation of the "liberal Utopia" into a program of "truly liberal radicalism which does not spare the susceptibilities of the mighty."[53] This conception stretches beyond the ideational task of (neo)liberal reconstruction, to embrace the institutional challenge, in Philip Mirowski's words, of "constructing and deploying elaborate social machinery designed to collect, create, debate, disseminate and mobilize neoliberal ideas."[54]

Although they would choose, as a group, to focus on questions somewhat "upstream" of actual policy advocacy, the Mont Pelerinians would hardly be reticent about seizing state power, when opportunities presented themselves. In fact, members of this highly selective free-market club would go on to run three countries (West Germany, Italy, and the Czech Republic), while occupying ministerial-level positions in numerous others (including Chile, New Zealand, the UK, and the US). Around this core group was an extended penumbra of intermediaries, disciples, and translators—not least amongst the free-market think tanks—whose task was to bridge between Mont Pelerin principles and the messy challenges of governance. This apparatus took thirty years to construct, but Hayek had been actively thinking in these terms since at least the mid-1940s.[55]

For all their shared convictions, in the beginning the Mont Pelerinians were also in some respects a heterogeneous group. One contingent was based loosely around Paris; having convened the "Colloque Lippmann" in 1938 this group was widely regarded as a precursor to the MPS, where it has been claimed the term *neoliberalism* was originally coined. There were the Austrians—together with an Austrian diaspora, now mostly based in the United States—whose allegiance was to Mises. (Most, in fact, were "graduates" of his formative *Privatseminar.*) The British group, with affiliations to Robbins and the LSE or the Manchester School, included Karl Polanyi's brother, Michael, whose increasingly conservative leanings contributed to the siblings' intellectual estrangement. Then there was the Chicago contingent, including Milton Friedman, George Stigler, Frank H. Knight, and Aaron Director, which in the words of the MPS historian, was "perhaps the most powerful and certainly in the long run the most influential."[56] And while there were also individual representatives from Italy, Switzerland, Belgium, Norway, Denmark, and Sweden, the largest group—and according to Hartwell, "in many ways the most interesting one"—came from Germany. Most conspicuous here was the Freiburg party, led by Walter Eucken, which had precariously maintained its liberal allegiances under the period of the Nazi ascendancy and through the war.[57] The most prominent member of the displaced Freiburg school, Wilhelm Röpke, then based in Geneva, was later anointed by Hayek as the most significant figure in "the neo-liberal movement" in the German-speaking world.[58]

The discussions at Mont Pelerin were, by all accounts, wide-ranging, constructive, and mostly convivial. But while there was a consensus on first principles, and on the prioritization of the most pressing challenges, such as the German reconstruction, Hayek's hope for some kind of programmatic statement on economic policy remained unfulfilled.[59] The grouping was meaningfully *neo*liberal in the sense of the participants' broadly shared understanding that a simple "restoration" of nineteenth-century classical liberalism was not appropriate for the times, politically, economically, or socially. However, demarcating a proper role for the state, beyond its minimalist rule-of-law function, proved beyond the reach of the meeting. Some felt that government had a role in the provision of public goods, others demurred. There was a shared recognition that the maintenance of a competitive market system required certain state powers, though there was a disagreement about how these should be restrained. Inescapably, though, the restoration and maintenance of market rule would call for *some form* of state engagement. The challenge was to restrain but also retask the state, determining a set of tightly constrained, yet positive, governmental functions, as the foundation for a *designed* market order.[60] The authorized history, based on notes and recollections from the meeting, conveys a clear sense of this:

Opinions varied, from those who believed that the government had the job of stabilizing the economy by fiscal measures to those who argued that the unresolved liberal problem was, as Robbins said, "to discover automatic stabilizers which will work for the system as a whole." Friedman saw the need for systems that are "automatically active in response to stimuli." But, asked Hayek, "how can monetary policy be automatic, and outside the range of politics?" "Can we agree," George Stigler asked, "that the first step [for monetary stability] should be to bring all money-making institutions under the control of the state?" They could not agree. It was the same for proposals to solve the problems of mass unemployment, monopolies, and poverty. Even the thought of industrial peace frightened Machlup [a displaced member of the Vienna school, based in the United States]: "Industrial peace is something we should be afraid of, for it can only be bought at the cost of further distortion of the wage structure." "Unemployment," declared Maurice Allais [of the Parisian delegation], "is inevitable in the free economy without controls."[61]

The founding statement of the MPS, sweeping and rhetorical in many respects, was appropriately circumspect on these enduring points of tension. Drafted by Lionel Robbins, it described the MPS as a group of "like minded persons," jointly motivated by the "crisis of our times"; but its consensus on the "constant menace from the development of current tendencies in policy" was unevenly matched with a rather cowardly commitment to "further study" on questions including... the "redefinition of the functions of the state so as to distinguish more clearly between the totalitarian and the liberal order," on "[m]ethods of reestablishing the rule of law" that would be resistant to "predatory power," and the "possibility of establishing minimum standards by means not inimical to initiative and the functioning of the market."[62] Beyond the unworkably minimalist conception of the "night watchman state" favored by Mises, the challenge was to re-engineer the state around the ideal of a market order.

Hayek was later forced to mediate between those factions within the MPS membership wanting to push for agreement on a specific policy agenda (led by Karl Brandt at Stanford and Hunold at Geneva) and those who sought to retain a more academic orientation (led by the LSE–Chicago pairing of Robbins and Director). While Hayek, so often the go-between, characteristically professed his sympathies lay somewhere between these positions, the outcome was closer to the Robbins–Director vision, the work of policy development later being taken up, from the mid-1950s onward, by an extensive network of MPS-aligned think tanks.[63] In the shorter term, the imperative was to construct the network, and to continue to hammer out shared principles. Beyond that, the MPS would define a zone of debate, not a site for the production of prescriptive strategies. The debates at Mont Pelerin, which according to insider accounts would sometimes later become "stormy," were never more disputatious than in relation to the question of "what the state does with the economy and with what results."[64]

The Mont Pelerinians shared a visceral distaste for the drift of "current policy," but were divided over the character of any positive neoliberal program. That they were talking at all may have been more a function of their shared sense of exclusion than it was a reflection of imminent consensus on the path forward. The MPS's "long range" approach might be considered visionary, but, in the shorter term, it also reflected the unique ideological chemistry of the group, the inchoation and dissension of which was managed under conditions of shared marginalization, if not victimhood. Hayek would later identify the three principal bases of the liberal reconstruction as Vienna, London, and Chicago.[65] While there were threads of connection between these embryonic nodes—not least through the vectors of Austrian economics and Hayek's personal peripateticism—these were, in important respects, in an early and somewhat fragile state of development in the late 1940s. For some time, Hayek had been focused on the urgent need for "re-education" efforts following the Allied victory, involving the selective rehabilitation of selected members of the German intellectual elite: "If these men are to be again made active members of the community of Western civilisation, they will soon have to be given an opportunity for exchanging opinions, for obtaining books and periodicals, and even for travel, which will for long be impossible for most Germans."[66] The inaugural MPS meeting was Michael Polanyi's "first glimpse of the Continent after these disastrous years," but also a chance better to appreciate "an important section of American opinion."[67]

The epicenter of this important section of American opinion was Chicago. Hayek had a long-established relationship with Henry Simons at Chicago, author of a 1934 pamphlet, *A Positive Program for Laissez-faire,* which for a while was regarded as a founding tract of *neo*liberalism,[68] even though the next Chicago School would later disown it. Simons had contended, contra the upstart practitioners of the Keynesian "new economics," that laissez-faire should not be a "do-nothing policy," but in fact necessitated a "positive" role for the state, in maintaining competitive conditions, controlling currencies, protecting property rights, curbing monopoly power, and (even) maintaining social welfare.[69] Simons himself had characteristically practiced a philosophical form of economic discourse, in many ways complementary to the style developed by Hayek. He had been struggling to find a way to use Volker Fund monies to bring Hayek to Chicago, as the figurehead of the "American Road" project. The resistance that he encountered allegedly contributed to Simons' decision to take his own life, in June 1946, a moment that Hayek described as a "catastrophe."[70] Eventually, Hayek was appointed to a position with the Committee on Social Thought at Chicago, enabled by Volker money,[71] where he would deepen his alliances with fellow MPS stalwarts like Aaron Director in the Law School, and Frank Knight, George Stigler, and Milton Freidman in economics. The rising generation of econometricians at Chicago, however, had no interest in Hayek, a sentiment that was thoroughly reciprocated—Hayek arrived in Chicago feeling "stale as an economist," later recalling that he "never sympathized" with the quantifiers, who considered him "old-fashioned."[72]

In fact, the Chicago School proper took shape as a recognizable "project" in the early 1950s. The origins and "true character" of the Chicago School have also long been matters of dispute, a subject that is taken up in the next chapter. In contrast both to the earlier Chicago tradition (personified by Simons), and to the economics profession in general, the modern Chicagoan would press "market-first" propositions to their (il)logical limits, combining a form of free-market scientism with principled antistatism. According to Laurence Miller,

A Chicagoan opposes occupational restrictions, price controls, and public transfers in kind such as public housing as a matter of course. In so doing, he automatically places the burden of proof on the person who would interfere with individual decision-making within the market. A Chicagoan, furthermore, looks continuously for new ways to introduce the market system of rewards and penalties.[73]

The postwar Chicago School placed the burden of proof on advocates of intervention, applying neoliberalism's "market test" in an unstinting manner, while portraying private monopoly as much the lesser evil. As Rob Van Horn and Philip Mirowski have argued, it came to represent "a theory of how to reengineer the state in order to guarantee the success of the market and its most important participants, modern corporations."[74] If the Old Chicago School was skeptical of government intervention, its successor was opposed—in a defining and doctrinaire fashion—to statist solutions.

Despite some significant affinities, postwar Chicago School economics was never synonymous with a Hayekian worldview. Hayek's instincts were closer to those of Simons, later reflected in the law and economics tradition—another Chicago product. The broader church of the MPS embraced all these strands, and more. Reder explained the relationship between the Chicago School and the Mont Pelerinians by way of a graphical metaphor:

[There are] two overlapping circles: one...labeled "Chicago-style economists" and the other "Friends and Members of the Mt. Pelerin Society." The small overlap of the two contains some of the most prominent and influential members of either group whose particular ideas are quite distinct from those in the non-overlapping portions of either circle.[75]

The challenge was creatively to manage the tensions within the overlapping zone of the MPS's venn diagram, a task to which Hayek seriously applied himself. The liberal revival proved to be a sustainable one, in large part, because symbiotic relationships were constructed between these various constituent parts, all of which retained some intellectual autonomy. Yet so closely intertwined were early developments in the Chicago School and the MPS—both intellectually and organizationally—that Van Horn and Mirowski have been moved to characterize them as "dual startups."[76] Chicago School economics was politicized from the outset; just as, from the beginning, the Mont Pelerin Society's conception of the market economy was, in its own way, "instituted."

To Freiburg, and back

Hayek spent the 1950s in Chicago, reveling in the libertarian intellectual environment, but never quite feeling "at home."[77] Despite arriving in Chicago as something of an iconoclastic celebrity, Hayek "never broke through to the popular consciousness" in the United States.[78] For some time, his dream had been to return to Vienna, establishing an institute for advanced studies funded by the Ford Foundation, but this was one of many schemes that did not come to fruition. A chair at Freiburg proved an attractive second choice, not least because the position promised greater financial security for Hayek's impending retirement. In 1962, he had "once again, to become an economist."[79] Hayek was also reestablishing his intellectual coordinates in other ways. Once part of the Austrian Empire, Freiburg was culturally familiar, and Hayek relished his fortifying walks in the Black Forest. This was also the spiritual home of Ordoliberalism, which had been part of Hayek's intellectual and political world since the 1920s.[80] Leading members of the Ordo group—notably Wilhelm Röpke and Walter Eucken—had long been close associates of Hayek. And in a more metaphorical sense, Freiburg felt "something like coming home," since it was more or less equidistant between Vienna and London, the two places which, Hayek recalled, had most "shaped me intellectually."[81] However, by the time he returned to Freiburg, Hayek's biographer recalls that the man was "largely forgotten in continental Europe."[82]

Hayek was returning to a very different Europe. The West German "economic miracle" had for more than a decade been delivering unprecedented prosperity, under the guidance of fellow Mont Pelerinian, Ludwig Erhard, who had been the Minister of Economic Affairs since the establishment of the new republic in 1949. Erhard had come to the attention of the US military command in the chaotic years of the postwar occupation, where he was appointed to run the economics directorate of *Bizonia,* the joint administrative zone of the British and American forces. The demanding brief, at a time when at least half of all economic activity was occurring outside the formal sphere and the *de facto* currency was Lucky Strike cigarettes, was to design a new monetary regime. A committed Ordoliberal, Erhard had smuggled copies of Rökpe's texts into Germany during the Nazi period. And he would work closely with Rökpe on what proved to be an audacious plan for the Deutschemark. In a radio announcement on June 20, 1948, Erhard declared that the new currency would be convertible at a rate of 1:10 to the Reichsmark, initiating a proto-monetarist cold bath which effectively reduced the money supply by 90 percent. But it was the second part of the "Erhard–Rökpe plan" which caused this event to be memorialized in conservative economic lore: the "bonfire of controls" removed, in a single act of administrative fiat, the entire structure of Nazi-era price and wage controls, while slashing taxes on incomes and capital, establishing what has since been celebrated as a deregulatory tabular rasa.[83] Erhard's actions were bold, to say the least. He was legally forbidden to modify the system of price controls without the explicit approval of the

Allied authorities, but the regulations said nothing about the outright abolition of the entire regulatory regime. It was through this loophole that Erhard leapt, causing the Allied Commander, General Clay, to fume: "Herr Erhard, my advisors tell me that what you have done is a terrible mistake," to which Erhard famously replied, "Herr General, pay no attention to them! My own advisers tell me the same thing."[84] To the contrary, of course, Erhard's Mont Pelerinian mentor, Wilhelm Röpke, not only supported the plan, he was, in effect, its joint architect. By any measure, this was a decisive moment. Three days later, the Russians established the Berlin blockade, in order to contain the effects of the currency reform, triggering the beginning of the Cold War.[85] Erhard's bold intervention has been authoritatively evaluated as the "most fateful event in the history of post-war Germany."[86]

It was in the wake of this moment of immaculate neoliberal intervention that the West German economy enjoyed a generation of "miraculous" growth, circumstances that helped elevate Erhard to the position of Chancellor in 1963. Ordo histories recount that his exit from office, in 1966, coincided with the country's surrender to the evils of bureaucratic intervention, welfarism, overregulation, and "penal" levels of taxation. Visitors to Hayek's home in the mid-1960s recall him complaining about his taxes.[87] He was also growing increasingly skeptical of the direction of West German economic policy, which since the early 1950s had been framed in the euphemistic discourse of the "social market economy." Coined by Alfred Müller-Armack in 1946 to refer to a rather pragmatic and elastic successor to Ordoliberalism, the social market economy would come to denote an "eclectic version of the neoliberal creed which was open to state interventionism," one that became consolidated as a "new hegemonic discourse coalition" following the recruitment of its creator to Erhard's Ministry of Economics in 1952.[88] During his six years in charge of German economic policy, Müller-Armack engineered a working conception of the social market economy as much through institutional action as programmatic intent. Operationalizing a guiding principle of Ordo economics, governmental interventions were supposed to be "market-conforming" (*marktkonform*), but in practice this would embrace a pragmatic accommodation of a wide range of barely-conforming interventions in social policy, the taxation system, industry policy, housing-market regulation, and so on.

Müller-Armack's retrospective attempt to clarify the meaning of the social market economy variously emphasized its ideological, sociological, philosophical, and spiritual character. He insisted that the social market economy should be understood as an "irenical formula, not a Utopian approach," favoring deliberate government action and the channeling of traditional values over simple faith in market forces: "This does not mean fixing a basis that sets a path for all time, but one pointing a road that must be taken now."[89] This was a way to signal Müller-Armack's (somewhat loose) adherence to an "end-state" rather than "procedural rules" variant of neoliberalism, the latter licensing a range of interventions and actions in the pursuit of a desired equilibrium state. This distinction points to continuities between the social market economy and Ordo-school neoliberalism, which at the time Müller-Armack was anxious to deny.[90] Rather than a straightforward extension of Ordoliberalism, the social market economy might be better understood as the first "Third Way" (re)formulation of neoliberalism, which after the Second World War had, in Keith Tribe's words, "reserved space between capitalism and socialism, without any specific characteristics of its own."[91] This reformulation was not only pragmatically consistent with the exigencies of postwar reconstruction, it also reflected the ideological Manicheanism of the time. As Müller-Armack saw it,

The whole world is in a state of tension between East and West, and within this framework fixed by the nuclear deterrent of either side, the possibilities for action by the free West are limited. So much more important, therefore, is the deliberate assertion of its inherent form of freedom. The Social Market Economy certainly cannot, and should not, be used as a counter-ideology, yet it is a formula by which the self-knowledge of the West can be organized in a form appropriate to it. If we make a conscious attempt to safeguard our way of life against the East, it is not enough to take this or that pragmatical step; the deliberate organization of our life under a guiding principle is required.[92]

The "flexible discourse" of the social market economy was also vulnerable to cooptation: the Social Democrats, the dominant party in Germany by the late 1960s, would later borrow the language of the social market economy to fashion a compromise between residual elements of the "Freiburger Imperativ" and both Keynesianism and corporatist bargaining.[93] Little wonder, then, that Hayek had always been suspicious of the term, which denounced the term "social" as a "weasel-word par excellence."[94]

This said, the kind of Ordo thinking with which Hayek was more sympathetic was also marked by a certain elasticity. While some of the founding Ordoliberals had gone into exile (or "half-exile") during the Nazi era, others remained in Germany, joining the Akademie für Deutsches Recht, helping to "realize the national-socialist program" in the field of law and economics, and engaging in a high-risk struggle with advocates of centralized planning in the context of Hitler's evolving economic philosophy.[95] Along with Walter Eucken and Franz Böhm, Müller-Armack was a member of the Akademie, exhibiting a facility for compromise that would later find reward in the social market era, when he would become the "guardian of neoliberal beliefs within the machinery of government."[96]

The Ordoliberals had long been vociferous opponents of Keynesianism, and would later contest Beveridgean welfare-statism no less vigorously,[97] but this did not mean that they were propelled towards the doctrinaire antistatism of the Chicagoans. Rather, the Ordo school believed in a visibly strong, but not expansive, state, arguing that concentrations of governmental power were acceptable where these enabled the maintenance of competitive conditions (and the *deconcentration* of private power, in the form of monopolies). This concern, to strike an appropriate balance between private and public power in order to *secure* economic freedom, can be traced back to the founding statements of the Ordo school, including Röpke's attacks on the restrictive association of liberalism with Manchesterism and the night watchman state in the early 1920s: true liberals, Röpke argued, should fight "for the idea of the state and against the lack of freedom in which private economic monopolies—supported by government leading a shadow existence—keep the economy captive."[98] This authoritarian strand of liberalism would later find a place within the National Socialist project. Rüstow defended a robust conception of the *Freie Wirtschaft–Starker Staat* [free economy–strong state] only months before Hitler's ascendancy: "The new liberalism ... which my friends and I represent, requires a strong state, a state above the economy, above interests, there where it belongs."[99]

While these arguments were closely consonant with the pre-Chicago School position of Henry Simons, they were explicitly—if not programmatically—antagonistic to Manchesterism, nineteenth-century laissez-faire, "paleoliberalism," and numerous strands of Austrianism.[100] Erhard described Manchester School liberalism as "virtually outmoded," while Eucken maintained that the experience of nineteenth-century laissez-faire "prove[d] that the economic system cannot be left to organize itself," concluding that there can be "no question of returning to *laissez-faire*."[101] The Ordoliberals shared with the Austrians strong critiques of bureaucracy, welfarism, central planning, and socialism, but they parted company with Mises and his followers in their contention that "the epoch of laissez-faire was a logical prelude to the interventionism and central planning which followed."[102] And in fact the postwar assessment of leading Ordoliberal theoreticians like Eugen von Böhm-Bawerk was that a "purified competitive order will have to go much further in admitting coercion and governmental control than in the past."[103] Ordo, in this respect, represented an alternative both to deregulated capitalism and centrally planned socialism; it envisaged a deliberately created, not a natural or spontaneous, order.

"The problem will not solve itself simply by our letting economic systems grow up spontaneously," Eucken wrote in his *Foundations of Economics,* "The history of the last century has shown this plainly enough."[104] Rather, he continued, "The economic system has to be consciously shaped." Writing to a senior official in Erhard's economics ministry in the same year, Eucken observed that the policy debates of the preceding years had, in fact, been closely modulated around this position:

The argument today is not at all that between *laissez-faire* and economic planning. It is not a matter of conflict about whether the state should interfere only a little or somewhat more. Actually the defenders of *laissez-faire* have completely disappeared. The conflict is a different one. One side, to which I belong, is of the opinion that the state must influence, or even directly establish, the forms and institutional framework within which the economy must work. It should, however, avoid the attempt to steer directly the everyday business of the economy. Others believe that the state must not just establish the framework, but must influence the day-to-day working of the economy on the basis of central planning.[105]

Writing to Röpke in 1946, Rüstow described Mises as "an old liberal ultra...who belongs behind glass in a museum [while] Hayek too...has never been quite transparent to me."[106] Parsing the differences more carefully, Müller-Armack styled the German variant of neoliberalism as a "regulative policy," albeit one dedicated to the notion that competition is "the primary principle of economic coordination."[107] According to Oliver, in their antimonopoly stance, in their embrace of market-conforming regulation, and "in their over-all program, most [German] neoliberals resemble the Chicago School"—albeit the *old school* of Henry Simons—"more than they do Von Mises."

The German variant of neoliberalism represented a search for a distinctive synthesis, located between the polar opposites of unfettered capitalism and state control. "It was not just a soggy compromise between the two—a receipt for a 'mixed economy,'" Nicholls maintained, but endeavored to "harness the dynamic forces of competition whilst ensuring that economic activity for private benefit should help to create a just and harmonious social order."[108] Defined against what was variously characterized as paleo-liberalism or "historical liberalism," the Ordoliberal project internalized a critique of laissez-faire with almost Polanyian undertones. Röpke assailed the rationalist assumption that the market was "something autonomous, something based on itself, as a natural condition outside the political sphere requiring no defense or support."[109] Neither would a minimalist, law-and-order state be sufficient to the task of effectively "embedding" the market economy, Röpke contending that this required a "firm framework... in short an anthropological–sociological frame."[110] His view was that "a pure free market economy... cannot float freely in a social, political, and moral vacuum":

[It] must be maintained and protected by a strong social, political, and moral framework. Justice, the state, traditions and morals, firm standards and values... are part of this framework as are the economic, social, and fiscal policies which, outside the market sphere, balance interests, protect the weak, restrain the immoderate, cut down excesses, limit power, set rules of the game and guard their observance... In other words, the final destiny of the market economy with its admirable and wholly irreplaceable mechanism of supply and demand is determined outside the sphere of supply and demand itself.[111]

Recognition of the necessity for extra-economic, indeed moral, regulation was therefore a defining characteristic of German neoliberalism, animated as it was by an idealized vision of a decentralized, but orderly, society—an unapologetically bourgeois order. Many of the contemporary threats to this order came from excessive concentration, in all its forms—private monopolies, sprawling cities, multilateral policymaking. Röpke, for his part, "shudder[ed] at the thought of an European Detroit," recoiled from the "noise and the stench of mechanized mass living," and gazed with incredulity at the life of the "typical office worker in New York."[112]

New York or Chicago?

Hardly typical office workers, Polanyi and Mises would both end their careers teaching economics in New York City. In 1947, Polanyi was appointed to a visiting professorship in economics at Columbia University, where he would teach institutional economics and economic history until his retirement in 1953.[113] Since the US authorities refused to grant his wife, Ilona Duczynska, resident status, on account of her Communist Party associations in Hungary and Austria, Polanyi commuted from Pickering, Ontario for most of this time. While he was to remain "a relatively neglected economist," according to his intellectual biographer, Polanyi was nevertheless remembered fondly by his students.[114] Just prior to his death in 1964, Polanyi wrote to a friend that his three decades in the wilderness seemed finally to be over, that the world had "caught up" with him.[115] But it was to take another three decades, arguably, for the world truly to catch up with Polanyi. Although he had remained essentially an optimist for most of his life, developments in the decades after Polanyi's death would earn his work a renewed, if unwelcome, relevance. "Polanyi's arguments are so important for contemporary debates about globalization because neo-liberals embrace the same utopian vision that inspired the gold standard," Fred Block has observed, even as "market liberalism makes demands on ordinary people that are simply not sustainable."[116] It had been somewhat prematurely, then, that Polanyi had pronounced "obsolete" the market mentality, and both ethnocentric and radically incomplete the formalist universalism of neoclassical economics.[117]

Something, apparently, provoked the Mises camp, the embattled remnants of which were also in New York City. Perhaps it was Polanyi's revisionist history of the origins of Austrian economics, which resurrected some of Carl Menger's late-in-life recalibrations of price theory,[118] that Mises, Hayek, Knight, and others apparently preferred to remain "lost." In 1961, the Volker Fund commissioned Mises-protégé Murray Rothbard to assemble a "thorough critique of Polanyi." Happy to oblige, Rothbard attacked *The Great Transformation* as "a farrago of confusions, absurdities, fallacies, and distorted attacks on the free market" in a response that was never published, perhaps never publishable.[119]

Mises' final decades were marked by much less contentment than those of Polanyi, though his followers would also stake a claim to a different kind of posthumous vindication. Appointed in 1945 to a visiting position at the Graduate School of Business Administration at New York University (NYU), Mises was embarrassingly dependent on the Volker Fund to pay his salary. According to Rothbard, he was "often treated as a second-class citizen by the university authorities," while he was effectively "neglected and forgotten" in the realm of public discourse.[120] At NYU, Mises was surrounded by colleagues to whom the "spirit of classical liberalism was alien and irksome," while it was dismissively observed of those accountancy and business-administration students who found their way into his classes, "few…really sought economic knowledge and comprehended what it was all about."[121] Mises maintained a prolific output, but his books— most of them published by rather marginal and subsidized libertarian presses—never found a wide audience. In *Bureaucracy*, as in all his works, he continued to display a combination of doctrinal fundamentalism, political consistency, and biting rhetoric: "Capitalism is progressive, socialism is not," he thundered. Meanwhile, the advocates of statism,

call themselves progressives, but they recommend a system which is characterized by rigid observance of routine and by resistance to every kind of improvement. They call themselves liberals, but they are intent on abolishing liberty. They call themselves democrats, but they yearn for dictatorship. They call themselves revolutionaries, but they want to make government impotent. They promise the blessings of the Garden of Eden, but they plan to transform the world into a gigantic post office. Every man but one a subordinate clerk in a bureau, what an alluring utopia! What a cause to fight for![122]

Mises soldiered on with his NYU seminar until 1969 when, at the age of 87, he retired. From this unprepossessing academic *"cul de sac . . . a tiny handful of graduate students did emerge . . . to carry on the Austrian tradition,"* but for the most part Mises remained a "lonely" voice in an "inhospitable world."[123] He had spent his life battling, more or less successively, though rarely successfully, the German Historical School, municipal socialists, positivists, National Socialists, Keynesians, American liberals, corporate bureaucrats, feminists, and even some of his former friends in the Mont Pelerin Society. Mises had become dismayed with what he saw as an "indiscriminate" policy of admitting "logical positivists and economic interventionists" to MPS meetings,[124] drifting away from the group during the 1960s. Storming out of an MPS meeting, during a session chaired by Milton Friedman, he is remembered for accusing his fellow delegates of being a "bunch of Socialists."[125]

Mises also had a tendency to fall out with his former students, many of whom went on to disappoint him. Hayek was always careful to remain on his right side. But Mises' estrangement from the orthodoxies of mainstream economics—vigorously opposing Keynesianism on theoretical and political grounds, while also finding fault with neoclassical formalism and mathematic proofs on methodological grounds—meant that his followers would have to plough an almost deserted furrow. While there are some affinities, at the level of principle, between Mises' originalist monetarism and the postwar variant established by Friedman and others, the trajectory of positive economics developed by the Chicago School was pretty much anathema to Mises.[126] The adoption of mathematics as the "language" of positive economics, after the Second World War, proved to be instrumental in the subsequent transnationalization of neoclassical economic discourse—a development most notably illustrated in the training of the Chicago Boys and their subsequent work in Chile.[127] It also left practitioners of an earlier art of economic discourse, based on oratorical and diagrammatic modes of analysis, seriously out of step. Garrison points out that a modern economist "who prefers not to use mathematics in his economic theorizing is held in the same regard as a sculptor who prefers not to use a chisel."[128] Mises, most conspicuously, had no interest in the new tools of positive economics. He remained, according to his wife, "uncompromising" to the very end. When he died, in 1973, there was more than a hint of irony in the statement that he remained "the undisputed doyen of the Austrian School of economics."[129]

Murray Rothbard concludes that Mises' long struggle against both the tides of history and the political-economic zeitgeist looked to many like a "hopeless cause," for his mentor "had the bad luck to be one of the foremost champions of laissez-faire in the history of economic thought, but during a century of aggravated statism."[130] It had been the burden of Mises' lifetime to "anxiously observe an almost continuous advance of socialism, which he opposed with all his strength and ability," Sennholz lamented, but he had continued to "resist every step of ill-conceived and counter-productive government intervention that invariably makes matters worse."[131] He had no time, needless to say, for those of his former students who drifted into Keynesian compromise and interventionist apologia, though he was almost as alarmed that others strayed into anarchistic forms of antistatism.[132] Allegedly in response to this latter development, he was forced to clarify his own position on the minimalist state. Seeing "unswerving enslavers and aggressors" all around him, Mises conceded that even freedom came at a price, one which justified public expenditures on "a government apparatus of courts, police officers, prisons, and of armed forces":

As isolated attempts on the part of each individual to resist are doomed to failure, the only workable way is to organize resistance by the government. The essential task of government is the defense of the social system not only against domestic gangsters but also against external foes. He who in our age opposes armaments and conscriptions is, perhaps unbeknown to himself, and abettor of those aiming at the enslavement of all.[133]

A year after Mises died, in 1974, Hayek was awarded the Nobel Prize for Economics. The tide was turning.[134] Mont Pelerinians would claim the prize on no less than eight subsequent occasions.[135]

Neither Washington nor Bonn

Neoliberalism's curse, as we have argued, has been that it can live neither with, nor without, the state. Marked by an abiding distrust of governmental power and the expansionist tendencies of bureaucracy, the post-laissez-faire credo of neoliberalism has struggled persistently with the question of how to define and delimit appropriate realms and roles for the state. For all its creativity, neoliberal discourse has never provided an elemental answer to this question. Mises may have had the most doctrinaire response, but it was also the most unrealistic. His brand of intransigent liberalism was an isolated and antiquated one, even within the MPS. Mises' fundamentalism, Hayek understood, represented but one of the ideational coordinates for the liberal revival. His attempt to construct an "integrated structure of liberal thought" had to begin with the scarce and scattered intellectual resources of postwar liberalism.[136] Against the tides of collectivism, these localized enclaves of liberalism were barely connected in the pre-Mont Pelerin years.

Hayek's decisive intervention established a transatlantic space of communication across an embryonic network of localized liberalisms. In a sense, the point of departure was defined by the Viennese group, grounded in Mises' efforts in the 1920s, with subsequent diasporic connections to Geneva and the East Coast of the United States. Then there was the London node, which had led the initial attack against Keynes—which was focused on Lionel Robbins at the LSE, with a strong lineage back to the work of Edwin Cannan before the First World War. More consequential for the mid-century revivalist project, however, were the Chicago School and the German Ordoliberals—the former espousing the most precocious manifestation of neoliberalism's theoretical project, and the latter representing the "actually existing neoliberalism" of the social-market economy. In some respects, the market-first model of Chicago School neoliberalism found its mirror-image in the state-first model of Ordoliberalism. Foucault went as far as to characterize them as "completely contrary" intellectual and political movements. These are better understood as countercurrents *within* an enfolding ideological dynamic of neoliberalism, which Hayek and the MPS placed in (mostly) productive tension. Denied the spontaneous utopia of laissez-faire, the architects of neoliberalism were engaged in the construction of what Foucault called a "regulative scheme," rooted in a trenchant critique of prevailing governmental practices. For Foucault, the plurality of

65

these practices partly accounts for the contextually specific character of the various strands of neoliberalism, since the liberal revival

constitutes—and this is the reason for both its polymorphism and its recurrences—a tool for criticizing the reality: (1) of a previous governmentality that one tries to shed; (2) of a current governmentality that one attempts to reform and rationalize by stripping it down; (3) of a governmentality that one opposes and whose abuses one tries to limit...I would be tempted to see in liberalism a form of critical reflection on governmental practice.[137]

The liberal revival was a polycentric and plural one from the beginning. The Mont Pelerinians may have been relatively unified in critique, but they were to remain divided over many of the practices and even some of the principles of its nascent transformative project. They may have all turned their backs on the road to serfdom, but they continued to differ on the question of the path forward. The Society's 1947 founding declaration, one of the few collective statements it would ever endorse, explicitly refused to commit to any "meticulous or hampering ideology," preferring instead to define the organization's goals in terms of "the exchange of views among minds inspired by certain ideals and broad conceptions held in common."[138] In this respect, the ideational project of neoliberalism was *formed as* a flexible and open-ended one; there never was a singular worldview, nor was there an expectation that one would be developed, at least in the short term.

Conservative historiographies are wont to highlight the "bonds of sympathy" that existed between, for example, the German neoliberals and Austrian paleoliberals, or between the European and the American free-marketeers,[139] but these were differences that, at all times, had to be *managed* within the framework of the MPS. Prior to the 1970s, these differences were counterbalanced by the visceral sense of shared alienation from the ideational and ideological mainstream. In this sense, the neoliberal credo was constructed at the margins, albeit at the margins of elite networks. The imperative to "save the books," to protect the flame of liberalism, clearly animated the project's pioneers. Yet rather than waging a titantic, dialectal battle against Keynesianism, socialism, and totalitarianism, they would prefer the image of a "Saving Remnant," an embattled band of true believers "huddled together," as one insider put it, "for warmth on a dark and stormy night."[140]

The beleaguered pilgrims may have had a shared vision of Hell, but they harbored no illusions about imminently entering Heaven. Instead, they debated which steps to take in the intellectual Purgatory into which they had been born. Agreement could be reached on which antithetical and alien institutions to "roll back," but there was no such consensus on the purposive shape of the preferred neoliberal order. This problem went back at least as far as Keynes' contention that Hayek was unable to demonstrate "where to draw the line" on the role of the state in the economy and Hansen's critique of *Serfdom*'s naïve impracticality.[141] Hayek insisted that dabbling with any "middle way" forms of planning would lead, inexorably, to serfdom, while at the same time grudgingly acknowledging that the extreme form of the unfettered market remained practically unattainable. In Keynes' mind, this meant that he was "done for," logically speaking: in practice, neoliberals would be no less reliant on intuition and judgment in determining appropriate forms of intervention than were their socialist foes.

The Ordo group's attempt to finesse the question of line-drawing, through their conception of "market-conforming" intervention, was ultimately unsuccessful, at least within the terms of the neoliberal project. The absence, in principle, of a "theoretical stopping point" led in practice to what the neoliberals saw as the unseemly governmental sprawl of 1970s-style German welfarism.[142] Subsequently, of course, the "German model" would acquire diametrically different signifiers, as the Ordo foundations of the social market economy became increasingly obscured, and as new historical geographies of capitalism began to celebrate the "coordinated form of 'Rhinish' capitalism" as an *alternative to* Anglo-Saxon neoliberalism. In its most elaborated form, the German model is sacrilegiously characterized in this literature as a form of "nonliberal capitalism."[143]

Of course, the social market economy always did represent an alternative to the "antistatism of traditional Anglo-Saxon laissez-faire,"[144] but it was also, crucially, an alternative cultivated *within* the framework of the neoliberal reconstruction. This explains why Foucault, in his lectures on biopolitics and neoliberal governmentality, chose the device of an extended comparison of Ordoliberalism and Chicago School economics. Rather misleadingly suggesting that the latter "derives from the former,"[145] Foucault nevertheless highlighted significant ontological differences between these foundational currents in neoliberal thought. Ordo implied an institutionally embedded and antinaturalist conception of the market, sanctioning social interventions *for* the market but not *in* the market—thereby redefining "economy" not as some autonomous sphere, but as a space for the "practice of government." As a constructed order, Ordo was therefore a necessary prerequisite for realizing the powers of the market, of competition, of entrepreneurialism. In contrast, the Chicago School developed an expansive vision of the market as the preeminent organizer of socioeconomic life, normatively and analytically superior to the state. Government, in this respect, became a space for the practice of economy. As Lemke explains Foucault's position,

> Whereas the *Ordo*-liberals in West Germany pursued the idea of governing society in the name of the economy, the US neo-liberals attempt to re-define the social sphere as a form of the economic domain . . . [F]or the neo-liberals the state does not define and monitor market freedom, for the market is itself the organizing and regulative principle underlying the state. From this angle, it is more the case of the state being controlled by the market than of the market being supervised by the state.[146]

If Keynes' burden, as Eric Hobsbawm reflected, was to strive "to save capitalism from itself,"[147] the Ordoliberals were also convinced that a different kind of "strong state was necessary to protect capitalism from the capitalists."[148] The more reckless Chicago solution put the market first, alternately starving the state while indulging finance and monopoly capital—and apparently oblivious to any need to protect capitalism from the market. The challenge implicit in Ordoliberalism was to ascertain where and when to put a brake on state creep; the challenge implicit in Chicago neoliberalism was to know where and when to put a brake on the market. As Keynes had immediately spotted, the neoliberals could not say where to draw the line in either case. Despite their rhetoric about the restoration of liberty, the neoliberals' more earthly goal was to save capitalism from Keynesianism—entailing a phase-shift *within* liberal regulatory practice, not beyond it.

While the ascendant Chicago School may have represented the most precocious strand/brand of neoliberalism, it never stood for the singular essence of the project. Rather, it established a key coordinate in the discursive space staked out by the Mont Pelerinians. Ordoliberalism defined another, though in retrospect its moment of realization as an actually-existing neoliberalism may have come too soon. Erhard himself was pressured to dabble with Keynesian measures in the mid-1960s, a prelude to the Social Democratic makeover of the social-market economy later in the decade.[149] Hayek would claim to have foreseen this slippery slope, although there were other Mont Pelerinians who found the neglect and marginalization of the German model "puzzling."[150] In different circumstances, it might even have been celebrated as a paradigmatic neoliberal transition story, rather than Chile, the US, or the UK . . . on the path to a different historical geography of capitalism.

By the time of the 1972 MPS meeting in Montreaux, Milton Friedman was arguing that the war of ideas within economics had now been won, and that it was time to consider dissolving the Society.[151] This proposal was defeated; there was still work for the Mont Pelerinians to do. And it was now time to press home the advantage. The economic dislocations of the 1970s created an environment in which neoliberal nostrums finally acquired real traction, then Thatcher and Reagan would both rise to power on the basis of economic advice delivered, quite disproportionately, by Mont Pelerinians.[152] Even after the fall of the Berlin Wall, one of Friedman's successors as MPS president, James Buchanan, was busy warning that, as socialism lay dead, the Leviathan-state continued to threaten. There was, he sensed, a pervasive "attitude of nihilism" around the question of economic organization: while the fallibility of command economics had been vividly demonstrated, there remained a "residual unwillingness" to defer to the free market, governed by the rule of law:

[Under these conditions], the natural forces that generate the Leviathan state emerge and assume dominance. With no overriding principle that dictates how an economy is to be organized, the political structure is open to exploitation by the pressures of well-organized interests. The special-interest, rent-seeking, churning state finds fertile ground for growth in this environment... There will be no escape from the protectionist-mercantilist regime that now threatens in both Western and eastern countries so long as we allow the ordinary or natural outcomes of majoritarian democratic processes to operate without adequate constitutional constraints.[153]

It was the rather less than ordinary functioning of majoritarian democratic processes, of course, that placed George W. Bush in the White House, ostensibly to resume the Reagan revolution. While Bill Clinton earned a knowing nod from the Mont Pelerinians for declaring the end of the era of big government,[154] the subsequent arrival of big-government conservatism under Bush II led Milton Friedman to complain that, "The second President Bush appears to have inherited the free-spending tendencies of the first."[155] The neoliberals, having ridden to power on the crisis conditions of the 1970s, had apparently created their own Leviathan, in the form of Republican pork barrel spending and neoconservative militarism. These circumstances must have been barely imaginable at the time of the birth of the neoliberal reconstruction.

Writing in the early 1930s, when "anti-capitalist sentiment threaten[ed] to engulf almost the whole intellectual class," when "deserters [were leaving] the capitalist for the socialist camp," and when there was a "distinct feeling of inferiority on the part of the capitalist world," Röpke scathingly decried the motives of those who would fan the flames of the crisis, recklessly announcing the arrival of "late capitalism," in the absence of persuasive proof of the sustainability of socialist economics.[156] The irony was a bitter one for Röpke, since in his eyes the demonstrable failures of Depression-era capitalism had less to do with the system itself than with the "grotesque" accretion of "alien elements" like collectivism and planning.[157] Röpke acknowledged that the present system had "defects," but that there was nothing to be gained from "emotional reactions" to exaggerated talk of the "crisis to end all crises," especially if this were to lead to yet-more wrongheaded interventionism:

It would be interesting to know today how this doomsday mood is going to be judged in fifty years' time, but my guess is that the chronicler of 1980 will find the mood very strange if he compares it to the technical feats achieved by capitalism during the ten years preceding the crisis... The chronicler of 1980 may have to record, sadly, how badly we failed when there was still time to prevent a catastrophic regression into poverty and barbarism. Maybe he will have to record that the civilization and the economy of the Western world perished because people allowed an economic system of unparalleled strength and resilience to rot or threw it overboard. And not without bitterness will he recall not only those who sinned against the economic system but also the pessimists and amateurish activists whose prophesies based on secret desires came true, just because their propaganda was more than anything else responsible for undermining the intellectual foundations of the system.[158]

Needless to say, the intellectual and political climate was dramatically different in 1980. On the occasion of the reissue of his 1962 tract, *Capitalism and Freedom,* Milton Friedman recalled that the original edition had been given the "silent treatment" by both the mainstream media and the Keynesian intelligentsia, who believed that its message would resonate only with a "small beleaguered minority [of] eccentrics."[159] A measure of the shift in the intellectual climate was that the book's sequel, *Free to Choose*—which was published as a mass-market paperback in association with a public television series—registered sales in the hundreds of thousands. It was the audience, rather than the basic message, which had changed—as evidenced, Friedman mused, in the stark contrast between the "overwhelming defeat" of Barry Goldwater in the presidential election of 1964 and the "overwhelming victory" of Ronald Reagan in 1980.[160] It was the crisis conditions of the 1970s, Friedman reflected, that finally delivered power into the hands of the pro-market reformers.

As one of the historians of the Chicago School has observed, "Intellectuals produce ideas which are received or rejected based on social conditions beyond their control"; the worldview of Friedman and many members of the Chicago School "never really changed. The world changed."[161] The neoliberal ideational project was designed—one might say planned—for this encounter with reality. Even as it recirculated utopian elements of the nineteenth-century vision of laissez-faire, its gaze was firmly fixed on the tawdry realities of economic governance. In this respect, the neoliberalism of the Chicago and Freiburg schools was not, in Foucault's words, "a dream that comes up against reality and fails to find a place within it," but a project knowingly formulated "'at the limit' of government action."[162] As Friedman later reflected,

To judge from the climate of opinion, we have won the war of ideas. Everyone—left or right—talks about the virtues of markets, private property, competition, and limited government. No doubt the Mont Pelerin Society and its many associates around the world deserve some credit for that change in the climate of opinion, but it derives much more from the sheer force of reality: the fall of the Berlin Wall; the tremendous success of the Far Eastern tigers . . . and, more recently, Chile.[163]

The sheer "force of reality" may have shaped the circumstances of the neoliberal ascendancy, but it did not functionally predetermine that ascendancy. The ideational projects of neoliberalism, and the painstakingly constructed networks that sustained and integrated them, had more than a little agentic capacity in this context. But of course they were not formulated, nor did they ever function, in isolation. Neoliberal nostrums gained widespread traction in the 1970s, purposefully narrating a set of crises that they had been designed to exploit. The genesis of neoliberalism as an ideational program, of course, had occurred much earlier, indeed in an earlier crisis, as a reaction to the socialist and Keynesian ascendancies of the 1930s. In this sense, neoliberalism can be seen as a kind of offspring of the Great Depression,[164] a deliberative and constructivist project that developed symbiotically with, but in the shadow of, Keynesianism's "new economics." It was a conservative, but creative, intellectual reaction to what was portrayed as the "crisis of capitalism" in the 1930s. The response, which got a false start at the Colloque Lippmann in Paris and then a kick start in Mont Pelerin, entailed the formation of a transnational network around the handful of localized incubators of liberal thinking. The epistemic community founded on Mont Pelerin could define, and debate, the critical problem space between the state and the market, elaborating areas of consensus and working on zones of disputation, but it was, as a mere critique of a historically dominant form of the state, radically incomplete. Only with the capture of state power could immanent critique become rolling autocritique. The space that the neoliberal intellectual project reserved, between the state and the market, had to be occupied.

"The epistemic argument against central planning," John Gray observes, "contains nothing to help us choose between different ways of organizing market economies."[165] The liberal revival stabilized and reapplied a trenchant critique of "totalitarian" government, a critique that was progressively broadened and deepened *in parallel with* the growth and development of its defining "other," the complex of postwar Keynesian welfare and developmental states. Yet the challenge of transforming critique into reconstruction could not be fully met until neoliberal principles *themselves* were explicitly melded with governmental practice, in Germany after 1947, in Chile after 1973, in the United States after 1980.

Neoliberalism redux

There is more than a hint of irony (and maybe some hope) in the fact that the official history of the MPS should invoke Polanyi's concept of the "double movement," the notion of alternating tides of liberalization and commodification, on the one hand, and regulation and social protection, on the other. Reading Polanyi in his own way, the MPS' in-house chronicler, Ronald Hartwell, adjudicates the historical sequence of economic epistemologies, since 1700, in cavalier and ultimately self-affirming terms, "from mercantilism (and state regulation) to liberalism (and laissez-faire) to neo-mercantilism (and the welfare state) to neo-liberalism (and deregulation and privatization)."[166] In a sense, though, one can see the appeal of such formulations for conservative intellectual historians: the war of ideas may have been won, but no victory is permanent, and the threat of collectivism and planning looms constant.[167]

The circuitous history of neoliberalism clearly reveals, moreover, that the battlefields over which such wars of ideas are prosecuted are deeply fissured and uneven ones. In its most recent iteration, those on the mountaintop may have possessed a tactical advantage, though they also made use of strategic alliances that would later prove to be critical, not least with financial and export-oriented capital, with the "taxpaying" middle classes, and with conservative forces in and around the state. As Rosanvallon observed with respect to Keynesianism,

Unlike scientific theories, economic ideas do not confront one another within a homogenous plane of knowledge. While the world of scientists is highly self-referential, economists act in a field that is deeply structured by other players: political decision makers, bureaucrats, and social agents. Economic theory, in this sense, is embedded within a highly complex system of articulation along with various ideologies and common sense.[168]

The winding path of neoliberalism from crank science to common sense surely reaffirms these insights. Had circumstances been different, the planned revival of the liberal creed may have been consigned to the dustbin of history, along with countless other revolutionary thought experiments. And certainly, its "success" was never preordained although, as an acute critique of the Keynesian orthodoxy, it was better placed than most to exploit incipient crises in the postwar order. This said, when the crises began to accumulate, and when the Keynesian orthodoxy itself entered a terminal spin, the neoliberal "alternative" did not amount to a full-service blueprint for a new political-economic order. The initial applications of shock therapy, it may be fair to say, had been meticulously planned, but when the patient refused to respond spontaneously to subsequent market stimuli, further rounds of treatment would be required. These post-monetarist turns had never been clearly visualized from Mont Pelerin; they would have to be rationalized on the hoof and realized experimentally. Thus, in a progressively deeper and ever-more contradictory sense, neoliberalism gradually morphed into a dynamic form of government practice.

The necessary melding of principle and pragmatism that followed would not have impressed neoliberalism's "natural intellectuals," like Mises, whose uncompromising purity came not only at the price of exclusion from the academic establishment, but even led to estrangement from the band of public economists, worldly philosophers, faceless technocrats, and "secondhand dealers in ideas," who comprised the extended social machinery of the neoliberal thought collective, and who later worked so purposefully to actualize the project. In contrast to Keynesianism, which laid out both a rationale and a rubric for governmental proactivity, complete with its own interventionist technology and economic ontology, the Mont Pelerinians were never successful in delimiting a set of *agreed* "positive" functions for the state, beyond law-and-order minimalism. The Austrians, the Ordoliberals, and the Chicagoans each had their own (shifting) responses to this defining, but elusive, problematic. If nothing else, this confirms the reactionary character of the neoliberal creed, the longevity of which owes much to the insistent denigration of alternatives. As

Mirowski has argued, neoliberalism has never been a "settled or fixed doctrine, but is better understood as a transnational movement requiring some time and substantial efforts to attain the modicum of coherence and power which it has achieved today... [N]eoliberalism remains a major ideology that is poorly understood but curiously, draws some of its prodigious strength from that obscurity."[169] The precise meaning of neoliberalism would remain elusive, even to its architects. This means that there are no fundamental "truth spots" in the neoliberal intellectual universe, only network nodes and transit points, the roles of which only make sense in relation to one another. This contention holds true, as we will see, even for the one of the preeminent cradles of neoliberal reinvention, Chicago.

Notes

1. Polanyi (1944); cf. Žižek (2009).
2. Hayek (1944: 17).
3. See Mirowski and Plehwe (2009), cf. Feulner (1999).
4. Friedman and Friedman (1998: 78).
5. Ebenstein (2003b: 163).
6. Polanyi (1944: 265).
7. See Silver and Arrighi (2003).
8. Friedman (1951: 93).
9. Polanyi (2000 [1925]) A letter to a friend, 1925. In K. McRobbie and K. Polanyi-Levitt, eds., *Karl Polanyi in Vienna*. Montréal: Black Rose Books, 317.
10. See Polanyi-Levitt, K. and Mendell, M. (1987: 317) Karl Polanyi: his life and times. *Studies in Political Economy* 22, 316–318.
11. Mises, L. (1935 [1920]) Economic calculation in the socialist commonwealth. In F. A. von Hayek, ed., *Collectivist Economic Planning*. London: George Routledge, 88.
12. Mises (1978: 73–74).
13. Mises (1978: 97).
14. Anticipating a later strand of neoliberal critique, Mises had tended to elide the problems of socialist economics with those of central planning. See Rosner, P. (1990) Karl Polanyi on socialist accounting. In K. Polanyi-Levitt, ed., *The Life and Work of Karl Polanyi*. Montréal: Black Rose Books, 55–65.
15. Hayek, F. A. (1992 [1963]: 27) The economics of the 1920s as seen from Vienna. In P. G. Klein, ed., *The Collected Works of F. A. Hayek,* volume iv: *The Fortunes of Liberalism*. Chicago: University of Chicago Press, 19–37.
16. Mises (1978: 97).
17. See Ebenstein (2003a).

18. See Craver, E. (1986) The emigration of Austrian economists, *History of Political Economy*, 18/1: 1–32.
19. Hayek (1992 [1956]: 133) Ludwig von Mises (1881–1973). In P. G. Klein, ed., *The Collected Works of F. A. Hayek*, volume iv: *The Fortunes of Liberalism*. Chicago: University of Chicago Press, 129–159; Hayek, quoted in Hoover (2003: 282, n. 93).
20. Hoover, K. R. (2003) *Economics as Ideology*. Lanham: Rowman and Littlefield, 72.
21. Hayek, F. A. (1994) London. In S. Kresge and L. Wenar, eds., *Hayek on Hayek: An Autobiographical Dialogue*. Chicago: University of Chicago Press, 98.
22. *Ludwig von Mises, Notes and Recollections*, 75.
23. Polanyi-Levitt, K. and Mendell, M. (1989: 22) The origins of market fetishism, *Monthly Review* 41/2: 11–32.
24. Polanyi (1944: 288).
25. Congdon, L. (1990) The sovereignty of society: Polanyi in Vienna. In K. Polanyi-Levitt, ed., *The Life and Work of Karl Polanyi*. Montréal: Black Rose Books, 81.
26. Mendell, M. (1990) Karl Polanyi and feasible socialism. In K. Polanyi-Levitt, ed., *The Life and Work of Karl Polanyi*. Montréal: Black Rose Books, 75.
27. Lewis, J. (1983) Red Vienna: socialism in one city, 1918–27, *European Studies Review* 13/3: 335–355.
28. Gamble (1996: 167).
29. As Milton Friedman recalled, "Hayek comes out very badly in those letters, in my opinion. Keynes comes out like a kindly, generous uncle, while Hayek comes out like a very arrogant, self-centered young man, which he was" (quoted in Eberstein, 2003a: 71 and 357, n. 13).
30. Hicks, J. (1967) *Critical Essays in Monetary Theory*. Oxford: Oxford University Press, 205.
31. Hayek, F. A. (1935) *Collectivist Economic Planning*. London: George Routledge, 241–243; Webb, S. and Webb, B. (1935) *Soviet Communism: A New Civilization?* London: Longmans, Green.
32. Caldwell (2004: 215).
33. Polanyi-Levitt, K. (2003) *The English experience in the life and work of Karl Polanyi*. Paper presented at the conference "Polanyian perspectives on instituted economic processes, development and transformation," Centre for Research on Innovation and Competition, University of Manchester, 2.
34. Ducyznska Polanyi, I. (1977 [1970]) Karl Polanyi: notes on his life. In H. W. Pearson, ed., *The Livelihood of Man*. New York: Academic Press, xvi.
35. Bienefeld, M. (1991) Karl Polanyi and the contradictions of the 1980s. In M. Mendell and D. Salée, eds., *The Legacy of Karl Polanyi*. New York: St. Martin's Press, 3–28.
36. Polanyi (1944: 142).
37. Polanyi (1944: 254).
38. Yergin and Stanislaw (2002: xiv).
39. Hayek, F. A. (2005 [1945]) The Road to Serfdom. In Institute of Economic Affairs, *The Road to Serfdom*. London: Institute of Economic Affairs, 39.

40. Blundell, J. (2005) Introduction: Hayek, Fisher and *The Road to Serfdom*. In Institute of Economic Affairs, *The Road to Serfdom*. London: Institute of Economic Affairs, 22–33.
41. Hayek, F. A. (2005 [1945]) The Road to Serfdom. In Institute of Economic Affairs, *The Road to Serfdom*. London: Institute of Economic Affairs, 37–38; Hayek (1944: 41, 48).
42. Keynes [1944], quoted in Skidelsky (2005: 723).
43. Polanyi (1944: 141).
44. See Plehwe (2009) and Mirowski (2009).
45. Hayek, F. A. (1994) London. In S. Kresge and L. Wenar, eds., *Hayek on Hayek: An Autobiographical Dialogue*. Chicago: University of Chicago Press, 77.
46. Hayek (1992 [1947]: 238, 240).
47. Hayek (1992 [1947]: 238).
48. Hayek (1992 [1947]: 239–240).
49. Hayek (1949: 417).
50. Hayek (1949: 428–429).
51. Hartwell (1995: xii).
52. Hayek (1994: 133).
53. Hayek (1949: 417, 432).
54. Mirowski (2009: 432).
55. See Hayek (1949) and Blundell, J. (2005) Introduction: Hayek, Fisher and *The Road to Serfdom*. In Institute of Economic Affairs, *The Road to Serfdom*. London: Institute of Economic Affairs, 22–33.
56. Hartwell (1995: 19).
57. Three of the Freiburg professors at the first MPS meeting had been kidnapped by the Gestapo during the war. Their survival was regarded by their exiled colleague, Wilhelm Röpke, as a "miracle" (quoted in Hartwell, 1995: 20). More recent commentators, while acknowledging the unique challenges of pressing economic-policy arguments under the Third Reich, have concluded that their survival was less than miraculous (see Nicholls, 1994; Ptak, 2009; Tribe, 1995). This might be seen as the first lesson in the subsequent neoliberal accommodation to authoritarianism.
58. Hayek (1967: 200).
59. Röpke and Hayek ensured that "the German question" was featured prominently on the agenda of the first MPS meeting (Nicholls, 1994).
60. See Friedman (1951) and Chamberlain, J. (1944) Foreword. In F. A. Hayek, *The Road to Serfdom*. Chicago: University of Chicago Press, iii–v.
61. Hartwell (1995: 36–37).
62. Mont Pelerin Society (1947), quoted in Hartwell (1995: 41–42).
63. See Plehwe (2009) and Cockett (1995).
64. MPS member John Davenport, quoted in Friedman and Friedman (1998: 160); Hartwell (1995: 227).
65. See Hayek (1967).

66. Hayek, F. A. (1992 [1945]) A plan for the future of Germany. In P. G. Klein, ed., *The Collected Works of F. A. Hayek,* volume iv: *The Fortunes of Liberalism.* Chicago: University of Chicago Press, 232.

67. Quoted in Cockett (1995: 115).

68. Compare Friedman (1951) and Kitch (1983).

69. Simons (1948) *Economic Policy for a Free Society.* Chicago: University of Chicago Press, 3); see also Friedman (1951), Stigler (1988), and de Long (1990).

70. Hayek (1994: 144). In his efforts to bring Hayek to Chicago, Simons had encountered "enormous opposition" from the economics department, Friedman recalled (quoted in Kitch, 1983: 189; see also Van Horn and Mirowski, 2009).

71. Mises, too, had required the assistance of the Volker Fund, along with other conservative foundations, to facilitate his position at New York University, an institution which "tolerated his teaching," and his prickly individualism, "provided it did not cost them a penny" (Sennholz, 1978: 156). As Chapter Three recounts, Volker also funded the lecture tour that yielded Friedman's (1962) *Capitalism and Freedom.* A major benefactor of Hayek's work, the Fund was wound up in 1965, its remaining resources passing to the Hoover Institution.

72. See Hayek (1994: 126) and Ebenstein (2003a: 175). In contrast to his professed sympathies with Simons' "positive program" for laissez-faire, Hayek actively considered writing a rebuttal to Friedman's invocation of "positive economics" (see Van Horn and Mirowski, 2009).

73. Miller (1962: 65, 66).

74. Van Horn and Mirowski (2009: 161).

75. Reder (1982: 32).

76. Van Horn and Mirowski (2009).

77. Hayek (1994: 131).

78. Ebenstein (2003a: 217).

79. Hayek (1994: 131).

80. In his inaugural lecture at Freiburg, Hayek pledged to "resume and continue the tradition which [Walter] Eucken and his friends have created at Freiburg and in Germany" (Hayek, 1967: 253). Eucken had died in 1950, while lecturing in London.

81. Hayek (1967: 251).

82. Ebenstein (2003a: 217).

83. See Lenel, H. A. (1989) Evolution of the social market economy. In A. Peacock and H. Willgerodt, eds., *German Neo-liberals and the Social Market Economy.* London: Macmillan, 16–39.

84. Quoted in Bark and Gress (1989: 202).

85. See Erhard, L. (1958) *Prosperity through Competition.* London: Thames and Hudson.

86. Bark and Gress (1989: 202).

87. See Ebenstein (2003a).

88. See Lehmbruch (2001).

89. Müller-Armack (1965: 94).
90. He claimed that the social market economy was not a "variety of Neo-liberalism" because it had "grown from different roots," though at the same time he chose to define neoliberalism narrowly, in terms of the "mechanical rules of competition" (Müller-Armack, 1965: 91).
91. Tribe (1995: 214–215).
92. Müller-Armack (1965: 90).
93. See Nicholls (1994) and Lehmbruch (2001).
94. Quoted in Ptak (2009: 128, n. 12). "I doubt very much whether anyone could really explain," Hayek (1967: 238) complained, "what the additional of this adjectival frill is supposed to denote." In slightly more conciliatory terms, he later reflected that "I regret this usage [of the social market economy] though by means of it some of my friends in Germany . . . have apparently succeeded in making palatable to wider circles the sort of social order for which I am pleading" (Hayek, F. A. 1976: *Law, Legislation and Liberty,* volume ii: *The Mirage of Social Justice.* London: Routlege and Kegan Paul, 180).
95. See Johnson (1989), Tribe (1995), and Ptak (2009).
96. Lehmbruch (2001: 84).
97. See Oliver (1960).
98. Quoted in Megay, E. N. (1970) Anti-pluralist liberalism: the German neoliberals, *Political Science Quarterly,* 85/3: 425.
99. Quoted in Johnson (1989: 47).
100. See Oliver (1960), Barry (1989), Willgerodt, H. and Peacock, A. (1989) German liberalism and economic revival. In A. Peacock and H. Willgerodt, eds., *Germany's Social Market Economy: Origins and Evolution.* New York: St. Martin's Press, 1–14.
101. Quoted in Barry (1989: 109).
102. Oliver (1960: 132).
103. Böhm-Bawerk (1950), quoted in Friedrich, C. J. (1955) The political thought of neo-liberalism, *American Political Science Review,* 49/2: 512.
104. Eucken (1950: 314).
105. Quoted in Nicholls (1994: 185).
106. Quoted in Nicholls (1994: 102).
107. Müller-Armack, A. (1989 [1956]) The meaning of the social market economy. In A. Peacock and H. Willgerodt, eds., *Germany's Social Market Economy: Origins and Evolution.* New York: St. Martin's Press, 83.
108. Nicholls (1994: 146).
109. Quoted in Barry (1989: 119).
110. Röpke, quoted in Ptak (2009: 103).
111. Röpke, quoted in Bark and Gress (1989: 208).
112. Röpke, W. (1960) *A Humane Economy: The Social Framework of the Free Market.* Chicago: Henry Regnery, 246, 50.

113. Mises' gung-ho pupil, Murray Rothbard, was a doctoral student in the Columbia economics department at the time. He and Polanyi did not get along.

114. Stanfield, J. R. (1986) *The Economic Thought of Karl Polanyi.* New York: St. Martin's Press, 21.

115. Quoted in McRobbie (1994b: vii).

116. Block, F. (2001) Introduction. In Polanyi, K., *The Great Transformation,* Boston, MA: Beacon Press, xxxiii–xxxiv.

117. Polanyi, M. (1947) Our obsolete market mentality, *Commentary,* 3/2: 109–117.

118. Polanyi, M. (1977 [1957]) Two meanings of economic. In H. W. Pearson, ed., *The Livelihood of Man.* New York: Academic Press, 19–34.

119. Rothbard, M. (2004 [1961]) *Down with Primitivism: A Thorough Critique of Polanyi,* accessed at <http://www.mises.org>.

120. Rothbard (1980: 35). In the mid-1950s, Mises became an advisor to the National Association of Manufacturers in Washington, DC, "working with their laissez-faire wing which finally lost out to the tide of 'enlightened' statism" (Rothbard, M. N. (n.d.) *Ludwig von Mises* (1881–1973), accessed at <http://www.mises.org>). Even here, he was on the losing side.

121. Sennholz (1978: 156).

122. von Mises, L. (1944) *Bureaucracy.* Grove City, PA: Libertarian Press, 125.

123. Rothbard (1980: 36).

124. Sennholz (1978: 170).

125. Quoted in Cockett (1995: 114).

126. From a Misean perspective, the twentieth-century trajectory in US economics was marked by a "grievous decline in the level of economic theorizing," for which the Chicago School was significantly responsible (Rothbard, 1980: 22).

127. See Valdés (1995) and Dezalay and Garth (2000).

128. Garrison, R. W. (1993) Mises and his methods. In J. M. Herbener, ed., *The Meaning of Ludwig von Mises.* Norwell, MA: Kluwer Academic, 103.

129. Butler, E. (1988) *Ludwig von Mises: Fountainhead of the Modern Microeconomics Revolution.* Brookfield, VT: Gower, 11–12. From the Chicago School, Stigler (1988: 167) tartly summarizes the span of the Austrian school from 1870 to 1930. On this count, Mises was intellectually "homeless" for more than four decades.

130. Rothbard, M. N. (1993) Mises and the role of the economist in public policy. In J. M. Herberner, ed., *The Meaning of Ludwig von Mises.* Norwell, MA: Kluwer Academic, 202, 197.

131. Sennholz (1978: 173).

132. Rothbard was once called "the most ideologically committed zero-State academic economist on earth" (North, G. (1988) Why Murray Rothbard will never win the Nobel Prize! In W. Block and L. H. Rockwell, eds., *Man, Economy, and Liberty.* Auburn, AL: Ludwig von Mises Institute, 99).

133. Von Mises, L (1963) *Human Action.* Chicago, IL: Contemporary Books, 282.

134. If Mises could have hung on for a further year, he would have also witnessed the long-anticipated bankruptcy of New York City, which produced a demented cheer from his dwindling band of followers, and an I-told-you-so from Milton Friedman (Rothbard, M. N. (1981) Felix the fixer to the rescue, *Inquiry*, April 27: 7–10; Friedman, M. (1983 [1975]) New York City. In M. Friedman, *Bright Promises, Dismal Performance*. New York: Harcourtrace Jovanovitch, 178–180).

135. After Hayek in 1974 came Friedman in 1976, Stigler in 1982, Buchanan in 1986, Allais in 1988, Coase in 1991, Becker in 1992, and Vernon Smith in 2002. Of these, four attended the first MPS meeting, in 1947, and five were past presidents of the Society (Hartwell, 1995).

136. Hayek (1967: 200). "It is perhaps difficult to realise today how little personal contact or intellectual exchange yet existed between the scientists of different countries [in the 1920s] . . . Before the First [World] War, few of the leading economists had ever met face to face" (Hayek, F. A. (1992 [1963]: 32) The economics of the 1920s as seen from Vienna. In P. G. Klein, ed., *The Collected Works of F. A. Hayek,* volume iv: *The Fortunes of Liberalism*. Chicago: University of Chicago Press, 19–37).

137. Foucault (1997: 78, 75, 77).

138. Quoted in Hartwell (1995: 42).

139. See Peacock and Willgerodt (1989: 6) and Hartwell (1995).

140. Feulner (1999: 25).

141. Keynes [1944], quoted in Skidelsky (2005: 723); Hansen, A. (1945) The new crusade against planning, *New Republic,* January 1: 9–12.

142. See Barry (1989: 120).

143. Streeck, W. and Yamamura, K., eds., (2001) *The Origins of Nonliberal Capitalism: Germany and Japan in Comparison*. Ithaca, NY: Cornell University Press; cf. Peck and Theodore (2007).

144. Allen C. S. (1989) The underdevelopment of Keynesianism in the Federal Republic of Germany. In P. A. Hall, ed., *The Political Power of Economic Ideas*. Princeton: Princeton University Press, 282.

145. Lemke (2001: 192)

146. Lemke (2001: 197, 200).

147. Quoted in Wattel, H. L. (1985) Introduction. In H. L. Wattel, ed., *The Policy Consequences of John Maynard Keynes*. Armonk, NY: M. E. Sharpe, 3.

148. Alexander Rüstow, quoted in Bark and Gress (1989: 207).

149. Allen C. S. (1989) The underdevelopment of Keynesianism in the Federal Republic of Germany. In P. A. Hall, ed., *The Political Power of Economic Ideas*. Princeton: Princeton University Press, 263–90.

150. Hartwell (1995: 215).

151. See the discussion in Feulner (1999) and Hartwell (1995).

152. See Anderson (1987) and Cockett (1995).

153. Buchanan, J. (1990) Socialism is dead; Leviathan lives, *Wall Street Journal,* July 18: A8.
154. See Feulner (1999).
155. Quoted in London (2003: 12).
156. Röpke (1969 [1931]).
157. "It is as though one poured sand into an engine and then hoped to start it up again by pouring in more sand" (Röpke, 1969 [1931]: 31).
158. Röpke (1969 [1931]: 43–44).
159. Friedman (1982: vi).
160. See Friedman (1980, 1982).
161. Kitch (1983: 231).
162. Foucault (1997: 75, 76).
163. Friedman and Friedman (1998: 583).
164. See Mirowski (2009), Denord (2009), and Ptak (2009).
165. Gray (1998: 150).
166. Hartwell (1995: 195).
167. See Blundell, J. (2003) *Waging the War of Ideas.* London: Institute of Economic Affairs.
168. Rosanvallon, P. (1989) The development of Keynesianism in France. In P. A. Hall, ed., *The Political Power of Economic Ideas: Keynesianism Across Nations.* Princeton: Princeton University Press, 171.
169. Mirowski (2009: 426).

3

Finding the Chicago School

January 29, 2007 was Milton Friedman Day in Chicago. The City Council's formal resolution, signed by Mayor Daley, called upon "the citizens of our great city to observe this day with appropriate ceremonies and activities that honor the significant contributions that Milton Friedman has made to our nation." The renowned free-market economist, who had died a few weeks earlier, was honored at a memorial service at the University of Chicago featuring, among others, fellow Nobel laureate Gary Becker, president of the Czech Republic, Václav Klaus, and chairman emeritus of the Chicago Mercantile Exchange, Leo Melamed. As the City of Chicago's resolution summarized Friedman's contribution:

It was here...that Friedman...synthesize[d] his theories of economics, based on the idea that government should be kept small and spending should be kept low... Though his embrace of free-market economics was very unpopular at the time, Friedman was tireless in championing his ideas. He knew that [the] free market was the answer, not only to allowing broad prosperity, but also to enduring political freedom... "The society that puts equality before freedom will end up with neither," Professor Friedman once wrote. "The society that puts freedom before equality will end up with a great measure of both."...Today, most nations in the world embrace the free market precepts he espoused and popularized...Milton Friedman's work, which began here at the University of Chicago, has served to advance America's economy...and spread the economic, political and social benefits of free-market economics throughout the world.[1]

Friedman was remembered by President Bush as a "revolutionary thinker [whose] bold ideas...serve as the foundation of many of America's most successful government reforms."[2] Characterized in the *New York Times* as the "grandmaster of free-market economic theory and a prime force in the movement of nations to less government," Friedman was credited with building the Chicago school of economics into a "counterforce" to

Keynesian hegemony and its East-Coast strongholds like Harvard and the Massachusetts Institute of Technology.[3] Friedman's iconoclastic contribution was not simply to mount a challenge to Keynesianism, but to "supplant it", as renowned conservative economist (and former student) Samuel Brittan proclaimed in the *Financial Times*.[4] Friedman had done so both as a remarkable "economic scientist" and as a skilled public intellectual, whose contributions had already been placed, by friends and foes alike, on a par with those of Keynes himself.[5] Indeed, the celebrated economist's passing led some to recall the observation of conservative columnist, George Will, following the death of George Stigler in 1991—Mr. Micro at Chicago, to Friedman's Mr. Macro: "The Cold War is over, and the University of Chicago won it."[6] The Dean of Chicago's Graduate School of Business amended the record on the occasion of Friedman's death: Who led the Chicago school, "armed [only] with a lot of facts and optimism and patience?" There could only be one answer, "It was General Friedman."[7]

The thirty-year war that Friedman and his colleagues waged against the Keynesian intellectual occupation began in earnest in the mid-1940s, reaching its moment of vindication in the mid-1970s. The arc of the ideational project of neoliberalism is closely synchronized with that of Chicago School economics, beginning with a postwar reconstruction, maturing into an increasingly assertive critique of Keynesian theory and practice, and mutating into a governmental project in the wake of the "Great Inflation" of the 1970s. Friedman himself recognized that these crisis conditions were decisive, simultaneously delegitimizing the faltering Keynesian orthodoxy, while prompting an urgent search for new approaches. In this context,

a major change in social and economic policy is preceded by a shift in the climate of intellectual opinion, itself generated, at least in part, by contemporaneous social, political, and economic circumstances. This shift may begin in one country but, if it proves lasting, ultimately spreads worldwide...All in all, the force of ideas, propelled by the pressure of events, is no respecter of geography or ideology or party label.[8]

In Naomi Klein's rendering, the Chicago School represents the epicenter of a historic process of "capitalist Reformation," with the 1970s experiment in Chile serving as an offshore "laissez-faire laboratory" for the restoration of a purified market order.[9] Here, the Chicago School itself is endowed with remarkable agentic capacity, with Friedman ("Dr. Shock") as the principal protagonist. Orthodox and sympathetic historiographies, in contrast, eschew the conspiratorial undertones, in favor of heroic narratives of scientific contestation and transformation, culminating in the righteous defeat of flawed Keynesian formulations and the revelation of enduring economic truths. Echoing Klein, the language of crusades is often invoked, minus the connotations of blind faith and fundamentalism. Johan Van Overtveldt's comprehensive history of the Hyde Park revolution, for example, begins with the observation that "Chicago is both a Mecca and a Rome for economic science," with due deference to the immaculate lineage: "If Adam Smith is the father of the dismal science called economics, then Chicago is arguably its capital."[10]

But why *Chicago*? Friedman was, according to financier Leo Melamed, "one of Chicago's most treasured icons."[11] Yet beyond the well-attended memorial service, and pulses of activity on conservative blogs and on the website of the Heartland Institute, the Chicago-based free-market think tank,[12] Milton Friedman Day passed without incident in the city of Chicago. That, locally, this should be a borderline non-event is curiously fitting. Friedman always had an ambivalent relationship with the city that was his intellectual home for three decades. And like most of his colleagues, he was never entirely comfortable with the Chicago School moniker.

For Van Overtveldt, the University of Chicago's location bubbles under as a "rather random" factor in his otherwise systematic account; there are passing references to what are, in effect, Chicago's locational deficits—such as the institution's "splendid isolation" both from its host city and from the primary centers of governmental and intellectual production on the East Coast—but for the most part his is a narrative of the force of personality and philosophy, rather than position and place. Maybe there was something in the air, since "the cowboy spirit of the pioneers . . . remains very much alive in Chicago,"[13] or perhaps the buccaneering derives from the city's unique history?

Chicago is a remarkable city which grew from 30 000 inhabitants in 1850 to the world's largest urban center a mere forty years later. It symbolized the global ability of capitalism to generate markets from nowhere—to the dismay of Left revolutionaries who expected collapse and social revolution.[14]

To be sure, Chicago has long been known for its especially unrestrained, if not raw, form of metropolitan capitalism, but in other ways the free-market reconstruction designed at the Hyde Park campus was out of synch with the city itself—a blue-collar *industrial* metropolis, notable for its Democratic machine politics and one-party local state, a cornerstone of New Deal federalism, and a center both of monopoly capital and big labor.[15] The Chicago of the Friedman years was also "Dick Daley's town," the largely uncontested terrain of the legendary machine boss—and father of the current mayor—who ruled the city almost uninterrupted, in any sense, from the mid-1950s through to the mid-1970s. Milton Friedman's parallel career was made just a few miles away from City Hall, but almost in a different world. This said, his Nobel Prize, which came at the end of his long tenure at the University of Chicago, in 1976, happened to coincide with something of a turning point for the city of Chicago, which was about to embark on its own kind of neoliberal transformation. This was the year that the first Mayor Daley died, in office, after more than two decades as the country's most powerful big-city mayor. And Chicago was about to enter a spiral of deindustrial retrenchment.[16]

The previous year, Friedman managed an extremely rare conciliatory nod in the direction of Daley's City Hall, but only in comparison with the municipal bankruptcy of New York City, where local government spending per head was running at twice Chicago's rate.[17] Friedman was no doubt more favorably predisposed towards the second Mayor Daley, whose economically-rationalist brand of good governance has been praised in stridently neoliberal circles, like the Manhattan Institute and the ChicagoBoyz blog.[18] But there were precious few signs of this urban-governance makeover when the architect of the Chicago School left for San Francisco in 1977, with barely a backward glance. In a sense, he was taking "Chicago" with him. "To economists the world over," Friedman once remarked, "'Chicago' designates not a city, not even a University, but a 'school'"— an apt observation, in many ways, for a public intellectual who may have been at Chicago, but was never *of* Chicago.[19]

The task of "finding" the Chicago School is therefore clearly not one of unearthing some long-buried organic-geographical essence. Rather, it is to take a journey to a quite appropriately contradictory "anti-capital" of the neoliberal intellectual project, a site of mutual ambivalences and fickle commitments, of often-creative tensions and not entirely disabling discordances. Never the place of doctrinal purity that, so often, it occupies in the conservative imagination, Chicago represented a vital staging post and transaction space in the intersecting ideational and institutional projects of the liberal reconstruction. As Friedman himself later claimed, the free-market project would probably never have been hatched had its originators been located in New York City, rather than Chicago. Can this be true?

Constructing the Chicago tradition

Milton Friedman went to Chicago in the Fall of 1932 to enter graduate school, his first time west of the Delaware River. If he left Rutgers as a frustrated insurance actuary, he arrived in Chicago an economist. A talented mathematician, as an undergraduate Friedman was converted to economics by two of his instructors at Rutgers, Homer Jones and Arthur Burns, who at the time were enrolled in the graduate programs at Chicago and Columbia, respectively. Burns, who went on to chair the Federal Reserve through the turbulent 1970s, would become a life-long friend and mentor to Friedman; but it was the Iowa farm boy, Homer Jones, who introduced the impressionable young statistician to what he recalled "even then was known as the Chicago view."[20] Jones' advisor, Frank Knight, epitomized this view at the time, combining a passionate defense of individual freedoms with a mordent skepticism (by some accounts, bordering on nihilism) with regard to government regulation and social intervention. Young Milton may have been many things, but a nihilist he was not. On the contrary, he was attracted to economics as an empirical, problem-solving science:

I graduated from college in 1932, when the United States was at the bottom of the deepest recession in its history before or since. The dominant problem of the time was economics. How to get out of the depression? How to reduce unemployment? What explained the paradox of great need on the one hand and unused resources on the other? Under the circumstances, becoming an economist seemed more relevant to the burning issues of the day than becoming an applied mathematician or an actuary.[21]

At Chicago, Friedman was soon learning life-changing lessons in both Economics and economics. He found part-time employment as a waiter—paying one meal a day, plus board—but even after securing a second job in a shoe store was unable to pay his own way without borrowing from family members. In the Economics Department, meanwhile, the mandatory, right-of-passage class in Price Theory, Economics 301, yielded revelations of a quite different kind. Taught by the department's other "star" professor, Jacob Viner, Econ 301 "opened up a new world" for Friedman, convincing him that "economic theory was a coherent, logical whole that held together, that didn't consist simply of a set of disjointed propositions."[22] An intimidating and unforgiving teacher, who George Stigler would later characterize as "the stern disciplinarian" of price theory,[23] Viner had his students sit in alphabetically ordered rows, which placed Friedman next to

Rose Director, the younger sister of one of the faculty, Aaron Director, and a research assistant of Knight's. Rose was to become Friedman's wife and life-long collaborator. And her brother, after a period in Washington, DC, returned to Chicago as a founder of the law and economics movement. In the same year, 1946, Friedman was appointed to a faculty position in Chicago (following spells in New York, Washington, DC, Wisconsin, and Minnesota), signifying the emergence of the Chicago School *qua* school.

While much is often made of the long conservative tradition in Chicago economics, dating back to the founding of the program in the 1890s, this was a necessary, but far from sufficient condition for the mid-1940s reboot of the Chicago School, which within a few years represented "the strongest group of free market economists not only in the country but in the world at this time."[24] Half a century earlier, when the department was founded, Chicago had been the "storm center" of roiling conflicts between the East-Coast industrial and intellectual establishment and the upstart West, while one prominent commentator adjudged "the chasm between capital and labor [to be] deeper and broader in Chicago than anywhere else in the country."[25] Into this fray stepped the first president of the University of Chicago, William Rainey Harper, whose aggressive hiring policy was already fueling a climate of resentment and suspicion around what critics liked to call Standard Oil University. Determined to build his new university on a "grand scale," Harper recruited research stars from the Ivy League, paying high salaries but requiring them to live "the life of frontiersmen . . . isolated from the rest of the country in a venture which had no past."[26] This was a "new university located on the outskirts of a new city," which to some seemed to embody "all the tensions, uncertainties, and hopes of America in the new century."[27] The formation of the University of Chicago as a private institution in a "new" city represented what Friedman later characterized as a "*tabular rasa* [since there was] no dead wood to be eliminated, no vested interests to be rooted out."[28] Moreover, in contrast to the great public universities of the Midwest, it was free from the "inevitable entanglements with state government."[29] As a result, Chicago became a place of robust intellectual independence, never "trucking in vulgar opinion," and riding out the political storms of the first half of the twentieth century as if securely moored in a "sheltered inland sea."[30]

Armed with deep reserves of Rockefeller money, Harper courted controversy by appointing the outspoken and doctrinaire J. Laurence Laughlin, "one of the most conservative economists in the country,"[31] to chair his new department of political economy. But if Laughlin's partisan reputation appeared to confirm received views of Chicago as a conservative redoubt, the new chair did not simply move to construct a department in his own image. Instead, he was to embrace the principles of robust heterodoxy and academic freedom, recruiting institutionalists like Thorstein Veblen and John Maurice Clark, among others. If there was a "school-like" economics program at the time, this was a much more fitting description of the progressive institutionalism of neighboring Wisconsin, under the influence of Ely and Commons, with which Chicago was often less-than-favorably compared.[32] Chicago, in contrast epitomized an early form of economic heterodoxy.

On his retirement in 1916, Laughlin's faculty line was filled by Jacob Viner, who would later be joined by Frank Knight as the dominant intellectual forces in the department. But if this reflected an incipient "Chicago tradition," it had more to do with a commitment to vigorous intellectual individualism than it did some programmatic or monocultural conservatism. While Knight and Viner are sometimes credited with the distinction of co-founding the Chicago School, or even of establishing a "first" Chicago School,[33] they had very different personal styles, and did not always see eye to eye. Viner's students never constituted a "club." In contrast, several of Knight's former students maintained "affinities" that would be crucial to the establishment of the Chicago School proper, after the Second World War, even though Knight himself played little or no direct role in this.[34] Curmudgeonly and idiosyncratic, according to his admirers, Knight believed that economics was neither an empirical nor a predictive science. "Knight's specialty was debunking," Friedman later recalled.[35] Libertarian and contrarian, he defended free-market capitalism not out of utopian conviction, but for want of a better arrangement for the coordination of human affairs.[36] Knight's notion of a far-from-idealized economic actor was "less *homo sapiens*, the knower, than *homo mendax*, the liar, deceiver, hypocrite, pretender, practicer of make-believe."[37]

Another Knight protégé, Henry Simons, who joined the Chicago faculty in 1927, fashioned critical elements of what would later be characterized as a Chicago School position, though some of its leading members would subsequently disown him. Very much "a midwest product," Simons was to develop a passion—and indeed a plan—for market-oriented reformism, but remained relatively detached from the political world, making "few trips to the nation's capital."[38] In a premonition of the law and economics movement, destined to grow into a pillar of Chicago-style neoliberalism, he also migrated between Economics and the Law School, though not entirely of his own volition, honing his "positive program for laissez-faire" along the way. A close friend of Hayek, Simons shaped a distinctive case for economic freedom, contra the economics of the New Dealers, against the backdrop of a 1930s economy "visibly ruined by banking and monopoly," but facing what Simons saw as a yet greater threat from FDR's techno-crats.[39] As his colleague, Aaron Director, remembered, "Simons thought that doomsday was upon us," which was also reflected, as another friend recalled, in his "never too peaceful" state of mind.[40] Although Stigler would posthumously enthrone Simons as the "Crown Prince of that hypothetical kingdom, the Chicago school of economics,"[41] his embrace of later heretical positions like redistributive taxation, limited public ownership, and the restraint of private monopoly would confuse the intellectual lineage. It seems to be for this latter reason that revisionist histories of the Chicago school often marginalize or exclude Simons, with Friedman, Coase, Stigler, and others branding Simons—who took his own life in 1946, at the age of 47—as an "interventionist."[42] For his part, Friedman was "astounded" on rereading, in the early 1980s, Simons' *Positive Program*, while conceding that its interventionist framing may have reflected the political and intellectual context of Depression-era Chicago:

I would say that close to a majority of the social scientists and students . . . at Chicago . . . were either members of the Communist Party or very close to it . . . It was an environment in which the general intellectual atmosphere was strongly prosocialist. It was strongly in favor of government going all the way to take over the whole economy [. . .] Relative to that kind of atmosphere, [Simons'] pamphlet created a great stir because it was widely interpreted as being, if you want, reactionary.[43]

Although Friedman neglected to mention it at the time, he himself had hardly been immune to the "general intellectual atmosphere." In fact, when Simons' intervention was published, Friedman was about to leave the "sheltered academic cloister at Chicago" to accept a posting at one of the New Deal agencies in Washington, DC—the National Resources Com-mittee—where along with Chicago alumnus Allen Wallis he would work on long-range planning in the statistical section. "New Deal Washington was a wonderful place for a young economist," Friedman later confessed, reveal-ing a reformist streak that he would never entirely lose, "There was a sense of excitement and achievement in the air [and we] had the feeling—or illusion—that we were at the birth of a new order."[44]

Aaron Director would also later concede that Simons' interventions were styled in such a way to render them "palatable" to his left-leaning collea-gues at Chicago. Just after Simons' death, Director wrote that he had been "slowly establishing himself as the head of a 'school'," which some believe to be the first printed reference to the existence of a Chicago school of economics.[45] Yet the Economics Department proper had been disinclined to tenure Simons—just as it would turn up its nose at the prospect of Hayek joining as a tenured colleague in 1950—prompting Simons' relocation to the Law School in the mid-1930s, albeit as a professor of economics. At the time of Simons' death, much of the groundwork for the establishment of the Chicago school of economics had been laid. Friedman had just been hired away from Minnesota, though following a recruitment snafu it would take more than a decade to secure a position for Friedman's former office mate, George Stigler, back in Chicago. Nevertheless, another strategically key hire had been prosecuted more smoothly—Friedman's brother-in-law, Aaron Director, had been brought back to the Law School from the Commerce Department in Washington, DC. And Friedman's old friend, Allen Wallis, also returned to Chicago to join the business school.

Plans had been afoot for some time to bring Hayek to Chicago. Simons had been the principal interlocutor in these discussions, along with the University's president, Robert Hutchins. While acknowledging the pressing need to rebuild, Hutchins liked to boast that he possessed "the most conservative economics department in the world."[46] Despite the availability of private foundation financing from the arch-conservative Volker Fund, the negotiations proved to be protracted and difficult. The eventual refusal of the Economics Department to offer Hayek a tenure home doubtless brought back painful memories for Simons; neither did the department demonstrate any enthusiasm for hosting the Volker Fund's proposed Free Market Project.[47] As Aaron Director—who had been identified by Simons and Hayek as the ideal leader of the Project—later recalled, it was almost through a process of elimination that Chicago became the "only place" that might host such a venture, while the Law School would be the "only part of the University of Chicago that would be accommodating."[48]

The Free Market Project, in fact, never did take shape in the form that Simons, Hayek, and their benefactors at the Volker Fund had envisaged. While the implicit responsibility for the Project lay with Director, his redoubtable skills as a debater and teacher were matched by a remarkable reluctance to commit to print. Nevertheless, Director occupied a galvanizing, leadership role in Chicago's conservative project, working alongside Friedman as the two "main intellectual forces" shaping the attendant policy program.[49] Following Simons' suicide, Director eventually managed to secure Hayek's move to Chicago in 1950. This would further consolidate the transatlantic bonds that had been developing since the inaugural Mont Pelerin meeting of 1947. What Stigler later described as a "junket to . . . save liberalism" had been Friedman's first time outside the United States, a journey that he made in the reassuring company of his brother-in-law, Aaron Director, his mentor, Frank Knight, and his former office-mate, George Stigler.[50]

The Mont Pelerin Society (MPS) meeting was a transformative one for most of the participants, but perhaps especially for the neophyte Friedman, who still "had some distance to travel on his road to *Free to Choose*," his Reagan-era statement of unadulterated neoliberal conviction.[51] Friedman acknowledged that Davenport's portrayal of the rather susceptible young economist suited him "to a T." Friedmanologist, Daniel Hammond likewise concluded that his public and private views had been "in the New Deal mainstream" throughout the 1930s and most of the 1940s,[52] when he was remembered as a competent, but unexceptional, young economist, with a publication record that was "undistinguished" and an air of "scholarly detachment."[53] Moreover, Friedman himself later admitted, on revisiting some Congressional testimony he had given in 1942, that he had "completely forgotten how thoroughly Keynesian I then was."[54] All this was about to change.

It was only at the 1947 MPS meeting that "Friedman's (classically or neo-) liberal commitments were cemented."[55] But this was not just the site of a personal transformation. The programmatic strategy of the Chicago School, as it was fashioned in the years after the Second World War, was constructed in dialogue with the evolving MPS network. Rather than reify some supposedly unbroken lineage, from Laughlin through Viner and Knight, to isolate a uniquely Chicagoan brand of economic theory, or to anoint moments of immaculate conception in Econ 301, Van Horn and Mirowski locate the origins of the Chicago School at this politicized nexus, underlining the mutual constitution of the MPS and the Chicago School:

[The] establishment of the Chicago School constituted just one component of a much more elaborate transnational institutional project to reinvent a liberalism which had some prospect of challenging the socialist doctrines ascendant in the immediate postwar period…That MPS and the Chicago School were joined at the hip from birth is verified by the fact that most of the major protagonists were present at the creation of both organizations: Director, Friedman, Wallis, and Knight.[56]

Viner later recalled that it was not until long after he had left the University of Chicago, in fact at a conference in 1951, that he "began to hear rumors of a 'Chicago School' which was engaged in an organized battle for laissez faire…against 'imperfect competition' theorizing and 'Keynesianism'."[57] Martin Bronfenbrenner also remembered hearing the somewhat pejorative soubriquet only after he left Chicago, in 1947, nevertheless countering that there was "not one but two Chicago schools; the departure of Jacob Viner and the passing of Henry Simons [both in 1946] are the watersheds between them."[58] Paul Douglas remembers returning from his wartime service to find that the battle with conservative forces in his department had been decisively lost. Douglas—a political activist and civil-rights campaigner, who was later elected to the United States Senate—had taught economics in Chicago since 1920, serving as an advisor to President Roosevelt. He returned from the war to find that Chicago had become "a different place ... Knight was now openly hostile, and his disciples seemed to be everywhere."[59] While the "first" Chicago School was characterized by its robust heterogeneity, embracing the mainstream currents of progressive interventionism along with a cell of free-market rebels, led by Knight and Simons, it was the "second" Chicago School that really earned the name. George Stigler was more emphatic, "There was no Chicago School of Economics when the Mt. Pelerin Society first met at the end of World War II."[60] That was to come.

Remobilization

If the political projects of neoliberalization have been characteristically associated with, not to say enabled by, crisis, several of its ideational antecedents seem also to have been (re)born amid considerable turbulence. In the immediate postwar years, when Friedman joined the faculty at Chicago, the Economics Department was "in turmoil."[61] Its reputation had been palpably diminished, and there was a strong sense of the need to "rebuild" after the war. Jacob Viner had just departed for Yale, while the socialist econometrician, Oskar Lange, had left for a political career with the Polish government. Paul Douglas, too, had decided to pursue elected office. By the time that Hayek arrived in Chicago for a sabbatical in the spring of 1946, it was clear that something was afoot. Simons had been maneuvering to construct a "project" around Hayek for some time, including a planned "raid" on Minnesota, for Stigler and Friedman. Simons was dead by the summer of 1946, but his plan was in motion. Before the year's end, the "Knight affinity group" had been reassembled in Chicago, consisting of Friedman in Economics, Allen Wallis in the Graduate School of Business, and Aaron Director in the Law School—now as Simons' replacement. Securing Hayek and Stigler would take several more years. Meanwhile, Knight's well-known social and leadership deficits meant that the paternal figure was neither inclined nor capable of sustaining any kind of programmatic project. Nevertheless, according to Emmett, he clearly "inspired those around him to go against the odds and oppose the progressive spirit of the age."[62] It was Friedman, most conspicuously, who would energetically grow into the leadership role.

This would be no simple takeover, however. In fact, a new source of opposition had just arrived on the scene. A talented group of young econometricians, assembled under the auspices of the Cowles Commission (motto: *Science is Measurement*), had been meeting at summer schools in the Rockies since the early 1930s, relocating to the University of Chicago during the war. A major shareholder in the *Chicago Tribune*, Alfred Cowles had come to realize, following the stock market crash of 1929, "that he did not understand the workings of the economy."[63] His response was to initiate a concerted effort to enhance the predictive power of economics, particularly through the adoption of mathematical techniques. Cowles was to become a powerhouse of the new science of econometrics, controversially favoring Walrasian approaches and general equilibrium modeling over the Marshallian tradition, as interpreted by Friedman. If the increasingly intense intramural disputes between Friedman and the Cowlesmen were primarily methodological and analytical, not far beneath the surface they were also political. Cowles was "stocked with self-identified socialists," with a range of affiliations ranging "somewhere between Keynes and [Oskar] Lange politically," while Friedman had begun to adopt what his biographer portrayed as an "extremist libertarian position."[64] Curiously, the *Chicago Tribune* seems to have looked the other way, continuing to bankroll the cabal of brilliant econometricians, despite the paper's avowedly McCarthyite sympathies.[65]

The battle was on, however, in the department. Friedman railed against the Cowles methods that in his mind sought to mimic, through ever-more elaborate forms of mathematical abstraction, "photographic descriptions of reality"; meanwhile Jacob Marschak, the Cowles research director, had taken to ridiculing Marshallian modes of *ceteris paribus* reasoning as a "refuge for lazy irresponsibles."[66] A pair of skits performed by graduate students at a department party some time in the late 1940s memorably dramatized the conflict. To the tune of "American Patrol," the Cowles boys sang:

> We must be rigorous, we must be rigorous,
> We must fulfill our role.
> If we hesitate or equivocate
> We won't achieve our goal.
> > We must elaborate our systems complicate
> > To make our models whole

Statistical control!
Our esoteric seminars
Bring statisticians by the score.
But try to find economists
Who don't think algebra's a chore.
   Oh we must urge you most emphatically
   To become inclined mathematically
   So that all that we've developed
   May some day be applied.

Then, in a reworking of the Gilbert and Sullivan ditty, "When I was a lad," Friedman was gently goaded:

When I was a lad I served a term
Under the tutelage of A. F. Burns.
I read my Marshall completely through
From beginning to end and backwards too.
   I read my Marshall so carefully
   That now I am Professor at the U. of C.
   (chorus) He read his Marshall so carefully
   That now he's a Professor at the U. of C.
Of Keynesians I make mince meat
Their battered arguments now line the street.
I get them on their weakest assumption:
"What do you *mean* by the consumption function?"
   They never gave an answer that satisfied me
   So now I am a Professor at the U. of C.
   (chorus) They never gave an answer that satisfied he
   So now he is a Professor at the U. of C.[67]

A frequent, yet pugnaciously combative, attendee at Cowles seminars, Friedman became the Commission's self-appointed "hair shirt."[68] It was during this time that his legendary debating skills were honed, with the benefit of what were formidable adversaries. Although relations between the Cowlesmen and the Friedman wing of the Economics Department were generally civil, by the late 1940s it was obvious that an "intense struggle" for intellectual dominance had been joined on both sides.[69]

This was not just a battle over local turf, since big guns were arrayed on both corners—counting back, the primary interlocutors included more than a dozen Nobel laureates and/or presidents of the American Economic Association. More than this, though, the tussles in the Social Science Research Building, not to mention their ultimate stakes, reflected and refracted the increasingly oppressive climate of ideological Manicheanism.

The Cold War was nothing if not a war of competing economic ideologies, with profound implications for the (re)constitution and dominant trajectory of American economics.[70] And although leading members of the Cowles Commission were to remain ambivalent about Keynes and Keynesian macroeconomics during the Chicago years, their preferred forms of general equilibrium modeling would later be associated with the formalization of a distinctly American version of the "Keynesian synthesis."[71]

In the decade after the Great Depression, Chicago had become a site of especially intense polarization in economic doctrines. No sooner had various "imported" forms of Keynesianism established a presence in both professional economics and governmental practice, during the 1930s and through the period of wartime planning, did substantial forces of institutional, political, and intellectual resistance begin to assert themselves. To many, the Keynesian approach invoked specters of interventionist planning and government control. It was the *Chicago Daily Tribune* that in 1940 branded Keynes "The Englishman who rules America," hinting darkly at the "communistic" threat behind Roosevelt's conversion to the principles of economic planning and deficit spending.[72] And the paper would periodically rail, including in front-page editorials, against Keynes' promotion of credit and inflation, his "mischievous economic schemes," the "amazing power" that he seemed to exert over Roosevelt and his administration, and his plans for a "future economic government of the world."[73]

As the grip of McCarthyite paranoia intensified, advocacy of even modest forms of economic intervention invited suspicion. Paul Samuelson, doyen of Keynesianism, later reflected that the climate created by McCarthy's witch-hunts "actually drove me a little to the right, as people vulgarly measure these things."[74] In fact, Chicago had attempted to recruit Samuelson in 1948, so that the Economics Department would then possess, in the words of Theodore Schultz, "two leading minds of a different philosophical bent." Samuelson declined, concluding that battling Friedman would unnecessarily "polarize [and] radicalize me," since, in engaging with arguments that he considered "too far right," there was a risk of repositioning himself "too far left."[75] And in an early sign of the "doctrinal and methodological cleansing" of the 1950s, an avowedly Keynesian cell was routed from the University of Illinois (culminating in the forced resignation of the dean of the School of Commerce, the chair of economics, and seven faculty members), following a concerted campaign on the part of conservative media and business interests.[76] Several Cowlesmen, many of whom had the additional misfortune of being heavily-accented Eastern European immigrants or refugees, were later caught up in these purges, while the Illinois legislature publicly contemplated the introduction of loyalty oaths for academic economists. As Philip Mirowski has mused, "Perhaps the midwesterners, mired in their mugwump xenophobia, could not be expected so willingly to concede to the Cowlesmen the right to 'plan' the economy of their newly adopted Arcadia."[77]

So Friedman was hardly acting alone in pressing home his unflinching attacks on the Cowles Commission. With the assistance of an increasingly combative cohort, including Allen Wallis and Aaron Director, Friedman was ultimately "instrumental" in winning the civil war with the Cowlesmen, who eventually decamped to Yale in the mid-1950s.[78] Friedman, who had energetically assumed the "intellectual leadership of the [ultimately dominant] faction of the department, had relished the 'intramural struggle'."[79] And when, the following year, Wallis recruited George Stigler to the "luxuriously upholstered" Walgreen Professorship of American Institutions, the "Knight affinity group" was duly reconsolidated, as indeed was the Chicago School itself.[80] This was more than a graduate school reunion for the Chicago Boys of the 1930s—who the precocious Paul Samuelson, as an undergraduate, had branded Knight's "Swiss guards."[81] It also represented a regrouping of the Statistical Research Group (SRG), which during the Second World War had conducted pioneering work on the challenges of ordnance management and materiel procurement, such that the Chicago School of the 1950s was a kind of "SRG in exile on the shores of Lake Michigan."[82] While the spell at the SRG may have deepened the bonds between Wallis, Stigler, and Friedman, their 9-to-5 work was primarily concerned with statistics, not economics. The SRG projects on which the Chicagoans worked included calculating the optimum size and number of pellets in anti-aircraft shells. Even though Friedman is credited, from this time, with some significant innovations in sampling theory, his ultimate conclusion was, in the words of fellow monetarist Alan Walters, that there was "little to be gained by the endless sharpening of statistical knives."[83]

Rationalizing positive economics

Battle-hardened from the tussles with the Cowlesmen, the Chicago School of the 1950s began to articulate its alternative vision in an increasingly assertive fashion. Hayek's move to Chicago represented his anointment, in Van Horn and Mirowski words, as the de facto "figurehead [of the] neoliberal project" at the University, which by the early 1950s was in "full swing."[84] An increasingly politicized Milton Friedman was now sensing that the ideological trend towards collectivism might be maxing out, and that the time was ripe to begin to "promote the ideas that can guide the next generation of legislators." In one of his rare uses of the word, he explained in 1951 that the "doctrine [of] neoliberalism... that, in America in particular, is connected to the name Henry Simons [seems to have been] created to fill the void."[85] The "Hayek tide" was beginning to rise, one that the Chicago School would ride both to academic recognition and political influence.

Somewhat ironically, Friedman was soon arguing—in his influential essay on methodology, published in 1953—for a strict separation of positive ("what is") and normative ("what ought to be") modalities of economic discourse. His concern was to elaborate a methodology of "positive economics," judged according to its predictive power (rather than the "realism" of its assumptions) and "in principle independent of any particular ethical position or normative judgments."[86] Harry Johnson, who for a time was the Chicago School's leading in-house rebel, later claimed that this form of positive economics was peculiarly suited not only to post-Cowles Chicago, but also to the proclivities (and limitations) of its diminutive author: rather than pursue the goal of descriptive realism, in the form of proliferating systems of general equilibrium equations, positive economics enabled Friedman and his followers to "select the crucial relationships that permit one to predict something large from something small, regardless of the intervening chain of causation... [an approach that] offered liberation to the small-scale intellectual, since it freed his mind from dependence on the large-scale research team and the large and expensive computer program."[87]

More and less sympathetic commentators seem to agree that the positive and political faces of Chicago School economics are intricately, if not deeply and definitively, intertwined.[88] In contrast to Hayek, who believed that his popular tract, *The Road to Serfdom* effectively destroyed his reputation as an academic economist, Friedman attempted to inhabit both worlds, more or less at the same time—issuing audacious and uncompromising policy advice on the one hand, while fiercely protecting his reputation as an empirically oriented economist on the other. While noting, *en passant*, that the 1947 MPS meeting "marked the beginning of my involvement in the political process," at least in his own mind Friedman maintained a sharp distinction between his efforts to "influence public policy" and his scientific endeavors: "I have led, as it were, two lives," he once said, "On the one hand, I have been a scientist, an economic scientist, an academic. On the other hand, I have been ... a public intellectual."[89]

I have spoken and written about issues of public policy. In doing so, however, I have not been acting in my scientific capacity, but in my capacity as a citizen, an informed one, I hope. I believe that what I know as an economist helps me to form better judgments about some issues than I could without that knowledge. But fundamentally, my scientific work should not be judged by my activities in public policy.[90]

These activities, however, were hardly mere diversions. Beginning in 1956, for example, Friedman played a leading role in a series of summer schools funded by the Volker Fund, which were designed to hone a set of popular arguments for "economic freedom." This represented, in effect, the long-frustrated American Road project, refitting Hayek's message for a US audience. Presented to groups of "twenty to thirty young academics," and recalled as "amongst the most stimulating intellectual experiences of my life," with Rose's assistance, these lectures were gradually shaped into the bestselling book, *Capitalism and Freedom*.[91] Although effectively shunned by the academic and journalistic establishment, the book went on to sell more than 500,000 copies, and has never since gone out of print.

The prefaces to successive editions of the book call attention to the tightness of the intellectual circles to which Friedman belonged, the author's irritation at the disdainful attitude of the East-Coast establishment, and the gradual change in the climate of public opinion. In the original 1962 preface, Friedman acknowledged his funders from Volker and the "incisive probing and deep interest" of the summer-school delegates, together with his current and former Chicago colleagues—Knight, Simons, Mints, Director, Hayek, and Stigler—from whom he had taken "so much ... [that] what I have learned has become so much a part of my own thought that I would not know how to select points to footnote."[92] In the 1982 preface, he complained about the failure of major national media outlets to review the first edition of the book, when its "views were [evidently] so far out of the mainstream," while welcoming the seismic shift in public opinion that had recently swept Reagan into office.[93] In the preface to the third edition, in 2002, Reagan and Thatcher were praised for having "curb[ed] Leviathan," though in retrospect neither had succeeded in "cut[ting] it down."[94]

Enclavization had clearly helped, in retrospect, to solidify and sharpen what Melvin Reder called the "Chicago subculture." In addition to the close intellectual affinities to which Friedman referred, this was rooted in a set of mutually reinforcing, locally institutionalized practices, including Chicago's rigorous and unforgiving graduate program, and the distinctive framework for intellectual exchange developed in the department. Chicago's graduate program simultaneously served the function of intellectual socialization (notably, at the alter of price theory, symbolized by Econ 301) and Darwinian selectivity (failure was commonplace). As if to underline the role of elemental proximity, accounts of the Chicago School invariably emphasize its treasured oral tradition, the insights of sacred texts being passed, literally, between successive generations of teachers and students.[95] Paul Samuelson, who had begun his undergraduate career at Chicago aged just 16, once remarked that while his Jesuit upbringing eventually "wore off," the searing impact of Chicago economics never did—he felt that he had been "somewhat brainwashed" at Hyde Park.[96] In the postwar period, alongside Friedman's dominating presence, as a teacher and as a "courteous but relentless" debater,[97] Aaron Director stands out as a truly remarkable verbal communicator, whom Stephen Stigler, likened to Socrates, while also conceding that he "published next to nothing."[98]

Another important feature of the Chicago subculture was the intensely combative workshop system, introduced by Friedman, which drew equally on graduate students and senior faculty. Here, rigorously formulated knowledge claims would be subjected to searching critique, "scientific progress [being achieved through] a process of creative destruction," though one strictly bounded by a locally cultivated and policed variant of a hyperrationalist economic orthodoxy—stylized as "tight prior equilibrium," or TP. Reder's sympathetic, insider account of the functioning of the TP regime invokes the notion of a locally calibrated scientific paradigm, if not a provincial form of scientific dogma:

The paradigmatic nature of TP gives its adherents a particular perspective upon empirical evidence ... [N]ew findings are accepted far more readily if they are consistent with the theory's implications ... This posture of TP causes its adherents to distrust reports (from historians, journalists, practitioners of other social sciences, and from some economists) of behavior incompatible with the implications of economic theory ... Resistance to paradigm-disturbing evidence is paralleled by a reluctance to accept disruptive theoretical innovations. A theoretical innovator must squeeze between the rock: "if an innovation is consistent with what is known, it serves no useful purpose" and the hard place: "if inconsistent with what was previously believed, it must be wrong" ... Consequently, at Chicago, a would-be theoretical innovator must be unusually self-confident and determined [while] Chicago-type innovations are "paradigm preserving" or "paradigm extending" rather than "paradigm shattering."[99]

A purified methodological space, circumscribed by tight intellectual and social networks, enabled Chicago to generate something large from something small, in Harry Johnson's words, and to do so from what might be called the theoretical "margins." Perhaps it is the case, as a key player in Chicago's law and economics movement has claimed, that scientific innovation is more likely to "come from the fringe, not the mainstream. Simons, Director, and Coase were all professors of economics who did not find a comfortable place in their own fields. Chicago, not Harvard or Yale, was the leading innovator."[100]

This shared marginality, tinged in some cases with a sense of righteous grievance, found its echo in the University of Chicago's cherished identity as an intellectual "haven," tolerant of renegade stripes of opinion. On the "inside," this made for extremely close intellectual, and often social, ties, and a culture that Stigler once characterized as "monastic."[101] The microgeographies of the Hyde Park campus happened to facilitate this. "Physical geography," Harry Johnson explained, made a difference: "the Harvard and Yale economists were scattered among widely separated buildings, whereas the Chicago economists lived on one, the fourth, floor with a single elevator around and in which they automatically met frequently and informally."[102] Relative isolation from the distractions of downtown further reinforced the academic monoculture, Deidre McCloskey being among those who attributed the vigor of intellectual engagement to the fact there was "literally nothing else to do" on the campus.[103] Most of the Economics faculty, in fact, lived within a mile of the department, making "informal social gatherings at home easy to arrange—in contrast to the far-flung suburban living patterns of Harvard, MIT and Yale."[104] Legend has it that it was at one such dinner party, at Aaron Director's house in 1960, that the "Coasean revolution" was launched. As David Warsh tells it, "The Chicagoans had gone into the room believing, along with liberals, that there were certain indispensable services that government had to provide because markets couldn't be made to offer them," but after several hours of intense debate, they left "with a new vision of what government might accomplish through the clever establishment of property rights."[105]

The Chicago School's theoretical and methodological proclivities therefore melded with a conducive local institutional environment to create the impetus behind what had become a redoubtable intellectual program, albeit one still located on the borderlands of "mainstream" or "establishment" thinking in the 1950s. Laurence Miller's assessment of the Chicago School during this time acknowledged that it was certainly "not monolithic," while maintaining that a "tendency toward a common position seems indisputable." Chicago's "polar position" within American economics was distinctive, Miller claimed, by virtue of its "unambiguous advocacy of a private-enterprise economy and limited government," since relative to the economics profession, the defining traits of the Chicagoan included:

the polar position that he [sic] occupies among economists as an advocate of an individualistic market economy; the emphasis that he puts on the usefulness and relevance of neo-neoclassical economic theory; the way in which he equates the actual and the ideal market; the way in which he sees and applies economics in and to every nook and cranny of life; and the emphasis that he puts on hypothesis-testing as a neglected element in the development of positive economics.[106]

Stigler, for his part, was unimpressed with this characterization, which he argued underestimated both the internal heterogeneity of the "Chicago tradition" and the scattered incidence of "Chicago-style" views across the economics profession. Perhaps not surprisingly, Stigler was willing to acknowledge the distinctiveness of the intellectual position represented in Miller's sketch, but he balked at the slippage into spatial stereotyping: "Whether this group deserves the name 'Chicago'—it once carried the name of an English town—is hardly for a literal Chicagoan to say."[107] In contrast to the nineteenth-century Manchester School, which was deeply—if not organically—embedded in a very particular urban political economy and a unique network of international trading relations,[108] the Chicago School dangled as a southern appendage to a somewhat inhospitable Fordist–Keynesian metropolis, the ideational and political currents within which were quite out of step with Chicago School economics.

Transplanted Chicagoan, Martin Bronfenbrenner, who had spent some time in the enemy territory of Wisconsin, was less inclined to quibble with Miller's use of geographical signification—he knew exactly what "Chicago School" meant. Bronfenbrenner recognized that "there is such a thing as the Chicago School, for better or worse," and more often than not the connotations were less than positive ones, particularly in institutionalist strongholds like Madison, where the Chicago School "meant Pangloss plus Gradgrind, with touches of Peachum, Torquemada, and the Marquis de Sade thrown in."[109] Even though *some* Chicago-style theoretical propositions and policy positions might have enjoyed quite broad support, much more common was the tendency for "Chicago School" formulations to be negatively stereotyped by a dogmatically unreceptive intellectual community: "That way," warned Bronfenbrenner, "lies not 'modernism,' not 'institutionalism,' not 'new economics,' but witch-hunting, book-burning, madness pure and simple."[110] Notwithstanding this sense of intellectual persecution, a familiar Chicago refrain, things were beginning to change. During the 1960s, it became clear that "Chicago"—which had always represented a normative/analytical space in the economic imagination, as well as a place—was beginning to "spread horizontally," including out to the coasts.[111] Among the most influential outliers on the mental map of free-market economics, by the 1970s, were those at UCLA and at Virginia, which prompted UCLA's Armen Alchian to coin the geographical neologism "*ChiVirLa*," in order to designate "where you've got what people typically call the Chicago type [...] whether or not it comes out of Chicago is irrelevant."[112]

While Chicago types remained a small minority, they were emboldened both by the strength of their convictions and by a sustaining belief that the collectivist-interventionist tide would eventually turn, the fervency of which has been likened to religious forms of devotion.[113] Then, the time would come for "classical" undercurrents in economic theory to reap their deserving revalidation. Both Friedman and Stigler ascribed to the Dicey-esque position, that intellectual transformation occurs in long waves, beginning with contestation among elites, before stabilizing as a common sense, and then falling prey to challenge.[114] In fact, Stigler once traveled to Harvard to labor the point, insisting that by specific training and general inclination, the economist was politically conservative. He acknowledged that Keynesian meddlers had sullied this long-standing reputation, facilitating a lay (mis)conception of the professional economist as a "wild-eyed visionary, whispering absurd schemes to Franklin Roosevelt," but nevertheless held to the conviction that—such "camp followers" aside—the underlying predisposition of the field was skeptical of egalitarian schemes and interventionist pretensions.[115]

Empirically oriented, skeptical, and conservative, Chicago therefore stood for the enduring spirit of the dismal science, Stigler maintained, noting that, "It is not a coincidence that [those] who have turned socialist or communist have usually been completely abstract theorists."[116] In fact, extremely tight analytical and normative parameters were erected around Chicago's search for economic truth. Reder concedes that the analytical and normative sides of the Chicago School, in this sense, were mutually constitutive. More than this, it was symbiotically related to the evolving political project of Hayek and the MPS:

The normative strain is held by a set of Chicago economists much smaller than the total, but a group which I believe would include most of the original Knight affinity group. An intellectual portrait of this group, many of whom would be members of the Mt. Pelerin Society, would be quite different from a description of Chicago economics [in toto], although the relation of the two can be (and has been) the subject of many a lunch table conversation.[117]

No doubt, the tight prior connections of those in the inner circle—which could be traced back to Knight and Chicago in the 1930s and the SRG and Columbia in the 1940s—were instrumental in establishing the preconditions for the postwar Chicago School, but this hard-earned reputation as an infamous intellectual outpost had yet to be converted into influence. Slowly, though, the tides were turning.

Economics, public and private

Milton Friedman claimed to have only narrowly avoided contracting "Potomac Fever" during his two years at the US Treasury in the early 1940s, where amongst other things he helped devise a plan for the withholding tax.[118] During this time, however, he had been mainly working as what he liked to call a "technical economist," his life's vocation, therefore limiting his exposure to the disease. Engagement with the worlds of policy and politics came later. And even though this "sideline" was, for him, practically a continuous one from the late 1950s onwards, Friedman always insisted that such interventions were calculated acts of professional transgression.

This policy stuff has been a strict avocation. If you really want to engage in policy activity, don't make it your vocation . . . Get a job. Get a secure base of income. Otherwise, you're going to get corrupted and destroyed . . . I think you'll make a mistake if you're going to spend your life as a policy wonk. I've seen some of my students who have done this. And some of them are fine, and some of them, especially those who have gone to Washington and stayed, are not.[119]

Cultivating an outsider identity, of course, suited Friedman's political message, but he would soon be drawing upon—and helping to reconstruct—elite circuits of his own. Some of this required organizational innovation as well as resources. For example, Friedman was instrumental in establishing the Philadelphia Society, a sort of American branch of the MPS. The Philadelphia Society's inaugural meeting, held in Chicago in 1965, where the organization was incorporated, was described by one observer as a "conclave of the brave."[120] Today, Philadelphia Society meetings are scheduled to coincide with the annual gathering of the Heritage Foundation's Resource Bank, the main event on the calendar for "more than 500 think tank executives, public interest lawyers, policy experts, elected officials, and activists from around the world to discuss issues, strategies, and methods for advancing free market, limited government public policies."[121]

Friedman was also present at the rebirth of the American Enterprise Institute (AEI), which took a free-market turn in the mid-1950s under the determined leadership of incoming president, Bill Baroody, ostensibly as a counterweight to the centrist, establishment presence of the Brookings Institution.[122] It was as an adviser to AEI that Friedman truly "entered the Washington political scene," shortly thereafter.[123] He was to provide academic stewardship for AEI's research and publication program for many years, but the offices of the think tank also enabled Friedman to make contact with a cabal of ideologically motivated Republican congressmen (including Melvin Laird, Gerald Ford, and Donald Rumsfeld), whose intelligence and commitment to a programmatic agenda for the party especially "impressed" the Chicagoan. During this same period, Friedman met Senator Barry Goldwater at one of Baroody's Washington dinner parties, which were positioning AEI as the "brains trust" for the candidate who would become the standard-bearer for free-market conservatives within the Republican Party.[124]

Friedman later served as Goldwater's senior economic advisor, in the Senator's iconoclastic but ill-fated presidential run of 1964. Prior to this, the closest that Friedman had come to electoral politics had occurred when Rose volunteered as a Republican observer in their Hyde Park electoral district, an act of symbolic futility in this "the most solidly Democratic precinct in a Democratic city."[125] Even though he shied away from making campaign-trail appearances with Goldwater, the presidential election was a baptism of fire for Friedman. Taking a visiting position at Columbia University during 1964–65, Friedman found himself in the thick of Democratic *and* Republican party opposition to Goldwater, who had defeated one of the scions of the East-Coast Republican establishment, Nelson Rockefeller, for his party's nomination, before losing to Johnson in an unedifying general election. (Among other things, Goldwater was branded an extremist, a racist, and a warmonger in the course of the campaign.) Friedman's prominent role on the Goldwater policy team prompted, he recalled, "disgust and dismay [from] most of my academic friends," hardly any of whom were "on our side."[126]

Called upon by the *New York Times* to articulate the "Goldwater view of economics," Friedman responded comprehensively, while also gently demurring that he was no hired gun.[127] Noting some differences between his own, more absolutist, policy positions and those of the comparative pragmatic Senator, the economist nevertheless called attention to what he saw as their closely overlapping convictions:

[Goldwater's] goal is always the same: to promote the freedom of the individual and to widen his opportunity; to stop the drift toward centralization and collectivism that has been underway in the past few decades, a drift that has not achieved its professed objectives but that has served to curtail individual freedom, to undermine individual responsibility and to weaken the moral fiber of the people... Senator Goldwater is often depicted as a reactionary mossback who wants to turn back the clock to an earlier but vanished era... [He] is, of course, inspired by ideas of an earlier age. So are we all... [But as] the Senator said in accepting the Republican Presidential nomination, "We must and shall return to proven ways—not because they are old, but because they are true."[128]

Paul Samuleson, in a characteristically erudite response, rejected what he characterized as Friedman's "Economic Libertarianism" as simply too "extreme" for mainstream American politics. In another flashback to his undergraduate days at Chicago in the 1930s, Samuelson confessed to having been seduced for a while by the "cold beauty" of the utopian worldview of Hayek, Mises, Simons, and Knight. But three decades later, he was no longer taken by such syllogistic reasoning, with its appeal to the "semantics of freedom": the electorate should not be presented with false choices between government regulation and individual freedom because, in the modern mixed economy, they could reasonably "hope to have the best of both worlds."[129] Manichean reasoning, however, suited Chicago's brand of cold-war economics. Particular invective, in fact, was aimed at the notion of a "mix-and-match" economy, a mere way station on the slippery slope to socialism.[130]

The discourse of public economics was beginning to pivot around a different axis. The Samuelson–Friedman exchange presaged the extended public debate around economic philosophy, policy, and practice that was starting to take shape in the mid-1960s. When *Newsweek* set out to recruit a troika of economists for a rotating sequence of columns on topical events, starting in 1966, they tapped Samuelson as the most articulate representative of "new deal liberalism," Henry Wallich of Yale as the voice of the "live center," and Friedman as the advocate of "old liberal" or "free enterprise" perspectives.[131] Friedman was happy to rise to the challenge, no doubt relishing this unprecedented opportunity to advance his position on more-or-less equal terms with the late-Keynesian mainstream, which *Newsweek* had repositioned on the left.[132] This had reached its zenith in the heady days of the Kennedy administration's "new frontier."[133] Even though the McCarthyite paranoia of the 1950s had thawed, cold-war sensibilities continued to shape the distinctive form of American economics in general, and the stunted and distorted form of US-style Keynesianism in particular. The repressive political atmosphere of the 1950s had served to "narrow the range of [economic] beliefs and to restrict the acceptable ways of expressing them," reinforcing the drift towards neoclassical formalism, technical introversion, and dependence on the "neutral" language of mathematics.[134] Bold policy advocacy had given way to technocratic tinkering within a narrow ideological bandwidth—the nexus of economic expertise and "high policy" having been reduced to "simple market analysis of the Marshallian kind, with a pinch of commercial Keynesianism thrown in."[135]

Nevertheless, in Chicago at least, resentments over the "academic oligarchy" continued to simmer. A veteran *Chicago Daily Tribune* journalist, sent out to assess the state of the field in the mid-1960s returned with a scathing indictment of the economics profession, "more than 90 percent of [whom] call themselves neo-Keynesians."[136] The techniques of modern economic governance were likewise dismissed as but one step away from revolutionary socialism—"transfer payments," for example, being read as code for the Marxian principle of "each according to his needs." Friedman, on the other hand, again chose to present himself on the opposite side of a crude ideological binary:

Fundamentally, there are only two ways of coordinating the economic activities of millions. One is central direction involving the use of coercion—the technique of the army and of the modern totalitarian state. The other is voluntary cooperation of individuals—the technique of the market place.[137]

During the mid-1960s, Friedman possessed a visceral sense of his location as a member of the intellectual anti-establishment. As he would later recall, Chicago was the ideal base in this respect, since he could advance contrary opinions, and even campaign for a candidate like Goldwater, "without losing the respect of either town or gown."[138]

Several degrees of separation from the dense circuits of opinion formation in the Boston–Washington corridor created the necessary space to work against the grain. Had he pursued his career in New York City, Friedman reflected, he would no doubt have been written off as a "kook." It was his visiting professorship at Columbia, in the thick of the Goldwater campaign, that had afforded him a rare entrée into the New York intellectual community. I talked to and argued with groups from academia, from the media, from the financial community, from the foundation world...I was appalled at what I found. There was an unbelievable degree of intellectual homogeneity, of acceptance of a standard set of views complete with cliché answers to every objection, of smug self-satisfaction of belonging to an in-group. The closest similar experience I have ever had was at Cambridge, England, and even that was a distant second [compared to] the homogeneity and provincialism of New York...This kind of intellectual homogeneity is destructive of tolerance. It is no accident that in the New York—or more generally, the eastern— environment, divergent views take the form of cults, not schools. One of the greatest economists of all time, Ludwig von Mises...was barely tolerated for years in a peripheral academic position at New York University...[He] had disciples but few students because of the stultifying intellectual atmosphere of New York.[139]

By way of evidence for his claim that Chicago stood for robust heterodoxy, Friedman recalled George Stigler's boast, that the University of Chicago was the only institution that could have staffed a Council of Economic Advisers for *both* Johnson and Goldwater, circa 1964. "If Chicago's geographical location had an effect," Friedman reflected, it was certainly not an isolation-induced proneness to "homogenous, if offbeat views"; rather it stemmed from a robustly liberal (in the old sense of the term) intellectual environment, actively dismissive of "narrowness, homogeneity, and inbreeding," New York-style.[140] Speaking at an annual dinner of the University's board of trustees, Friedman went on to conclude his "amateur exercise in the sociology of knowledge" by speculating that the intellectual fecundity of the various Chicago schools could be explained by the fact that

we were established in Chicago, a new, raw city, bursting with energy, far less sophisticated than New York, but for that very reason far more tolerant of diversity, of heterodox ideas. New York looked east, to the Old World [while looking] down its nose at the New...Chicago, like other cities this side of the Appalachians, looked west, to the frontiers...Chicago [became] characterized by diversity in every dimension, by a willingness to experiment, to judge people by their performance rather than their origins, to judge ideas by their consequences rather than their antecedents.[141]

This certainly was reflected in the Chicago School's geopolitical outlook, which favored perpetual experimentation and relentless competition between local jurisdictions over loyalties to place or, worse still, commitments to sociospatial equalization. In policy terms, this was translated into advocacy for decentralized and privatized strategies—a sort of dynamic, competitive federalism, galvanized by a determination to disperse power away from established centers like New York City and Washington, DC.

Insulated from the establishment-and-entitlement power blocs of the East coast, "Chicago" served as a kind of geographical symbol of Friedman's relative independence, the fact that he was "firmly based in a scientific academic discipline [rather than] simply a preacher or an ideologue or an unconnected philosopher" facilitating a constructively safe distance from the suffocating intellectual and political culture of New York, which tended to transform conservatives into cultists,[142] and from Washington, where the fetid ranks of think tanks and policy wonks could not help but dilute and distort, if not derail, truly pathbreaking ideas.[143] Friedman oscillated between these worlds through the 1960s and 1970s, while Chicago remained his touchstone and his base of operations. Summers, however, were always spent in New England—typically within striking distance of the library at Dartmouth College. It was here that the Friedmans built their dream home, named "Capitaf," in recognition of the role that royalties from *Capitalism and Freedom* had played in its purchase.

Neoliberalismo

The spring of 1975 marked the beginning of Chile's "silent revolution." General Augusto Pinochet, who—beyond suppressing labor unions and other "subversive" elements, "knew little about economics"—had set the country on a path of radical free-market reconstruction.[144] His guide was a monetarist tome known as "the brick" (ostensibly due to its 189-page length, rather than its lack of subtlety), which had been drafted in secret during the Allende period by a group of economists at the Pontificia Universidad Católica de Chile, under the leadership of Sergio de Castro. In one of the most storied episodes in the history of neoliberalism, Pinochet effectively handed control of economic policy over to "Los Chee-Ca-Go Boys," as they became known—a group of Chicago-trained economists, led by de Castro, who would staff the key positions in his administration.[145] In this notorious application of "shock treatment," the Chicago Boys went to war against inflation, which had spiked at 370 percent in the first year of the junta, their actions driving the economy immediately into recession, while at the same time setting about an uninhibited program of trade liberalization, tax reform, privatization, deregulation of foreign investment flows, and monetary restraint. An early move was to invite two of their Chicago professors, Arnold Harberger and Milton Friedman, for a week of seminars, public lectures, and meetings with military managers, culminating in an audience with Pinochet—all designed to bolster the credibility of the reform program. Not surprisingly, Harberger and Friedman signed off on the plan, which they might have authored by proxy. The Chicago School was about to learn a lesson in the politics of outsourcing.

Pointedly negative press commentary soon followed on the *New York Times* editorial page: here, the Chilean visit raised "troubling questions… about the social role of academics," given the instrumental role of the "ideas of Milton Friedman…and his Chicago school" in legitimizing the junta's "draconian" program.[146] A campus movement to censure Friedman and Harberger was eventually stifled by the University of Chicago's president, John Wilson, but sporadic protests would dog Friedman for years to come. Although he continued stridently to defend Pinochet's economic program—later dubbing Chile "an economic miracle" in a *Newsweek* column of 1982—Friedman had to learn to make his way to public speaking engagements "via the kitchen."

The protests organized by the united front [against the Friedman/Harberger Collaboration with the Chilean Junta] were annoying, especially when they included pickets marching up and down with signs in front of the apartment house in which we lived, but they were not very serious […] I never could decide whether to be more amused or more annoyed by the charge that I was running the Chilean economy from my office in Chicago.[147]

As Friedman and his supporters also insisted on pointing out, Harberger was actually the architect of the program that had brought Chilean economists to Chicago, beginning in the mid-1950s. As late as Friedman's ninetieth birthday, setting the record straight remained a priority: "I realize the 'Chicago-Boys-with-Milton' is the premise of numerous fine articles in the *New York Review of Books*," Deidre McCloskey huffed, "But they and you are wrong. Milton didn't do it."[148] It was, apparently, the entire Economics Department that did it, and most conspicuously Harberger. A fluent Spanish speaker with a Chilean wife, Harberger served as the chair of the Economics Department most of the time between 1964 and 1980. Worried that Chicago was losing out in the competition for talented graduate students with the East-Coast programs, Harberger had established a relationship with the Pontificia Universidad Católica de Chile in 1955, with financial assistance from the United States Agency for International Development and the Ford Foundation.[149] Sergio de Castro, who would eventually become Pinochet's finance minister, was among the first three students to arrive in Chicago, the following year. More than one hundred would follow. Harberger continues to credit the Chicago Boys with playing a catalytic role not only in the transformation of economic education in Latin America, but also in the wave of modernization and liberalization of economic policy that has swept Latin America in recent decades... [Prior to this], interventionism, paternalism, and socialism [had been the] watchwords... As good economics came to Latin America, all of this changed.[150]

Authorized histories of the Chicago School prefer to make light of these controversial connections, albeit conceding that they "must be covered."[151] Ebenstein contends that Friedman had only "minimal contact" with the Chilean students when they were in Hyde Park, though they all participated in his (mandatory) foundation course on economic theory, and some were invited to join his workshop on money and banking.[152] Normally among the first to proclaim the "power of ideas,"[153] Friedman's declaration of the Chilean economic miracle ironically occurred on the eve of the Chicago Boys' monetarist meltdown, in 1982,[154] when unemployment surged to 30 percent, the poverty rate climbed to 50 percent, and the banking sector collapsed. The government-led bailout of the banks yielded the ironic epithet, the "Chicago road to socialism."[155] A less doctrinaire form of neoliberal economic management was subsequently adopted, with diluted inputs from the discredited Chicago Boys. Appropriately, perhaps, a prime factor in the economic collapse of 1982 had been the prior pegging of the peso to the US dollar, which proved disastrous when the incoming Reagan administration launched its own experiment in monetarism.

While supporters of Chicago School economics would later claim vindication, when Chile eventually transitioned to both economic growth and democratic rule,[156] there has been continuing defensiveness about the fact that the first full-scale implementation of the Chicago method had occurred in the context of an authoritarian regime. McCloskey contends that "the economic advice that Chicago economists gave Chile was very, very good," adding with a characteristic flourish: "I, Deidre McCloskey, probably taught more future Chilean economists associated with torturing and murdering citizens in soccer stadiums than Milton did."[157] But for many critics, the Pincohet episode merely confirmed the suspected relationship between political repression and the economic violence of free-market governance.[158] In the space of a few fateful months in 1975, the "image of the 'Chicago Boys' was born," Van Overtveldt complains, in the form of "a group of amoral, ruthless, and antidemocratic hyper-technicians, who believed that the free-market economy was the only thing worth worrying about."[159] Not only would the associated controversy cast a cloud over the remainder of Friedman's teaching career at Chicago, following his award of the Nobel Prize in 1976, it brought an estimated 5,000 protesters onto the streets of Stockholm, one of whom made it into the ceremony itself, interrupting the pleasantries by shouting, "Down with capitalism, freedom for Chile."[160] Many years later, when an interviewer put it to Friedman that Chile did, in fact, deserve "a place in history [as] the first country to put Chicago theory into practice," he sputtered, "No, no, no. Not at all. After all, Great Britain put Chicago theory into practice in the 19th century [and the] United States put Chicago theory into practice in the 19th and 20th century. I don't believe that's right."[161]

Reaganomics

While Friedman continued to be the public face of the Chicago school of economics, he was to become somewhat estranged from domestic politics during the 1970s.[162] He had served on Nixon's economic advisory group, which was chaired by his mentor, Arthur Burns, but pointedly had little or nothing to do with the doomed president after he imposed price controls— "I saw him only once after that."[163] In fact, Friedman seemed to enjoy reiterating the principled overstatement that the enactment of wage and price controls, in August 1971, "did far more harm to the country than any of the later actions that led to [Nixon's] resignation."[164] The Chicago School version of the long national nightmare began with this craven act of misintervention—"not so much wrong as ridiculous," as Stigler recalled it—and then continued with a veritable "explosion in regulatory activity," more than doubling the number of pages in the Federal Register between 1968 and 1974.[165] Stigler was not alone in noting the irony that the Nixon Administration represented a high water mark in terms of the participation of professional economists in political positions—George Shultz left the office across from his at the Graduate School of Business to become Nixon's Labor Secretary, and later Treasury Secretary; proto-Chicagoan Arthur Burns was elevated to the position of chair of the Federal Reserve; and Friedman and Stigler both occupied senior advisory roles for a time. For some on the libertarian right, this unseemly rush to Washington merely confirmed what they had always suspected about the Chicago School. In 1971, Murray Rothbard launched a scornful attack on Friedman, portraying him as not just a closet "statist," but as "the Establishment's Court Libertarian."[166] Sensing personal animosity, Friedman did not rise to the bait, but later explained that, while he would "*like* to be a zero-government libertarian," his reading of history had taught him that this was "not a feasible social structure," outside perhaps Iceland, and the United States between 1780 and 1929.[167]

And then came Reagan. For Friedman, at least, this represented a long-awaited sea change. He and Rose had first encountered Reagan as they listened to the speeches at the 1964 Republican Convention, on the radio at their summer place in New Hampshire. This was when Reagan had stepped onto the national stage, as a Goldwater Republican, with a speech that many regarded as a highlight of the election season.[168] Sixteen years later, Reagan—as heir to the Goldwater project—was himself on the path to presidential power. Friedman served on Reagan's fourteen-member Economic Policy Coordinating Committee, chaired by George Shultz, which was tasked with engineering an advance plan for the new Administration.[169] Amongst the Committee's recommendations was the immediate removal of price controls on oil, which was duly enacted by the incoming President. Friedman later joined the President's Economic Advisory Board, which also included Alan Greenspan, Arthur Laffer, and William Simon—a cabal that he portrayed as "independent thinkers" with a "free-market orientation," and all professional economists rather than "'yes' persons."[170] Of the twelve members of Reagan's economic "brains trust," fully half had substantial Chicago connections.[171] The President's eyes would reportedly twinkle whenever he joined this group of true believers for a working lunch. In the words of one of Reagan's senior policy advisors, Martin Anderson, this was "truly the board of directors for the development of Reaganomics."[172] Friedman, Anderson disclosed, was one of the President's "favorites."

The same could not be said of George Stigler. One day in late October 1982, Chicago's Mr. Micro learned that he had been awarded the Nobel Prize—"a marvelous surprise," and at the time still a tax-free gift—in recognition of his contributions as "the intellectual Father of Deregulation."[173] On the face of it, this was a timely shot in the arm for Chicago economics, the achievements of which in theory had been overshadowed by some very public failures in practice—notably, in the first domestic applications of monetarism and in the Chilean experiment.[174] The United States was in the second, painful part of an unprecedented "double dip" recession, and the Republicans were facing major setbacks in the midterm elections. Seizing the opportunity for some free publicity on the eve of the vote, the White House paraded Stigler in front of the Washington press corps.

The President joked with reporters that, "Our critics are saying that the economy is on its knees, well you know something, if the economy is back on its knees, that's quite an improvement because two years ago it was flat on its back." The unemployment rate had topped 10 percent, but Reagan quipped that his Administration need only take responsibility for 2.7 percent, since it had stood at 7.4 percent when he entered office. Misplaced levity aside, it was expected that the newly minted Nobel laureate would at least offer a vote of support for the Administration's experiment in "supply-side economics." But when reporters invited Stigler to comment on Reagan's economic program, he curtly dismissed supply-side economics as "a gimmick [if not] a slogan...Where they went too far was in claiming so much for it and saying that if we do that, that alone will take care of inflation and things like that. I don't think that was in the cards."[175] When Stigler went on to use the word "depression," he was practically bundled from the platform, "in a manner reminiscent of vaudeville days."[176] The liberal use of what Stigler rather proudly described as his "unruly tongue" had apparently confirmed, for both sides, the Chicagoan's long-held view that politicians and economists were breeds apart.

Stigler had long before grown skeptical of the potential for even well-intentioned reform efforts. His work on the microeconomics of regulation, in particular, had extended the rational-choice paradigm deep into the sphere of politics itself, yielding the conclusion that policymakers should be seen as "endogenous participants in a political-economic process," whose preoccupations with the calculus of utilitarian and electoral gain rendered them, in the words of Melvin Reder, "incapable of acting on advice as to the promotion of general welfare, and unlikely to be much interested in receiving such advice."[177] These arguments had been articulated most forcefully, of course, by James Buchanan, who after working with Frank Knight in Chicago—a defining moment in his intellectual formation—went on to found the Virginia school of public choice.[178] "The language of public interest," Stigler once observed, "surely covers a good many acres of self-interest." His autobiography is replete with witty anecdotes about the manipulation of economic expertise, and experts, by self-serving politicians. His conclusion: that, "If I had worked in the White House, I assume I would have learned to be discreet and possibly also to be illegal."[179] There is clearly more than a suggestion, in both Stigler's and Buchanan's formulations, of the shadier kinds of economic motivations described by their mentor, Frank Knight.

While a studied cynicism concerning the prospects for constructive governmental intervention might be considered typical of the "Chicago view," a rather conspicuous exception is provided by Friedman himself, who repeatedly flew perilously close to the governmental flame. Like Stigler, Friedman had come to regard congressional testimony as a "waste of time,"[180] but quite unlike Stigler, Friedman did not extend this interpretation to the governmental process *in toto*. To the contrary, he grew increasingly preoccupied with public-policy interventions, both in the popular media and as a high-level policy advisor. Friedman possessed a sense of the progressive role of reform, at least when allied to a market-oriented program and the "right ideas."[181] Stigler's joke, which they shared, was that, "Milton wants to change the world. I just want to observe it."[182]

Friedman had pursued public-policy objectives with increasing vigor in the second half of his career, after he relocated to the Hoover Institution, pushing *inter alia* for education vouchers, the abolition of the military draft and professional licensure, flat taxes, and the privatization of social security. These policy positions, as Reder points out, were all broadly consistent with the Chicago School worldview—since they invoked market logics and incentives, favoring private over public systems of delivery, and voluntary provisions over mandation. But they bluntly contradicted the public-choice fatalism of Stigler and Buchanan, with its principled rejection of the notion "economist-reformer could move the economy in a desired direction simply by persuading a beneficent ruler, constrained by prices but otherwise omnipotent, to behave appropriately."[183] Stigler's position, in the final analysis, represented a more positive variant of positive economics than its original proponent was willing to accept, undermining the rationale for normative economics, and leaving would-be economist-reformers either with "nothing to do" or, worse still, suggesting the unpalatable conclusion that policy agitators might be in it, as Reder put it, "for their own amusement or private advantage."[184]

The full implications of this interpretation were never fully explored in Chicago, at least while Friedman was still on the faculty. At the start of the Reagan era, however, by which time Friedman had relocated to the West coast, the mood in the Economics Department was somewhat paradoxically one of disengagement, if not fatalism. As Reder observed, in the first months of the Reagan Administration:

[M]any of the younger Chicago economists are quite apolitical. In current lunch time discussions, the political question is at least as likely to be: "Why take the time and trouble to vote?" as it is: "For whom should one vote?" Nevertheless, the aversion to government activity built into the Chicago sub-culture remains strong … Fortunately, affection and good sense have prevented serious intellectual disagreement from causing any breach of personal relations between Stigler and Friedman … But despite the lack of public debate the fact of the disagreement has been well-known in Chicago for the last decade.[185]

Experience would soon temper Friedman's reforming zeal, however. While remaining fiercely defensive of the President himself, Friedman was soon dismayed to find that the radical policy program advocated by Reagan's band of free-thinking economists was being diluted, delayed, and derailed. His *Newsweek* columns became increasingly shrill, accusing the US Congress and even the White House of "hypocrisy," "schizophrenia," and unprincipled backsliding.[186] From their new perch in San Francisco, Milton and Rose were soon complaining about the *Tyranny of the Status Quo*, to which the Reagan project had apparently also succumbed. Their retrospective read on the situation was that the body politic would only respond to shock treatment: "a new administration has some six to nine months in which to achieve major changes; if it does not seize the opportunity to act decisively during that period, it will not have another such opportunity."[187] Following a brief honeymoon period, a new incumbent inevitably confronts regrouped political forces, the ranks of which may have been swelled by the "losers" from the first round of reforms. The Friedmans' conclusion was that pre-election advance planning was, somewhat ironically, essential, if status quo interests in the state were to be overcome.

Insider accounts invariably testify to the singular influence of Friedman on both Reagan and his Administration's program.[188] "Before there was Reaganomics," the chief economist at *Newsweek* summarily wrote, "there was Milton Friedman."[189] And even though Friedman "expected so much of the Reagan administration [only to be] disappointed,"[190] his retrospective assessment was that, "No other president in my lifetime [came] close to Reagan in adherence to clearly specified principles dedicated to promoting and maintaining a free society."[191] He was to remain relatively pessimistic about the prospects for genuine governmental reform, having apparently concluded that the means had yet to be found truly to tame Leviathan. If the drift of the Reagan administration represented a disappointment, in Friedman's eyes, the Bush succession compromised much of what had been achieved. On the cusp of the mid-90s Gingrich revolution, he remained "skeptical" about whether the Contract with America would get beyond the "talk."[192] Friedman would be even less impressed by the second President Bush, in particular due to his administration's indifference to fiscal restraint.[193] Certainly, the younger Bush violated a fundamental principle in prosecuting the Iraq War while recklessly cutting taxes, since as Friedman had concluded as a tax analyst in the Second World War, "one of the ways to avoid inflation [is] to finance as large a percentage of current spending with tax money as possible."[194] In fact, Friedman had been consistently underwhelmed by the Bushes, evaluating Reagan's selection of a vice-presidential running mate as "the worst decision not only of his campaign but of his presidency." His own choice for vice-presidential slot had been his longtime friend, Donald Rumsfeld.[195]

Reliberalization

The Chicago School may have achieved its paradoxical apogee in the early 1980s, the point at which both its doctrinal principles and its policy prescriptions passed—secularized and sullied, at least by Chicago standards—into the mainstream. Within a few years, one of the school's most astute chroniclers, Melvin Reder, was reflecting that, if "the vitality of [the Chicago] tradition is threatened," it was, ironically, more a product of "the growing acceptance of many of its key ideas than [due to] resistance to them"; what was once a highly distinctive Chicago emphasis on competition and the money supply having "become mainstream economics."[196] In retrospect, the moment of Reaganomics represented a crossroads—and the first of many, rather than some final "destination"—in the Chicago School's long trek from local epistemology to elite consensus, if not common sense. Like many such local epistemologies, the Chicago School's distinctive form of economic knowledge began life in a somewhat insulated socioinstitutional space, though hardly a consensual or homogenous one. And while its dominant predilections were clearly not functionally determined by the local institutional and political–economic "environment," a case can certainly be made that a combination of conjunctural circumstances and network positionality shaped the way in which this insurgent project was manufactured, refined, and later propagated.

For his part, economic historian William Breit is convinced that, to the extent that "environmental" influences shaped Milton Friedman's worldview, these were rooted in the Great Depression.[197] It was the events of the 1930s that positioned Friedman as a monetarist outsider, surrounded on all sides by interventionists and collectivists, but with a handful of local allies, like Frank Knight and Henry Simons. At least initially, brilliant rhetoricians on the other side, like Galbraith, possessed the notable advantage of working with the grain of popular conceptions of the underlying causes of the 1930s crisis, while Friedman's only option was to operate at the margins, meticulously marshalling evidence in support of his dissenting propositions—empirical precision, rather than artful persuasion, was at the time his "most powerful asset" in what amounted to the construction of an alternate economic reality.[198] In this respect, the various forms of exclusion and marginalization experienced by, and even engendered by, the Chicago School, were in a sense productive. The defeat of the Cowlesmen represented an important early victory, even if it yielded only local turf in the short term. Subsequently, relative isolation from the heavily trafficked corridors of the East coast did more than enable the cultivation of a discrete "strain" of economics, out on the Great Plains, it also generated an urgent imperative to reach out for *extralocal* sources of support and sustenance. Mont Pelerinian networks, in particular, were decisively important in the early development of the school. Similarly, what Harry Johnson dubbed the department's "social 'outsider'" status, compared to the Ivy League schools, with their inside tracks to Washington, fueled an aggressive publishing culture.[199]

Local pedagogic and mentoring practices would later reinforce these distinctive characteristics. Chicago's famous workshop model, for example, which was introduced by Friedman in the early 1950s and continues to this day, was consciously modeled on the hermetically sealed, closed system of the scientific laboratory.[200] Likewise, the Chicago style of academic mentoring became more, rather than less, effectual, by virtue of the imperative to "protect" alumni from a hostile world outside, coupled with the programmatic desire to extend the reach of their minoritarian project. Friedman was known to have especially "long arms," in this respect, as his first- and second-generation students are always amongst the first to attest.[201] The sheer intensity of the relationships forged at Hyde Park, particularly during the period of Keynesian hegemony, translated into an almost tribal form of loyalty amongst faculty, students, and alumni, transforming what in some circumstances might have been an inert diaspora into an active network, spanning the worlds of business, government, consulting, and the law, as well as the universities.[202] As Gary Becker recalled, this boot camp for intellectual combat produced students that often had "chip[s] on their shoulder," but who were also "aggressively proud of being Chicagoans,"[203] an often unedifying combination that reportedly generated a form of zip code discrimination amongst other economics departments, only redoubling the sense of victimhood. Hence the traits of stridency and self-righteousness often found amongst Chicago alumni were very much consequences of the place and the position of the program.

In this context, what is often stylized as the "Chicago tradition" looks less like a transmission belt for some purified form of price theory, more like a sociologically distinctive regime for the intergenerational transfer of instincts, temperaments, and prejudices. Knights and Simons, in this light, might at least be considered the spiritual "godfathers" of the Chicago

117

School. Stigler once reflected that it was "possible" that "if I had gone to Harvard instead of Chicago, I would have been a believer in monopolistic competition, a student of input-output tables, or a member of the Mason school of industrial organization," but he did not "attach high probabilities to these possibilities"; going on to clarify that he was "no longer a faithful follower," but "still an admirer" of Knight and Simons.[204] Yet clearly there was something about Chicago in the 1930s that made it, in Robert Sobel's words, "one of the great breeding grounds for economists."[205] The Chicago temperament was evidently both a distinctive and an ingrained one, maybe more so than were the principled positions on theory, method, and policy, which while often presented as inviolable, were in fact rather more flexible. Friedman concedes as much when he observes that, on close examination, there were multiple slippages and similarities between Chicagoan and Keynesian positions during the 1930s, but a clear separation between their respective "intuitions." There was, he felt, something

in the air in Chicago in the early and mid-1930s that [meant that] the Chicago students were much less susceptible to the Keynesian virus than their contemporaries in London, England, and Cambridge, Massachusetts, who were taught that the Great Depression was a necessary and ultimately healthy purgative... *The major differences between Keynes and Simons on policy reflected differences in temperament...* Keynes the reformer [placed] emphasis on short-run problems [and] confidence in civil servants to control and regulate... Simons the radical, who always took the long view, who had the mid-westerner's suspicion of bureaucrats in Washington, who regarded a large measure of laissez faire as an essential prerequisite for the preservation of political liberty, the solution was to go to the root of the problem by reforming drastically the financial structure.[206]

The journalist, and founding Mont Pelerinian, John Davenport, likewise portrayed Simons as a liberal in the sense that he was "profoundly prejudicial to all collectivist solutions."[207] His posthumous review of Simons' sparse and scattered writings paints a picture of a radical conservative, an interventionist libertarian, and a moody utopian—indeed, something close to a protosynthesis of the oxymoronic and contradictory bundle of attributes that would later come to be known as *neoliberalism*:

The vision that Simons offered this country was old, and it was new. It was old in that it rested on the dignity and worth of the individual and on the belief that the bulwark of individual liberty cannot be disassociated from the preservation of the free competitive market. [Yet] it was likewise his business to reassert what is implicit in all liberal thinking but too easily forgotten, that free competition cannot be preserved without a government able and willing to lay down the rules of the road. "The representation of laissez-faire as a do-nothing policy is unfortunate and misleading [Simons wrote]. The so-called failure of capitalism may reasonably be interpreted as primarily a failure of the political state in the discharge of its minimum responsibilities under capitalism" ... The issue that Simons drew was therefore not between plan and no plan but between planning for freedom and planning against it.[208]

Stigler agreed that Simons, had been "closely tuned to the time and place in which he lived: America in the Great Depression. It was a time for great fears and bold reforms—indeed bold reforms require great crises, and Simons frequently invoked utter catastrophe as the justification of his proposals." But while this may sound like a kind of crisis theory, "Simons was the utopian [one who envisaged] a decentralized, unpoliticized world in which personal freedom and economic efficiency find wide scope and strong defense."[209]

It was, perhaps, the futility of this premature expression of neoliberal utopianism that eventually overcame Simons—the "decentralized, unpoliticized world" would remain forever elusive. Friedman, in contrast, was always more willing to engage with the purveyors of politicized and even centralized power, more or less as he found them, albeit with the option of beating occasional tactical retreats to the Social Science Research Building or the Quadrangle Club. Quite unlike Simons, Friedman was repeatedly drawn to power, only to find his relatively uncompromising ambitions frustrated. It might be said that he was substantially defined by the lived contradiction between his professional and political roles. While choosing to exaggerate the distance between Friedman and the corridors of power, Deirdre McCloskey conveys a sense of this when she defensively observes, "He has in fact been notably careful about advising *any* government, including even the American one ... [He] advised Goldwater, Nixon, Reagan, but always as an outsider, never ... as a paid employee."[210] It was, of course, his *tenure* at the University of Chicago—a system he personally opposed—which facilitated this measure of principled freedom.[211]

Friedman's contrarian colleague, Harry Johnson, famously made the case, at the 1970 Ely lecture, that—like the Keynesian revolution before it—the monetarist counterrevolution was in large part propelled by careerism, cynical calculation, and conjunctural circumstance. By the late 1960s, Keynesianism had become vulnerable, by virtue of its failure to adequately deal with a major social problem (inflation), and as a result of complacency borne of its establishment status. The moment of maximum overreach occurred with the hubristic "new economics" of the Kennedy era, and the opportunity to strike back came with the escalation of the Vietnam War after 1965. According to Harry Johnson, the monetarists, who had been preparing for this moment of gathering inflationary crisis, saw the opportunity to "cash in," while misrepresenting both their means and their motives in rhetorical appeals to a pre-Keynesian, even transhistorical, orthodoxy:

[This entailed] the *invention* of a University of Chicago oral tradition that was alleged to have preserved understanding of the fundamental truth amongst a small band of the initiated through the dark years of the Keynesian despotism … [But] there was no lonely light constantly burning in a secret shrine on the Midway, encouraging the faithful to assemble in waiting for the day when the truth could safely be revealed to the masses; that candle was made, and not merely lit, only when its light had a chance of penetrating far and wide.[212]

This public accusation of "scholarly chicanery," no less, directed squarely at Friedman and the Chicago School project, again warrants no more than passing reference from sympathetic historiographers. In their brief comments on the episode, Ebenstein prefers to discuss Johnson's "very heavy drink[ing]," while Leeson avers that the attack was "clearly fuelled by a variety of inputs and motives," including academic jealousy.[213]

In contrast, the stories that Chicago likes to tell about itself favor (principled) lineage and tradition over (situated) calculation and opportunism. Alan Walters observed that Friedman's attempt to revive and revise this tradition, in the face of the Keynesian orthodoxy of the late 1950s, seemed to many like "flogging a decomposing horse."[214] A decade later, when Friedman presented his monetarist thesis from the presidential podium at the American Economic Association, the critique of Phillips-curve assumptions was beginning to enroll a wider audience.[215] "Like Keynes's *General Theory*," Alan Walters reflected, "it was one of the very few contributions that changed both the approach of professional economists and the policies adopted by finance ministers [once it was] recognized that the road to fuller employment did not lie over the high sierra of soaring inflation."[216] This echoed Friedman's Nobel citation, which stated that, "It is very rare for an economist to wield such influence, directly and indirectly, not only on the direction of scientific research but also on actual policies."[217] Conjuncture and context, apparently, did matter after all.

By the early 1970s, certainly, there was evidence that the balance of opinion was beginning to shift decisively against the Keynesian orthodoxy. But even if the political class had become disinclined to follow their economic advisors from the Keynesian establishment "over the high sierra," this did not mean that would automatically fall into line behind the Midway monetarists. As Friedman captured this moment, early in 1973, in his interview with *Playboy*:

There are some faint stirrings and hopeful signs. Even some of the intellectuals who were most strongly drawn to the New Deal in the Thirties are rethinking their positions, dabbling just a little with free-market principles. They are moving slowly and taking each step as though they were exploring a virgin continent.[218]

Monetarism, of course, *did* represent uncharted territory, no matter how confident were the directions provided by its advocates. The monetarist turn would have to be an abrupt one, moreover, since there could be no half measures, according to the absolutists from Chicago. Characteristically, when the turn came, it arrived, rudely unannounced, in the form of the "Volcker shock" of 1979, triggering not only a domestic recession—which the Chicagoans had dispassionately "predicted"—but also initiating the Latin American debt crisis.[219] "In this way," Naomi Klein writes, "crisis is built into the Chicago School model."[220]

If Henry Simons was a frustrated crisis theorist of the 1930s, then Milton Friedman would assume this role in the more propitious 1970s. But whereas Simons' variant of Chicago's oral tradition was largely confined to the classroom and occasional pamphleteering, Friedman's was extensively disseminated and telemediated. Through his *Newsweek* columns and *Wall Street Journal* op-eds, and just as importantly through his mastery of the staged, studio debate and the TV sound bite, Friedman fabricated a new form of public economics.[221] Stigler frequently acknowledged Friedman's distinctive skills as a "master peddler," even as he came close to implicitly endorsing Harry Johnson's accusation of opportunist hucksterism—in acknowledging that progress in economics, more often than not, occurs through controversy, while effective public intellectuals will inevitably have to "adapt" their arguments to appeal to potential consumers, not the other way around.[222] This called for careful weaving on Friedman's part, if not concerted spinning. Whether the resulting crime rises to the level of "scholarly chicanery," as Harry Johnson put it, may have to remain an open question.[223] But Paul Samuelson once snipped that Friedman's "style surpasses his integrity."[224] And one of the period's most important wholesale buyers of economic ideas—Alfred Malabre, economics editor at the *Wall Street Journal* for twenty-five years—later concluded that he had been "misled" by Friedman's sales pitch, which at the time he had very much wanted to believe.

I would rather think of Friedman and his monetarist colleagues as super salespeople, successfully merchandising, after much frustration, an economic medicine that promised far more than it could possibly deliver... [Friedman's arguments in *Newsweek* and elsewhere] came close to guaranteeing recession-free growth—if only Washington would follow his recommendations... With the benefit of hindsight more than two decades later, these claims seem wildly utopian. In 1972, however, they sounded to many of us remarkably credible and highly desirable.[225]

The bromide that Friedman was selling was a cure for inflation, but as Harry Johnson had pointed out, there would be no market for such a remedy until inflation assumed the status of a social problem on a par with mass unemployment. Johnson fully recognized that inflation was the Achilles heel of Keynesianism, but he believed that the monetarist project would eventually "peter out" for want of serious public concern about the "evils of inflation."[226] On this score, at least, he would be proved wrong. The influence of the Chicago School was to rise in lockstep with the misery index—a simple measure of the late-Keynesian ordeal of unemployment *plus* inflation—the historic peak of which coincided, exactly, with the presidential election of 1980. And it is no coincidence that this moment of macroeconomic rupture also represented the moment of rapture for the Chicago brand of crisis theory. Friedman's infamous concession that only crises produce "real change," was rooted in the pragmatic understanding that tectonic shifts in the climate of opinion are wrought by "experience, not by theory or philosophy."[227]

Notwithstanding supply-side arguments about the power of ideas emanating from Hyde Park, it is difficult to escape the conclusion that it was the conjunctural opening provided by the stagflation crisis that ultimately established an international market for Chicago's brand of provincial economics—even though it must also be acknowledged that Friedman and his colleagues had assiduously prepared for this moment—for far longer, infact, than Johnson had suggested. But the selection of Illinois 60637 as the US location of the incubator for the free-market reconstruction was anything but "random."[228] The University of Chicago's robust conservative "tradition" and its proud defense of intellectual dissent were vital preconditions, as were the concerted efforts of Knights and Simons—respectively, as the motivator and the enabler of the Chicago School's postwar (re)construction. This said, the remobilization of Knight's "Swiss guard" of the 1930s—Friedman, Wallis, Director, and eventually Stigler—would surely not have had the effect that it did absent the mercurial presence of Hayek, who had been a correspondent in the 1930s, an episodic presence in the 1940s, and then a fixture in the 1950s. Above all, it was Hayek who cemented Chicago's *latitudinal* networks, across the Atlantic in particular, that were essential for the original constitution of the project (qua project), at a time when its vital intellectual connections were both frail and far-flung. Friedman's subsequent function extended far beyond the purification and parameterization of the Chicago School (qua school), the role that is conventionally celebrated, but more consequentially involved the construction of a set of *longitudinal* networks, to centers of state power in Washington and Santiago, and to zones of political–economic transformation across Latin America and the US South. And, for all the fêting of its endogenous capacity, the power and potency of the Chicago School—the Chicago effect/affect, if you like—was decisively dependent upon these crosscutting, constitutive networks of intellectual and political influence, each of which was animated by charismatic agents, whose transformative capacity was only fully realized in the context of an enabling set of conjunctural circumstances.

Finding Chicago in the Chicago School is therefore more a matter of specifying the relational, rather than the idiographic, "uniqueness" of this historically transformative place–project. Chicago was located, in effect, at the crossroads of the cogenerative currents of the free-market reconstruction—its ideational project, rooted in the effort to construct a mid-twentieth-century liberalism, and its governmental project, oriented to the goal of institutional-normative transformation. And, in this context, Chicago's very particular blend of provincialism and cosmopolitanism, and its classically *liberal* urban culture, found a most appropriate echo in the semi-detached ambivalence of the Chicago School. Just like the neoliberal project it was propagating, the Chicago School bore no loyalties to place per se; as a mobile rationality it was formally indifferent to place, indeed *designed* for travel. The relatively *dis*embedded character of the Chicago School project, which was shorn of potentially complicating obligations to the city that provided its name, would find an echo in the fickle and flighty political rationality of neoliberalism. "No respecter of geography," Friedman would explain, in his field guide for *homo neoliberalismus*, that if

I do not like what my community does, be it in sewage disposal, or zoning, or schools, I can move to another local community, and though few may take this step, the mere possibility acts as a check. If I do not like what my state does, I can move to another. If I do not like what Washington imposes, I have few alternatives in this world of jealous nations.[229]

When asked why he had forsaken Chicago for the left-leaning city of San Francisco, on his retirement from teaching, Friedman joked, "Where is there [the most] work to do?"[230] Henry Spearman would no doubt have agreed. Spearman, the fictional economist-sleuth, modeled on Friedman, was the principal character in a series of novels that applied free-market principles to the solution of intractable crimes, finding trouble wherever he went.[231] The books' pseudonymous authors playfully relocated Spearman to Harvard, no doubt because Cambridge represented a more credible backdrop for the preferred crop of 1970s adversaries, "collectivists of all shades—anthropologists, sociologists, environmentalists, social democrats, Keynesians, and Marxoids."[232] Maybe there are fewer potential (socialist, statist...) suspects today than there were when Spearman began his detective work, but it is surely going too far to concur with Guy Sorman that "We are all Chicagoans now."[233] Perhaps there are, however, reasons to agree with Andrei Shleifer—superstar economist at a much-changed Harvard and architect of Russia's privatization program—that the quarter century after 1980 will be remembered as "the decade of Milton Friedman."[234]

Notes

1. City of Chicago (2006) Declaration of January 29, 2007 as "Milton Friedman Day" in Chicago, Agreed Calendar, 90577, November 1. Accessed at <http://www.chicityclerk.com/journalofproceedings00.php>.
2. Accessed at <http://www.edchoice.org/friedmans/statementworld.jsp>.
3. Noble, H. B. (2006) Milton Friedman, the champion of free markets, is dead at 94, *New York Times*, November 17, A1.
4. Brittan's assessment of Friedman's counter to Keynesianism was that "to some extent [he] supplanted it." (Brittan, S. (2006) Iconoclastic economist who put freedom first, *Financial Times*, November 17, 13.)
5. See Galbraith (1987); Walters (1987); and Warsh (1993).
6. Will, G. (1991) Passing of a prophet, *Washington Post*, December 8, C7.
7. Nobel Prize-winning economist Milton Friedman dies at age 94, *Newshour* transcript, www.pbs.org/newshour/bb/remember/july-dec06/friedman_11-16.html.
8. Friedman and Friedman (1988: 455, 466).
9. Klein (2007: 53).
10. Van Overtveldt (2007: 1).
11. Accessed at <http://www.edchoice.org/friedmans/statementworld.jsp>.
12. The Heartland Institute (<http://www.heartland.org>) was formed in 1984 with a mission "to discover and promote free-market solutions to social and economic problems." Heartland has been active on issues like privatization, climate-change denial, smokers' rights, public-education reform, the deregulation of health care, and school vouchers.

13. Van Overtveldt (2007: 42).
14. Leeson (2000: 1).
15. See Sinclair, U. [1906] (2003) *The Jungle*. Tucson, AZ: See Sharp Press; D'Eramo, M. (2002) *The Pig and the Skyscraper*. London: Verso.
16. See Doussard *et al.* (2009).
17. Friedman, M. (1983 [1975]) New York City. In M. Friedman, *Bright Promises, Dismal Performance*. New York: Harcourt Brace Jovanovich, 178–80.
18. On Daley as one of the Manhattan Institute's "supermayors," see Center for Civic Innovation (1999) *The Entrepreneurial City: A How-to Handbook for Urban Innovators*. New York: Manhattan Institute; Glastris, P. (1993) Chicago's hands-on mayor, *City Journal*, 3/4: 78–84. See also <http://chicagoboyz.net.>
19. Friedman (1974: 11).
20. Friedman and Friedman (1998: 32).
21. Friedman (2004: 69–70).
22. Friedman (2004: 70).
23. Stigler (1988: 19).
24. Friedman, R. D. (1976) "Milton Friedman: husband and colleague—(3)," *Oriental Economist*, 44/7: 23.
25. Lyman Abbott, quoted in Coats (1963: 488).
26. Shils (1991: x).
27. Emmett, R. C. (2002) Introduction. In R. C. Emmett, ed., *The Chicago Tradition in Economics, 1892–1945*, volume 1. New York: Routledge, xvii.
28. Friedman (1974: 15).
29. Kitch, E. W. (1998) Chicago school of law and economics. In P. Newman, ed., *The New Palgrave Dictionary of Economics and the Law*, volume 1. London: Macmillan, 228.
30. Shils (1991: xv).
31. Coats (1963: 489).
32. Lampman, R. J. (1993) *Economists at Wisconsin: 1892–1992*. Madison: University of Wisconsin Press.
33. See Bronfenbrenner (1962); Formaini, R. L. (2002) Frank H. Knight: origins of the Chicago School of Economics, *Economic Insights*, 7/3: 1–4.
34. See Reder (1982).
35. Quoted in Van Overtveldt (2007: 72).
36. See Breit and Ransom (1998).
37. Knight, F. H. (1947) *Freedom and Reform*. London: Harper, 341.
38. Davenport (1946: 116).
39. See Simons (1934).
40. Director, quoted in Kitch (1983: 179); Davenport (1946: 119).
41. Stigler (1982: 166).
42. See Kitch (1983) and de Long (1990).
43. Milton Friedman, quoted in Kitch (1983: 178–179); see Simons (1934).
44. Friedman and Friedman (1998: 55). See also Silk (1976).

45. Director, A. (1948) Prefatory note. In H. C. Simons, *Economic Policy for a Free Society*. Chicago: University of Chicago Press, v.
46. Robert Hutchins, 1946, quoted in Van Horn and Mirowski (2009: 169, n.5).
47. Also known as the "American Road" project (see Chapter 2). In the months prior to his death, Simons had been working on a plan to establish an Institute of Political Economy at Chicago, on the grounds that classical economics had been reduced to a minority pursuit in the Economics Department (Ebenstein, 2007: 131).
48. Quoted in Kitch (1983: 181).
49. Stigler (1982: 170).
50. Quoted in Friedman and Friedman (1998: 158).
51. John Davenport, quoted in Friedman and Friedman (1998: 160). See also Friedman (1980).
52. On the occasion of Friedman's engagement to his sister, Director wrote to Rose: "Tell him I shall not hold his very strong New Deal leanings... against him" (quoted in Hammond, J. D. (2000) Columbia roots of the Chicago School: The case of Milton Friedman, *Mimeo*, Department of Economics, Wake Forest University, 29).
53. Sobel (1980: 151–152).
54. "I was apparently cured, or some would say corrupted, shortly after the end of the war" (Friedman and Friedman, 1998: 113).
55. Hammond, J. D. (2007) Markets, politics, and democracy at Chicago, *Mimeo*, Department of Economics, Wake Forest University, 9.
56. Van Horn and Mirowski (2009: 158–159).
57. Patinkin, D. (1981) *Essays on and in the Chicago Tradition*. Durham, NC: Duke University Press, 266.
58. Bronfenbrenner (1962: 72–73).
59. Douglas, P. H. (1971) *In the Fullness of Time*. New York: Harcourt Brace Jovanovich, 127. Douglas and Knight had earlier fallen out over the tenure case of Henry Simons, which Knight strongly supported, but which Douglas (successfully) opposed (Stigler, 1988).
60. Stigler (1988: 148).
61. Van Overtveldt (2007: 178). See also Reder (1982) on the need to rebuild.
62. Emmett, R. C. (2002) Introduction. In R. C. Emmett, ed., *The Chicago Tradition in Economics, 1892–1945*, volume 7. New York: Routledge, viii.
63. Christ (1994: 30).
64. Van Horn and Mirowski (2009: 151); Ebenstein (2007: 55).
65. Warsh (1993: 67).
66. Friedman (1953: 91); Warsh (1993: 68).
67. Quoted in Christ (1994: 34–35).
68. Friedman and Friedman (1998: 197).
69. Reder (1982: 10).
70. See Morgan and Rutherford (1998) and Mirowski (2002).

71. See Van Overtveldt (2007: 37–39), Warsh (1993: 67), and the discussion in Mirowski, P. (2011) The Cowles Commission as an anti-Keynesian stronghold 1943–1954. In P. Duarte and G. Lima, eds., *Historical Explorations in the Micro-foundations of Macroeconomics*. Cambridge: Cambridge University Press, forthcoming.

72. Cahn, R. (1940) The Englishman who rules America! *Chicago Daily Tribune*, January 7: G2.

73. *Chicago Daily Tribune* (1943) Inflation promoter, *Chicago Daily Tribune*, October 3: 18; *Chicago Daily Tribune* (1943) The Keynes mission, *Chicago Daily Tribune*, September 23: 1.

74. Quoted in Silk (1976: 21).

75. Quoted in Silk (1976: 18).

76. For its part, the *Chicago Daily Tribune* bade the departing professors "good riddance"; they had received their just deserts for propagating the heresy of deficit spending, "shifting [instruction] in the direction of Keynesian doctrine and socialism" (*Chicago Daily Tribune* (1951) Economics at Urbana, *Chicago Daily Tribune*, July 29: 24). See Solberg, W. U. and Tomlinson, R. W. (1997) Academic McCarthyism and Keynesian economics, *History of Political Economy*, 29/1: 55–81.

77. Mirowski (2002: 245).

78. See Ebenstein (2007: 57) and Mirowski (2002).

79. Reder (1982: 10).

80. Stigler (1988: 157). "In an important sense, 'Chicago economics' in the 1950s and 1960s was simply an extension of the ideas of the Knight coterie of the 1930s" (Reder, 1987: 415).

81. Quoted in Silk (1976: 10). Friedman later recalled that he "ate almost every lunch and dinner together" with George Stigler, Allen Wallis, and Rose during their time shared in Chicago in the early 1930s (quoted in Doherty, 1995: 34).

82. Mirowski (2002: 203).

83. Walters (1987: 423).

84. Van Horn and Mirowski (2009: 165).

85. Friedman (1951: 91). Translated by Anette Nyqvist and Jamie Peck.

86. Friedman (1953: 4).

87. Johnson (1971: 9).

88. See Coats (1960), Reder (1982), and Van Horn and Mirowski (2009).

89. Friedman and Friedman (1998: 159). Milton Friedman, quoted in Abate, 2006: J1.

90. Friedman (2004: 75).

91. Friedman and Friedman (1998: 57).

92. Friedman (2002 [1962]: xvi).

93. Friedman (2002 [1982]: xi).

94. At the time of the 1956 summer school, non-defense spending amounted to 12 percent of national income in the United States; in 2000, it stood at 30 percent, having been at 31 percent in Reagan's first term (Friedman, 2002: vii).

95. See Hammond (1999) and Steindl, F. G. (1990) The "oral tradition" at Chicago in the 1930s, *Journal of Political Economy*, 98/2: 430–432.
96. Quoted in Silk (1976: 20).
97. Shils, E. (1991) Harry G. Johnson. In E. Shils, ed., *Remembering the University of Chicago*. Chicago: University of Chicago Press, 203.
98. Stigler, S. M. (2005) Aaron Director remembered, *Journal of Law and Economics*, 48/2: 307.
99. Reder (1982: 19, 20, 21–22).
100. Kitch (1983: 233).
101. See Nelson (2001: 164).
102. Johnson (1977: 100).
103. Deidre McCloskey, quoted in Van Overtveldt (2007: 43).
104. Johnson (1977: 100).
105. Warsh (1993: 115).
106. Miller (1962: 65).
107. Stigler (1962a: 70).
108. See Sheppard (2005).
109. Bronfenbrenner (1962: 72).
110. Bronfenbrenner (1962: 75).
111. Frazer (1988: 324); see also Stigler (1962a), Friedman (1974).
112. Quoted in Frazer (1988: 301–302).
113. See, especially, Nelson (2001).
114. See Friedman (1951), Stigler (1959) and, especially, Friedman and Friedman (1988).
115. Stigler (1959: 522, 525).
116. Stigler (1962b: 530).
117. Reder (1982: 32).
118. Friedman (2004: 72).
119. Milton Friedman, quoted in Doherty (1995: 34).
120. Crocker, G. N. (1965) New torch burns, *San Francisco Examiner*, March 7: 30.
121. See <http://www.heritage.org/About/Community/resourcebank.cfm>.
122. See Cockett (1995).
123. Friedman and Friedman (1998: 344).
124. See Doherty (1995) and Friedman and Friedman (1998).
125. Friedman and Friedman (1998: 367).
126. Friedman (1974: 16); Milton Friedman, quoted in Rossant, M. J. (1964) A talk with a Goldwater man, *New York Times*, October 8: 63.
127. Friedman would later recall that Goldwater possessed an "IQ [that] is perfectly reasonable," though this was not necessarily a requirement for those seeking high political office (quoted in Doherty, 1995).
128. Friedman, M. (1964) The Goldwater view of economics, *New York Times*, October 11: 37.

129. Samuelson, P. (1964) The case against Goldwater's economics, *New York Times*, October 25: 131, 134.
130. Klein (2007: 53).
131. See Friedman (1983), Friedman and Friedman (1998: 356–365).
132. In contrast, Silk's (1976: xi) authoritative survey located Samuelson at the "vital center" of the American economics establishment, with Friedman as the dominant symbol of the right, and Galbraith as his counter on the left.
133. See Wilkins, B. H. and Friday, C. B., eds. (1963) *The Economists of the New Frontier*. New York: Random House.
134. Morgan and Rutherford (1998: 15).
135. Goodwin, C. D. (1998) The patrons of economics in a time of transformation. In M. S. Morgan and M. Rutherford, eds., *From Interwar Pluralism to Postwar Neoclassicism*. Durham, NC: Duke University Press, 63.
136. Manly, C. (1966) More scholars than ever now wielding power, *Chicago Tribune*, July 17: B2.
137. Milton Friedman, quoted in Manly, C. (1966) More scholars than ever now wielding power, *Chicago Tribune*, July 17: B2.
138. Friedman (1974: 16).
139. Friedman (1974: 16).
140. Friedman (1974: 14).
141. Friedman (1974: 16).
142. Milton Friedman, quoted in Doherty (1995: 37). This had been not only Mises' fate, in Friedman's view, but also helped explain the behavior of figures like Ayn Rand and Murray Rothbard, whom he considered to be "cult builder[s] and dogmatist[s]" (quoted in Doherty, 1995: 35).
143. Echoing Hayek's observations on the role of think tanks as secondhand dealers in ideas, Friedman commented that, "There are only a relatively small number of manufacturers of ideas [but there are] a very large number of wholesalers and retailers ... I think there are too damn many think tanks now ... You don't have the talent for it" (quoted in Doherty, 1995: 37).
144. Yergin and Stanislaw (2002: 239).
145. In the words of a fellow Chilean economist, these intellectual compradors had returned from their training in Chicago "even more Friedmanite than Friedman himself" (quoted in Klein, 2007: 61).
146. *New York Times* (1975) Two years of Pinochet, *New York Times*, September 21: 32; Lewis, A. (1975) For which we stand: II, *New York Times*, October 2: 38.
147. Friedman, M. (1983 [1982]) Free markets and the generals. In M. Friedman, *Bright Promises, Dismal Performance*. New York: Harcourt Brace Jovanovich, 391–393; Friedman and Friedman (1998: 404, 402, 400).
148. McCloskey (2003: 144).
149. See Valdés (1995) and Dezalay and Garth (2002).

150. Harberger, A. C. (1997) Good economics comes to Latin America, 1955–95. In A. W. Coats, ed., *The Post-1945 Internationalization of Economics*. Durham, NC: Duke University Press, 301–302.

151. Van Overtveldt (2007: 346). See also Frazer (1988), Leeson (2000), and Skousen, M. (2005) *Vienna and Chicago: Friends or Foes?* Washington, DC: Regnery.

152. See Ebenstein (2007).

153. See Friedman and Friedman (1988).

154. Hayek made a similar pronouncement, though by this time in his life he was growing increasingly dismissive of conventional democratic governance (Hoover, K. R. (2003) *Economics as Ideology*. Lanham, MA: Rowman and Littlefield). The MPS also chose to take one of its peripatetic meetings to Chile, in 1981.

155. Yergin and Stanislaw (2002: 240).

156. See, for example, Sorman, G. (2008) Cheers for Chile's Chicago Boys, *City Journal*, 18/1: 7–9.

157. McCloskey (2003: 144).

158. See Green, D. (1995) *Silent Revolution: The Rise of Market Economics in Latin America*. London, Cassell, and Klein (2007).

159. Van Overtveldt (2007: 346).

160. Quoted in Friedman and Friedman (1998: 451).

161. Milton Friedman interview, conducted in 2000, accessed at <http://www.pbs.org/wgbh/commandingheights/hi/resources/pdf_index.html>.

162. He did, however, find time to dabble in the real economy, playing an instrumental role, in the early 1970s, in establishing the market in currency futures. Friedman reassured his friends at the Chicago Mercantile Exchange that the Bretton Woods agreement would not be resuscitated, and that new market opportunities beckoned, unleashing a fateful adventure in avant-garde finance which also flew in the face of the East-coast conventions of the time. According to the Chicago Mercantile Exchange's Leo Melamed, it was Friedman who gave him "the courage to proceed" with his plan for a futures market in Chicago: "By 1970, I had become a committed and ardent disciple in the army that was forming around Milton Friedman's ideas … [His] was the voice of supreme economic authority saying that the system of fixed exchange rates was wrong, that it was time for its demise" (Memorial service for Milton Friedman, University of Chicago, January 29, 2007, accessed at <http://www-news.uchicago.edu/releases/07/070129.friedman-webcast.shtml>).

163. Milton Friedman, quoted in Doherty (1995: 33).

164. Friedman and Friedman (1998: 384–385).

165. Stigler (1988: 135); Friedman and Friedman (1998: 387–388).

166. The most loyal follower of Mises in the United States, Rothbard argued that the Chicago School's "particular brand of 'free-market economics' is hardly calculated to ruffle the feathers of the powers-that-be" (Rothbard, M. N. (2002) [1971] Milton Friedman unraveled, *Journal of Libertarian Studies*, 16/4: 37–54).

167. Quoted in Doherty (1995: 35), emphasis added.

168. Reagan, R. W. (1989) Televised nationwide address on behalf of Senator Barry Goldwater, October 27, 1964. In R. W. Reagan, *Speaking My Mind: Selected Speeches*. New York: Simon and Schuster, 22–36.

169. The Heritage Foundation's *Mandate for Leadership* also played a critical role in this process, and was closely keyed into Chicago School thinking (see Cockett, 1995).

170. Friedman and Friedman (1998: 391).

171. Shultz, Friedman, and Laffer had been on the faculty; Thomas Sowell and Herbert Stein earned their doctorates from Chicago; Burns was a lifelong mentor to both Friedman and Stigler.

172. Anderson (1988: 267). David Stockman Reagan's controversial budget director, also pronounced himself a "disciple" of Friedman and Hayek (Stockman, D. A. (1986) *The Triumph of Politics*. New York: Avon, 33–34).

173. Stigler (1988: 87); Warsh (1993: 84).

174. See Greider (1989) and Malabre (1994).

175. Quoted in ABC News Transcripts, *World News Tonight*, November 1, 1982.

176. Stigler (1988: 137).

177. Reder (1982: 26).

178. While Buchanan confessed to entering the University of Chicago program as a socialist, albeit a libertarian one, the course of his life changed following his "immediate conversion upon exposure to teachings that transmitted the principle of market coordination" (Buchanan, J. M. (2004) James M. Buchanan. In W. Breit and B. T. Hirsch, eds., *Lives of the Laureates: Eighteen Nobel Economists*. Cambridge, MA: MIT Press, 141). Somewhat cowed by Friedman's "dominating intellectual brilliance," Buchanan opted to cut his own path into what became public-choice economics. He was awarded the Nobel Prize for this work in 1986 and served as president of the MPS between 1984 and 1986.

179. Stigler (1962b: 6), (1988: 137), and (1982).

180. Milton Friedman, quoted in *Playboy* (1973: 52).

181. See Nelson (2001).

182. An Interview with Milton Friedman, Podcast Transcript, Library of Economics and Liberty, Russ Roberts and Milton Friedman September 4, 2006, accessed at <http://www.econlib.org/library/Columns/y2006/Friedmantranscript.html>.

183. Reder (1982: 25–26).

184. Reder (1982: 26).

185. Reder (1982: 26).

186. See Friedman (1983).

187. Friedman and Friedman (1984: 3).

188. See Anderson (1988); Meese, E. (1992) *With Reagan*. Washington, DC: Regnery; Regan, D. T. (1988) *For the Record*. New York: Harcourt Brace Jovanovich.

189. Thomas, R. (1988) The magic of Reaganomics, *Newsweek*, December 16: 33.

190. Quoted in Doherty (1995: 33).

191. Friedman and Friedman (1998: 396).

192. Quoted in Doherty (1995: 33).
193. Quoted in London (2003: 12).
194. Friedman made this observation in defense of his work on the withholding tax (quoted in Doherty, 1995: 33). He later opposed the Iraq War, unlike Rose, and believed that excessive spending was "killing" the Republican Party (Varadarajan, T. (2006) The romance of economics, *Wall Street Journal*, July 22: A10).
195. Friedman and Friedman (1998: 391). "Had [Rumsfeld] been chosen, I believe he would have succeeded Reagan as president, and the sorry Bush–Clinton period would never have occurred" (Friedman and Friedman, 1998: 391).
196. Reder (1987: 417).
197. See Breit (1990).
198. Breit (1990: 8).
199. Johnson (1977: 100).
200. Friedman, R. D. (1976) "Milton Friedman: husband and colleague—(4)," *Oriental Economist*, 44/8: 21–26.
201. Carlstrom, C. T. and Fuerst, T. S. (2006) Milton Friedman: teacher, 1912–2006, *Economic Commentary*, Cleveland, OH: Federal Reserve Bank of Cleveland, 3. See also Hammond (1999).
202. "Largely because of the intellectual loyalty of former students, the influence of the Chicago School extends far beyond the University of Chicago to the faculties of other universities, the civil service, the judiciary and private business" (Reder, 1987: 413). See also Breit (1990) and Kogut and Macpherson (2008).
203. Becker (1991: 143).
204. Stigler, G. J. (2004) George Stigler. In W. Breit and B. T. Hirsch, eds., *Lives of the Laureates: Eighteen Nobel Economists*. Cambridge, MA: MIT Press, 79–94.
205. Sobel (1980: 148).
206. Friedman (1967: 8–9, emphasis added).
207. Davenport (1946: 116).
208. Davenport (1946: 116).
209. Stigler (1982: 170).
210. McCloskey (2003: 144).
211. Friedman, R. D. (1976) "Milton Friedman: Husband and colleague—(4)," *Oriental Economist*, 44/8: 21–26.
212. Johnson (1971: 11, emphasis added).
213. Ebenstein (2007: 164); Leeson (2000: 30). It was also common to recycle comments pertaining to Johnson's alleged inconsistency, that he had a deeply contrarian tendency to become "more Keynesian" when he was in Chicago, where he was employed from 1959 until his death in 1977, and more monetarist whenever he was in the UK, in Cambridge or London.
214. Walters (1987: 425).
215. Friedman, M. (1968) The role of monetary policy, *American Economic Review*, 58/1: 1–17.

216. Walters (1987: 426).
217. Nobel Committee (1990) [1976] The Nobel Prize in economics 1976. In J. C. Wood and R. N. Woods, eds., *Milton Friedman: Critical Assessments*, volume 2. London: Routledge, 436.
218. Milton Friedman, quoted in *Playboy* (1973: 74).
219. Friedman and Friedman (1998: 405).
220. Klein (2007: 160).
221. See Malabre (1994), Nelson (2001), and Dezalay and Garth (2002).
222. Stigler (1975: 321). When "intellectuals sell their wares to customers [it is] they—and not the customers—[who] do most of the adapting" (Stigler, 1975: 315).
223. Johnson (1971: 11).
224. Quoted in Sobel (1980: 145).
225. Malabre (1994: 144–145).
226. Johnson (1971: 12, 7).
227. Friedman (2002 [1982]: xiv, xiii).
228. Compare Van Overtveldt (2007: 42).
229. Friedman and Friedman (1988: 466); Friedman (1962: 3).
230. Quoted in Abate, T. (2006) Decades don't douse Milton Friedman's fire, *San Francisco Chronicle*, February 12: J1.
231. The Marshall Jevons mysteries are required readings on many introductory economics courses: Jevons, M. (1978) *Murder at the Margin*, Sun Lakes, AZ: Thomas Horton and Daughters; (1986) *Fatal Equilibrium*, New York: Ballantine Books; (1995) *A Deadly Difference*, Princeton: Princeton University Press.
232. Skousen, M.(1996) Who is Henry Spearman? *The Freeman* 46/6: 462.
233. Sorman, G. (2007) The market revolution, *City Journal*, accessed at <http://www.city-journal.org/html/rev2007-08-24gs.html>.
234. Shleifer, A. (2009) The age of Milton Friedman, *Journal of Economic Literature*, 47/1: 123–135.

4

Between Gotham and the Gulf

In 1976, a fateful meeting took place between two businessmen in New York City. The rather aristocratic Brit, sometime fighter pilot and chicken farmer Antony Fisher, had an appointment with Wall-Street financier and former spy, William Casey, to lay plans for the city's first free-market think tank. Casey, a longtime Republican Party activist of the Goldwater generation, was looking for innovative ways to galvanize and energize the ascendant conservative movement. (Well-connected, Casey would later serve as Reagan's campaign manager in 1980 and, following that, as Director of the Central Intelligence Agency until his death in 1987, in the midst of the Iran Contra scandal.) Fisher was, however, more interested in Casey's connections in the business community than in his party affiliations. Following an encounter with Hayek some thirty years earlier, Fisher had dedicated his life to the furtherance of the free-market cause. Just after the Second World War, the recently demobilized fighter pilot had made an approach to Hayek after reading the *Reader's Digest* version of the *Road to Serfdom*, sharing as he did Hayek's consternation at the rise of what both saw as socialist totalitarianism in Britain. The advice, Fisher recalled, was explicit:

Hayek first warned me against wasting time—as I was then tempted—by taking up a political career. He explained his view that the decisive influence in the great battle of ideas and policy was wielded by intellectuals whom he characterized as the "second-hand dealers in ideas." It was the dominant intellectuals from the Fabians onwards who had tilted the political debate in favor of growing government intervention with all that followed. If I shared the view that better ideas were not getting a fair hearing, his counsel was that I should join with others in forming a scholarly research organization to supply intellectuals in universities, schools, journalism, and broadcasting with authoritative studies of the economic theory of markets and its application to practical affairs.[1]

Fisher took the advice to heart, making a trip to one of the outposts of free-market thinking, the Foundation for Economic Education, in upstate New York in the late 1940s. There, Fisher met F. A. "Baldy" Harper, an agricultural economist who had been driven out of Cornell University a few years earlier, ostensibly on the grounds that he insisted on teaching from Hayek's heretical tome. Fisher was impressed by the Foundation's approach to popularizing free-market ideas, which at the time included a no-holds barred critique of the Tennessee Valley Authority experiment,[2] but was later convinced that his planned British think tank would achieve greater traction with a more scholarly style. The visit was certainly not wasted, however, since Fisher also picked up from Harper some tips on the latest developments in US-style agricultural technology—the factory farming of poultry. It was with the introduction of intensive chicken farming to the UK that Fisher would later make his fortune. But no sooner was his company *Buxted Chickens* established, did Fisher turn his attention back to Hayek's assignment. Along with what were alleged to have been "the last two economists who believed in free markets," Fisher founded the Institute of Economic Affairs (IEA) in London in 1955.[3] The modern think tank movement had been born.

The IEA would grow, but hardly prosper, over the next two decades—a lonely free-market voice in a sea of Keynesian planning and corporatist intervention. Dispirited, Fisher left England in 1975 at the invitation of a Canadian industrialist, Patrick Boyle, to help establish Canada's IEA, the Fraser Institute. Boyle had been alarmed by the circulation of a socialist manifesto in British Columbia, not to mention Prime Minister Trudeau's public musing over the "unreliability" of market capitalism.[4] Fisher relished this second chance to make a difference, and was more convinced than ever that it was not so much the production, but the *retailing* of free-market ideas that was the primary challenge. As he liked to say, "The echo is more important than the message." Writing to an American banker to solicit support for the cause of economic liberty he stressed that, "Proliferation is required because it is vitally necessary that common sense should be made available from as many directions as possible, particularly *not* just from one source in one place."[5]

It was this quest that would later carry Fisher from Vancouver to Bill Casey's office in New York City, which was at the same time both the right and the wrong place for such an endeavor. While adjacent to the financial spigots of Wall Street, this near-bankrupt, crime-ridden city was after all "the embodiment of urban liberalism's worldview, a municipal welfare state, Moscow-on-the-Hudson," and a stronghold of social advocacy

movements and public-sector unionism.[6] Yet as Alice O'Connor has pointed out, New York City's reputation as a liberal bastion, complete with the
full panoply of urban contradictions, conferred a sort of dialectical logic on
the subsequent rise, in that uniquely hostile setting, of the conservative
"counterintelligentsia."[7]

It might have been scripted to be so. In the summer of 1977, a citywide
electricity failure had been the occasion of widespread looting, especially in
low-income and minority neighborhoods, an event that emboldened conservative critics in their mounting attacks on the perceived pathologies of
urban liberalism, which in the words of Midge Decter had "proclaim[ed]
that race and poverty were sufficient excuses for lawlessness."[8] The city was
apparently at boiling point. Indeed, as Fisher and Casey were plotting their
challenge to New Deal New York, local movie theaters were running Martin
Scorcese's *Taxi Driver*, perhaps the signature statement of this apocalyptic
moment in New York City's history. Recall the scene in which Travis Bickle,
the De Niro character in the film, has occasion to pick up a (presumably
conservative) presidential candidate in his cab. Travis declares that he is
one of the candidate's "biggest supporters," which prompts the clichéd
response, "I'll tell you, Travis, I've learned more about this country sitting
in taxi-cabs than in the boardroom of General Motors." The following
exchange ensues:

PALANTINE Travis, what single thing would *you* want the next President of this
country to do most?
TRAVIS I don't know, sir. I don't follow political issues much.
PALANTINE There must be something...
TRAVIS (*Thinks*) Well, he should clean up this city here. It's full of filth and scum;
scum and filth. It's like an open sewer. Sometimes I can hardly take it. Some days I go
out and smell it then I get headaches that just stay and never go away. We need a
President that would clean up this whole mess. Flush it out.

   (*Palantine is not a Hubert Humphrey-type professional bullshitter, and Travis's intense
reply stops him dead in his tracks. He is forced to fall back on a stock answer but tries to give
it some meaning.*)
PALANTINE (*After a pause*) I know what you mean, Travis, and it's not going to be easy.
We're going to have to make some radical changes.
TRAVIS (*Turning the wheel*) Damn straight.[9]

Radical changes were exactly what Fisher and Casey had in mind when
they launched their think tank, the International Center for Economic
Policy Studies, in November 1977, with a mission to win "new respect for
market-oriented policies and [help] make reform a reality." Fisher's third
think tank would, as his biographer later put it, "explain the virtues of the

free market to the mostly liberal (i.e. mildly socialist) New York City, the home of international capitalism."[10] Barry Goldwater had captured the prevailing sentiment of an increasingly ex-urban, South and West-leaning US conservative movement when he argued that the "country would be better off if we could just saw off the eastern seaboard and let it float out to sea."[11] For Milton Friedman, as we have seen, the political and intellectual atmosphere of New York City was alien, "stultifying."[12] Reflecting this somewhat paradoxical location, the organization soon adopted the more neutral name of the Manhattan Institute, a persistent—if in its own way audacious—signifier of the "urban" issues that would later make its reputation: welfare reform, policing, schools policy, race relations, local government restructuring, and culture.

The extent to which conservative policy innovations like workfare and zero-tolerance policing have since become mainstreamed is a measure both of the specific successes of the Manhattan Institute in "turning intellect into influence" and the broader shift to the right in American politics.[13] This represents a major ideational and ideological realignment. In fact, one "could argue that the modern conservative movement had its birth in New York... a reaction to what some felt were the misguided excesses of mid-century liberalism, which was found most fully developed in New York City itself."[14] In this context, even the think tank's name change represented a calculated gamble, since as one of those involved recalled, "Manhattan had become a synonym for incivility, crime, and urban decay," such that many of its board members "did not want anything to do with the name *Manhattan*."[15] Eventually, the argument was won on the grounds that the rebranded organization would "envision New York as it could be—and should be."[16]

Despite their characteristic, if quirky, reluctance to declare any conclusive victories in the war of ideas, these pioneers of the new urban right can certainly count some successes in reframing the debate around America's cities, their alleged pathologies, and their putative salvation. If the Manhattan Institute began life as a "speck on the margins of the city's political landscape,"[17] as a profile in the *New York Times* put it, by the 1990s it was pulling off the "improbable feat of helping change the course of the country's most liberal city... challeng[ing] the rules by which New York was governed."[18] The *New York Post* went as far as to editorialize that the Institute "has literally changed the terms of the American debate on a host of social issues... Its ideas and proposals formed the basis of [Mayor] Rudy Giuliani's governing philosophy and his determination to challenge the long-accepted notion that New York City was simply ungovernable."[19]

With a budget of around $10 million and a dedicated staff of about sixty, the Institute's scale is modest by public-policy standards, but this belies a significant record of influence. A conspicuous New York conservative Tom Wolfe, channeling Henry Kissinger, allowed himself to boast on the occasion of the Institute's twenty-fifth anniversary, "it helped that we were right."[20]

Being right has been the Manhattan Institute's method and mission since the late 1970s, a period that has witnessed a dramatic shift in both the character and the content of the urban policy debate in the United States. Charting some of the traces in this long transformation, the chapter examines the far-reaching ways in which American's urban condition has been successively reimagined by the ideational activists and policy retailers of the right—those "organic intellectuals" in the think tanks. These efforts, it will be argued, have helped facilitate a transformative rethinking of the city, both as an object and a subject of regulation. After Gramsci, this intellectual project can be seen as one of practical construction and successive reorganization of the ideological program of a new urban right, in the vanguard of which sits a newly empowered class of "permanent persuaders."[21] Intellectual contestation, Gramsci argued, is at no time more consequential than in moments of crisis, when ideational cadres rise to prominence as fabricators and rationalizers of putatively transformative programs. This is a vital clue to the "organic" function of the neoliberal think tanks, a new organizational form that rose to prominence under just such conditions.

The span of the analysis here is defined by two generative moments of urban crisis, thirty years apart: beginning with New York City, after the fiscal crisis of 1975, and ending with New Orleans in the wake of Hurricane Katrina in 2005. The think tanks, in this context, have not only narrated urban crises, they have also acquired critical new roles as mediators of putative policy solutions, suturing their favored "second-hand ideas" to contemporary forms of urban governance. The neoliberal think tanks are not simply peddling a new urban vision, their words, formulations, and policy frames both express *and put to work* an increasingly pervasive political rationality. Functioning under stress also helps reveal how this invisibly ubiquitous process of "permanent persuasion" actually works. Hence the concern here with what the new urban right says, where it says it, and to what apparent effect. The torrent of "conservative solutions" for New Orleans—in policy briefs, blogs, and editorials—was not merely commentary. It was also, in important respects, *constitutive* of subsequent policy responses. New Orleans' post-Katrina policy makeover—comprising a gentrified, free-market city on top, and the disciplinary reregulation of the poor underneath—*came from* somewhere. Granted, the Manhattan Institute and other conservative think tanks may have been paying no more attention to New Orleans than the Bush Administration prior to Katrina; but within days of the hurricane they were hyperactively engaged in managing the policy fallout—reining in spending commitments, while moving to ensure that the "right" policy response was in place. The crisis on the Gulf of Mexico was, in other words, purposefully reframed.

Borrowing the Manhattan Institute's tag line, this raises the question of how neoliberal think tanks "turn intellect into influence," how they have worked to redefine urban "problems" and reconfigure urban-political practice. A form of "fast urban policy" has been manufactured, it will be argued, in which ideologically drenched policy frames and strategies circulate not only with increased velocity but also with intensified purpose. In this respect, there has just been a rapid, and profoundly consequential, shortening of the "policy distance" between New York and New Orleans. As the editorial team of the Manhattan Institute's house magazine, *City Journal*, argued, New Orleans has long symbolized "How Not To Do It," Katrina having belatedly exposed what they would portray as a decadently corrupt, welfare-dependent, and murderously uncontrolled city, "a poster child for an unreformed town, stuck in a time warp before policy innovators sparked America's urban renaissance."[22] New Orleans, in other words, had it coming. And the "storm-after-the-storm," as the *Wall Street Journal* aptly called it,[23] would reveal both subtle and stark realities of postwelfarist urban policymaking in the United States, its complex circuitry and its structural orientations. In exposing the ideational networks of neoliberalism, operating at full stretch, it also hints at some of the *limits* of the project of the new urban right.

Towards postwelfare Gotham

"Ford to city: drop dead" read the now-infamous *Daily News* headline in October, 1975, the day that President Ford declared that there would be no federal bailout of New York City. The fiscal crisis of the mid-1970s was a signature event for the new urban right, if not for the transnational project of neoliberalism more generally,[24] both because it necessitated a protracted period of budgetary restraint, and in its role as a potent symbol of the effective exhaustion of the welfarist status quo. It represented, for David

Harvey, the "iconic case" of what would later be understood as a crisis-assisted transformation to neoliberal urbanism. What for Harvey was a de facto "coup," engineered by the city's financial elites, was for Kim Moody, a dramatic premonition of regime change:

> The fiscal crisis and financial troubles of the mid-1970s were the call to action and the opportunity to act. The city's fragmented politics, along with the decline of the social movements and the relative "maturity" of the municipal unions, cleared the way for a reversal of priorities via the establishment of a "crisis regime," a series of state-sponsored organizations and offices imposed on the financial governance of New York City...New York City in the mid-1970s was a sort of rehearsal for the larger neoliberal reorganization of national priorities that would take place in the United States under Ronald Reagan and in the United Kingdom under Margaret Thatcher. Restraint on social spending, privatization, deregulation, and most importantly, the reassertion of class power...are at the center of the neoliberal project... The crisis regime shaped in 1975 would in many ways be an example of how government could be used to reassert class power and shift priorities toward both the traditional goals of business and the new ideas that would be known as neoliberalism.[25]

New York City had become "ungovernable," so the argument went, because, together, the poor, programs for the poor, deliverers of programs for the poor, and political advocates of programs for the poor had suffocated the city with unsustainable financial and social commitments. Businesses and middle-class taxpayers would only return to the city, the new conservative script read, if tax bills and the social state were simultaneously downsized.

The Manhattan Institute can itself be seen as a product of New York City's signature urban crisis, plans for its launch being hatched during the immediate aftershocks of the bankruptcy. Exploiting its epicentral location, it would subsequently work to apportion blame—mostly targeted at managers of, advocates for, and beneficiaries of New York's welfare state—while developing an ambitious suite of outside-the-box policy rationales, responses, and routines. In retrospect, these were clearly based on neoliberal principles, though at the time many of these were being actively worked out. As Kim Moody has explained, the Manhattan Institute sought to groom a "new generation of right-wing intellectuals and to provide alternative analyses and policies to what [was seen], more or less correctly, as a moribund liberalism."[26] Its meta-strategy has been to name and narrate this structural crisis, not in a fatalistic manner, but in a fashion generative of free-market and (neo)conservative *solutions*—the purposeful flipside of these tales of urban failure. It would serve, in effect, as an intellectual incubator for an emergent form of neoliberal urbanism.

The feds, Manhattan Institute senior fellow Steven Malanga later argued, had been entirely right to refuse to bail out his "profligate city," ensnared as it was in the "toxic vestiage[s] of the New Deal."[27] But if this was the wake-up call, the task of governmental transformation proved to be a massive, and prolonged, one. As Stephen Berger, one of the key players in New York City's fiscal recovery effort confessed more than fifteen years later, in the pages of *City Journal*, "we who were involved in resolving the crisis of the mid-1970s failed to define in any serious way the proper limits of city government's activities," the absence of structural reform meaning that that "budget deficits... reappear every spring, each bringing with it a new round of service cuts and tax increases."[28] These problems were seen to be exacerbated by an entrenched *expansionist-Keynesian* urban political culture, which Berger tartly summarized in two perverse principles: first, "no problem can be dismissed as outside the scope of city government," which was expected to deal with "every imaginable problem"; and second, the fundamental rationale of city government lay in its role as "an elaborate system for dispensing benefits to service providers," essentially as a form of sacrament to the all-powerful public-sector unions. For Berger, the solutions to New York City's recurrent "political tragicomedy" had, by definition, to be radical ones:

Getting them won't be easy. [None of the city's political leaders] has shown the willingness to go beyond conventional short-term budget-cutting strategies, or to risk the wrath of entrenched interests that proposals for more fundamental change would provoke. Those who consider themselves realists will no doubt respond that, in New York's current state of mind, sweeping changes in city government are not politically possible. But true realism now requires not only the recognition that there isn't enough money to support the bloated government New York's politicians have created, but that there never will be enough money. In the face of that reality, conventional ideas about what is "politically acceptable" become irrelevant. *Measures that are acceptable in this sense are by definition inadequate...* What New York faces today is not just a fiscal crisis. It is, to borrow Arthur Schlesinger's phrase, *a crisis of the old order*. We cannot afford to keep paying for New York's governmental sprawl—nor should we want to.[29]

The insistent message emerging from the Manhattan Institute and the pages of *City Journal* was that successive rounds of financial belt-tightening and tinkering reform were just short-term distractions—bankruptcy was a characteristic not simply of the municipal accounts but of the "old order" itself. The alternative "new urban vision," Myron Magnet explains, "totally rejects the old municipal welfare-state ideology, whose decades of failed policies led the nation's cities to the brink."[30] For too long, the Manhattan Institute scholars argued, conservatives had been content with the "benign neglect" approach to "urban decay [which] was simply to spend less on the same old programs." While the recurrent threat of "fiscal Armageddon" in New York City might call attention to some of the underlying problems, the more strategic challenge facing the Manhattan Institute, qua think tank, was tirelessly to "expose the bad ideas of the 1960s and come up with better ones."[31]

This meant taking the fight to the liberal defenders of the Keynesian urban settlement at the level of ideological principle—at the level of the rationale and rationality of policy itself. Trafficking in policy evaluation, tinkering with programs, and street-fighting over budgets would certainly not be sufficient. In contrast to other conservative think tanks, most notably the combative Heritage Foundation in Washington, DC,[32] the Manhattan Institute spent much of the 1980s focused on "big ideas," rather than the shorter-term challenges of policymaking and governmental reform. It is not without significance that Heritage is located within walking distance of Congress, while the Manhattan Institute occupies prime Midtown real estate—each is strategically insinuated at the particular nexus of the policymaking complex that is their target. Their efforts have essentially set the terms and the tone for neoliberal (urban) policymaking in the ensuing period: supply-side economics and rolling tax cuts in place of reflationary, investment-based, or "tax-and-spend" Keynesianism; workfare in place of welfare; "broken windows"-style policing, restoring social order in the name of (potential) victims of crime, in place of overweening social policies ostensibly addressing the causes of crime; the compassionate conservativism of private charity, faith-based interventions, and voluntarism, in place of government-led approaches and entitlement programming; privatization and choice in services like education and heath, in place of municipal monopolies. As the following discussion will reveal, these interventions have *incrementally* shaped the worldview of the new urban right, borrowing on well-established conservative and free-market themes (those "second-hand ideas"), but framing them into a practical, governing philosophy, along with the ebb and flow of political opportunity. Maybe the transition to neoliberal urbanism was structurally induced in some respects, but the minoritarian intellectuals of the Manhattan Institute never seemed to see it that way. They were battling, as they saw it, from the margins.

For Manhattan, this meant attacking welfarist policy rationalities at their source, engaging in "upstream" debates around the basic presumptions, premises, and constitutive terms of the policy settlement itself. A new common sense would be developed as a dialectical alternative to the old common sense. Echoing the form of scholarly engagement that had initially been so important to Antony Fisher, the Institute initially concentrated its energies on the production and promotion of orthodoxy-challenging books, sufficiently well written and engaging to attract commercial publishers. The results included some of the best-selling, and most fundamentally transformative, public-policy books of the 1980s. The first major contribution of this kind, which was to sell more than half a million copies, was George Gilder's *Wealth and Poverty*—often credited with the distinction of bringing the theory of supply-side economics into wide currency for the first time.[33] Gilder's book would anticipate many of the Manhattan Institute's defining themes—the overriding imperative of sustaining economic growth, the costs of "confiscatory" tax systems, the corrosive effects of the welfare state, the virtues of entrepreneurialism and individualism. As *Wall Street Journal* stalwarts, and friends of Manhattan, Bartley and Shlaes note, this radical challenge to the Keynesian orthodoxy was predicated on the "disasters" of the 1970s: New York City was suffering from its very own form of tax-and-spend-induced economic crisis, calling for a supply-side offensive against the municipal tax burden, its apologists and beneficiaries.[34] Gilder himself spent little time dealing with urban economies (apart from passing reference to the seething underclass resentments of the wealthy and the deadening hand of state intervention in cities) in what in many ways was a paean to the mobile (and implicitly internationalizing and exurban) market, from which the institutionally sclerotic cities had much to fear. Bartley and Shlaes explained that,

"Supply-side economics" was new. But it also made new the old faith of classical economics—a faith in the individual, a faith in the producer, and a faith that... "Supply Creates Its Own Demand." Economics were not about clever work at the top; they were about providing a stable environment with a reliable currency, removing excess burdens from business, and, finally, getting out of the way. The Keynesians' hero was a single smart man at a command post in a national capital managing the macroeconomy—an image like that of the Wizard frantically pulling levers behind his curtain in the *Wizard of Oz*. The supply-siders' hero, by contrast, was an anonymous simple entrepreneur, operating alone—in the cornfields, perhaps, or in a small town shop—far from Emerald City.[35]

If supply-side economics was promptly put to work by the incoming Reagan Administration, the same could not be said of the Manhattan Institute's next paradigm-shifting contribution, Charles Murray's *Losing Ground*. Here, the superficially compassionate but trenchantly anti-welfare argument was that, "We tried to provide more for the poor and provided more poor instead. We tried to remove barriers to escape from poverty, and inadvertently built a trap."[36] The attendant policy prescription—that the entire welfare system should be scrapped, since it ensnared the ghetto poor in a state of "dependency"—was allegedly too rich for the Reagan White House, which denied the underemployed political scientist a job.[37] It is a measure of the long-run impact of *Losing Ground*, however, that Murray is now widely credited with inspiring the welfare overhaul of 1996, his contention that welfare dependency, rather than poverty per se, represented the basic policy "problem" having been accepted by centrist liberals as well as conservatives.[38] According to Manhattan's Myron Magnet, "Not only did *Losing Ground* have the distinction of being the 'book that many people believe begat welfare reform,' as the *New York Times* described it when the momentous bill passed, but Murray's arguments also had the virtue of being right."[39] It also, quite literally, helped to change the terms of the debate, by rehabilitating and rejuvenating the concept of welfare *dependency*, which was to become one of the most potent public-policy keywords of the 1980s and 1990s.[40]

If the Manhattan Institute's agenda during the 1980s was focused on the critique and roll-back of antithetical institutions and practices, like the welfare state, progressive taxation, and Keynesian planning, the 1990s brought concerted attempts to claim new territory, often entailing the limited license of new forms of intervention. Gradually, the agenda of welfare reform morphed into the advocacy of alternative means of regulating the poor, via workfare.[41] New York City under the Giuliani Administration became a center for workfarist experimentation. But New York's path to workfare was a distinctive one: it has been more oriented than most to public-sector placements, in part due to weaknesses in the city's low-wage labor market, in part as a means of facilitating a parallel conservative objective—the downsizing of the municipal labor force.[42] The muscular companion to workfare, for which New York City would also become the principal proving ground, was another Manhattan Institute product—zero-tolerance policing. According to the "broken windows" thesis of George Kelling, disorderly neighborhood environments serve as incubators for both fear and crime, the appropriate response to which is relentless, street-level policing of all forms of public disorder, including prostitution, public urination, vandalism, fare-dodging, pan-handling, and vagrancy.[43] While the thesis remains an intensely contro-versial one in criminological circles, the dramatic reduction in the crime rate that accompanied the program's introduction in the mid-1990s has meant, according to advocates, that "the New York story adds up to a textbook on how to police any big city."[44] In turn, the falling crime rate is widely hailed by Manhattan Institute scholars as an essential prerequisite to the restoration of order and civility in the city. According to Myron Magnet

For years, the nation's inner-city neighborhoods were anarchies. The public hous-ing projects would crackle with gunfire every night. Residents would eat their dinner sitting on the floor, because they were afraid of stray bullets coming in the window. They'd be afraid, and justly, to send their kids out for a loaf of bread, for fear of violence, and they'd often not take night courses to get ahead or not take a night-shift job for fear of crime . . . Now, this is tyranny . . . the first of all civil rights [is] the right to be safe in your home and in the streets . . . [W]hen formerly crime-ridden inner-city neighborhoods are policed [intensively] and order returns, civil society can begin to put forth shoots. Neighbors can watch the streets together—can begin to know one another—and so people can have a sense of being in control of their own lives. It's astonishing, too, what a powerful economic conse-quence for cities as a whole, not just for poor neighborhoods, the restoration of public order has. When people aren't afraid to go out at night, restaurants and movie theaters flourish, and tourists aren't afraid to come. So crime turns out to be a huge tax on urban economies, big enough to kill businesses, as we've learned from experience.[45]

Magnet's *The Dream and the Nightmare* never won mainstream recognition at the time of its publication in 1993, though it was in its own way highly influential. Texas gubernatorial candidate George W. Bush was passed a copy by his political handler Karl Rove, and it is said to have had a greater impact on the future president than any book after the bible.[46] An indictment of the if-it-feels-good-do-it culture of the 1960s, Magnet's book is regarded as one of compassionate conservatism's progenitive texts, its Gilderesque mes-sage being that the prevailing culture of permissiveness brought devastating consequences for have-nots, ensnaring them in a dysfunctional culture of poverty. Arguing that "[c]ompassionate conservatism is above all an urban agenda," Magnet makes the case for a bundle of neoliberal, neoconservative, and neoDickensian social policies, including school vouchers, intensive policing, "restigmatizing illegitimacy," liberal immigration policies, work-fare, and behaviorally appropriate forms of support for the deserving poor, "mak[ing] sure that government doesn't subsidize the unruly non-working poor to move to neighborhoods that the near-poor are...trying to keep decent and orderly."[47] Compassionate conservatives flatly rebut the liberal argument that, in order to reduce crime, "government has to remove crime's supposed 'root causes,' poverty and racism," their populist, no-nonsense position being that the (actual and potential) *victims* of crime must be protected.[48] This, however, is not a recipe for simple deregulation or state abandonment.

Restoration and reclamation are the dominant motifs in the urban ideology of Myron Magnet and other Manhattan Institute scholars—the restoration of an unapologetically bourgeois urban order and a reclamation of the city for the (hard-)working and middle classes. The "Manhattan of the early 1990s," Michael Barone wrote, "boasted the greatest accumulation of cultural capital of any city in human history but...was at the same time a place in which criminals prowled the streets and the deranged fouled the sidewalks."[49] Taking the city back, restoring the "natural order of things," meant attacking the institutions that, according to the neoliberal critique, actually produced these urban dysfunctions.[50] As contributors to *City Journal* repeatedly argue, the fundamental challenge is to downsize urban government, reduce the tax burden, and refocus the public effort on a handful of priorities—policing and social order, choice and accountability in education, housing-market deregulation. This postwelfare urban fix is, in principle, within reach, since "our money worries arise almost entirely from the fact that New York is the only American city that is trying to run its own welfare state."[51] The deceptively simple solution is for urban government to do a few (essential) things well—maintaining *order*—instead of many things badly, thereby simultaneously reconnecting with the middle class, lowering the tax burden, unshackling the dependent poor, and making space for economic growth. Dismantling the urban welfare state therefore pays its own reform dividend—interventionist pathologies are snuffed out at source, taxes are not levied, the wages of dependency do not have to be paid.

The conflicted conservatives that launched *City Journal* at the start of the 1990s liked to present themselves as exiles in Gotham, living a "vivid tension: to be in love and yet to be on the edge—poised for flight."[52] On the one hand celebrating the possibilities of the talent and information-driven economy, on the other sensing that the city teeters at the "point of no return," the new editorial board extended a worldly, half-ironic welcome to its anticipated audience of wonks, activists, journalists, and opinion (re)formers:

It would not take much to turn New York around. Just the basics: a working school system, a reasonable housing market, civility on the streets, faith that there is some law operating here besides the law of the jungle. If we could only come so far in restoring the quality of private life our other natural advantages would make us sure winners in the competition for people . . .

For too long now, along with working schools, bridges, and subways, New York City has lacked a working politics. [Our] goal is to restore to the city something it has lacked for decades: real debate about the city's very real problems . . . We are interested in fundamental reforms, not simply ways of coping . . .

Many who enter the city abandon all hope. Not all of them leave. Some remain, carefully cultivating cynicism, wearing irony like a badge of honor. These voices of New York, despairing of making the city livable, have instead come to celebrate the unlivable, to wallow in the dirt and the drugs and the degradation, to call it "real," "gritty," "authentic." A whole generation of New Yorkers have been offered only these alternatives: to flee or to shrug. To these people, and to every concerned citizen, [we offer] that rare commodity: hope. If in facing New York's serious problems we occasionally sound grim, it is not because we are grim at heart. This is a labor of love. Like all labors, it begins in pain and ends, we hope, in the rebirth of America's greatest city.[53]

Recalling one of Antony Fisher's favorite topics, the stoical hopemongers at *City Journal* would occasionally wonder whether New York was afflicted with its own version of the "British disease," a pervasive form of fatalism that chokes off innovation at source,[54] but an abiding intellectual optimism has never been far from the surface. Locating themselves at the basic-knowledge end of the policy "supply chain," they could hardly have been expecting immediate results, though clearly they hoped for gradual realignment of the intellectual climate. As Tanenhaus points out, the Manhattan Institute differs from the majority of conservative think tanks, which are crowded inside the Washington beltway, since it addresses itself to the city, striving to "create a 'public space' for thinking and advocating policy."[55] Befitting their self-image as "universities without students" (or for that matter, left-leaning professors), neoliberal think tanks like the Manhattan Institute like to address blue-skies and fundamental issues, with all the scholarly trappings of hefty books, lectures, and journals. Rather than making "noise," the Institute practices what its president, Larry Mone, likes with a Gramscian twist to call the art of "quiet persuasion"—cerebral, engaged, serious, respectful—with (in public at least) "no Hillary Clinton jokes."[56]

The ideological demeanor of the Manhattan conservative can be characterized as a kind of inverted Gramscianism: there is a certain pessimism of the will, or at least an abiding, weary sense that the city's leadership lacks the resolve to confront "reality," coupled with a transcendental optimism of the intellect, borne from a conviction that the better, more righteous ideas must win through in the end. Enveloped by an alien political culture, the Manhattan conservative sees corruption, dysfunction, and bureaucratic bloat, quite literally, all around—a city addicted to an unsustainable existence alternating tax hits and spending rushes, unable to break the "governmental habit."[57] The tone is typically more stoical than finger-wagging, since the desire to find solutions is clearly a genuine one. It is not uncommon for Manhattan conservatives, in fact, to be recovering liberals, or as Irving Kristol memorably put it, "liberals who'd been mugged by reality."[58]

This said, frequent resort to sky-falling rhetoric, entailing an incessant narration of urban crisis, is very much the modus operandi: at a Manhattan Institute roundtable on the failure of old-deal liberalism and the potential for liberal reconstruction in 1991, for example, William Stern warned that "the city could come down"; Elaine Kanarck contended that "[u]nlike other cities that are evolving...entrepreneurial forms of government, what will propel New York into the future is a tax revolt"; Fred Siegel imagined New York becoming the next Detroit; and Sol Stern characterized the city's hospital system as "probably the only central command economy left in the world today."[59] Taking a leaf from Milton Friedman's evocation of the jurisdiction-hopping tax refugee, brought to life in *Capitalism and Freedom,* the threat of accelerating middle-class (and often white) flight is frequently invoked, the selfish acts of those dependent upon government salaries and benefits having apparently brought the city to the "tipping point" of depopulation.[60]

Recognizing that it would be self-defeating to preach to the converted, the Institute seeks to engage with the mainstream of elite opinion-makers. The aim, according to the Institute's president, Larry Mone, is to "influence the influential...some people matter more than others. [So] that's our constituency."[61] Reflecting this aspiration, the high-design *City Journal* has a print run of around 10,000, most of which is distributed free to a "carefully chosen" list of current and would-be urban players, politicos, and thought leaders.[62] The range of opinion is somewhat heterodox—befitting the oxymoronic label *New York conservative*—encompassing libertarians, social conservatives, fiscal and market conservatives, right-leaning and centrist Democrats, "old-style aristocratic conservatives," and various lost and/or mugged liberals, all of whom dissent, in one way or another, from the "New York establishment point of view."[63] The Institute will often deny that it is even conservative, maintaining instead that it is committed to pragmatism—policies that work.[64]

Under the mercurial leadership of its founding president, William Hammett, the Manhattan Institute blended intellectual chutzpah and a maverick ethos with an affected, anti-establishment stance. From the *new* urban right, Hammett castigated the city's Republican leadership, for example, as "just a bunch of brain-dead assholes," and neither had he any interest in those "you see at the musty establishment get-togethers held by the Association for a Better New York or the New York City Partnership."[65] While it is common for conservative intellectuals, especially members of think tanks, to portray themselves as outsiders, excluded from the universities, the liberal media, and even from mainstream intellectual life,[66] this sense of cerebral victimization is experienced with self-indulgent intensity in New York City. Constantly carping that the city is barely livable, that it is being suffocated by high taxes and red tape, and that another suburban exodus is around the corner, New York's conservative intellectuals could not, of course, bring themselves to live anywhere else.

It is perhaps appropriate, then, that when the city's conservative moment eventually came, it arrived in the enigmatic form of Rudolph Giuliani, whose somewhat anomalous political character was powerfully shaped by the Manhattan Institute. An avid reader of *City Journal*, Giuliani was to be seen scribbling feverishly at the Institute's events in the months preceding his successful campaign for mayor, actively participating in an internal seminar series, organized by his aides, with broken-windows guru George Kelling and arch-supply-sider Lawrence Kudlow, amongst others.[67] Giuliani's policy program, particularly in his first term as mayor (1994–1997) might almost have been downloaded from the *City Journal* web site—tax cuts, budget reform, zero-tolerance policing, workfare, public order. And the Mayor was never less than generous in sharing the credit, acknowledging the journal for "spark[ing] a lot of the reanalysis, reinvention, reinvigoration of government [with its] provocative and very good ideas."[68]

As if in reciprocation, the drumbeat of urban doom in the pages of *City Journal* almost stopped, and the refrain instead became one of the "opportunity city." In this halcyon period for the urban right, the crime rate plummeted and the economy boomed, tourists finally returned, and Wall Street registered record highs. While clearly enjoying the ride, Manhattan Institute scholars nevertheless sought also to maintain the momentum of reform, pressing the Mayor to enact further tax cuts, which for all Giuliani's efforts remained stuck at "Canadian" levels,[69] while creating more space for economic growth through deregulation, rezoning, and development incentives.[70] In its Summer 2001 issue—as New York's world was about to change dramatically—*City Journal* was engaged in what had become its usual business: pressing for radical hospital reform, attacking the teaching unions, debating urban race relations in the age of affluence, even finding time to reflect on "the greatest of all American urban disasters," the San Francisco earthquake of 1906.[71]

"When the Twin Towers fell, *City Journal* shelved almost all the stories that were to go into [the] Autumn issue and started over," the result of which was a hastily assembled prospectus for rebuilding Lower Manhattan, including articles on terrorism, restrictive immigration reform, celebrations of "the civilization we are fighting to preserve," and a specific plan for the redevelopment of the World Trade Center site.[72] Dismissing the ruined structure, with more than a little post-Keynesian sangfroid, as "the quintessential New York-style centrally planned government-authority project—ill-suited to the marketplace and unsuccessful for years," Steven Malanga reassured readers that the "terrorists hit a city that was at the top of its form:"

[T]he fundamentals are in place for the opportunity city to recover and rebound ... Nothing we decide to do must impede that recovery, fueled as it must be by the energy of free-market entrepreneurs. We must do nothing out of fear that our city is crippled or mortally wounded, needing some kind of government-funded life support. Such defeatism would be an admission that the terrorists won a victory. They did not ... To clear the way for the city's natural energies to reassert themselves, the first, most urgent task is to replace the 18 million square feet of modern office space lost in the attack ... [This] means clearing away the choking jungle of impediments to private builders that New York has allowed to grow up over decades. It means, above all, getting government out of the way.[73]

Now-objective conditions of crisis, Malanga insisted, necessitated a single-minded focus on the city's most urgent problems: rezoning, development incentives (not subsidies), deep tax cuts, and a private-sector led rebuilding effort, since "no government agency or authority, new or existing, should under any circumstances be put in charge of planning or executing the project."[74] Nevertheless, Malanga maintained that the federal government must provide infrastructural investment, that it should finance the clean-up of the World Trade Center site, and that it might also fund a memorial to those killed—as long as the accompanying expenditures were tightly controlled. *City Journal's* palpable fear of government overreach was only compounded by anxieties associated with the term-limited Giuliani's imminent departure, after seven years in office. Significantly, 9/11 cemented Giuliani's reputation as an urban "crisis manager" without equal.[75] If his successor should drift back to deficit spending, Malanga warned, the State Governor should immediately place the city's finances in the hands of the Financial Control Board—the body that imposed what Ken Auletta called "fiscal martial law" in the mid-1970s.[76]

City Journal emitted an unambiguous "Bravo" on the occasion of Giuliani's exit from office, pronouncing him New York's greatest mayor and living proof that "history is made not by ineluctable forces but by men, sometimes even great men."[77] In contrast, incoming Mayor Bloomberg— nominally the Republican candidate, but a well-known political chameleon and "lifelong liberal"—was extended only the most muted welcome, in an article bemoaning the lack of small-government Republicans in "one-party" New York City.[78] In the post 9/11, Bloomberg years, *City Journal* has reverted to a subdued version of its pre-Giuliani posture: the city's fiscal problems, structural as they are, remain chronically untended; the quality-of-life record is decidedly mixed; and the man the magazine likes to sarcastically call "the businessman mayor" seems to lack both the spine and the sensibility to do what is necessary.[79] Damned with the faintest of praise for competently *managing* the city's day-to-day finances, Bloomberg has been faulted for his tax hikes and his reluctance to seriously tackle "out-of-control spending"—now portrayed as the city's most pressing problem since Giuliani's war on crime.[80] Under "let-them-eat-cake" Bloomberg, Malanga morbidly concluded in the mid-years of the Bush Administration, "New York is slipping back into an all-too-familiar pattern" of slow growth, slack spending, and high taxes.[81]

Giuliani's triumph had been nothing less than the salvation of New York—erasing what Magnet characterized as "the squalid dystopia depicted in movies like *Taxi Driver*"—through the combinatorial application of supply-side economics and a robust package of policing, education, and welfare reform, and "revers[ing] decades of ultra-liberal policies that had brought the city to the brink of disaster.[82] Not a single mention was there, in Magnet's welcome note Republican to conventioners during the 2004 presidential campaign, of the current (Republican) mayor. The Manhattan Institute's corporate view of the new administration was better summarized in an earlier tirade against the city's recurrent budgetary incontinence, entitled "Bloomberg to city: drop dead."[83]

Drowning the beast

Tropical Depression 12 formed over the Bahamas on August 23, 2005, triggering a sequence of events that would result in a most unnatural urban crisis. When Hurricane Katrina made landfall in Louisiana, some six days later, the city of New Orleans was bracing itself for what Mayor Ray Nagin had called the "storm most of us have long feared."[84] The Mayor had ordered the city's first mandatory evacuation, but many of its poorest and sickest residents had been unable to evacuate. Although the eye of the storm narrowly missed the city itself, a series of catastrophic breaches of the levee system on August 29 inundated four-fifths of the urban area with several feet of toxic floodwater. If the level of preparedness for this long-anticipated disaster was lamentable, the management of the subsequent emergency was tragic. A fatally slow and ill-coordinated response from the Federal Emergency Management Agency (FEMA) compounded the problems faced by state and local agencies, whose limited organizational capacities were quickly overwhelmed. The abject failure of the evacuation effort was captured in searing media images of tens of thousands of displaced New Orleanians crowded, in unsanitary and dangerous conditions, into the city's Convention Center and Superdome. Lacking adequate food, water, and medical supplies, these "refuges of last resort" were not themselves fully evacuated until a week later. Yet more shocking, for many commentators, was that in the days after the storm, the city's social order apparently ruptured: the police lost control of the streets, looting and violence ensued, all of which was broadcast, in occasionally hysterical form, by the global media.

The full scale of the human, environmental, and social catastrophe wrought by Katrina may, quite literally, never be known. The immediate death toll quickly rose to over one thousand, while long-term assessments of the number of direct and indirect fatalities now exceed four times this figure. One-and-a-half million people were displaced by the storm, a sizable share of whom were never to return to the Gulf Coast. Early damage estimates, quickly politicized, ranged from $40 to $120 billion. The costs of reconstruction, independently pegged at least twice the size of the largest damage estimates, soon became effectively unknowable—for they implied very different takes on the *kind* of reconstruction that might, or should, take place. What was imagined by some as "the greatest urban renewal project in American history" was immediately countered by sternly neoliberal visions of a new New Orleans—leaner, more entrepreneurial, smaller, *and whiter* than the pre-Katrina city.[85] The slow and selective rebuilding of New Orleans, which has been gradually taking shape in the years since the storm, says a lot about the new urban orthodoxy in the United States and its accompanying, profoundly ideological forms of crisis management.

Together, New York and New Orleans had acquired reputations as "bastions of 'new deal' civic liberalism and expansive government spending."[86] And New Orleans, for its part, had also been embroiled in a decades-long urban crisis before the storm hit—characterized by structurally embedded poverty, a flagging economy, crumbling infrastructure, dysfunctional services, and untended legacies of racism. Post-Katrina New Orleans seems to be experiencing yet another chapter in this long history of urban neglect. In October 2009, on the occasion of his first visit to New Orleans as President, Barack Obama was reportedly greeted by a "weary city." Some 91,000 homes remained in a state of abandonment or disrepair, more than four years after the storm. In a town hall meeting, a local resident pressed the fundamental question: "I expected as much from the Bush administration. But why are we still being nickel-and-dimed?"[87]

If the emergency response of Hurricane Katrina was lethally tardy, the ideological response was certainly not. As the Bush Administration floundered, both institutionally and politically, in the days following the flood, the conservative think tanks did not hesitate to wade in. The initial reactions of these ideological first-responders were occasionally off key, but before long they were acting in concert. Working off a series of well-established scripts, many of them crafted in New York City, the think tanks were within days constructing a "principled response" to Katrina, predicated upon fiscal restraint and "offsetting" budget cuts in Washington, DC, but at the same time elaborating what amounted to a new urban agenda for the Crescent City—enlarging the role for private enterprise, in market-led development, governmental outsourcing, and urban governance; selective institutional roll-backs, focused on the social state; redoubled crime control, making the city safe for tourists and gentrifiers; and an interventionist program of "moral reconstruction," targeted at those who had been stranded in the storm's wake.

Within hours, the free-market think tanks were at work, hitting some discordant tones at first before more purposefully suturing well-established narratives of urban crisis to an "imperative" package of pro-market responses. While the media was transfixed by the real-time social catastrophe on the Gulf, think-tank operatives had their gaze fixed on the longer-term policy horizon. In a sense, though, this was their moment: even though the political optics looked extremely bad for the Bush Administration, circumstances clearly demanded game-changing interventions. Detached from the immediate challenges of emergency management, the free-market think tanks were soon completely engaged in the task of managing the fiscal and policy *aftermath* of the crisis. In these techniques, at least, they had been well schooled.

"No American city has ever gone through what New Orleans must go through," wrote Manhattan Institute analyst Nicole Gelinas in the midst of the inundation, since notwithstanding the short-term problems, no city has had to contend with "flight of its most affluent and capable citizens, followed by social breakdown among those left behind, after which must come the total reconstruction of economic and physical infrastructure by a devastated populace."[88] Herself one of the city's former residents, Gelinas confessed in a *New York Sun* editorial that "The truth is that even on a normal day, New Orleans is a sad city." Worse still, apparently, it had also become a "dependent" city:

New Orleans can't take care of itself even when it is not 80 percent underwater; what is it going to do now, as waters continue to cripple it, and thousands of looters systematically destroy what Katrina left unscathed?... The city's government has long suffered from incompetence and corruption... On television this week, the mayor has shown no clear inclination to take charge and direct post-Katrina rescue and recovery efforts for his population, as Mayor Giuliani did in New York on and after 9/11... New Orleans teems with crime, and the NOPD [New Orleans Police Department] can't keep order on a good day... Socially, New Orleans is one of America's last helpless cities.[89]

The underlying explanation for New Orleans' "helplessness" here is the city's subjection to a hypertrophied form of the American urban condition, as graphically portrayed in the pages of *City Journal:* the breakdown of social control triggers a middle-class exodus, leaving behind a racialized, welfare-dependent underclass whose proclivity to cultural dysfunction and economic disconnection then goes unchecked; a complicit and corrupt municipal administration is unable—by definition, since it is part of the problem—either to read the causes or manage the consequences. Having traveled further than most down this spiral of self-fulfilling decline, New Orleans may now lack the capacity even to save itself: "Sure, the feds must provide cash and resources for relief and recovery—but it's up to New Orleans, not the feds, to dig deep within itself to rebuild its economic and social infrastructure," Gelinas counseled. Yet her sense was that this would take nothing less than "*a miracle*. New Orleans has experienced a steady brain drain and fiscal drain for decades, as affluent corporations and individuals have fled, leaving behind a large population of people dependent on the government."[90] The only way to avert a still-greater urban crisis, Gelinas opined, was with a large injection of Giuliani-style leadership. New Orleans Mayor Nagin, visibly reeling in the face of his city's destruction, would have to *manage* first himself, then the crisis: "He must not waver, or a priceless city will be borne by the waters into Newark, 1967."[91]

The following day, as media portrayals of the city's descent into chaos began to focus on reports of violence and looting, Gelinas' analysis turned yet more pessimistic. In what had become a "perfect storm of lawlessness," she announced, the New Orleans "criminal class [had] taken over the stricken city." The circumstances may have been unique, but the cast of characters was a familiar one, at least to the readers of *City Journal*:

> Katrina didn't turn innocent citizens into desperate criminals. This week's looters ... are the same depraved individuals who have pushed New Orleans' murder rate to several multiples above the national average in normal times...Today may not be the best day to get into New Orleans' intractable crime problem, but it's necessary, since it explains how this week's communications and policing vacuum so quickly created a perfect storm for the vicious lawlessness that has broken out... On a normal day, those who make up New Orleans' dangerous criminal class—yes, likely the same African-Americans we see looting now—terrorize their own communities...Failure to put violent criminals behind bars in peacetime has led to chaos in disaster...Now, no civil authorities can re-assert order in New Orleans. The city must be forcefully demilitarized, even as innocent victims literally starve.[92]

If American think tanks are often criticized for their tendency to rush to prefabricated policy prescriptions,[93] a somewhat different dynamic seems to have been at work here. Perhaps reflecting the Manhattan Institute's role as a supplier of basic ideational resources for neoconservative/neoliberal policymakers—as opposed to quick-fire policy formation—Gelinas was (re)presenting her own form of causal interpretation. Recirculating staples of underclass analysis, she drew reassuring distinctions between the behavior and motivations of the "core criminal class" and the hapless group of benign dependents ("impoverished women, children, and elderly folks") who had trudged en masse to the Superdome and the Convention Center "expecting their government to take care of them."[94] Like Charles Murray's imaginary inner-city couple, Harold and Phyllis, these segments of the underclass were seen to be behaving rationally, if dysfunctionally, within a governmentally engineered universe of perverse incentives. And echoing the broken-windows thesis, untended lawlessness is intrinsically degenerative, spawning a hypertrophied culture of urban crime. While the new urban right has developed responses to these entrenched problems—reform the poor with systemic welfare reform and zero-tolerance policing; bring back the middle classes with tax breaks and quasi-privatized schools—these are not, realistically speaking, short-term policies. Hence the undercurrent of weary fatalism in these initial dispatches from New York. *City Journal* stalwarts Theodore Dalrymple and David Brooks reflected this sentiment, Dalrymple expounding on the "thin line" separating civilization from "barbarism and mob rule," while Brooks detected not a tipping but a "bursting point," from which New Orleans had emerged as an "anti-9/11 [in which] nobody took control."[95] Market forces alone, evidently, would not be enough. This form of neoliberal triage would require bold, if not authoritarian, leadership. *Order* would have to be restored before the market could do its work.

As the Bush Administration fumbled and local administrators reeled, the post-Katrina policy vacuum sucked in prefabricated conservative diagnoses of the American urban condition—the usual cocktail of race, crime, and dependency—but even professional opinion-shapers seemed initially at a loss how to construct much more than a rhetorical response. It was if, in a period in which the governmental system itself temporarily lost all traction, the most persistent critics of the misinterventionist state also momentarily lost their bearings. And nowhere was the vacuum more profound than at the federal level, where the White House appeared paralyzed, successively, by indifference, incomprehension, indecision, and incompetence.[96] Reluctantly returning from vacation in Texas, President Bush had taken an aerial detour over the flood zone to assess the damage for himself. Acknowledging that New Orleans' recovery would be a "difficult road," the President reaffirmed his confidence in Michael "Heckuvajob" Brown, then head of FEMA, as the Administration's point man in the stricken region, praised the "armies of compassion" for their charitable responses, and appealed lamely for better coordination of the emerging relief program. While his Administration contemplated a "comprehensive relief effort," Bush symbolically underlined the absence of federal control of the situation by standing in the Rose Garden and reading out the Red Cross emergency number, 1–800-HELPNOW.[97] One of the few decisive acts of the day was to open up the Strategic Petroleum Reserve, in order to relieve pressure on the nation's gas prices.

Initially at least, the response of the Washington think tanks was almost as flat-footed. Even the Heritage Foundation, the most closely attuned to the daily rhythms of the political cycle, had its attention focused elsewhere at the beginning of the crisis. With harrowing images of corpses floating in New Orleans floodwaters dominating the national media, Heritage's opening salvo in the post-Katrina policy debate was to warn of the perils of price controls, including a remarkably detached meditation on the "disaster" of governmental intervention in the oil market during the 1970s.[98] This discordant tone continued the next day, when the off-key opportunism of Heritage operatives was plainly exposed for what it was. Still lacking a coherent narrative, there was an unseemly, reflexive push for both Arctic drilling and the deregulation of emission controls, ostensibly as means of easing post-Katrina gas prices.[99] Not until veteran fiscal hawk, Ronald Utt, joined the fray did a more rounded, apposite, and self-assured Heritage response begin to take shape. Having praised private and charitable responses to the disaster, Utt rhetorically asked if members of Congress would also be prepared to make a "sacrifice"—recognizing this "higher purpose" by renouncing "frivolous pork barrel spending" in the recently enacted highway bill. Impishly, Utt proposed that funds earmarked for the now-infamous "bridge to nowhere" in Alaska could be reallocated to the Gulf Region, perhaps for a bridge reconstruction project gifted by "the People of Alaska."[100]

The metaphor of the politically indefensible bridge to nowhere would become a staple for fiscal conservatives in the following weeks. Codifying a theme that reverberated across the conservative blogs and letters-to-the-editor pages, Heritage posted a set of "instructions for writing an op-ed" on the members' section of its web site, echoing the message that essential spending for Katrina recovery efforts should be clawed back from the "fiscally reckless" highway bill.[101] This line of attack was amply echoed by other free-market think tanks, most notably by Cato and the American Enterprise Institute (AEI), themselves still smarting over the passage of the $244 billion highway bill in early August, 2005—which infamously contained some 6,373 "earmarks," a bloated package of congressional members' local projects with a total value of nearly $25 billion.[102] By now, the free-market and conservative think tanks had recovered their footing, and were concertedly moving ahead of the public debate.

Consistent with the view of think tanks as the ideological "outriders," relative to mainstream political discourse,[103] Washington's conservative intelligentsia was actively engaged, during this time, in stretching the envelope of the politically palatable and the governmentally feasible. This involved constantly redrawing a series of fiscal lines in the sand, offering occasional encouragement to budget hawks—particularly members of the

Republican Study Committee (RSC), the inheritors of the Contract with America project on the right of the party—while castigating or ridiculing moderates. While think tanks often take pride in their intrepid exploration of the "unthinkable" reaches of policy,[104] in the immediate aftermath of Katrina this extended into saying the unsayable. While mainstream politicians quickly learned that contemplating anything less than a complete reconstruction of New Orleans was practically unacceptable, at least in the full media blare generated by the disaster itself,[105] think-tank scholars pondered much more freely the possibly "doomed" fate of New Orleans, the city's long-standing cultural association with death, its possible loss "to the forces of nature"; indeed, the very "improbability" of the place, which—like Venice—"was created in defiance of the forces of nature."[106] The natural order had apparently been defied, and now the price was being paid.

Who framed New Orleans?

Less than two weeks after Katrina's strike, by September 12, Heritage was ready to announce a full package of "principled solutions" to the challenge of Gulf reconstruction. Presenting a tightly framed small-government strategy, the team of senior Heritage researcher-operatives outlined a strategy based on restrained federalism, market-oriented interventions, and the strict prioritization of public-spending priorities (see Box 4.1).[107]

The comprehensive plan developed by Heritage deployed what would become a keyword in the subsequent reconstruction debate—*offsets*. Any new federal spending commitments, Heritage argued, must be "offset by reductions in other spending," since under no circumstances must there be "mission creep" into uncompensated spending, new programs, or worse still, "any entitlement expectations for disaster relief."[108] The Bush Administration was applauded for its "courage" in suspending the Davis–Bacon Act, which requires that contractors working on federally funded construction projects should pay the prevailing wage, on the grounds, ostensibly, that this would both hold down rebuilding costs and stimulate job creation.[109] Beneath the veneer of reconstruction talk and conservative compassion came a potpourri of neoliberal staples—rolling back the Clean Air Act and restrictions on oil drilling; removing tariffs; accelerating tax cuts within the "Opportunity Zone," including voucher schemes for healthcare, education, and job training; incentives for private providers and faith-based organizations across these and other policy fields; expansion and retasking of the National Guard; capping Medicaid entitlements; streamlining FEMA while rolling out a network of regional offices for homeland security, managed by political appointees; and the repeal of the Estate (or "death") Tax. Pressing a broad package of conservative proposals, the Vice President of Heritage editorialized in the *Los Angeles Times* against "reflexively pouring money into the Gulf" through Congressional displays of "checkbook compassion."[110]

On the other hand, "unexpected" events, like hurricanes, must not, under any circumstances, disrupt the defining programmatic element of the conservative agenda: tax cuts. In a less than subtly titled intervention entitled "New Orleans vs. New York?"—just two weeks after the storm—the

---

Box 4.1. HERITAGE'S GULF RECONSTRUCTION STRATEGY

The federal government should provide support and assistance *only in those situations that are beyond the capabilities of state and local governments* and the private sector. State and local governments must retain their primary role as first responders to disasters. The federal government should avoid federalizing state and local first response agencies and activities.

- Federal financial aid, when necessary, should be provided in a manner that promotes accountability, flexibility, and creativity. In general, tools such as tax credits and voucher programs, which *allow individuals and families to direct funds,* should be utilized to encourage private-sector innovation and sensitivity to individual needs and preferences.
- Consistent with genuine health and safety needs, *red tape should be reduced or eliminated* to speed up private-sector investment and initiative in the rebuilding of facilities and the restoration of businesses. Regulations that are barriers to putting people back to work should be suspended or, at a minimum, streamlined.
- Congress should reorder its spending priorities, not just add new money while other money is being wasted. *Now is the time to shift resources to their most important uses and away from lower-priority uses* . . . It is critical that America focus on building capabilities for responding to a catastrophic disaster, not on catering to the wish lists of cities, parishes or counties, states, and stakeholders.
- *Private entrepreneurial activity and vision, not bureaucratic government, must be the engine to rebuild.* New approaches . . . such as enhanced choice in public school education should be the norm, not the exception . . . The critical need now is to encourage investors and entrepreneurs to seek new opportunities within these cities. Bureaucrats cannot do that. The key is to encourage private-sector creativity—for example, by declaring New Orleans and other severely damaged areas "Opportunity Zones" in which capital gains tax on investments is eliminated and regulations eliminated or simplified.

Source: Meese *et al.* (2005: 1, emphasis added).

Manhattan Institute's Steven Malanga advised compassionate conservatives to check their impulses: New Yorkers had "already done their share to lend aid" to the victims of Katrina; the more serious concern was that a "post-Katrina mindset in Washington" might lead to a postponement of the scheduled extension to dividend and capital-gains tax cuts, badly needed for Wall Street's continued recovery.[111] Never one to flinch in the face of potential controversy, Grover Norquist of Americans for Tax Reform had struck while the Superdome tragedy was still unfolding, brazenly accusing those politicians considering a pause in the rolling program of tax cuts of "exploiting this tragedy"; instead, the long-awaited repeal of the Estate Tax should proceed immediately, on the grounds that it would stimulate economic growth.[112] Norquist, who has been described as the "V. I. Lenin of the anti-tax movement," continued to press for deep tax cuts on principle, irrespective of the immediate political–economic climate—a measure of the long-term horizons of the conservative movement, where according to Graetz and Shapiro there is "no interest in politics on the margin or in managing the next recession or the one after that."[113]

By mid-September, with President Bush about to give a major speech in New Orleans on the reconstruction effort, the drumbeat for offset accounting had intensified to the point that real pressure was being exerted on the Republican leadership. The strategic line was that every dollar of reconstruction spending in the Gulf should be offset by cuts in Washington, with federal cutbacks being most effectively targeted at the bone of entitlement programs rather than the flesh of the current account; meanwhile, disaster-related spending outlays must be targeted and temporary, detached from future federal responsibility or entitlement entanglements. Then House Leader Tom DeLay's remark that "there is simply no fat left to cut in the federal budget" had caused consternation amongst fiscal conservatives.[114] Heritage and AEI got into something of an "offset" race to identify the longest and most inflammatory list of "dispensable" federal programs. In addition to the fiscally conservative "gimmies" of highway pork and bridges to nowhere, the AEI proposed terminating the United States Agency for International Development program for malaria prevention and the National Endowments for the Arts and for the Humanities, while privatizing air traffic control, National Aeronautics and Space Administration, the US Postal Service, and Amtrak; meanwhile, Heritage took aim at just some of the "easy places to start cutting," like Americorps, the Corporation for Public Broadcasting, community development block grants, 130 programs serving the disabled, 90 early childhood development projects, and 342 economic development initiatives.[115]

The temporary period of disorientation and wheel-spinning had now evidently passed. The free-market think tanks had again found their more assertive and strategic voice. Heritage and AEI operatives began placing media stories that pushed back against "distorted" reporting on the Katrina tragedy in Europe and elsewhere, where the politically motivated were seen to be too ready "to blame President Bush for the actions of Mother Nature," while being tragically unaware that "a Hobbesian world waits explosively, just below [the] skin—here in America, just as in any place."[116] The suggestion that Katrina's might could have been related to global climate change was also rebuffed, portrayed by the AEI as "disgusting exploitation" on the part of "environmental extremists" like Sir David King, the British Government's chief scientific adviser.[117]

The overriding concern, however, in the run-up to Bush's New Orleans speech, was to influence not only the price-tag but the governing principles of what would inevitably be a massive rebuilding effort. In this latter respect, there was a high degree of consonance in the positions of the free-market think tanks. Like Heritage, AEI was pressing for emergency assistance tied more to people than places, and based on short-term loans, vouchers, and temporary provisions; yes, there should be a concerted effort to repair the damaged infrastructure, but once the proper framework was established, "it's important to let markets decide how fast New Orleans springs back."[118] An AEI colleague, James Glassman chimed in that the "revival should be as spontaneous as possible." But since New Orleans was never a city that "worked" in the first place—"the world got a taste of that dysfunctionality... during the storm... [C]orruption, squalor and stupidity do not equal charm"—then a radically new approach would be called for:

New Orleans could become a laboratory for ideas like tax-free commercial zones and school reform. This is the ultimate libertarian city and the last thing it needs is top-down planning... I'm optimistic. New Orleans has a unique chance to make a fresh start and, in fact, become more like cities that do work (Chicago and Phoenix come to mind) while retaining its spirit of mystery, absurdity, beauty and decadence.[119]

At least some of this neoliberal optimism was well founded. When President Bush addressed the nation from New Orleans' Jackson Square two days later, he promised that an entrepreneurial city would rise from the flood-waters, assisted by a package of tax-breaks, short-term loans and guarantees for small businesses branded the "Gulf Opportunity Zone" (GO Zone); there would be temporary jobs and short-term extensions to unemployment benefits, and evacuees would not "have to travel great distances or navigate bureaucracies to get the benefits that are there for them"; there would be an Urban Homesteading Act, to encourage homeownership, and Worker Recovery Accounts, to help individuals re-enter the workforce; the federal government would join forces with the "armies of compassion—charities and houses of worship, and idealistic men and women" in the rebuilding effort; the flood protection system would be rebuilt "stronger than it has ever been"; and there would be a "team of inspectors general reviewing all expenditures" in order to ensure that the taxpayers' money was being spent honestly.[120]

If the free-market think tanks were quietly satisfied with many aspects of the Administration's proposals—indeed they were uncredited originators of several of them—there was a frisson of panic with what would become the headline-generating line from Bush's speech—"we will do what it takes, we will stay as long as it takes." Fearing an open-ended spending commitment, Cato reflexively warned of an impending "budget disaster," in a front-page op-ed in the *Washington Times*.[121] For their part, Heritage functionaries were somewhat more circumspect, working feverishly through less public channels, but also highlighting "dangers" with aspects of the Administration's plan. They welcomed the announcement of the GO Zone—practically a Heritage creation, in any case—reiterating the demand for offsets (a word Bush did not use once in his speech), chiding Congress for its reluctance to make tough choices,[122] while gravely warning that "local officials [will] see this as an opportunity to put forward an extensive wish list." Obliviously extending its own wish list, Heritage called for Education Smart Cards, more support for charter schools, and—fearing a "cost explosion"—a cap on emergency healthcare provisions, together with the appointment of an Emergency Regulatory Relief Board in order to minimize bureaucratic creep. AEI likewise called for the appointment of a "red tape tsar," and would have preferred more emphasis on vouchers and private-sector financing: "Once responsible intervention to restore order and infrastructure has occurred, individual desires and market forces should continue to shape the design of cities, not a federally financed return to the status quo ante."[123]

While presenting their intricate plans for the reregulation of housing, education, labor market, health, national security, and transport policy, the free-market think tanks remained fearful of the wrong kind of governmentalism—involving the proliferation of "paper plans," the growth of command-and-control decision-making through "vast bureaucracies," and "out-of-control" spending. While the nightmare scenario of Senator Edward Kennedy's New Deal-style Gulf Coast Regional Redevelopment

Authority never represented a serious threat, it was one that the conserva-tive think tanks liked to ventilate frequently, at least for effect.[124] More serious, in just about every way, was the very real and imminent menace of "Big Government Conservatism," Bush-style. As the president of Heritage editorialized, just after the Administration's plans for the Gulf region had been announced:

At some point, a hurricane is downgraded from a crisis to a problem... But as lawmakers scramble to throw money at the problem, it's worth remembering that no level of government has distinguished itself in the last several weeks... [We] shouldn't respond to government failures by making the government larger and still more unwieldy. The best way to rebuild New Orleans will be for the government to get out of the way. Congress and state governments can do this by eliminating or reducing regulations and allowing communities to decide for themselves how best to rebuild... Let's make sure that in responding to the temporary problems of Katrina, we don't simply create the permanent problem of ever more—and ever more expensive—bureaucracy.[125]

Similar concerns were generously amplified by the *Wall Street Journal*'s editorial page, which has long had a symbiotic relationship with the free-market think tanks. Under the headline, "Hurricane Bush" the *Journal* bloviated to the effect that, "The people who couldn't flee the storm were not ignored by 'small government conservatism,' as if that still exists outside Hong Kong. The city's poor have been smothered by decades of corrupt, paternal government—local, state and federal," concluding that, "It was certainly a collapse of government, but more accurately of bureau-cracy and the welfare state."[126] A week earlier, the *Journal*'s deputy Wash-ington editor, David Wessel, had gloomily proclaimed that, "The era of small government is over. Sept. 11 challenged it. Katrina killed it"—a statement that reverberated widely around the conservative blogs and the free-market think-tank community.[127] Illustrating the tight nexus between the financial press, the free-market think tanks, and fiscal conservatives in Washington, the Republican Study Committee had been meeting at the Heritage Foundation to hatch their own version of the rebuilding plans, yielding a "sea of conservative ideas" that were subsequently published by the *Journal*. Parroting Heritage's reconstruction blueprint, the RSC's chair, Representative Mike Pence, declared that, "We want to turn the Gulf Coast into a magnet for free enterprise. The last thing we want is a federal city where New Orleans once was. [We want] a flat-tax free-enterprise zone."[128] What began as a series of talking points was beginning to evolve into textual coherence. Soon, the RSC's foot soldiers were at least marching in unison, and the echo chamber of the blogosphere was being primed with inflammatory stories about waste, corruption, and runaway spending commitments.

The RSC followed up with the launch of "Operation Offset"—proposing more than $71 billion in cuts from the 2006 federal budget, in order to cover the costs of Gulf Coast reconstruction, while pressing for a much wider and deeper program of "savings" (totaling more than $500 billion) over the ensuing decade.[129] Not surprisingly, Heritage warmly welcomed the package, much of which had been hatched in its own offices, while at the same time presenting the initiative as an outcome of "grassroots energy."[130] The *Wall Street Journal* also voiced its support, declaring the White House's position on Katrina spending to be "irresponsible and even insidious," having previously accused members of Congress of getting "in the way of this natural economic recovery by exploiting Katrina to spend like they're back on Bourbon Street."[131] A parallel effort was also beginning to gain ground in the Senate, led by spending hawks John McCain and Tom Coburn, who called on the President to present his own package of offsets and rescissions.[132] This initiative was loudly welcomed on the conservative/libertarian blog, *Porkbusters,* which had been established in mid-September, 2005 to deal with the urgent challenges of offset accounting, post-Katrina.[133]

At the same time, the think tanks were stepping up their attacks on the spendthrift ways of the Republican leadership,[134] taking the calculated taunting to the national press.[135] Perhaps the mood in Washington was already beginning to shift, then, prior to the presentation of the Louisiana delegation's $250 billion reconstruction package in early October—the "extensive wish list" that Heritage had predicted on the day of Bush's Jackson Square speech. The line, apparently, had now been crossed. The President immediately called a press conference to declare a subtle, but critical, shift in policy: "The heart of America is big enough to be generous and responsible at the same time...As the federal government meets its responsibilities, the people of the Gulf Coast must also recognize its limitations." Bush emphasized that the recovery effort would be private-sector led, going on to promise, in language emboldened by the keyword of conservative accounting that the think tanks had been anxious to hear, to "work with members of Congress to identify offsets, to free up money for the reconstruction efforts."[136] The chair of the RSC, Representative Mike Pence, immediately issued an obsequious press release, calling attention to the President's new-found commitment to the principle of offsets.[137] And the fiscally conservative think tanks dutifully reiterated the same line, also crediting the Administration's far-sighted embrace of offset budgeting.

Louisiana's PELICAN (Protecting Essential Louisiana Infrastructure, Citizens, and Nature) Plan was immediately besieged. Heritage characterized it as a "breathtaking display of parochial self-interest," favorably citing the criticisms of RSC stalwart, Representative Jeff Flake, in the *Wall Street Journal*, that "we risk setting...an unsustainable precedent that it is the responsibility of the federal government to ensure that the victims of natural disasters are made whole."[138] PELICAN was similarly dismissed by the AEI as "pork gumbo," resident scholar Newt Gingrich stepping into the fray to portray the funding request as deficit-busting audacity from a cabal of local lawmakers historically prone to corruption. "While we all feel for Louisiana's residents," Gingrich opined,

there are limits to what American taxpayers can—and should—be asked to contribute on top of their already large tax bill. More worrisome, too much federal largesse can have negative consequences on behavior. What are the odds, for instance, of more responsible behavior by state and local officials when the federal government picks up all costs? And will private individuals and businesses make sound decisions...when Uncle Sam bails out poor choices?[139]

Compassion fatigue, it seemed, was now extending beyond the tight circuit of fiscally conservative activists. But more importantly, a conservative position on New Orleans had now stabilized, with the aid of insistent incantation from the think tanks via briefings, blogs, editorials, and daily policy memos. The dominant motif, or policy "frame,"[140] was now those of *responsibility:* fiscal responsibility in Washington; personal and local (government) responsibility in New Orleans. And by very clear implication, various forms of *irresponsibility* had effectively invited the inundation.

As Heritage noted, the House Leadership was finally succumbing to a combination of orchestrated pressure and relentless reason, while acknowledging that it would take "political courage" to respond to what they could now describe as the *President's* call for a fiscally responsible offset package.[141] Unless a line was drawn in the sand, Heritage president Ed Feulner predicted that federal spending would balloon to the point that taxes would have to rise by 50 percent—and then "France will look good by comparison."[142] Cajun Keynesianism apparently threatened. The Washington version of "behaving responsibly," it now seemed, was defined by sending less, not more, money to the Gulf Coast.[143] And more than this, the twin cases of Katrina spending and the Alaskan bridge provided an object lesson in the determination of legitimate federal responsibility and spending. The spontaneously choreographed challenge, to which all the free-market think tanks would rise, was to intensify the drumbeat on the need for offset spending, to brand all nonessential forms of spending as "pork," and as the AEI put it, "to get the federal government out of the disaster-relief business [in order] to promote responsible behavior on the part of individuals and businesses."[144] The provision of flood insurance, or for that matter no-strings-attached welfare payments, would only encourage what de Rugy described as "dangerous" and irresponsible behavior, inducing "people to constantly make the same mistake." The small print in the PELICAN Plan that suspended work requirements and welfare time limits in New Orleans had also irked the neoliberal intelligentsia, a Heritage analyst concluding that this meant that "welfare recipients would not be expected to play a constructive role in the recovery."[145] Meanwhile, others at Heritage saw an opportunity to roll back federal labor policies, including Unemployment Insurance coverage in the effected area, fearing that the Administration's proposed $5,000 Worker Recovery Accounts might re-induce an entitlement mindset, encouraging cooks, taxi drivers, and bartenders to invest in training that they patently did not need.[146]

When Senator John Kerry (quite plausibly) observed that the Republicans' plans for the Gulf Region would transform it "into a vast laboratory for right-wing ideological experiments...recycling all [the conservatives'] failed policies and shipping them to Louisiana," Heritage immediately countered that the root cause of the problems facing the region were those Great Society programs in welfare, housing, education, and job training, which had in effect rendered the poor defenseless.[147] Since it was the welfare state that placed the poor in the path of the storm, so the argument went, it would be no less than perverse to pour money into programs that destroy work ethics and encourage illegitimacy: "The poor of New Orleans have been victims twice," Cato's Michael Tanner editorialized in the immediate aftermath of the disaster, so "let's not victimize them a third time."[148] The Hoover Institution's Thomas Sowell likewise presented the main challenge as one of "rebuild[ing] New Orleans' moral levees."[149] Less compassionately, George Neumayr, Executive Editor of *The American Spectator* and a recent media fellow at Hoover, railed against those New Orleans residents whom he alleged had "no intention of leaving," since the criminally inclined foresaw a "target-rich environment," while a passive majority were "just waiting for their welfare checks at the beginning of September." Like Harold and Phyllis, they had submissively followed the rules, stayed put, and drowned. Had "chronically craven and indolent" local officials had the wit to announce that the next round of welfare checks would be issued in Baton Rouge, Neumeyr raved, then no doubt "people would have somehow found a way to get out."[150]

Similar forms of deregulated venting were by this time, less than three months after the storm, increasingly common. But there was work still to do on the inside, too. The ideological thought police in the free-market think tanks had been dismayed to hear President Bush acknowledge, in the Jackson Square speech, the existence of "deep, persistent poverty [with] roots in a history of racial discrimination," and what was characterized as a "legacy of inequality."[151] The Bush Administration's achievements in the area of welfare reform had been regarded, in these circles, as modest, if not timid and tokenistic—a boost in funding for a compassionate conservative program of "marriage incentives," but little else. The Heritage Foundation's welfare guru Robert Rector, amongst others, sensed another occasion for "experiment[ing] boldly." Lecturing the dependent residents of New Orleans "how not to be poor," Rector contended that the root cause of the city's poverty was neither racial discrimination nor an absence of job opportunities, but derived from the collapse of the nuclear family, coupled with low levels of parental work—both trends that have disproportionately affected the black community. The falling marriage rate was fueling welfare dependency amongst blacks, while propagating the dysfunctional "culture of the underclass: drug abuse, promiscuity, and violence"; and the appropriate response should be "moral renewal." Rector complained that the post-Katrina debate had been unecessarily preoccupied with

jobs and construction, joined with occasional proposals about relocating dysfunctional families or voucherizing services. But it is families, not houses, that really need rebuilding. If the proposals continue to ignore the social causes of poverty, they will merely reproduce the original slums of New Orleans in fresh concrete. Twenty years from now, another hurricane will swamp the city and pundits will wonder again where all the poor folks have come from.[152]

Likewise, for George Neumayr, "The countless images of stranded women, children, and elderly were explained far more by the absence of fathers than by the tardiness of FEMA."[153] Striking his trademark tone, Charles Murray, now W. H. Brady Scholar at AEI, informed the readers of the *Wall Street Journal* that the conventional repertoire of policy responses simply does not work for the underclass, whose defining characteristic is "behaving destructively." The underclass, he cautioned, should not be confused with the responsible poor, who can be identified by their willingness to work and get married; rather, they are the "looters and thugs" and "inert women" for whom conventional policies simply fail:

We already know that the programs are mismatched with the characteristics of the underclass. Job training? Unemployment in the underclass is not caused by lack of jobs or of job skills, but by the inability to get up every morning and go to work. A homesteading act? The lack of home ownership is not caused by the inability to save money from meager earnings, but because the concept of thrift is alien. You name it, we've tried it. It doesn't work with the underclass.[154]

It was this brand of argumentation, of course, that had first made Murray's name, more than a quarter century earlier, at the Manhattan Institute. And it has been one that his followers have pursued with gusto. "For a while it looked like Hurricane Katrina would accomplish what the NAACP [National Association for the Advancement of Colored People] never could," *City Journal* contributing editor Kay Hymowitz reflected, "reviving civil rights liberalism as a major force in American politics."[155] *Newsweek*'s post-Katrina cover story, "The Other America" had vividly recalled Michael Harrington's formative contribution to the War on Poverty, just as Senator Edward Kennedy's Gulf reconstruction proposals explicitly begged comparisons with the achievements of the Tennessee Valley Authority.[156] But, as Hymowitz now felt able to bluster, this moment of retro-liberalism had "only lasted about five minutes"; the panic having passed, it was down to conservatives to respond to the real problem—the breakdown of the nuclear family, together with its racially and socially uneven consequences. Hymowitz's Manhattan Institute colleague, Nicole Gelinas likewise dismissed as mere "amorphous talk" the President's evocation of racism, poverty, and inequality in the aftermath of the hurricane. What New Orleans really needed, she contended, was the minimalist supply-side infrastructure of better levee protection, since "civil engineering actually works, unlike the social engineering that Bush has invited with his lament about urban Southern poverty." With the physical infrastructure appropriately fixed, then it might be possible to deal with New Orleans' "immutable civic shame, before and after Katrina," the city's "culture of murder."[157]

City Journal's photo editors joined the cause, unambiguously providing an answer to the cover story question, "Who's killing New Orleans?" The lineage was now being invoked even more explicitly, not just to the riots in Newark in 1967, but to those in New York City in 1977—catalytic events for the new urban right.[158] After documenting in gruesome detail the city's pre-and post-Katrina "murder rampage"—together with glossy images of black men caught in the commission of ostensibly illegal acts, in one case in the gunsights of a white police offer—Nicole Gelinas argued that the problem was a supply-side one, since "New Orleans' legions of weak, female-headed, underclass black families supply generation after generation of ... 'lightly parented' young men to fuel the carnage." In the short term, there could be no regeneration of New Orleans, not until public safety could be assured. The pressing need was for a New York-style public-order makeover, including tough drug laws and policing practices.

Day in and day out, Katrina or no Katrina, New Orleans is America's most dangerous city ... But New Orleans's long history of street carnage is not a topic for polite discussion in Katrina's aftermath. [Politicians] and pundits have a million solutions for the city, from building more affordable housing to ensuring better schools to creating an incubator for the nation's "creative class" to offering tax credits for resettlement. But none addresses the city's most obvious, and intractable, problem, the one that has kept New Orleans from thriving for years ... Evacuees—and businesses—know that even Cat-5 levees can't protect them from the day-to-day mortal fear of living in New Orleans ... Only when New Orleans can assure safety can it begin to make up some of the losses it has sustained over a generation of mismanagement. Only then can it build a real private economy and robust public institutions that will attract a thriving middle-class population.[159]

Pointedly drawing attention to Houston's late-2005 crime spike, Gelinas went on to claim that these were no longer problems for the Crescent City alone, since "Katrina's floods dispersed throughout the unprepared South the uniquely vicious New Orleans underclass culture of drugs, guns, and violent death."[160]

Writing in the AEI's monthly magazine, *The American Enterprise,* urbanist Joel Kotkin moved to cement this solidifying conservative orthodoxy from the center, detailing his vision of post-Katrina urban policy. Announcing that the storm had torn "the lid off a virtual Superdome of liberal illusions," Kotkin launched a scathing attack on "rotten administration" at the state and local level, and the "collapse of responsibility and discipline" that in his mind was a function of Cajun welfarism:

By becoming mass dispensers of welfare for the unskilled, playpens for the well-heeled and fashionable, easy marks for special interests, and bunglers at maintaining public safety and dispensing efficient services to residents and businesses, many cities have become useless to the middle class, and toxic for the disorganized poor. Today's liberal urban leadership across America needs to see the New Orleans storm not as just a tragedy, but also as a dispeller of illusions, a revealer of awful truths, and a potential harbinger of things to come in their own backyards. Look beyond the tourist districts. Few contemporary cities are actually healthy in terms of job growth or middle-class amenities. Most are in the grips of moral and economic crisis. If we are lucky, the flood waters of Katrina will wash away some of the '60s-era illusions that fed today's dysfunction. Honest observers will recognize that this natural disaster, which hit the nation so hard, was set up by the man-made disaster of a counterproductive welfare state.[161]

Conventional urban bromides would be singularly unequal to this challenge. The much sought-after creative class, for example, was certainly not likely to initiate a middle-class return to New Orleans by way of hipster gentrification. The city's Richard Florida-style "port of cool" strategy—which had been promoted at a flashy conference just a month before the hurricane struck—was chronically ill-fitted to "the problem of isolated, immobile African-American remnants mired in urban poverty," Kotkin complained, because the talent-magnet model assumes that "the urban underclass will just fade away, and leave the cool hipsters unbothered to enjoy their entertainment districts."[162]

As the next chapter will show, the soft neoliberal consensus that has been constructed around the creative-cities fix has also been assailed by social conservatives and economic rationalists for legitimating new forms of public spending (and wrongheaded intervention) in the guise of a faux-cultural form of urban economic development.[163] Fundamentally, the agenda of the new urban right is about setting the "ground rules" for appropriate behavior in cities, modeled on middle-class norms; establishing the preconditions for economic growth, largely through the kinds of minimalist supply-side interventions metaphorically represented, in this case, by the cat-5 levee; and maintaining social order through ruthless application of the force of law, facilitated by zero-tolerance policing. This, clearly, is anything but a noninterventionist program, but its interventions are profoundly selective and strategically targeted. It represents a form of revanchist neoliberalism, practiced at the urban scale.[164] The neoliberal face of this program caters explicitly *to* business, taxpayers, and the middle classes, for whom the restructured city must be made safe and welcoming. Meanwhile, the program's revanchist face justifies a new round of socially invasive interventions *on* a criminalized, feckless, and morally bankrupt class of the urban poor, from whom "legitimate" citizens must be shielded at all costs. This is a form of urban policy not so much *for* cities, or even in the interest of cities, but one that is applied *to* them—restoring bourgeois urbanism by way of a kind of postwelfare policy corrective.

Urban involution

There is no record of Antony Fisher ever having visited New Orleans, but the godfather of the free-market think tank movement was certainly there in spirit when, in April 2003, the joint meeting of Heritage and the Atlas Economic Research Foundation took place in the city's Sheraton Hotel. Atlas had been established by Fisher in 1981 with a charge to capture enemy territory, "litter[ing] the world with free-market think tanks," especially in those "countries where the struggle for economic liberalism is at a relatively early stage of development."[165] In raising funds for Atlas, Fisher had the benefit of a letter of support from Hayek, who praised the entrepreneur's "*method*" of persuading, as a matter of priority, "the intellectuals, the makers of opinion" of the virtues of economic freedom in the "race against the expanding Socialist tide."[166] As Fisher's sometime neighbor, Milton Friedman recalled, the former chicken farmer had been remarkably successful in the "breeding of think tanks," first on a retail basis (with the Institute of Economic Affairs, the Fraser Institute, and the Manhattan Institute), and then on a wholesale basis—through the formation of Atlas.[167]

Riding the neoliberal wave, Atlas today claims to have had a hand in the formation of more than 275 free-market think tanks in 70 countries, from China to Costa Rica, France to Kenya, Lithuania to Bangladesh. It often assumed that the scrupulously free-market Atlas Economic Research Institute took its name from Ayn Rand's foundational libertarian treatise, *Atlas Shrugged*, though this is apparently incorrect. In fact, Fisher's inspiration was more classical, befitting an old Etonian perhaps, in its appeal to Archimedean principles as a means of invoking the odds against which the small band of true believers were prosecuting the free-market revolution: "Give me a lever and I will move the world." The lever, Fisher averred, was the Institute of Economic Affairs—his first think tank—and the fulcrum, "nothing less than market forces."[168] Writing to Fisher, during the planning phase for Atlas, in January 1980, Hayek explained that

I entirely agree with you that the time has come when it has become desirable and almost a duty to extend the network of institutes [internationally]. The future of civilization may really depend on whether we can catch the ear of a large enough part of the upcoming generation of intellectuals all over the world fast enough. And I am more convinced than ever that the *method* practiced by the IEA is the one that promises real results. I have sometimes despaired that this can be done at all. But the last thirty years of the Institute's work has made me more optimistic.[169]

While Fisher—who died in 1988, shortly after being knighted in Margaret Thatcher's honors list—would have no doubt celebrated Atlas' widespread successes in the marketing of market principles, this would have been tempered by a visceral, Hayekian sense of the remaining challenges. As his biographer put it,

Antony would have enthusiastically welcomed these developments and focused his energies on identifying obstacles and proposing remedies. He would have rejoiced that think tanks in remote places, inspired either by the success of the IEA, Manhattan or Fraser, and some supported by Atlas, are doing just this, some with distinction. But he would have been perturbed that new developments threaten to restrict economic freedom—most notably hyper-regulation (much of it coming from Brussels) and radical environmentalism. He would also have been dismayed that despite his heroic attempts to undermine the welfare state, its fractured and decaying edifice remains intact [and that] the proportion of national wealth consumed by the state shows no early sign of declining. There would nevertheless be encouragement for think tanks who have explored the (non-economic) factors that account for the longevity of the welfare state, and plaudits for those who have found innovative ways to advance the argument for private provision of health care, education and welfare.[170]

Fisher would surely have noticed the irony of a joint Heritage–Atlas meeting in New Orleans, a city that the *American Spectator*'s George Neumayr characterized as a "sewer of applied liberalism."[171] The free-market revolution's distinct lack of traction in the immediate environs of the conference stood in stark contrast with both its firm grip on national institutions and its precocious international reach. Huddled in the Sheraton Hotel, the 400-plus contingent of free-market delegates explored strategies for liberalizing the Chinese economy, worked on ways to maintain the momentum of Bush tax cuts while controlling the deficit (answer: widespread privatization), and listened attentively to then-Attorney General John Ashcroft's thoughts on the "spirit of justice." One of the gala events of the meeting was the presentation of the Sir Antony Fisher International Memorial Awards, which on this occasion, attracted forty nominations from seventeen different countries.[172]

Yet while the delegates could celebrate their evident successes in the transnational diffusion of the free-market *doxa*, there were sobering reminders all around of how little headway had been made in the state of Louisiana. Indeed, the most visible symbol of New Orleans' failed experiment in urban entrepreneurialism is, ironically, the loss-making Superdome. The State Policy Network—which works closely with Atlas within the United States, on professional and leadership development, fundraising, and the dissemination of organizational best practice for free-market think tanks at the state level—could at the time boast a membership of fifty-five such institutes in some forty-four states, but when the hurricane hit Louisiana was still a white space on their map.[173] Heritage's phone book-sized compendium of conservative policy "experts" lists a few contacts in New Orleans-based universities, but likewise identified no free-market think tank in the state.[174] And the state-level network of conservative movement activists, a group modeled on Grover Norquist's "Wednesday meetings" at Americans for Tax Reform, boasted coverage of some forty-two states, but had yet to make any inroads in Louisiana.[175]

While a handful of pioneering urban think tanks, like the Manhattan Institute, can be traced to the 1970s, it was during the following decade that "Conservatives . . . realized that the battle of ideas [was] increasingly being waged at the state and local levels."[176] By the end of the 1980s, there were twelve market-oriented think tanks working on state and local issues; today, there are more than sixty. For a long time, however, New Orleans seems to have been impervious to these developments, perhaps partly a function of its history of left-leaning political leadership, no doubt also due to the city's long-run social and economic decline. Cold indifference surely played a part too. The market showed little interest in New Orleans; the free-market think tanks apparently followed suit. Like New York City and much of urban America, New Orleans was alien territory for conservatives. Yet in marked contrast with New York City, there seems historically to have been little to fight for, or over, in New Orleans.

Hurricane Katrina, however, dramatically raised the stakes, transforming New Orleans into a "laboratory" for experiments in free-market statism. *Progressive* change has, however, been slow to arrive. While candidate Obama visited New Orleans five times, President Obama did not make his first trip until his ninth month in the White House—a four-hour stopover on the way to a San Francisco fundraiser.[177] The free-market ideational offensive, managed from the East Coast, has yet to be countered. Meanwhile, the new urban right now has boots on the ground, locally: New Orleans' first free-market think tank, the Pelican Institute, opened its doors in March, 2008, its planning and launch having been actively assisted by Atlas and by Heritage's State Policy Network. Quickly outed by some locals as a minimally staffed "astroturf" think tank, recycling materials from other free-market institutes, but with little capacity of its own,[178] Pelican nevertheless got quickly to work, attacking local tax proposals, liberally blowing the corruption whistle, while rushing out an inaugural *Louisiana Pork Report*.[179] Interviewed by an Atlas fellow, Pelican's founding director explained how the political culture of New Orleans was now beginning to change:

Even before Katrina...there has been a shift in the culture, and more and more people around the state have recognized that these populist policies, going back to the Huey Long days—of tax corporations and take that money and throw it around—and everyone will be happy as long as there are jobs [no longer work]. Well, eventually those companies packed up and moved to Texas, or went elsewhere, and along with them a lot of the educated workers and taxpayers...The people of Louisiana have recognized that those policies were bad, that we paid a price for the corruption. And then of course Katrina didn't do a lot to instill faith in big government...This was the perfect time for this kind of organization to get started. *Katrina demonstrated the limits of government ability at the federal, state and local levels.*[180]

Pelican remains little more than an outpost in the world of free-market think tanks—a kind of redistribution center. But it has, nevertheless, been generously praised by the *Wall Street Journal* for its energetic form of "bottom up" sound-policy advocacy.[181] Clearly, Pelican has the right connections, and it has pulled Louisiana into "startup" status on the State Policy Network's map of free-market think tanks, which by the end of the Bush Administration had achieved blanket coverage (see Figure 4.1).[182] Most charitably, this startup institute epitomizes Fisher's guiding maxim, that "the echo is more important than the message." The *Wall Street Journal* also envisages a promising future for Pelican and its entrepreneurial president, Kevin Kane, since New Orleans now attracts national attention, as "a boom town for charter schools [and a] crucible of the school-choice movement," hoping that "Mr. Kane can emulate the Manhattan Institute, the think thank that helped Rudy Giuliani revolutionize New York City in the 1990s." After all, this too was a communications strategy as much as anything else: "Mr. Giuliani's note-taking at the [Manhattan] institute's forums was important, but perhaps more so was *City Journal,* the institute's magazine and a model of down-to-earth analysis."[183]

The Atlas fellows that traveled to New Orleans to interview Kane later posted a web video of what they called their "government destruction tour" of the city, in the company of Loyola College of Business's resident anarcho-capitalist, Daniel D'Amico. The city's extreme state of dependency on public housing and welfare handouts had induced social paralysis in the face of the storm, D'Amico explained, while recovery efforts were being strangled at source by excessive regulation—"it's like a ghost town."[184] As Atlas fellow, Jason Talley, rhetorically put it to Pelican's Kevin Kane, "I think

States with a free-market think tank

States with a startup free-market think tank

Established think tanks:

ALABAMA
Alabama Policy Institute
www.alabamapolicy.org

ALASKA
Institute of the North
www.institutenorth.org

ARIZONA
Goldwater Institute
www.goldwaterinstitute.org

ARKANSAS
Arkansas Policy Foundation
www.arkansaspolicyfoundation.org

CALIFORNIA
Pacific Research Institute
www.pacificresearch.org

COLORADO
Independence Institute
www.i2i.org

CONNECTICUT
Yankee Institute for Public Policy
www.yankeeinstitute.org

FLORIDA
James Madison Institute
www.jamesmadison.org

GEORGIA
Georgia Public Policy Foundation
www.gppf.org

HAWAII
Grassroot Institute of Hawaii
www.grassrootinstitute.org

ILLINOIS
Illinois Policy Institute
www.illinoispolicyinstitute.org

INDIANA
Indiana Policy Review Foundation
www.inpolicy.org

IOWA
Public Interest Institute
www.limitedgovernment.org

KANSAS
Flint Hills Center for Public Policy
www.flinthills.org

KENTUCKY
Bluegrass Institute for Public Policy Solutions
www.bipps.org

MAINE
Maine Heritage Policy Center
www.mainepolicy.org

MARYLAND
Calvert Institute for Policy Research
www.calvertinstitute.org

Free State Foundation
www.freestatefoundation.org

Maryland Public Policy Institute
www.mdpolicy.org

MASSACHUSETTS
Pioneer Institute
www.pioneerinstitute.org

MICHIGAN
Mackinac Center for Public Policy
www.mackinac.org

MINNESOTA
Center of the American Experiment
www.americanexperiment.org

Freedom Foundation of Minnesota
www.freedomfoundationofminnesota.com

MISSISSIPPI
Mississippi Center for Public Policy
www.mspolicy.org

MISSOURI
Show-Me Institute
www.showmeinstitute.org

NEBRASKA
Platte Institute for Economic Research
www.platteinstitute.org

NEVADA
Nevada Policy Research Institute
www.npri.org

NEW HAMPSHIRE
Josiah Bartlett Center for Public Policy
www.jbartlett.org

NEW JERSEY
Center for Policy Research of New Jersey

NEW MEXICO
Rio Grande Foundation
www.riograndefoundation.org

NEW YORK
Empire Center for New York State Policy
www.empirecenter.org

NORTH CAROLINA
John Locke Foundation
www.johnlocke.org

John William Pope Civitas Institute
www.jwpcivitasinstitute.org

NORTH DAKOTA
North Dakota Policy Council
www.policynd.org

OHIO
Buckeye Institute for Public Policy Solutions
www.BuckeyeInstitute.org

OKLAHOMA
Oklahoma Council of Public Affairs
www.ocpathink.org**oreGon**

Cascade Policy Institute
www.CascadePolicy.org

PENNSYLVANIA
Commonwealth Foundation
www.commonwealthfoundation.org

SOUTH CAROLINA
South Carolina Policy Council
www.scpolicycouncil.com

SOUTH DAKOTA
Great Plains Public Policy Institute
www.greatplainsppi.org

TENNESSEE
Tennessee Center for Policy Research
www.tennesseepolicy.org

TEXAS
Texas Public Policy Foundation
www.texaspolicy.com

UTAH
Sutherland Institute
www.sutherlandinstitute.org

VERMONT
Ethan Allen Institute
www.ethanallen.org

VIRGINIA
Thomas Jefferson Institute
www.thomasjeffersoninst.org

Virginia Institute for Public Policy
www.virginiainstitute.org

WASHINGTON
Evergreen Freedom Foundation
www.effwa.org

Washington Policy Center
www.washingtonpolicy.org

WEST VIRGINIA
Public Policy Foundation of West Virginia
www.westvirginiapolicy.com

WISCONSIN
MacIver Institute for Public Policy
www.maciverinstitute.com

Wisconsin Policy Research Institute
www.wpri.org

Startup think tanks:

DELAWARE

Caesar Rodney Institute
www.caesarrodney.org

IDAHO
Idaho Freedom Foundation
www.idahofreedom.net

LOUISIANA
Pelican Institute for Public Policy
www.pelicaninstitute.org

MONTANA
Montana Policy Institute
www.montanapolicy.org

RHODE ISLAND
Ocean State Policy Research Institute
www.oceanstatepolicy.org

WYOMING
Wyoming Liberty Group
www.wyliberty.o

Figure 4.1. "Contact the free-market think tank in your state": State Policy Network members, October 2009

Source: <http://www.spn.org/>

most unfortunate [is] the faith that people put into government, because you have a natural disaster that happened, and then you have people that are, like, 'OK, now save me,' as opposed to self-reliance."

The crisis was a "natural" one in that the hurricane laid bare a disaster waiting to happen in New Orleans, the root causes of which were duly reinterpreted by the neoliberal think tanks in terms of government failure and social incapacity. For George Neumayr, New Orleans—as one of urban America's lost causes—was rotting from the inside:

New Orleans did not fall from without; it fell from within. The chaos after Hurricane Katrina did not cause a civilizational collapse; it simply exposed and magnified one that had already occurred...A strange admixture of upper-class decadence and underclass pathology, New Orleans has long been a stew of disorder and dysfunction, convincing many New Orleans residents, years before Hurricane Katrina, to evacuate what they regarded as an increasingly unlivable city...The squalor and crime in the Superdome represented nothing more than the squalor and crime transferred from New Orleans' legendarily hellish housing complexes [and the] countless images of stranded women, children, and elderly were explained far more by the absence of fathers than by the tardiness of FEMA.[185]

From this perspective, "the city's fall was inevitable," a predestined outcome of the orgy of welfare dependency, crime, family breakdown, and corruption that preceded the storm, conditions that rendered the city socially, economically, and morally defenseless—and then both "nature and human nature ran amok."[186] The fall of New Orleans was, for the neoliberal "counterintelligentsia" a governmental-assisted cultural implosion, merely exposed by the hurricane. When they looked at the devastation of New Orleans, what they saw was a "hurricane of entitlements."[187] This historic process of *urban involution* created the vacuum subsequently filled by the Gulf Opportunity Zone and the accompanying panoply of postwelfare urban policies. The package of neoconservative and neoliberal ideas that has dominated the post-Katrina policy debate did not prevail simply because it was simply "out there." It was aggressively and effectively peddled by a network of "organic intellectuals" with close connections to the levers of conservative state power.

Permanent persuasion

The think tanks' influence can be read in the changing posture of the Bush Administration, from defensiveness and disorientation in early September,

2005, through cautious and ultimately confident containment of the "Katrina problem" by the year's end. By the time of the January 2006 State of the Union address, New Orleans barely rated a mention. No longer was the rhetoric about "doing what it takes"; by the new year Bush was snippily retorting at a press conference, "I want to remind the people in that part of the world, $85 billion is a lot."[188] In the years that have followed, evidence of systematic evasion and unfulfilled promises in the Gulf reconstruction program has continued to accumulate. The tone certainly changed with Obama's election victory, but the on-the-ground social, environmental, and financial realities look depressingly similar.[189]

In his own way reaffirming some of Hayek's arguments, George Lakoff has argued that the political efficacy of the conservative movement in the United States is substantially rooted in the capacity of politicians and intellectuals of the right to "frame" issues and problems in ways that have facilitated their ideological objectives, by supplying the language and the supporting arguments for the radical reframing of issues like tax cuts ("tax relief," the "death tax"), or welfare retrenchment ("welfare reform," "dependency").[190] If conservatives were initially placed on the defensive by Katrina—having manifestly failed to provide basic security and protection, having publicly demonstrated both ineptness and indifference—they responded by "filling the framing gap so quickly and so effectively" that Katrina became an occasion for "an even greater power grab than . . . September 11."[191] The outpouring of conservative commentary, editorializing, and detailed policy advocacy, particularly from the think tanks, does indeed seem to have been decisive in substantially reframing the issue of New Orleans' fall and reconstruction. But for all its prefabricated nostrums, the new urban right took some time to establish a relatively coherent post-Katrina policy stance, which in turn called for significant interventions on the part of the class of "permanent persuaders" in the think tanks. None of this was easy and nothing about it was inevitable. The Washington think tanks, led by Heritage, went to work almost immediately on the challenge of managing the costs of the reconstruction, deploying the frame of fiscal responsibility to contain and corral the Republican-controlled Congress and White House. Meanwhile, the Manhattan Institute and its sundry followers labored to (re)construct their portable model of urban transformation for the inhospitable setting of New Orleans—advocating what amounts to a shock-therapy program of moral reconstruction, social control, and economic discipline. In the space of a few months, these interventions helped fashion a gradual realignment of the post-Katrina debate.

First, initial accusations of abject governmental failure disproportionately impacted the party with complete control over federal institutions, and the Bush White House in particular; but, with growing intensity, the roots of the problem were subsequently portrayed as *state and local ones*—a function of the "craven and corrupt" governance of New Orleans and of incompetent leadership at the state level—while the question of federal *political* responsibility soon morphed into an(other) indictment of federal *bureaucracy.* So contained, this narrative of governmental failure actually serves neoliberal ends: the "solution" becomes one of downsizing, reforming, and/or retasking government, outsourcing further functions to corporate contractors and faith-based organizations. It became an apt moment, for example, for Milton Friedman to press the case, one more time, for vouchers and charter schools. In the *Wall Street Journal,* he argued that Katrina represented

an opportunity to radically reform the educational system [...] If, by a political miracle, Louisiana could overcome the opposition of the unions and enact universal vouchers, it would not only serve itself, it would also render a service to the rest of the country by providing a large scale example of what the market can do for education when permitted to operate.[192]

Second, the enormous financial cost of the recovery effort—which plainly exceeded not only state and local fiscal capacities, but also challenged a federal government overextended by an unsustainable program of tax cuts, military commitments, and deficit spending—was effectively translated into a debate about *fiscal responsibility,* prioritizing "higher purposes," and "offset" spending reductions. In a reworking of the "starve the beast" strategy developed in the Reagan era, the necessity of Katrina-related expenditures (themselves minimized through processes of delay and obfuscation), became translated into *imperative* budget reductions, initially directed at indefensible "pork," but more ominously focused on the historic target of entitlement programs. In this manner, an urban catastrophe that disproportionately impacted the poor, the infirm, and the elderly perversely resulted in the paring of programs designated for precisely these groups.

Third, early narratives emphasizing victimization, particularly along race and class lines, were progressively displaced by a familiar discourse of *individual responsibility,* even personal culpability. Most egregiously, this is exposed in the portrayal of New Orleans residents *choosing* to disregard evacuation orders in anticipation of beginning-of-the-month welfare checks and post-hurricane opportunities for looting. It was therefore not a lack of resources, private transportation, or out-of-town support systems that placed some of the most-needy New Orleans residents in the storm's path; it was the long-run consequences of urban welfarism—and its racialized cast of supported characters, including the workless, the feckless, and the lawless, absentee fathers, inert mothers, and criminalized youths.

It is these narrations of the post-Katrina crisis that came to dominate both the discourse and (more unevenly) the practice of reconstruction. They have helped transform what began as a "decidedly unnatural disaster," in Neil Smith's words, into a malformed reconstruction program that blames, and morally reregulates, the most vulnerable victims, while setting in train "[w]holesale gentrification on a scale unseen in the United States."[193] This is about as far from Naomi Klein's "people's reconstruction" as one could imagine—a program of contracted-out urban structural adjustment, designed in Washington and New York.[194] Amongst other things, this has helped redefine (and recalibrate "down") what remained of a federal commitment to America's cities—one that the Obama Administration has yet seriously to address, let alone reverse. The process of urban abandonment that began in the 1970s seems to have arrived at its most hypertrophied form—federal responsibilities should be tightly circumscribed even in the face of "extreme events," like hurricanes, and need only be dispensed when complemented by what Heritage framed as "'bottom-up' preparedness from individuals and communities."[195]

Meanwhile, the Heritage Foundation feels free to sermonize (from its offices in Washington, DC) that, "The worst thing that the U.S. could do is try to run disaster response out of an office in Washington." For all the rhetorical faith that the neoliberal think tanks place in responsive and responsible "local communities," their idealized bourgeois-urban world seems only to be populated by utilitarian abstractions (atomized rational actors), privileged social forms ("traditional" nuclear families), and surrogate institutions (private contractors and faith-based deliverers), an awkward fact revealed in the apparent paucity of both deserving recipients and reliable compradors in New Orleans. What, then, could New Orleans expect but a form of shock-treatment urban policy, imposed from the outside, and designed by ideational technocrats on the East Coast?

There is a tragic truth in the ways in which Katrina "laid bare" the operating model of American neoliberalism, its inequities and limitations.[196] But by the same token, the relentless political management of the hurricane's protracted aftermath exposes the continuing grip of this project, manifest in what has been a forceful display of orchestrated ideological recoil. The only partly hidden hands of think-tank protagonists were feverishly at work in fashioning this "free- market" response. These new cadres of organic intellectuals are more than mere "orators," they also *construct, organize,* and give direction to state projects.[197] As such, their strenuous and concerted actions in the wake of Katrina again reveal the essential truth that in as far as the neoliberal project demonstrates unity, this is very much a *constructed* unity. It is also a contradictory unity. Beneath the veneer of common purpose, for example, there are sharp—and potentially fatal—differences in the means and ends of small-government fiscal conservatives and big-government social conservatives.

Even though the new urban right was ready with a prefabricated crisis narrative when Katrina struck, the subsequent performance of the free-market think tanks reveals not only the potency, but also some of the incipient limits, of this postwelfare *doxa*. The bourgeois urban vision of the Manhattan Institute, just like the truncated, small-government federalism of the Heritage Foundation, did not emerge through a simple process of historical succession, as a singular and ready-formed alternative to Keynesian-welfarist urbanism. Rather, it has been formed incrementally, albeit in the context of a radical and overarching vision, as a tendentially consonant hybrid of a range of conservative, libertarian, pro-business, anti-statist, neoliberal and "post-liberal" ideological arguments, claims, propositions, and "second-hand ideas." What might be characterized in retrospect as a (formidable) neoliberal project, or even a hegemonic "market order," was of course a socially constructed one, the product of several decades of ideological investment and intellectual entrepreneurship, going back at least as far as the Hayek–Fisher encounter of 1945, and all facilitated by a favorable political–economic climate.

While the speed and force with which neoliberal nostrums filled the post-Katrina void can be read as a somber commentary on America's contemporary realpolitik, and the circuits of power and persuasion that sustain it, at the same time, the tensions and differences that were exposed along the way represent manifestations of the *problematically* hybrid character of the market order. For example, the post-Katrina debate reveals that fiscal constraint is evidently easier to preach than to practice; that the morally interventionist impulses of compassionate conservatives routinely try the patience of libertarians, just as they alarm budget hawks; that wholesale contracting out risks compromising fiscal accountability; that small-government conservatives find it increasingly difficult to trust big-government conservatives; and so on. In principle, the exhaustion of the neoliberal project might just as easily result, therefore, from *internal* ideological fractures—or for that matter from various forms of social, political, and fiscal overreach—as from "external" contestation. For now, if the fast-policy relays between New York City, Washington, and New Orleans tell us anything, it is a story of evolving neoliberal hegemony, for all the project's shaky foundations and flawed realization. Only for a relatively brief moment did the manifest urban tragedy of New Orleans—the likes of which has never been seen before in the contemporary United States—disrupt business-as-usual neoliberalism. Within the space of a few months, if not weeks, it had become clear that the longer-run outcomes of Katrina would not be a reversal, nor even a midcourse adjustment of the process of neoliberalization, but in fact an *acceleration* of its extant programs of social regression and market governance.

Notes

1. Fisher, A. (1978) *Fisher's Concise History of Economic Bungling: A Guide for Today's Statesmen*. Ottawa, IL: Caroline House Books, 79–80.
2. Russell, D. (1949) *The TVA Idea*. Irvington-on-Hudson, NY: Foundation for Economic Freedom.
3. Blundell, J. (2003) *Waging the War of Ideas*. London: Institute of Economic Affairs, 41.
4. Abelson, D. E. (2002) *Do Think Tanks Matter?* Montreal and Kingston: McGill-Queen's University Press.
5. Quoted in Frost (2002: 136–137).
6. Magnet, M. (2004) Gotham, GOP poster child, *City Journal*, August 24, accessed at <http://www.city-journal.org>: 1.
7. See O'Connor (2008).
8. Midge Decter in *Commentary*, September 1977, quoted in O'Connor (2008: 346).
9. Elsewhere in the movie, there is reference to candidate Palatine's commitment to workfare ("this new mandatory welfare program") and to his determination to tackle the evils of inflation (Schrader, P. (1990) *Taxi Driver*. London: Faber and Faber, 28, 11).
10. Frost (2002: 145).
11. Quoted in Micklethwait and Wooldridge (2004: 58).
12. Friedman (1974: 16).
13. Tanenhaus, S. (2005) The Buckley effect, *New York Times Magazine*, October 2: 68–115.
14. Shorto, R. (2005) All political ideas are local, *New York Times Magazine*, October 2: 60.
15. The Atlas Economic Research Foundation, another "Fisher think tank," provides explicit advice on naming, among other things, in its various primers, toolkits, and how-to guides for the international community of think tanks. "[S]ome

institutes deliberately pick names that convey little information in the hopes that it will enable them to participate in a wider variety of opportunities," Atlas observes, before issuing the caution, "if the name you choose is likely to generate hostilities because of misplaced assumptions associated with certain words, you might want to go with something less descriptive" (Kwong, J. and Dyble, C. (2006) *Guidelines and Recommendations for Starting an Institute.* Washington, DC: Atlas Economic Research Foundation, 6).

16. Roger Hertog, Chair of the Manhattan Institute, at the 2003 Alexander Hamilton Awards, accessed at <http://www.manhattan-institute.org>.

17. Kaplan, F. (1998) Conservatives plant a seed in NYC: think tank helps Giuliani set his agenda, *Boston Sunday Globe,* February 22: A4.

18. Scott, J. (1997) Turning intellect into influence: promoting its ideas, the Manhattan Institute has nudged New York rightward, *New York Times,* May 12: B1.

19. *New York Post* (2003) Ideas matter, *New York Post,* January 30: 26.

20. Wolfe, T. (2004) The Manhattan Institute at 25. In B. C. Anderson, ed., *Turning Intellect into Influence.* New York: Reed Press, 7.

21. Gramsci (1971: 10); see also Desai (1994) and Peck and Tickell (2007).

22. *City Journal* (2005) In prospect, *City Journal,* 15/4: 5.

23. *Wall Street Journal* (2005) Beltway hurricane, *Wall Street Journal,* September 8: A18.

24. See Sites (2003), Moody (2007), and O'Connor (2008).

25. Moody (2007: 17–18); Harvey (2005: 44–45).

26. Moody (2007: 127).

27. Malanga, S. (2003) I'm outta here, *City Journal,* 13/4: 8.

28. Berger (1992: 54).

29. Berger (1992: 54, 60, emphasis added).

30. Magnet, M. (2000) Introduction. In M. Magnet, ed., *The Millennial City: A New Urban Paradigm for 21st Century America.* Chicago: Ivan R. Dee, 3.

31. Barone (2004: 48, 49).

32. Ever since Ed Feulner reluctantly declined the offer, extended by Fisher and Casey, to run the newly-formed International Center for Economic Policy Studies/Manhattan Institute, deciding instead to accept the position of president of the Washington-based think tank, the Heritage Foundation (Frost, 2002), the two organizations have evolved symbiotically, with a clear division of labor. Heritage focuses on day-to-day policy management; Manhattan is concerned with longer-term, bigger-picture issues. The financial, personal, and ideational circuits connecting the network of think tanks have always been tight ones. Feulner, who remains Heritage's president, had previously worked as an intern for the IEA in London, and later served as Executive Director of the Republican Study Committee, which itself continues to have close connections to Heritage (see Edwards, 1997). He is also a past present of the Mont Pelerin Society.

33. Gilder, G. (1980) *Wealth and Poverty*. New York: Basic Books; Bartlett, B. R. (1981) *Reaganomics: Supply Side Economics in Action*. New Rochelle, NY: Arlington House.

34. See Bartley and Shlaes (2004: 37).

35. Bartley and Shlaes (2004: 35).

36. Murray (1984: 9).

37. Miller, J. J. (2002) Eight books that changed America, *Philanthropy*, July/August, accessed at <http://www.philanthropyroundtable.org>.

38. See Albeda, R. and Withorn, A., eds. (2002) *Lost Ground: Welfare Reform, Poverty, and Beyond*. Cambridge, MA: South End Press; Peck (2001).

39. Magnet, M. (2005) Ending welfare as we knew it, *National Review*, December 19: 111.

40. See, especially, Fraser, N. and Gordon, L. (1994) A genealogy of dependency: tracing a keyword of the U.S. welfare state, *Signs*, 19/2: 309–36; Schram, S. F. (1995) *Words of Welfare*. Minneapolis: University of Minnesota Press.

41. See, for example, Mead, L. (1991) Kicking New York's dependency habit, *City Journal*, 1/4: 41–49.

42. See Peck (2001); Goldberg, C. A. (2008) *Citizens and Paupers: Relief, Rights, and Race, from the Freedmen's Bureau to Workfare*. Chicago: University of Chicago Press; Krinsky, J. (2008) *Free Labor: Workfare and the Contested Language of Neoliberalism*. Chicago: University of Chicago Press.

43. Kelling, G. L. and Coles, C. M. (1996) *Fixing Broken Windows: Restoring Order and Reducing Crime in Our Communities*. New York: Free Press.

44. Bratton, W. J. and Andrews, W. (2000) What we've learned about policing. In M. Magnet, ed., *The Millennial City: A New Urban Paradigm for 21st Century America*. Chicago: Ivan R. Dee, 70–80. Compare Harcourt, B. (2002) *Illusions of Order*. Cambridge: Harvard University Press.

45. Magnet, M. (2001) Solving President's Bush's urban problem, *City Journal*, 11/1: 20–21.

46. Magnet, M. (1993) *The Dream and the Nightmare: The Sixties Legacy to the Underclass*. New York: William Morrow. See Brustein (2003), and Miller, J. J. (2002) Eight books that changed America, *Philanthropy*, July/August, accessed at <http://www.philanthropyroundtable.org>.

47. Magnet, M. (2001) Solving President's Bush's urban problem, *City Journal*, 11/1: 16, 22.

48. Magnet, M. (2001) Solving President's Bush's urban problem, *City Journal*, 11/1: 21.

49. Barone (2004: 51).

50. Vigilante, R. (1991) How to save the city, *City Journal*, 1/5: 7.

51. Vigilante, R. (1991) How to save the city, *City Journal*, 1/5: 10.

52. Editors (1990) Welcome to NY, *City Journal*, 1/1: 2.

53. Editors (1990) Welcome to NY, *City Journal*, 1/1: 3.

54. See Siegel, F. (1993) The New York disease, *City Journal*, 3/1: 18–19; McMahon and Siegel (2005).

55. Tanenhaus, S. (2004) A laboratory for change. In B. C. Anderson, ed., *Turning Intellect into Influence*. New York: Reed Press, 82.

56. Quoted in Gupte, P. (2005) Lunch at the Four Seasons: on being a high-profile conservative in a liberal city, *New York Sun*, March 24: B14.

57. Berger, S. (1993) Breaking the governmental habit: proposals for the Mayor. *City Journal*, 3/1: 20–27.

58. See Magnet (2001: 21).

59. *City Journal* (1991) Liberalism and the city, *City Journal*, 1/5: 20–34.

60. Malanga, S. (2005) The real engine of blue America, *City Journal*, 15/1: 66–73; Malanga, S. (2003) I'm outta here, *City Journal*, 13/4: 8.

61. Larry Mone, quoted in Brustein (2003: 2).

62. See Brooks, D. (2004) A walker in *City Journal*. In B. C. Anderson, ed., *Turning Intellect into Influence*. New York: Reed Press, 9–18; Kaplan, F. (1998) Conservatives plant a seed in NYC: think tank helps Giuliani set his agenda, *Boston Sunday Globe*, February 22: A4.

63. Scott, J. (1997) Turning intellect into influence: promoting its ideas, the Manhattan Institute has nudged New York rightward, *New York Times*, May 12: B1.

64. See Brustein (2003).

65. Quoted in Siegel, F. (2005) *The Prince of the City: Giuliani, New York and the Genius of American Life*. San Francisco: Encounter Books, 60–61.

66. See Blumenthal (1988).

67. See Brustein (2003); Scott, J. (1997) Turning intellect into influence: promoting its ideas, the Manhattan Institute has nudged New York rightward, *New York Times*, May 12: B1.

68. Rudi Giuliani, quoted in Scott, J. (1997) Turning intellect into influence: promoting its ideas, the Manhattan Institute has nudged New York rightward, *New York Times*, May 12: B1.

69. Stern, W. J. (1998) Restoring the opportunity city, *City Journal*, 8/1: 14–25.

70. Malanga, S. (2001) Building the opportunity city, *City Journal*, 11/2: 72–81.

71. Page, C. (2001) The last big one, *City Journal*, 11/3: 102–109.

72. *City Journal* (2001) In prospect, *City Journal*, 11/4: 5.

73. Malanga, S. (2001) How to rebuild New York, *City Journal*, 11/4: 2.

74. Malanga, S. (2001) How to rebuild New York, *City Journal*, 11/4: 3.

75. "[If] indeed one man proved he could govern a city that seemed ungovernable before him, then any man can govern the city—provided he believes in the right things and does the right things at the right times" (Podhoretz, J. (2005) The greatness that was Giuliani. In W. Kristol, ed., *The Weekly Standard—A Reader: 1995–2005*. New York: HarperCollins, 163).

76. Auletta, K. (1979) *The Streets Were Paved with Gold*. New York: Random House. See also McMahon and Siegel (2005) and Brustein, J. (2005) The fiscal crisis after 30

years. *Gotham Gazette,* October 10, accessed at <http://www.gothamgazette.com>.

77. *City Journal* (2002) In prospect, *City Journal,* 12/1: 5.

78. Malanga. S. (2002) Gotham needs a GOP, *City Journal,* 12/1: 56–65.

79. McMahon, E. J. (2005) Rating Mayor Mike, *City Journal,* 15/3: 64–67; Malanga, S. (2005) Reformer Bloomberg? *City Journal,* 15/4: 6.

80. Gelinas, N. (2005) *Mayor Bloomberg and the Limits of Pragmatism.* Civic Report No. 46. New York: Center for Civic Innovation, Manhattan Institute for Policy Research.

81. Malanga, S. (2005) Gotham stalls out, *City Journal,* 15/3: 50.

82. Magnet, M. (2004) Gotham, GOP poster child, *City Journal,* August 24, accessed at <http://www.city-journal.org>: 2, 4.

83. Malanga, S. (2003) Bloomberg to city: drop dead, *City Journal,* 13/1: 27–35.

84. Quoted in Snadowsky, L. T., Robinson, E., and de Krester, L. (2005) Beast of bayou! *New York Post,* August 29: 2.

85. MacQuarrie, B. (2005) A battle to rebuild looms in New Orleans, *Boston Globe,* October 2: A1; *Houston Chronicle* (2005) How New Orleans might change, *Houston Chronicle,* September 29: A1.

86. Gotham and Greenberg (2008: 1043).

87. Obama disappointed many, Maureen Dowd observed, with this "technocrat's answer," concerning the "complications between the state, the city and the feds in making assessments of the damages." Obama continued to explain that "The damage from Katrina was not just caused by a disaster of nature, but by a failure of government, a government that wasn't adequately prepared and didn't adequately respond" (see Parsons, C. and Fausset, F. (2009) Welcomed by a weary city, *Los Angeles Times,* October 16: A18; Dowd, M. (2009) Fie, fatal flaw! *New York Times,* October 18: A9.

88. Gelinas, N. (2005) Will New Orleans recover? *New York Sun,* September 1: 9.

89. Gelinas, N. (2005) Will New Orleans recover? *New York Sun,* September 1: 9.

90. Gelinas, N. (2005) Will New Orleans recover? *New York Sun,* September 1: 9, emphasis added.

91. Gelinas, N. (2005) Will New Orleans recover? *New York Sun,* September 1: 9. Newark, NJ was the site of significant urban unrest in the summer of 1967, focused on confrontations between segments of the African-American community and the police, and triggered by a long history of political disenfranchisement, inadequate housing and social-service provision, and police brutality. On the riots, which left 26 dead and hundreds injured, see Mumford, K. (2007) *Newark: A History of Race, Rights, and Riots in America.* New York: NYU Press.

92. Gelinas, N. (2005) A perfect storm of lawlessness, *City Journal,* September 1, accessed at <http://www.city-journal.org>: 2–4.

93. See McGann, J. G. (2004) *Scholars, Dollars and Policy Advice.* Philadelphia: Foreign Policy Research Institute.

94. Gelinas, N. (2005) A perfect storm of lawlessness, *City Journal,* September 1, accessed at <http://www.city-journal.org>: 1.

95. Dalrymple, T. (2005) The veneer of civilization, *National Review,* September 26: 24; Brooks, D. (2005) The bursting point, *New York Times,* September 4: 11.

96. Amongst the torrent of (largely scathing) media commentary on the federal government response to Katrina, see Mulrine, A. (2005) Lots of blame, *U.S. News & World Report,* September 19: 26–35; Elliston, J. (2005) Confederacy of dunces, *The Nation,* September 26: 4–5.

97. President outlines Hurricane Katrina relief efforts, White House, Office of the Press Secretary, August 31, 2005.

98. See Lieberman, B. (2005) A bad response to post-Katrina gas prices, *Web Memo,* No. 827, Heritage Foundation, Washington, DC; Lott, J. R. (2005) *A Look at the Positive Side of Price-Gouging and Greed.* Washington, DC: American Enterprise Institute.

99. Lieberman, B. (2005) No easy answers for post-Katrina gas prices, *Web Memo,* No. 831, Heritage Foundation, Washington, DC.

100. Utt, R. D. (2005) The Katrina relief effort: Congress should redirect highway earmark funding to a higher purpose, *Web Memo,* No. 832, Heritage Foundation, Washington, DC: 2. On the Alaskan bridge controversy, see Clarren, R. (2005) A bridge to nowhere, *Salon.com,* August, 9.

101. Heritage Foundation (2005) Congress should redirect highway pork to the Katrina relief effort, September 9, accessed at <http://www.heritage.org>.

102. See Edwards, C. (2005) *Both Parties Find Trough to Their Liking.* Washington, DC: Cato Institute; Slivinkski, S. (2005) Congress should make some sacrifices, too, *Newsday,* September 16: A58; de Rugy, V. (2005) Fools rush in, *Tech Central Station,* September 7, accessed at <http://www.tcsdaily.com>.

103. See the discussion in Peck and Tickell (2007).

104. See Cockett (1995) and Edwards (1997).

105. When Republican Speaker of the House, Dennis Hastert, candidly mused that the rebuilding of New Orleans might not "make sense," he was forced, within hours, to retract the statement (quoted in Taylor, G. (2005) Rebuilding the city will change its face, *Washington Times,* September 2, 2005: A1).

106. Dale, H. (2005) Preventing future catastrophes: answers needed on Katrina response, *Washington Times,* September 8: A21; Ledeen, M. (2005) The doomed cities, *National Review Online,* September 1, accessed at <http://www.nationalreview.com>.

107. Meese *et al.* (2005: 1, emphasis added).

108. Meese *et al.* (2005: 2).

109. See Utt, R. D. (2005) President's bold action on Davis-Bacon will aid the relief effort, *Web Memo,* No. 836, Heritage Foundation, Washington, DC.

110. Butler, S. M. (2005) Lose the rules, *Los Angeles Times,* September 13: B13.

111. Malanga, S. (2005) New Orleans vs. New York? *City Journal,* September 15, accessed at <http://www.city-journal.org>.

112. Americans for Tax Reform (2005) Death tax repeal/Katrina: Memorandum to Members of the United States Senate, September 2, accessed at <http://www.atr.org>.

113. Graetz and Shapiro (2005: 28–29). On Norquist's philosophy, see his (2008) *Leave us Alone*. New York: HarperCollins. Norquist's treasure trove of neoliberal one-liners includes the now-infamous: "I don't want to abolish government. I simply want to reduce it to the size where I can drag it into the bathroom and drown it in the bathtub" (quoted on National Public Radio, May 25, 2001; Peck, 2004: 392).

114. Utt, R. D. (2005) Congress faces pressure to surrender pork for flood relief, *Web Memo*, No. 841, Heritage Foundation, Washington, DC; de Rugy, V. (2005) Hurricane relief spending: how will we pay for it? *Tech Central Station*, September 12, accessed at <http://www.tcsdaily.com>.

115. de Rugy, V. (2005) Pork gumbo, *Tech Central Station*. October 7, accessed at <http://www.tcsdaily.com>; Riedl, B. M. (2005) A "victory" over wasteful spending? Hardly, *Web Memo*, No. 839, Heritage Foundation, Washington, DC.

116. Dale, H. (2005) Post-Katrina frenzy, *Washington Times,* September 14: A19; Novak, M. (2005) Hurricane hysterics: a message to Europe about Katrina. *National Review Online,* September 14, accessed at <http://www.nationalreview.com>.

117. See Glassman, J. K. (2005) Katrina and disgusting exploitation, *Tech Central Station,* August 31, accessed at <http://www.tcsdaily.com> and Hayward, S. F. (2005) Katrina and the environment, *Environmental Policy Outlook,* September/October, American Enterprise Institute, Washington, DC.

118. Hassett, K. A. (2005) Let's tie Katrina aid to people, not just places, *Bloomberg.com,* September 12.

119. Glassman, J. K. (2005) How to rebuild a great city, *Scripps Howard News Service,* September 12, accessed at <http://www.shns.com>: 2.

120. President discusses hurricane relief in Address to Nation, Jackson Square, New Orleans, Office of the Press Secretary, White House, Washington, DC, September 15, 2005.

121. Quoted in Weisman, J. and VandeHei, J. (2005) Bush to request more aid funding, *Washington Post,* September 15: A1.

122. Butler *et al.* (2005: 3).

123. Hubbard, R. G. (2005) A post-hurricane action plan should focus on people, *Financial Times,* September 19: 19.

124. Franc, M. (2005) Legislative lowdown—week of September 19th, *Human Events,* September 19, accessed at <http://www.humaneventsonline.com>.

125. Feulner, E. J. (2005) Don't bind New Orleans in red tape, *San Francisco Chronicle,* September 19: B5.

126. *Wall Street Journal* (2005) Hurricane Bush, *Wall Street Journal,* September 15, A20.

127. Wessel, D. (2005) Small government rhetoric gets filed away, *Wall Street Journal*, September 8, A2.

128. Quoted in Wilke, J. R. and Mullins, B. (2005) After Katrina, Republicans back a sea of conservative ideas, *Wall Street Journal*, September 15: B1.

129. Republican Study Committee (2005) *Operation Offset: RSC Budget Options 2005*, Washington, DC: Republican Study Committee.

130. See Acosta Fraser A. and Muccio, M. (2005) The growing disconnect: federal spending and congressional leadership, *Web Memo*, No. 865, Heritage Foundation, Washington, DC.

131. *Wall Street Journal* (2005) Cuts for Katrina, *Wall Street Journal*, September 21: A26; *Wall Street Journal* (2005) Beltway hurricane, *Wall Street Journal*, September 8: A18.

132. The Senate's self-styled Fiscal Watch Team called for a "package of offsets" totaling $130 billion, including a 5% reduction in spending on all federal programs except those which impact national security, a pay freeze for federal employees, and a two-year delay in implementation of the Medicare prescription drug benefit.

133. *Porkbusters,* now at <http://porkbusters.org/secrethold.php>, featured advocacy of the Pork Barrel Reduction Act (S.2265) and a Pork Hall of Fame (#1 being, not surprisingly, Senator Ted Stevens of Alaska, of "bridge to nowhere" infamy).

134. Frustration with the Republican leadership, however, had been building for some time amongst fiscal conservatives, particularly since the passage of the Medicare bill in 2003. See de Rugy, V. and Gillespie, N. (2005) Bush the budget buster, *Reason*, October 19, accessed at <http://reason.com>; Slivinski, S. (2005) *The Grand Old Spending Party: How Republicans Became Big Spenders*. Policy Analysis No. 543. Washington, DC: Cato Institute.

135. Utt, R. D. (2005) Give up your bike path, bridge for hurricane relief, *USA Today*, September 28, A11.

136. President holds press conference, Office of the Press Secretary, White House, Washington, DC, October 4, 2005. Bush also made the case that post-Katrina realities called for an extension of the Patriot Act and increased oil-refining capacity ("The storms that hit our Gulf Coast also touched every American, with higher prices at the gas pump").

137. Republican Study Committee (2005) *Pence Praises President's Call for Budget Cuts*. Washington, DC: Republican Study Committee.

138. Franc, M. (2005) Legislative lowdown—week of October 4th, *Human Events*, October 4, accessed at <http://www.humaneventsonline.com>: 1.

139. Gingrich, N. and de Rugy, V. (2005) Pork, pelicans, and Louisiana, *Washington Times*, October 18: A19; de Rugy, V. (2005) Pork gumbo, *Tech Central Station*. October 7, accessed at <http://www.tcsdaily.com>.

140. For a discussion of policy framing, see Lakoff, G. (2002) *Moral Politics*. Chicago: University of Chicago Press.

141. See Feulner, E. J. (2005) *Getting Serious about Spending*. Washington, DC: Heritage Foundation; Muccio, M. and Acosta Fraser, A. (2005) House Leadership reacts to calls for fiscal responsibility, *Web Memo*, No. 879, Heritage Foundation, Washington, DC.

142. Feulner, E. J. (2005) *A Line in the Sand on Spending*. Washington, DC: Heritage Foundation: 3.

143. The "rainbow in the aftermath of Katrina," as Heritage President, Ed Feulner put it, was that the "tipping point" had finally been reached, "Now excessive spending is on everyone's mind." (Feulner, E. J. (2005) A rainbow in the aftermath of Katrina: realization that overspending must stop, *Investor's Business Daily*, October 31: A21).

144. de Rugy, V. (2005) Taming the spending beast, *Press-Enterprise*, November 20: D1.

145. Franc, M. (2005) Legislative lowdown—week of October 4th, *Human Events*, October 4, accessed at <http://www.humaneventsonline.com>: 1.

146. Kane, T. and Muhlhausen, D. B. (2005) Should federal labor policy be any different after the 2005 hurricane season? *Backgrounder*, No. 1893, Heritage Foundation, Washington, DC.

147. Franc, M. (2005) Legislative lowdown—week of September 26th, *Human Events*, September 26, accessed at <http://www.humaneventsonline.com>: 1.

148. Tanner, M. (2005) No longer out of sight; chance for an effective war on poverty, *Washington Times*, September 9: A23.

149. Sowell, T. (2005) Who will rebuild New Orleans' moral levees? *Investor's Business Daily*, September 7: A14.

150. Neumayr (2005: 50).

151. President discusses hurricane relief in Address to Nation, Jackson Square, New Orleans, Office of the Press Secretary, White House, Washington, DC, September 15, 2005.

152. Rector, R. (2005) How not to be poor, *National Review*, October 24: 26–28.

153. Neumayr (2005: 50).

154. Murray, C. (2005) The hallmark of the underclass, *Wall Street Journal*, September 29: A18.

155. Hymowitz, K. S. (2006) Marriage and caste, *City Journal*, 16/1: 29.

156. Harrington, M. (1962) *The Other America*. New York: Macmillan.

157. Gelinas (2005: 16).

158. See O'Connor (2008) on the riots of 1977 and the Manhattan Institute's urban agenda.

159. Gelinas (2005: 22, 21, 24–25).

160. Gelinas, N. (2006) Katrina refugees shoot up Houston, *City Journal*, January 4, accessed at <http://www.city-journal.org>.

161. Kotkin, J. (2006) Ideological hurricane, *The American Enterprise*, January/February: 29.

162. Kotkin, J. (2006) Ideological hurricane, *The American Enterprise*, January/February: 26, 28.

163. The Manhattan Institute has been a prominent skeptic in this regard. See Malanga (2004) and Kotkin and Siegel (2004).

164. See Smith (2002) and Peck and Tickell (2002).

165. Antony Fisher, 1981, quoted at <http://atlasnetwork.org/>; Frost (2002: 157).

166. Quoted in Atlas (2004) *Atlas Year-in-Review*. Arlington, VA: Atlas Economic Research Foundation, 32.

167. Friedman, M. (2002) Foreword. In Frost, G., *Antony Fisher: Champion of Liberty*. London: Profile, xvi.

168. Frost (2002: 154). On Ayn Rand, see Rand, A. (1957) *Atlas Shrugged*. New York: Random House; Heller, A. C. (2009) *Ayn Rand and the World She Made*. New York: Doubleday.

169. Hayek to Fisher, January 1, 1980, quoted in Frost (2002: 155).

170. Frost (2002: 171–172).

171. Neumayr, G. (2005) Masques of death, *American Spectator*, September 2, accessed at <http://www.spectator.org>.

172. The winners came from the Cato Institute, Canada's Atlantic Institute for Market Studies, and Libertad y Desarrollo in Chile.

173. See <http://www.spn.org>.

174. Heritage Foundation (2005) *Policy Experts 2005–2006*. Washington, DC: Heritage Foundation.

175. ATR (2005) *Center-Right Coalition Meetings in the States*. Washington, DC: Americans for Tax Reform.

176. Moore, W. J. (1988) Local right thinkers, *National Journal*, October 1, 2455.

177. Shear, M. D. (2009) Residents of New Orleans losing patience with Obama, *Boston Globe*, October 15: 10.

178. White, L. (2009) The Pelican Institute: Louisiana's first "astroturf" think tank, *CenLamar* blog, August 1, accessed at <http://cenlamar.com/>. Pelican's top-heavy staff only a President and Vice President, plus three "adjunct scholars" based at sister organizations in Los Angeles and Washington, DC.

179. Pelican Institute (2009) *Louisiana Pork Report*. New Orleans and Washington, DC: Pelican Institute and Citizens Against Government Waste.

180. Kevin Kane, interviewed on Motor Home Diaries, June 5, 2009, accessed at <http://www.freestateblogs.net/node/6633>, emphasis added.

181. Feith, D. (2008) How to bring innovative ideas to a machine-politics state, *Wall Street Journal*, August 9: A9.

182. Membership in the State Policy Network (SPN), its web site states, "is voluntary and by invitation-only." Founded in 1992, the SPN has been franchising free-market think tanks at the state level across the United States. The *Wall Street Journal* obfuscates its real identity by characterizing the SPN as "Oregon-based" and "a small but robust organization that operates as a trade association for the think-tank industry." The SPN's headquarters are located, in fact, in Arlington,

Virginia, not Oregon—literally next-door neighbors to the Atlas Economic Research Institute. See Feith, D. (2008) How to bring innovative ideas to a machine-politics state, *Wall Street Journal,* August 9: A9; DeParle, J. (2006) Right-of-center guru goes wide with the gospel of small government, *New York Times,* November 17: A24.

183. Feith, D. (2008) How to bring innovative ideas to a machine-politics state, *Wall Street Journal,* August 9: A9.

184. Motor Home Diaries, Government destruction tour, September 25, 2009, accessed at <http://www.freestateblogs.net/taxonomy/term/1765?page=1>.

185. Neumayr (2005: 48, 50).

186. Neumayr (2005: 50).

187. Franc, M. (2005a) Hurricane of entitlements, *National Review Online,* September 20, accessed at <http://www.nationalreview.com>.

188. Press conference of the President, White House, Office of the Press Secretary, January 26, 2006.

189. See Hsu, S. S. (2006) Post-Katrina promises unfulfilled, *Washington Post,* January 28: A1; Cutter, S. L. *et al.* (2006) The long road home: race, class, and recovery from Hurricane Katrina, *Environment,* 48/2: 8–20; Katz, C. (2008) Bad elements: Katrina and the scoured landscape of social reproduction, *Gender, Place and Culture,* 15/1: 15–29; Gotham and Greenberg M. (2008).

190. See Lakoff (2002) and, for an instructive case, Graetz and Shapiro (2005).

191. Lakoff, G. and Halpin, J. (2005) Framing Katrina, *The American Prospect,* October 7, accessed at <http://www.prospect.org>: 1.

192. Friedman, M. (2005) The promise of vouchers, *Wall Street Journal,* December 5: A.20.

193. Smith, N. (2005) There is no such thing as a natural disaster. In SSRC, *Understanding Katrina: Perspectives from the Social Sciences,* accessed at <http://understandingkatrina.ssrc.org>.

194. Klein, N. (2005) Needed: a people's reconstruction, *The Nation,* September 26: 12.

195. Meese *et al.* (2005: 9).

196. Bakker, K. (2005) Katrina: the public transcript of "disaster," *Society and Space,* 23/6: 795–802; Braun, B. and McCarthy, J. (2005) Hurricane Katrina and abandoned being, *Society and Space,* 23/6: 802–809.

197. See Gramsci (1971: 10).

5

Creative Liberties

"Be creative—or die" is how Christopher Dreher summarized the new urban imperative: "cities must attract the new 'creative class' with hip neighborhoods, an arts scene and a gay-friendly atmosphere—or they'll go the way of Detroit."[1] The occasion was an interview with Richard Florida, whose book, *The Rise of the Creative Class, And How it's Transforming Work, Leisure, Community and Everyday Life* was already on the way to becoming both an international bestseller and a public-policy phenomenon. The book's thesis—that urban fortunes increasingly turn on the capacity to attract, retain, and even pamper a mobile class of "creatives," whose aggregate efforts have become the primary drivers of economic development—has proved to be a hugely seductive one for civic leaders around the world. As Shea explains, "civic leaders are seizing on the argument that they need to compete not with plain old tax breaks and redevelopment schemes, but on the playing fields of what Florida calls 'the three T's [of] Technology, Talent, and Tolerance.'"[2] According to this increasingly-pervasive urban-development script, the dawn of a "new kind of capitalism based on human creativity" calls for funky forms of supply-side intervention, since cities now find themselves in a high-stakes "war for talent," one that can only be won by developing the kind of "people climates" valued by creatives—urban environments that are open, diverse, dynamic, and cool.[3]

Hailed in many quarters as a cool-cities guru, assailed in others as new-economy huckster, Florida has made real waves in the brackish backwaters of urban economic-development policy. As the Manhattan Institute's, Steven Malanga has observed, the "notion that cities must become trendy, happening places in order to compete in the twenty-first century economy is sweeping urban America... A generation of leftish policy-makers and urban planners is rushing to implement Florida's vision [just as] an admiring host of uncritical journalists touts it."[4] In the field of urban policy, which has hardly been cluttered with new and innovative ideas lately, creativity strategies have quickly become the policies of choice, where they license both a discursively distinctive and an ostensibly deliverable development agenda. No less significantly, though, they also work entirely with the grain of extant development agendas, framed around inter-urban competition, gentrification, middle-class consumption, and place-marketing. *The Rise of the Creative Class* has been described as "the most popular book on regional economies in the past decade,"[5] having garnered awards and acclaim from sources as varied as the *Washington Monthly, Harvard Business Review,* the Modesto *Bee,* Entrepreneur.com, *Money* magazine, the Phoenix *New Times,* and actress Cybill Sheppard. "Although the idea of a professor of regional development being a celebrity," Dreher knowingly observes, "seems like a contradiction in terms... Richard Florida is managing that feat."[6]

Somewhat implausibly, the architect of this feat claims not to have seen this coming. Apparently, some confluence of the deep currents of historical destiny and the froth of happenstance placed this particular surfer atop the wave of creativity, one who purports to be "amazed by how quickly city and regional leaders began to use my measures and indicators to shape their development strategies."[7] The critiques and attacks were also ostensibly unanticipated. Pointed, sarcastic, and in some cases plain nasty criticisms have come from the right, from conservative bastions like the Manhattan Institute and from a tawdry band of anti-immigrant and homophobic groups, who variously construct Florida's thesis as an attack on (big) business-oriented development strategies and suburban lifestyles, if not a frontal assault on "family values." Responses from the left have been more patchy but in some respects just as vigorous, ranging from skeptical screeds in the Democratic Leadership Council's *Blueprint* magazine, through snide cultural critique in *The Baffler,* to outright opposition from dissident segments of the arts community.[8] Innocent, aloof, or tactically perching on the fence, Florida maintains that:

Such heated rhetoric puzzles me; I harbor no hidden agendas. I am a political independent, fiscal conservative, social liberal, and believer in vigorous international competition and free trade. Over the course of a twenty-year academic career, I have voted for and served under Democrats and Republicans. Today, I work closely with mayors, governors, business, political, and civic leaders from both sides of the aisle on economic development issues, and a good deal of the time, I cannot even tell who is Republican and who is a Democrat.[9]

This ambiguity is echoed in the politically-ambivalent arguments contained in *The Rise of the Creative Class,* which mixes cosmopolitan elitism and pop universalism, hedonism and responsibility, cultural radicalism and economic conservatism, casual and causal inference, and social libertarianism and business realism. Florida may have inadvertently trodden on some socially conservative corns in his paeans to social tolerance and smart municipal intervention, not least at the Manhattan Institute, but the wide appeal of his message and method reveals a great deal about the soft center of neoliberal urban politics.

Florida's irreverent, informal, sometimes preachy, but always business-friendly delivery is in many ways a familiar one, echoing as it does the lifestyle guides, entrepreneurial manuals, and pop sociologies of the new-economy era.[10] As one of Florida's former teachers, Peter Marcuse, said of the book: "Well written in an almost chatty style, it reads like a series of well-crafted after-dinner speeches at various chamber of commerce dinners."[11] Recall also that the new-economy discourse of the late 1990s, epitomized by magazines like *Fast Company,* was replete with paeans to the creativity, if not artistry, of its casually-dressed entrepreneurial heroes.[12] Florida's street-level analog of such attempts to "harness" creativity comes in the form of a celebration of the buzzing, trendy neighborhood, a place where everyday innovation occurs through spontaneous interaction, a place literally "seething with the interplay of cultures and ideas; a place where outsiders can quickly become insiders."[13] For Florida, such places are the very fonts of creativity, essentially because they attract creative *people.* Ensuring that creatives are "welcomed," by extension, becomes the new task for cities. "Thus, the old mode of people moving to follow jobs is turned on its head," Baris writes, as in order to compete in the new race for talent, cities "must restructure themselves ... much as companies have already done."[14]

Even as *The Rise of the Creative Class* retreads some familiar ground, as a new-economy fairytale for the inner city, it also opens up new territory by yoking these entrepreneurial orthodoxies to a specific, and in many translations strikingly concrete, urban development agenda. The creative-cities script has found, constituted, and enrolled a widened civic audience for projects of new-age urban revitalization, anointing favored strategies and privileged actors, determining what must be done, with whom, how, and where. It is addressing, and simultaneously helping to constitute, creative growth coalitions in city after city, repacking creative development packages for these new urban actors in these new times. And the tone is appropriately declarative and direct: "I like to tell city leaders," Florida declares, "that finding ways to help support a local music scene can be just as important as investing in high-tech business and far more effective than building a downtown mall."[15] This is a script that gives urban actors significant new roles, while prodding them with talk of new competitive threats. On recent evidence, they have been extremely keen to get in on the act. A bewilderingly large number of cities have willingly entrained themselves to Florida's creative vision.

Notwithstanding the issue of the intrinsic value of Florida's insights, a more pertinent question concerns why they have struck such a chord among urban elites. Where, in other words, did the *audience* for Florida's arguments come from? Apart from his obvious promotional and presentational skills, what made him "the toast of city conferences from Toronto to Auckland"?[16] Why was the government of Singapore moved to relax its medieval laws on homosexuality, and for that matter absurd restrictions on busking and bungee-jumping, in the name of spurring talent-rich economic growth?[17] Why was the Governor of Michigan so profoundly taken by Florida's arguments that she posed in fashionable shades when launching a "Cool Cities" program across the state, in order to attract and retain those "urban pioneers and young knowledge workers who are a driving force for economic development and growth"?[18] Why did a large group of chosen ones embark on a creative pilgrimage to Memphis, TN in order to appoint themselves as "the Creative 100,"[19] issuing a *Memphis Manifesto* (see Box 5.1), and publicly committing to its principles of "helping communities realize the full potential of creative ideas"? What, in other words, motivates the disciples of new-found cult of urban creativity?

Creative juices

Florida's argument is that we have entered an age of creativity, comprehended as a new and distinctive phase of capitalist development, in which the driving forces of economic development are not simply technological and organizational, but *human*. His is a celebratory account of a *new*, new economy, in which human creativity has become the "defining feature of economic life . . . [It] has come to be valued—and systems have evolved to encourage and harness it—because new technologies, new industries, new wealth and all other good economic things flow from it."[20] Creative types have always been critical to capitalist growth, of course, but in the past few decades, so the argument here goes, they have grown both in number and influence, such that they now account for some 38 million US workers (or about 30 percent of the workforce), and therefore justify proper-noun status—"the Creative Class has become the dominant class in society."[21] This discovery having been made, the challenge is to understand what makes the members of this class tick, how they like to spend their money and their (precious) time, what they *want*. As the source, apparently, of all good economic things, the Creative Class must be nurtured and nourished,

---

Box 5.1. THE MEMPHIS MANIFESTO

The Creative 100 are dedicated to helping communities realize the full potential of creative ideas by encouraging these principles:

1. Cultivate and reward creativity. Everyone is part of the value chain of creativity. Creativity can happen at anytime, anywhere, and it's happening in your community right now. Pay attention.
2. Invest in the creative ecosystem [including] arts and culture, nightlife, the music scene, restaurants, artists and designers, innovators, entrepreneurs, affordable spaces, lively neighborhoods, spirituality, education, density, public spaces and third places.
3. Embrace diversity. It gives birth to creativity, innovation and positive economic impact. People of different backgrounds and experiences contribute a diversity of ideas, expressions, talents and perspectives that enrich communities. This is how ideas flourish and build vital communities.
4. Nurture the creatives. Support the connectors. Collaborate to compete in a new way and get everyone in the game.
5. Value risk-taking. Convert a "no" climate into a "yes" climate. Invest in opportunity-making, not just problem-solving. Tap into the creative talent, technology and energy for your community. Challenge conventional wisdom.
6. Be authentic. Identify the value you add and focus on those assets where you can be unique. Dare to be different, not simply the look-alike of another community. Resist monoculture and homogeneity. Every community can be the right community.
7. Invest in and build on quality of place . . . This will make communities more competitive than ever . . .
8. Remove barriers to creativity, such as mediocrity, intolerance, disconnectedness, sprawl, poverty, bad schools, exclusivity, and social and environmental degradation.
9. Take responsibility for change in your community. Improvise. Make things happen. Development is a "do it yourself" enterprise.
10. Ensure that every person, especially children, has the right to creativity . . .

We accept the responsibility to be the stewards of creativity in our communities. We understand the ideas and principles in this document may be adapted to reflect our community's unique needs and assets.

Source: <http://www.norcrossga.net/user_files/The%20Memphis%20Manifesto.pdf>.

---

its talents must be harnessed and channeled. This means adopting an entirely new analytical and political mindset. The old categories of class analysis are manifestly inadequate to this task, because in what Florida calls this "post-scarcity, post-material" stage of capitalism, the ownership and control of property in the physical, bricks-and-mortar sense no longer matters, since the only property with any salience is the new überclass's "creative capacity [which] is an intangible because it is literally in their heads."[22] Such is the radical nature of this challenge to extant systems of social and economic order, which Florida equates to the transition from feudalism to factory capitalism, the rules of the game have forever changed:

Economic shifts are . . . altering the structure of everyday life. The rise and decline of the New Economy did not cause these changes, though it did help push them to the surface and make them more noticeable. In a deeper and more pervasive way, the September 11, 2001, tragedy and subsequent terrorist threats have caused Americans, *particularly those in the Creative Class,* to ask sobering questions about what really matters in our lives. What we are witnessing in America and across the world extends far beyond high-tech industry or any so-called New Economy: It is the emergence of a new society and a new culture—indeed a whole new way of life. It is these shifts that will prove to be the most enduring developments of our time. And they thrust hard questions upon us. For now that forces have been unleashed that allow us to pursue our desires, the question for each of us becomes: *What do we really want?*[23]

If the dot.com crash exposed the lie that technology alone would secure the economic future, 9/11 sent the Creative Class on a search for its Calling.

It is this shared awakening of an incipient Creative-Class consciousness that Florida sets out both to chronicle and to enable, typically adopting a second-person mode of communication, while weaving often-excruciating details of his own biography, lifestyle, and consumption habits into a new-age narrative of individual freedom, economic destiny, and slowly-dawning social responsibility. By implication, the choices made by Florida and his Creative Class, which right down to the selection of kitchen utensils and hair styles, are minutely documented in the book, are validated because they are being made by the Chosen Ones. And play and consumption really matter here because creatives confront the unique challenge of fitting these in around their demanding work schedules,[24] squeezing in a quick bike ride or latte at the art gallery before logging on for the second shift. While many members of this class are understandably absorbed in the tasks of nurturing their own creativity through work and play, Florida informs his fellow creatives that they "need to see that their economic function makes them the natural—indeed the only possible—leaders of twenty-first century society... [W]e must harness all of our intelligence, our energy and most important our awareness. The task of building a truly creative society is not a game of solitaire. This game, we play as a team."[25]

Glimpses of the kind of society the creatives might build are to be found, we learn, in the distinctive locational decision-making of the talented, the revealed preferences of whom are quite unambiguous. The Creative Class seek out tolerant, diverse, and open communities, rich in the kind of amenities that allow them precariously to maintain a work–life balance, together with experiential intensity, in the context of those demanding work schedules. Uniquely suffering from a relentless "time warp," creatives gravitate towards "plug and play" communities, where social entry barriers are low, where heterogeneity is actively embraced, where loose ties prevail, where there are lots of other creatives to mingle with, where they can work hard and "validate their identities."[26]

One of the primary indicators of these diagnostically-critical conditions—of openness and tolerance—is the conspicuous presence of gays and lesbians, characterized here as the "canaries of the creative economy," due to the way in which they signal a "diverse, progressive environment," thereby serving as "harbingers of redevelopment and gentrification in distressed urban neighborhoods."[27] Should these avant-garde economic indicators somehow be overlooked, more concrete clues—which have not been lost on urban planners and consultants—include "authentic" historical buildings, converted lofts, walkable streets, plenty of coffee shops, art and live-music spaces, "organic and indigenous street culture," and a range of other typical features of gentrifying, mixed-use, inner-urban neighborhoods. Creatives want edgy cities, not edge cities. They contemptuously reject suburbia, the "generica" of chain stores and malls, and places that are oriented to children or churches. Indeed, many of the mundane and time-consuming tasks of social reproduction are also spurned by creatives, among whom "marriage is often deferred and divorce more common"; they prefer more spontaneous associations in localized "mating markets."[28] Meanwhile, the "absence of a support spouse crunches time" even further, inducing yet greater reliance on a wide range of local services and "amenities."[29] *Homo creativus* is an atomized subject with a preference for intense but shallow and noncommittal relationships, mostly played out in the sphere of consumption and on the street.

Celebratory descriptions of the work, play, and consumption habits of the Creative Class are occasionally punctuated by finger-wagging over the negative externalities of these forms of free-market self-actualization. At various points, Florida concedes that the crowding of creatives into gentrifying neighborhoods might generate inflationary housing-market pressures, that not only run the risk of eroding the diversity that the new overclass craves but, worse still, could smother the fragile ecology of creativity itself. He reminds his readers that they depend on an army of service workers trapped in "low-end jobs that pay poorly because they are not creative jobs," while pointing soberly to the fact that the most creative places tend also to exhibit the most extensive forms of socioeconomic inequality.[30] Ultimately, though, since it is the creatives' destiny to inherit the earth, it is they who must figure out how to solve these problems, in their own time and in their own way, as part of what Florida characterizes as their "growing up." The uncreative population, one assumes, should merely watch and wait (and maybe learn). Certainly, there is no space here for their institutions, or for "obsolete" forms of politics, like unions and class-aligned political parties—all of which are breezily dismissed; what matters is the capacity of the Creative Class *internally* to generate "new forms of civic involvement appropriate to our times," based on a "shared vision" of universal and humanistic creativity.[31]

Biscotti and circuses

Cities loom significantly in Florida's account of the Creative Class, as settings for the most salient of (new) social processes, as the germinal sites of new cultural and economic imperatives, and as reconstituted places of culturally-inflected political agency. His argument goes that all three T's—technology, talent, and tolerance—are necessary to ignite the economic sparks of creativity. Technological capacity is a prerequisite, but on its own is manifestly insufficient—just look, we are told, at the bleak social landscapes of the suburban nerdistans. Flows of talented individuals, the second T, are essential and necessary, since this restless-but-critical factor of production has become the carrier of creativity. But the third T, tolerance, is the crucial magnet, the supply-side foundation upon which creative clusters are built. Florida's principal method is to rank cities according to multiple direct and stand-in measures of these phenomena, both in isolation and combination—a transparently calculated but also highly effective means of popularizing the creative cities thesis. Urban regions are ranked on everything from the number of patents per head to the density of bohemians and gays, on their respective shares of immigrants, credentialed knowledge-workers, and even "fit versus fat" residents, the endlessly manipulated combinatorial outcome of which is the "Creativity Index." The declared winners in the big-city race are San Francisco, followed by Austin, TX, Boston, and San Diego; atop the midsize cities category is Albuquerque, NM, Albany, NY, and Tucson, AZ; and at the next level down in the new urban hierarchy comes Madison, WI, Des Moines, IA, and Santa Barbara. "Nothing," Paul Maliszewski observes, "can quite guarantee a book national media attention, reviews in local newspapers, and a shot at becoming a best seller than a list like this, declaring authoritatively that some stuff is better than other stuff, but only one is best of all."[32] The received and, one might say, fairly obvious appeal of cities like Seattle and San Francisco is translated into a new kind of currency in Florida's rankings. Rather than plodding through a complex causal argument, the mobilization and manipulation of extant urban images functions here to great effect. Positive urban images are crudely quantified, then recast as objects of deference—as places to be emulated. As Florida explained to *Money* magazine, "what makes a place hot" is, well, being hot:

As a paid consultant, Florida often suggests that cities should look to successful role modes like Austin or Seattle at the same time that they nurture their own unique qualities... [Florida believes] that buzz and energy are very real factors in a city's popularity.[33]

Almost at a stroke, a new dimension of urban competition was constituted by Florida's league tables and the relentless marketing of his supporting thesis. They allow some city leaders to congratulate themselves on a job well done, even if this had been achieved subconsciously, while the rest all have something, or somewhere, to aim at. Playing to this newly-constituted gallery, Florida confidently asserts that *any* big city, with the right political will, "can turn it around," and most of the other urban centers at least have a shot, if they possess the essentials—like a good university, some "authentic" neighborhoods, a handful of high-tech employers. In fact, there are very few entirely "hopeless places," like Enid, OK and Youngstown, OH, which languish as technologically-backward and tragically-unhip locations at the very bottom of the league table, where it is not even worth the effort, because these are "small places with huge working-class backgrounds, or places that are service-class centers that aren't tourist destinations."[34] These are, in other words, the wrong kinds of places.

Outside Youngstown and Enid, most cities do have hope, at least once they have recognized the significance of the creativity imperative. These aspirant cities are Florida's audience, and his market. And a large number have been ready, willing, and able to join the new market for hipsterization strategies. Those cities seeking a more finely-grained analysis of their creative health may purchase (off-the-shelf or custom) consultancy products from Florida's own consulting company, Catalytix, or from a now-countless number of emulators.[35] Another option is to book Florida, today one of the world's best-known "economic-development troubadours," for a speaking engagement, at a price tag well into the five-figure range.[36] This provides an opportunity for the mayor and other civic leaders to appear on platforms, usually in appropriately bohemian locations, with local creative entrepreneurs and arts activists. And typically there will be several hundred in the audience, including the local press, and as many people with purple hair as gray. Florida attends scores of such events every year, in major (and not so major) cities all around the world.

In a fashion that recalls the way in which a few "turnaround" entrepreneurial cities, like Cleveland and Baltimore, were celebrated during the 1980s for pioneering property-led and partnership-facilitated downtown revitalization,[37] a new set of extant and aspirant creative cities has quickly risen to prominence on the back of the work of Florida and his followers. Cities like San Francisco and Austin are continuously invoked, and are subject to instrumental practices of "case study," since these are the places that define the new urban genre. Typical of such emulative efforts was the response of Memphis, TN. Spurred into action by its near-bottom location on the Creativity Index, the chamber of commerce and several local-government agencies commissioned a study of the city's image among "young urban knowledge workers," benchmarking themselves against "high-performing" creative cities, and dissecting Austin's experience in order to identify "hopeful signs of what happens when a city actively fosters creativity."[38] Similarly, Portland, OR has also been promoted as a "compelling case study" of urban creativity, the replication-friendly lessons for other cities including: identifying creative leaders; building new systems of communication within the local community; enabling artists and other creatives to build sweat equity in emerging creative neighborhoods; promoting the adaptive reuse of buildings; supporting festivals and other street-level events; and, above all, being "authentic."[39]

But rhetorically and practically more important, in many ways, are the earnest efforts of creative strivers, since these experiences suggestively place the goal of creative transformation within reach, even for "ordinary" places. They also help materialize the creativity script in the domain of everyday urban policy. So, Providence, RI, for example, is (perhaps prematurely) celebrated for "emerging as one of the nation's and the world's leading Creative Hubs," apparently on the basis of the city's "commitment to a creativity-driven economic development strategy," the efficacy of which will surely be reflected in "move[ment] steadily upward in the rankings."[40] Notwithstanding the presentational benefits of splicing contemporary art and culture to economic-development efforts, the awkward question is what is meaningfully deliverable from a public-policy standpoint. Investments in the "soft infrastructure" of the arts and culture are easy to make, and need not be especially costly, so the creativity script easily translates into certain forms of municipal action. Whether or not this will stimulate creative economic growth, however, is quite another matter.

This may not be the biggest challenge for Providence, however, since its weakest T is perhaps the most expensive one: "Technology is frankly the region's weakspot,"[41] the evidence of which is to be found in its sorry, bottom-half position in the national "Tech-pole" league table. While Florida's consulting group, Catalytix, has talked up the "strong local universities," these are apparently not strong enough when it comes to Florida's own measures like the rate of registration of patents, while mere "proximity to the Cambridge-Boston intelligence complex" sounds like a point-stretching attempt to ride someone else's creative coat-tails. However, there remains important work for Providence's dons to do, in their unrealized role as agents of gentrification—creating "a whole new model of university-community redevelopment," universities can play a leading role in the "adaptive reuse of older urban facilities, renovating the downtown core and surrounding areas as a seamless work-live-learn-play environment."[42] This initiative is embedded within a strategic framework for the city, which combines creative exhortation with the prioritization of a series of "doable" projects. In addition to plucking some low fruit—like using creativity as a keyword in marketing and promotion campaigns, establishing new offices of cultural affairs and (creative) economic development in City Hall, and fixing up the bike paths—Providence also pledges, in a much more bold but unspecified way, to "grow the biomedical industry."

Now, while such strategies may have some limitations, certainly if measured against Schumpeterian-cum-Kontratievian rates of technological productivity and economic growth, the delivery of most of their modest supply-side components is at least feasible within the parameters of local electoral horizons and fiscal constraints. They also have an apple-pie quality, which has the dual effect of generating a certain degree of warm-and-fuzzy support, while disarming local opposition. This said, there is often a rather large credibility gap between the means and ends of creativity strategies. Consider Michigan's Cool Cities program, which seeks to reverse the state's "alarming" negative balance of trade in young "knowledge workers" on the basis of an "economic development strategy that puts 'creative people' first."[43] Governor Granholm, despite having recently enacted the largest spending cuts in state history—"twisting the wet towel of government tight, to wring out ounce after ounce of inefficiency" (including limiting cell-phone usage and out-of-state travel, turning off lights and canceling subscriptions)—was nevertheless able to eke out funds for the Cool Cities program, a central component of the state's strategy for economic and social revitalization:

Michigan's greatest economic successes have always been tied to the creative and productive power of our cities. From the Furniture City to the Motor City to the Cereal City—the fates of our industries and cities have been intertwined from their beginnings. [W]e will grow... by spurring strong regional economies anchored by cool cities... [T]his is a bottom-up movement in which nearly 80 of our communities have local commissions on cool that are uncorking the bottle of creativity and unleashing the genie of possibility—planning everything from bike paths to bookstores to attract more people and new businesses. I applaud the creativity and enthusiasm of these cities from Calumet to Kalamazoo from Saginaw to Saugatuck.[44]

The mechanism for achieving this feat is a series of $100,000 "catalyst" grants (awarded to cities that have demonstrated some measure of faith by establishing a Local Cool Cities Advisory Group), to be spent along with funds from the state's "Resource Toolbox"—a package of 113 preexisting funding measures, modestly retasked around cool-cities goals. These grants are expected to achieve measurable results within one year in neighborhoods that are—*already,* to an identifiable extent—"vibrant, mixed-use [and] happening."[45] Neighborhoods that are not experiencing at least early-stage creative gentrification, in other words, need not apply. A more concrete sense of what it takes to meet the criterion of "neighborhoods with potential" is provided by the following indicative list of characteristics, the specification of which implies the targeting of public resources not to socioeconomic need, but to creative *potential*:

- Mixed-income housing opportunities
- Pedestrian-friendly environment
- Commercial retail (basic goods and services, as well as entertainment venues)
- Champion neighborhood/organizing mechanisms ...
- Higher density
- Clean/cared for public and private space
- Food venue options (restaurants, grocery stores, etc.)
- Historic districts ...

- Recreation opportunities/parks
- Arts—galleries, shops, venues
- Accessibility

Eligible activities within the Cool Cities program include rehabilitation or new construction of buildings (specifically, theaters, galleries, mixed-use housing), physical infrastructure development, farmers' markets, streetscaping and public art, façade improvements, outdoor recreation facilities, green space, parks, pavilions, and demolition ("where viable historic resources are not damaged"). Even though the creative-cities thesis rests precariously on a series of illusive "intangibles—excitement, attitude, open-mindedness, buzz,"[46] its translation into urban-development development practice, in states like Michigan, entails both literal and metaphorical forms of concretization.

In Michigan, the creative awakening was an abrupt one. Within a few weeks of the Cool Cities program announcement, some 129 communities across that state had been mobilized for action, and just a few weeks later 20 had developed full proposals for funding, nearly all of which are unimaginatively parroted from the State Government's guidelines. Most proposed mixed-used, pedestrian-friendly initiatives, leveraging public and private resources to revalorize historic districts through the construction of lofts, bike paths, river walks, and other street-level cultural amenities. In their specifics, each of these proposals recycles a rather narrow repertoire of newly-legitimized regeneration strategies. The recurrent themes are unmistakable, and they are already on the way to being routinized. With apologies for repetition, for this is really the point: The City of Saugatuck proposed to convert a dilapidated pie factory into an arts center; Flint's Uptown Reinvestment Corporation sought assistance in converting an historic bank building into a sixteen-unit loft development; turning a parking lot into an ice-rink and performance space was the priority project for the City of Marquette; Detroit Jefferson East Business Association called on the State to subsidize desirable business clients—in the technology and entertainment sectors—for a mixed-use complex containing twenty-eight lofts, a TV studio, an ice cream parlor, "an upscale bar, an art gallery . . . and a coffee shop that will double as a music production and education café"; a heritage river walk was the centerpiece of the proposal from the City of Alpena; Grand Rapids proposed streetscaping and public art installations around a thirty-five-unit loft complex; the City of Ypsilanti sought help to make its historic downtown neighborhood "more intriguing," ostensibly by turning a vacant office building into a retail gallery and overflow space for the nearby Riverside Arts Center; the City of Warren, along with General Motors Corporation, sought help with the construction of a new city square, part of a $75 million downtown plan, which also includes ninety-six new-build brownstones and a few public facilities in order to "provide an environment necessary to help businesses like GM attract the most talented young professionals [to its Warren Technical Center]"; and in practically the only proposal that did not tout its pedestrian-friendliness, the Southwest Detroit Business Association sought subsidies for the renovation of an historic building to house a "Neighborhood that built the car" cultural-tourism center.[47]

While such bricks-and-mortar methods have become increasingly commonplace in the competitive race to attract talented workers, other cities have focused on "softer" strategies to build and sustain their communities of talent. CreativeTampaBay—the compressed text is apparently now necessary for all such organizations—was established in the wake of Richard Florida's visit to the city in 2003, boasting four signatories of the Memphis Manifesto. Like many such organizations, its energies are focused on cultural events, social activities, and information-sharing, including "regular discussion salons and cultural encounters." And in another widely-emulated strategy, the city's cultural pioneers like to recharge their creative batteries by getting together regularly for early-evening walks. The Creative TampaBay web site mixes yuppie futurology with an undercurrent of urban entrepreneurialism—so alongside the universalizing statements to the effect that "[c]reativity resides in everyone, everywhere," and that "building a community of ideas means empowering all people with the ability to express and use the genius of their own creativity," come sobering revelations that "a demographic wave is sweeping across our nation."[48] This will be "a decisive force in shaping the economic destiny of Tampa Bay [because as] cities move increasingly into a knowledge-based economy, the kind of talented people each attracts will determine whether it wins or loses in the campaign for future prosperity." The spur for action in this case is the yet-more-sobering fact that Tampa Bay has been on the losing side of the inter-urban war for talent—the area being ranked almost bottom of fifty metro regions in terms of its attractiveness to the "young and restless" population of 25–34-year-olds.[49] The formation of CreativeTampaBay, which rushed to host the first creative cities "summit" in September, 2004, represents a response to this newly-appreciated strategic deficit. While describing itself as a "grassroots organization," CreativeTampaBay also has the backing of a number of local institutions, including Greater Tampa Chamber of Commerce, Tampa Bay Partnership, the Pinellas and Hillsborough Arts

Councils, Tampa Downtown Partnership, Tampa Bay Technology Forum, and the Florida High Tech Corridor.

The region's civic leaders have begun to focus on the vexing question of how to reproduce a "San Francisco or Austin or Boston on Florida's gulf coast [albeit] with a uniquely Tampa Bay flavor."[50] However, the consultants hired to probe the hopes and desires of the young and restless reported that Tampa Bay has a long way to go to realize this goal. Genuflecting before focus groups of young creatives, and earnestly reporting their lifestyle preferences as indicators of some new cultural reality, has become modus operandi for this form of creative consultancy. So, the faltering public-school system is not simply a social and public-policy problem in its own right, but worse still, it is producing an insufficient supply of "equally educated partners" for the rising class. The city's creative leaders were also informed that the radio stations must be improved and that the nightlife-deficient downtown just "sucks." Potential remedies were, however, conveniently at hand in the form of a "Toolkit for Cities," which is illustrative of the kind of new consultancy products that are being developed to serve the new market for (ostensibly authentic and home-grown) creativity strategies. It included the conduct of "exit interviews" with fleeing creatives; initiatives to celebrate young entrepreneurs and civic contributors; and efforts to promote young-adult lifestyles—without fear that this might "scare off the soccer moms."[51]

For his part, Florida also emphasizes that "an environment attractive to young people *must* be part of the mix" for contemporary cities.[52] In some cases, following this advice has led cities to endorse targeted promotional campaigns as a substitute for, or low-cost complement to, orthodox urban-regeneration policies. Another Florida-inspired, though also ostensibly "grassroots" group, Cincinnati Tomorrow, has produced a strategy that focuses almost exclusively on redefining the city's battered image, proposing that marketing brochures should hitherto feature fewer "cityscape photos" and more "shots of busy streets in the urban core." It is advisable, moreover, that neighborhoods should have "more pronounced identities," in order that the "creative class can better find the area that best suits their needs," the less-than-creative Creative City Plan suggesting that marketing consultants be brought in to help with this pressing task, while a new web site will help employers and realtors "locate new residents that fit the broad 'creative class' profile."[53] As public and private agencies are mobilized around these goals—which the Mayor was prepared to endorse, if for no other reason than "Our image sucks"—they are also reminded of the "demanding" nature of the creatives' lifestyle requirements: "Creative class members are looking for experiences, not commitments. Their busy schedules and tangential approach to life constrain them from joining organizations or taking on new responsibilities. Instead, they seek out activities . . . where they can make quick, temporary, and stringless attachments."[54] This insight is presented next to an image of a group of well-dressed young women, drinking.

While Florida has voiced concerns about how "some cities have oversimplified his ideas,"[55] at the same time, he lambastes those places that "just don't get it," since these cities are clearly "trapped by their past," suffering as they do from a form of "institutional sclerosis" that blinds them to the emergence of new social and economic norms, norms that he finds dazzling. The city that defines this negative condition, for Florida, is Pittsburgh: "Trapped in the culture of a bygone era, it has great difficulty opening up the social space in which members of the Creative Class can validate their identities."[56] As if to prove his own theory, Florida left Pittsburgh, his home for seventeen years, in 2004, taking time before his departure to inform the local newspaper, the *Tribune-Review,* that the city needed to get rid of both its Mayor and its "1950s country club" culture.[57]

Florida recount

The Rise of the Creative Class found a policy audience, as well as a popular one, in part because it was able to show "cities how to operate within the new paradigm," taking the form of a "smart, energetic 'how to' manual, loaded with supporting statistics and examples."[58] The foundation for this policy advocacy is a sweeping theoretical assertion. "With little in the way of academic studies or literature to guide me," Florida reports, he street-tested his homegrown theory in interviews and focus groups, later turning to regression analyses for verification, before confidently concluding that "regional economic growth is driven by the locational choices of creative people—the holders of creative capital—who prefer places that are diverse, tolerant and open to new ideas." The basis of this argument, that urban growth is a function of a privileged set of supply-side, human-capital attributes, has some support in the orthodox urban economics literature.[59] What is distinctive in Florida's thesis is the more specific claim that bohemian places function as "talent magnets," and the urban-policy prescriptions that are derived from this assertion.

Harvard's Edward Glaeser, while conceding the point that human capital (broadly defined) has become a principal determinant of urban fortunes, risked an alliterative brawl by insisting that the fundamental forces at work were not Florida's three T's but, instead, the three S's of "skills, sun, and sprawl": Most creative people "like what most well-off people like," Glaeser insists, "big suburban lots with easy commutes by automobile and safe streets and good schools and low taxes."[60] Running his own regressions against Florida's data, Glaeser concludes that human-capital endowments basically explain US urban population growth in the 1990s, with little or no evidence of an independent "Bohemian effect." In the service of a much more critical, conservative critique of Florida's thesis, the Manhattan Institute's Steven Malanga contends that the best-performing cities, on measures like employment and population growth, or the rate of formation of high-growth companies, are not creative capitals like San Francisco or New York, but low-tax, business-friendly cities like Las Vegas and Memphis, ostensibly the "creative losers."[61] Demonstrating, if nothing else, the ease with which urban league tables can be manipulated, Malanga mischievously suggests that Florida constructed his measures in such a way as to elevate a predetermined set of favored liberal-leaning cities, linked to the 1990s technology boom. In a classic circular fashion, certain conspicuous features of these cities are then ascribed causal significance as foundations of economic creativity. But the arguments are scrambled. Street-level cultural innovation and conspicuous consumption may just as easily be consequences of economic growth, rather than causes of it. And loose correlations between economic development and certain cultural traits may be no more than contingent, or easily challenged by counterfactual cases. This is the Las Vegas critique: high growth, lousy culture, *how come?* For their part, conservative critics like Malanga will use such arguments, but rather than taking issue with the eccentric economics, they seem more offended by the liberal cultural politics and exhortations to urban intervention that they see all over the Florida thesis:

Yes, you can create needed revenue-generating jobs without having to take the unpalatable measures—shrinking government and cutting taxes—that appeal to old-economy businessmen [sic], the kind with starched shirts and lodge pins in their lapels. You can bypass all that and go straight to the new economy, where the future is happening now. You can draw in Mr. Florida's creative-class capitalists—ponytails, jeans, rock music and all—by liberal, big-government means: diversity celebrations, "progressive" social legislation and government spending on cultural amenities. Put another way, Mr. Florida's ideas are breathing new life into an old argument: that taxes, incentives and business-friendly policies are less important in attracting jobs than social legislation and government-provided amenities...Not only does he believe that marginal attractions like an idiosyncratic arts scene can build economic power, but he thinks that government officials and policy makers like himself can figure out how to produce those things artificially...Concerned with inessentials, cities under Mr. Florida's thrall can easily overlook what residents really want.[62]

Writing in the New Democrats' *Blueprint* magazine, Kotkin and Siegel also took issue with both the analysis and the policy prescription in what they dismissively characterize as a "creativity craze."[63] Like Malanga, they contend that in the aftermath of the dot.com bubble, growth has been shifting to "less fashionable but more livable locales" like Riverside, CA and Rockland County, NY. Such "family-values" places are the locus points for a still-suburbanizing economy, Kotkin argues, dominated as they are with far-from-trendy characteristics like "single-family homes, churches, satellite dishes, and malls," all of which are held to add up to the kind of "cultures attractive to ordinary families."[64] The deliberately marked contrast here is to Florida's favored population of "homosexuals, sophistos, and trendoids." After all, if the geography of economic growth does not align with the spatial distribution of this population, then the basis of Florida's argument—which rests on correlation rather than causality—is undermined.

Florida's oeuvre has also attracted criticism for its neglect of issues of intra-urban inequality and working poverty. A swelling contingent economy of under-laborers may, in fact, be a necessary side-effect of the creatives' lust for self-validation, 24/7 engagement, and designer coffee. *The Rise of the Creative Class* both glorifies and naturalizes the contracted-out, "free-agent" economy, discursively validating the liberties it generates, and the lifestyles it facilitates, for the favored class of creatives. Baris observes that the "overall tone [of the book] is unequivocally celebratory," the possibility that there might be serious downsides to unrestrained workforce and lifestyle flexibilization strategies warranting no more than a passing—if moralizing—mention.[65] Florida is inclined to revel in the juvenile freedoms of the idealized no-collar workplaces in this flexibilizing economy, while paying practically no attention to the divisions of labor within which such employment practices are embedded. There is little regard for those who are on the thin end of Florida's "thick labor markets," beyond the forlorn hope that, one day, they too might be lifted—presumably by acts of sheer creative will—into the new overclass. There is certainly no role for unions or large-scale government programs, creativity-stifling institutions that these are held to be, since Florida's vision of a creative meritocracy is essentially a libertarian one.[66]

Rather evasively, the creativity credo holds that *everyone* is—at least potentially—creative, that "[t]apping and stoking the creative furnace inside every human being is the great challenge of our time."[67] If only a way could be found, Florida muses, to pull the two-thirds of society currently stranded in "deadening" jobs within the working and service classes into the creative economy, then all might share the fruits of the creative Eden. Leaving unanswered, then, the nagging question of who will launder the underwear in this creative paradise, Florida exhorts his fellow creatives to show others the (bike) path—indeed portraying this as a moral duty. Ultimately, however, the solution seems to be that the working and service classes need to find a way to pull themselves up by their creative bootstraps. So while all people are creative, some are evidently more creative than others, and there are some, still, that simply "don't get it."

The Creative Class, in other words, are the drivers, the rest are merely passengers; the Creative Class generates growth, the rest live off the spoils. In his interview with *Salon*, Florida insists that his "supercreative core" of scientists, artists, and techies "is really the driving force in economic growth," just as it has become evident that "[w]hat drives a city...are good places to live, great neighborhoods, great cafes, night life, places to have fun"; and then comes the moral imperative:

We have to take responsibility for the society we're driving. If not, the social and political consequences are dire. The creative class has to look beyond itself and offer members of society a vision in which all can participate and benefit from [sic]. That's the challenge of our age.[68]

Such resort to driving metaphors not only sends strong signals about who is in the driving seat and the direction of the traffic, it also implies causality. So, growth derives from creativity and therefore it is creatives that make growth; growth can only occur if the creatives come, and the creatives will only come if they get what they want; what the creatives want is tolerance and openness, and if they find it, they will come; and if they come, growth will follow. The causal mechanisms themselves, however, are not specified. Instead, Florida's arguments are largely fashioned on the basis of a handful of suggestive correlations, for example between gays and technology-intensive growth, whereas in the text, "the arguments for [the] connection" between various stand-in measures of cultural openness and "the actual processes of regional economic development are virtually nonexistent."[69]

Florida has responded to his critics in a number of ways. Some he has dismissed as "squelchers [who] divert human creative energy by posing road blocks and saying 'no' to new ideas," offering offhanded, evasive, and selective responses.[70] When challenged on his rankings, Florida has responded by effortlessly requantifying urban economic performance in various ways, thereby restoring the chosen creative cities to the top positions. The clear implication from Florida's responses to the "squelchers" is that his critics on the right are afflicted by tunnel vision, tinged with social nostalgia, while those on the left seek to restore a lost era, their affliction being economic nostalgia: "if social conservatives can't turn back the moral clock to a time when every family resembled the Cleavers, neither can the left magically restore a time when forty or fifty percent of the workforce toiled in blue-collar factory jobs," the get-with-the-program conclusion being that, "The creative economy is not going away."[71]

If you look at the critics of my work, look at where they come from, they come from the socially conservative right and they come from the far left...I can show you two quotes, one coming from the Democratic Leadership Council's *Blueprint* magazine and the other coming from the (conservative Manhattan Institute's) *City Journal*. Both critiques are political. And both critiques are essentially saying, "Don't let the genie out of the bottle. Don't let these creative people get their way. Let's control, control, control. Let's squelch."

The task of "building a...prosperous, creative society," Florida implausibly counters, is a "nonpartisan, nonideological issue."[72]

As for the argument that creativity and inequality may be mutually dependent, Florida increasingly portrays such negative externalities as a pressing analytical, political, and indeed moral challenge for the Creative Class, not least since his own subsequent researches have confirmed the connection between creativity and polarization.[73] Having recognized that the creative haves actually rely upon, as well as preferring occasionally to mingle with, the creative have-nots, and that this "massive functional division of human labor produces the bulk of our income divide [and also] threatens our national competitiveness,"[74] Florida is left with little, however, but a series of "open questions." Having lauded the creative overclass for its achievements, having accounted for its privileged position as the consequence of intrinsic talent, and having made the case for increased public subsidy for this elite group, Florida's own arguments reduce the uncreative two-thirds to an afterthought, defined largely in terms of creative deficits. While some members of this majority underclass appear in Florida's account—usually waiting tables or cutting hair—most are absent. In terms of economic growth and development, those who are not dependent on the Creative Class seem to be little more than deadweight. But if only in response to the looming threat of "social unrest,"[75] or to realize this untapped reservoir of potential creativity, *something* must be done.

The problem is that the Creative Class, having become a uniquely restless factor of production, motivated by extrinsic rewards and the "pursuit of happiness," is apparently sorting itself into like-minded enclaves,[76] with little concern for the wider social consequences, maybe little concern for wider society. Entrenched inequality in the creative capitals tends to blur, in Florida's idealized stories, into a soft-focus recognition of urban "diversity." If the pop sociologies of the Creative Class are to be trusted, then openness to cultural diversity may indeed be more of a lifestyle choice than a political trait, which might explain why it can coexist with apparent indifference to social inequality. Creatives, fellow traveler Charles Shaw writes, seem to have little interest in public-sector jobs, neither are they "big on Solidarity"; they "don't care much for news or politics, and hold a special contempt for things that they are not directly involved in."[77] Asking creatives to pay higher taxes is bound to be a "tough sell," Florida warns, because "[h]igh-end creative workers, who often send their kids to private or elite public schools, may have to be persuaded to pay higher taxes for educating children other than their own."[78] The challenge is to persuade this group of precocious individualists that they should become less self-absorbed and self-oriented, though the main lever that Florida and his followers have is moral exhortation. This may fall on deaf ears, however. As Shaw observes, the politics of the Creative Class stem from their self-image as an unruly tribe of independent consultants—"the *elan vital* of the Creative Class is 'take me as I am and facilitate the use of my unique skills, but don't expect me to buy into some corporate culture that requires me to change who I am.'"[79]

Earnest attempts to graft social inclusion and antipoverty objectives onto the basic creative-cities script—which have been evident in the Canadian and British debates, for example,[80] pay insufficient attention to the script's predication on, and infusion with, the realpolitik of neoliberal urbanism, premised on market allocations and unequal outcomes. This is the terrain out of which the creativity thesis emerged, of course. The less-than-creative underclasses have only bit parts in this script. Their role is secondary and contingent, in economic terms, to the driving and determinant acts of creativity. Their needs and aspirations are implicitly portrayed as wrong-headed and anachronistic; their only salvation being to become more creative. And the libertarian politics that envelops the creativity thesis in as far as it concerns itself with the underclasses at all—for the most part, these are portrayed as servants of the Creative Class, or the stranded inhabitants of "hopeless" cities—peddles only voluntaristic and usually moralizing solutions. This, in effect, is a recipe for creative (market) distribution, not social redistribution, one that is entirely compatible with a low-tax, competitive polity. For example, pre-crash Dublin was praised for offering "tax breaks to culturally creative people," like the members of U2, Liam Neeson, and Andrew Lloyd Webber.[81]

Skeptical of big government solutions, Florida instead advocates a form of creative trickle down, with the lumpen classes of non-creatives eventually coming around to that which the overclass has already figured out, that "there is no corporation or other large institution that will take care of us— that we are truly on our own."[82] This is familiar neoliberal snake-oil. Insecurity as the new freedom: "we simply accept it as the way things are and go about our busy lives."[83] Once contingent workers and the laboring poor come fully to share this revelation, throwing off their entitlement mindset, then they too may be able to join the Creative Class. Florida concedes that while a "living wage is still essential," what the poor really want is not so much a "chance to get rich," but an opportunity to "reap intrinsic rewards from [their] work," just like the creatives.[84] As he explains of his politics:

Where I share common ground with some Republicans and libertarians, is that I think that old-style government programs have become a huge impediment to leveraging the creative age and allowing it to emerge. That said, I think there is still a role for government to set up the parameters in which market-based actions take place ... If you asked me what the problems of our current structure are, I'd say it is oriented toward large-scale political institutions and large companies when it should be oriented to entrepreneurial efforts, small firms and to people's energy. We have to move away from large-scale government programs to community-oriented efforts.[85]

While Florida implores his fellow creatives to "grow up,"[86] his critics bristle at how the discourse of creativity simply sidesteps many of the concerns of grown-up politics, intractable challenges, and distributional questions. From the right, Malanga characterizes this form of liberal hedonism as "the equivalent of an eat-all-you-want-and-still-lose-weight-diet," which evades what he sees as the most pressing imperative of cutting taxes and downsizing government.[87] Addressing an audience of New Democrats, Kotkin and Siegel reveal where the center of gravity has moved in the American political conversation when they complain that the Memphis Manifesto is "an urban strategy for a frictionless universe [with] no mention of government or politics or interest groups [and] no recognition of the problems produced by outmoded regulations, runaway public spending, or high taxes."[88] Yet this neoliberalized urban environment provides the constitutive context for Florida's performance. His plea is really for a new kind of urban *liberalism*, framed in this restructured context, and some of the reactions to his work say as much about this context as they do about the thesis itself.

Florida's understandable skepticism about the value of old-school urban-economic development techniques—based on business subsidies, convention centers, sports stadia, and shopping malls—has produced a conservative cultural recoil in the form of a rejection of his brand of hipster elitism: affordable and safe suburban lives, his critics respond, is what the middle classes *really* want.[89] And Florida's relatively modest proposals for fostering creative ecosystems—things like small-scale arts subsidies, support for grassroots cultural activities; communitarian creativity strategies, if you like—are derided by fiscal conservatives of the center-left as well as the right. On the right, they are hysterically portrayed as a "kind of aggressive, government-directed economic development (albeit with a New Age spin)."[90] In the broad political center, where Florida has been accused of offering the false promise of an easy way around those urban roadblocks that ostensibly *really* deter business—"schools that fail to improve, despite continuous infusions of money; contentious zoning and regulatory policies; and politically hyperactive public-sector unions and hectoring interest groups that make investment in cities something most entrepreneurs studiously avoid."[91]

(Over)reactions like these allow Florida to position himself outside the neoliberal mainstream and above the political fray, but they belie the fact that the creative credo is barely disruptive of neoliberal models of development. Self-described as fiscally conservative and socially liberal, Florida's proposals ultimately amount to a plea for grassroots agency with a communitarian conscience amongst a privileged class of creatives, lubricated by modest public-sector support for culturally-appropriate forms of gentrification and consumption. There is no challenge to the extant "order" of market-oriented flexibility; indeed, this environment is presented as the natural habitat of the Creative Class. Florida is not asking for a blank check for new government programs, for major concessions to be made to the non-creative underclasses, nor even for regulatory transformation. His calls for creative empowerment can be met in relatively painless ways—by manipulating street-level façades, while gently lubricating the gentrification processes. This, critics justly complain, is cappuccino urban politics, with plenty of froth.

In this sense, Florida's ideas may have traveled so far, not because they are revolutionary, but because they are so modest. Kotkin and Siegel recognize this in a curious way when they state that, "mayors, city councils, and urban development officials seem ready to embrace any notion of reform that holds out hope without offending entrenched constituencies that resist real reform."[92] While Kotkin and Siegel's version of "entrenched constituencies" evidently does not extend far beyond public-sector unions, big bureaucracies, and social-advocacy groups, the shared enemies of most neoliberals and many third-wayers, the rather more deeply entrenched constituencies of the business community and mainstream city politicians are, in practice, no less positively inclined towards this low-cost, market-friendly urban placebo. Surely, Florida's notions would not be "sweeping urban America" if they fundamentally ran counter to these latter interests?[93] In truth, establishment constituencies have little to fear from conspicuous urban consumption, key-worker attraction strategies, and gentrification-with-public-art. For the average mayor, there are few downsides to making the city safe for the Creative Class—a creativity strategy can quite easily be bolted on to business-as-usual urban-development policies, at relatively little cost. The reality is that city leaders are embracing creativity strategies not as *alternatives* to extant market-, consumption-, and property-led development strategies, but as low-cost, feel-good *complements* to them. Creativity plans do not disrupt these established approaches to urban entrepreneurialism and consumption-oriented place promotion, they *extend* them. Florida perhaps implicitly concedes as much when pointing out, in response to what he continues to portray as axe-grinding attacks from critics, that he works with "civic leaders from both sides of the aisle on economic development issues," disarmingly observing that "[w]hatever pundits might say about our findings, business and civic leadership in city after city has taken them to heart."[94]

Fast urban policy

Two decades ago, David Harvey called attention the rise of "entrepreneurial" urban strategies, pointing to emergent features of the city-political terrain that have since been, to all intents and purposes, normalized.[95] Describing the responses of deindustrializing cities in the 1980s, where the accelerating retreat of the Fordist economy was compounded by diminished urban fiscal capacity and a political turn against redistributive spending and social programming, Harvey portrayed the rise of interurban competition as a disciplining and coercive force. Confronted by an extremely limited repertoire of politically-feasible options, cities threw themselves into a series of zero-sum competitions for mobile public and private investments, thereby inadvertently facilitating (indeed subsidizing) the very forms of capital circulation and revenue competition that were major sources of the problem in the first place. In this climate of beggar-thy-neighbor competition, cities turned to a restrictive suite of supply-side and promotional strategies, which were serially reproduced and emulated in the scramble for mobile investment, jobs, and discretionary spending. None of this, of course, increased the aggregate amount of available investment, though it certainly contributed to its increasing rate of circulation.

Recall, though, that the 1980s imperative was not only to attract jobs and mobile corporations, both of which were in short supply, but to reposition cities within the spatial division of *consumption*. "Above all," Harvey explained, "the city has to appear as an innovative, exciting, creative and safe place to live or visit, to play and consume in," as festivals, spectacle and display, cultural events, and the arts were increasingly appropriated as "symbols of [a] dynamic community."[96] Symptoms of this intensification of urban competition included the overproduction of certain urban forms, resulting in their simultaneous devaluation and—hamster-wheel style—even more aggressive, anxious, and ultimately futile competitive behavior. In terms of the built form of cities, these moves were associated with the abandonment of comprehensive planning in favor of the selective and piecemeal development of "urban fragments," particularly those with some kind of market potential, usually with the aid of gentrification and image makeovers. Harvey observed that:

[The] urban terrain is opened for display, fashion, and the "presentation of self" in a surrounding of spectacle and play. If everyone, from punks to rap artists to the "yuppies" and the haute bourgeoisie can participate in the production of an urban image through their production of social space, then all can at least feel some sense of belonging to that place.[97]

From these inauspicious origins, it is but a short hop to one of Florida's creative epicenters, where members of the Creative Class today indulge their "passionate quest for experience" and expressive consumption amid the throb of "indigenous street-level culture—a teeming blend of cafes, sidewalk musicians, and small galleries and bistros, where it is hard to draw the line between participant and observer, or between creativity and its creators."[98] This is not simply a matter of learning to live with gentrifying cities, not even merely to accommodate the process; it is to go several steps further, in asserting the ostensibly *productive* nature of creative gentrification.

The ethos of the Creative Age is an anti-entitlement one; it is about nurturing and rewarding creativity, not compensating the creative have-nots. The hard news for civic leaders is that while they can, and must, do whatever is in their power to cultivate creativity, there is no way of knowing where the creative sparks will ignite. As Florida counsels, "We cannot know in advance who the next Andy Warhol, Billie Holiday, Paul Allen, or Jimi Hendrix will be, or where he or she will come from";[99] yet it would appear to be a racing certainty that these as-yet unborn super-creatives will want to live in Austin, TX, or somewhere very much like it. And they will likely ride into town by mountain bike. The duty of civic leaders, in the meantime, is to make sure that a network of bike paths connects the funky neighborhoods and authentic entertainment districts, so that the creatives will feel "welcomed." This is another variant of the Papua New Guinean cargo cults, in which airstrips were laid out in the jungle in the forlorn hope of luring a passing aircraft to earth.

The creative cargo cults of today are consequently little more than retreads of some very familiar local strategies. These facilitate and extend "third generation" forms of gentrification, in which the (local) state, as Neil Smith puts it, assumes an increasingly active role in "[r]etaking the city for the middle classes."[100] Discourses of creative competition, moreover, serve to enroll cities in more far-reaching forms of cultural commodification and artistically-inflected place promotion, targeted at a new audience. Pioneers of some of the early rounds of urban entrepreneurialism, like Baltimore, quickly discovered that the allure of "innovations" like waterfront redevelopment schemes and tourist-retail complexes can quickly fade.[101] The leapfrogging logic of these investments meant that cities could never stand still, but always had to be on the lookout for the next big thing. No surprise, then, that we should find the City of Baltimore unveiling its own strategy for the Florida Age, rather-less-than-creatively entitled *Creative Baltimore*. Here, where civic leaders joke that they "should be so lucky to have [the] problem" of gentrification,[102] the scope for actually delivering on creativity-led urban regeneration may be limited, but the costs of trying are not especially high. The city's plan involves the creative retasking of a long list of existing programs, complemented with a rather shorter set of "new ideas," including, in addition to the mandatory bike paths . . . establishing a mentoring scheme for creative wannabes; extending licensing hours to 4 a.m.; ridding Howard Park of its drug dealers and vagrants, so that it might be made safe for dog-walkers; creating a street performers program; converting unused industrial buildings to art studios and live–work spaces; setting up a city-wide music festival and arts parade; memorializing creative locals like Frank Zappa and Billie Holiday; initiating a duckpin bowling tournament, in which City Hall insiders take on challengers from the business and cultural communities; welcoming newcomers to the city with a "fun networking event," including three minutes face time with the mayor; promoting offbeat and eccentric events that are unique to Baltimore, including the American Dime Museum, John Waters and Edgar Allan Poe, and the Night of 100 Elvises; developing "stick around stipends" for creatively-inclined college students; and overcoming residual "squeamishness," which apparently stretches to "covert bigotry" in some quarters, around the idea of a strategy for attracting gays—about which "Florida makes no bones" in his advice to city leaders.[103]

Creativity strategies, even as they have promptly become clichés in their own right, are in many ways tragically appropriate for late-entrepreneurial cities like Baltimore, the cities that have already tried practically everything, including of course building stadiums and offering corporate inducements. Today, hopes are pinned on such hackneyed forms of culturally-inflected economic development. But rather than "civilizing" urban-economic development by "bringing in culture," creativity strategies achieve the opposite: they commodify the arts and cultural resources, even social tolerance itself, suturing them as putative economic assets to evolving regimes of urban competition. They enlist to this redoubled competitive effort some of the few remaining pools of untapped resources; they enroll previously-marginalized actors for this effort, enabling the formation of creative growth coalitions; they constitute new objects of governance and new stakes in inter-urban competition; and they enable the script of urban competitiveness to be performed—quite literally—in novel and often eye-catching ways. And they do all of this within the framework of an inherited complex of new urban "realities," that variously contextualize, channel, and constrain "creative" urban politics—including the material and social artifacts of gentrification, as a definitionally-uneven process of financial and symbolic valorization; a proclivity for "soft," pliable and task-oriented modes of urban governance, organized around short-term, concrete projects (like funding competitions or development schemes), rather than progressive and programmatic goals (such as poverty alleviation or environmental sustainability); and a substantially neoliberalized urban policy environment, within which a range of competitive and market-oriented metrics, techniques, and rule regimes are displacing urban-Keynesian systems, like comprehensive planning, bureaucratic delivery, needs-based approaches, and progressive sociospatial redistribution. In the short run at least, the discursively-privileged actors on this stage and not the (distracted and self-absorbed) members of the Creative Class itself, since these are the ones who must be *catered to,* but those "regional leaders" with the vision and the will to adopt "aggressive measures."[104]

Creative-city strategies are predicated on, and designed for, this neoliberalized terrain. They repackage urban cultural artifacts as competitive assets, valuing them (literally) not for their own sake, but in terms of their (supposed) economic utility. They presume and work with gentrification, conceived as a positive urban process, while making a virtue of selective and variable outcomes, unique neighborhood by unique neighborhood. And with almost breathtaking circularity, it is now being proposed that these gentrification-friendly strategies should be evaluated, not according to old-school metrics like job creation or poverty alleviation, but according to more relevant measures like...increased house prices! So Robert Sirota, an advocate of the *Creative Baltimore* plan, enthuses that many of the city's newly-constructed downtown housing units "are leasing for higher than anticipated rents to what we might call Creative Class types,"[105] while Florida himself muses that there may be a need to develop alternative measures of economic growth, like "house prices [since these] indicate how the market views the 'attractiveness' of various places—the real *demand* for place, if you will."[106] As if this were not circular enough, it is increasingly common for cities to evaluate the effectiveness of their creativity strategies according to their shifting position in Florida's league tables.[107]

Both the script and the nascent practices of urban creativity are peculiarly well-suited to entrepreneurialized and neoliberalized urban landscapes. They provide a means to intensify and publicly subsidize urban consumption systems for a circulating class of gentrifiers, whose *lack* of commitment to place and whose weak community ties is perversely celebrated. In an echo of the Creative Class's reportedly urgent need to "validate" their identities and lifestyles, this amounts to a process of public validation for favored forms of consumption and for a privileged class of consumers. In fact, indulging selective forms of elite consumption and social interaction is elevated to the status of a public-policy objective in the creative-cities script. "The challenge before us," Cincinnati Tomorrow ludicrously intones, "is to help young creatives develop ties with each other and connect with the events, places, and experiences they crave."[108]

Moreover, and no less significantly, the notion of creative cities extends to the urban domain the principles and practices of creative, flexible autonomy that were so powerfully articulated in the libertarian business ideologies of the 1990s,[109] for all the knowing distinctions that creativity advocates ritually draw with their new-economy forebears. As Lehmann notes, "the core values that Florida charts as the key to the 'creative ethos'— individuality, meritocracy, diversity, and openness—are all by now slogans of first resort for the same corporate economy that [he] claims is being displaced by high-tech innovators in no-collar workplaces and edgy neighborhoods."[110] Discourses of urban creativity seek to normalize flexible labor-market conditions, lionizing a class of workers that can not only cope with, but positively revel in, this privatized environment of persistent insecurity and intense, atomized competition, just as they enforce modes of creative governmentality based on "compulsory individualism, compulsory 'innovation,' compulsory performativity and productiveness, compulsory valorization of the putatively new."[111] This is achieved, in part, by the suggestive mobilization of creativity as a distinctly positive, nebulous-yet-attractive, apple-pie like phenomenon: like its stepcousin flexibility, creativity preemptively disarms critics and opponents, whose resistance implicitly mobilizes creativity's antonymic others—rigidity, philistinism, narrow mindedness, intolerance, insensitivity, conservativism, *not getting it.*

The urban creativity script also enables a subtle reworking of the scalar politics of the post-Keynesian era. Reflecting on the way in which Florida's work is being *read* by city leaders, it would seem that there is a predisposition to accept the most controversial steps in his thesis—that creativity is the root cause of growth and this is borne by a mobile class of elite workers—in order to jump to the chase on the question of how to lure the creatives to town. The cities that grow will be those with cool people in them, and cool people will only go to cool cities. But "what makes a city cool?" Michigan Governor Granholm rhetorically asks, "We understood that the best place to look for the answer to this question was at the local level."[112] Uncool cities, it seems, have no-one to blame but themselves, while creative places stand to be rewarded both with economic growth and targeted public spending. Thus, the creativity script works seamlessly with the new urban realpolitik, neoliberal-style. Apparently operating on the presumption of a distant, dysfunctional, largely irrelevant, if not terminally hollowed-out national state, creativity discourses privilege the local and bodily scales as the loci both of determinate processes and meaningful social action: creativity resides in mobile individuals, and the interventions that make a difference are focused on neighborhood ecosystems. Florida insists that creative "environments cannot be planned from above,"[113] just as he endows cities with significant degrees of agency: So Austin was not merely fortunate or well placed, according to Florida's account, its civic leaders "really hustled," reportedly declaring that, "We're going to make Austin really unique."[114] Meanwhile, the problem with "institutionally sclerotic" cities that have not participated in the creativity explosion, like Detroit and Pittsburgh, is that they still "just don't get it," or worse still, "they don't want to change."[115] In this respect, the creative-cities script is a mobilizing discourse: it spells out the nature of the challenge and the necessity for action, framed as an historic *imperative*; then it outlines a simple urban formula for creative turnaround, sternly warning that civic leaders had better take heed, or else. And increasingly, the threat is a global one:

[A] new global order will not pit Boston against Austin for jobs, but Boston against Dublin. "I believe the U.S. has the most amazing transformative capacity," [Florida] says, "and also that we're still the leading country. But those places are beginning to become more open. They are beginning to see that our strength in the U.S. has not been our market size, nor our own intrinsic genius, but that we've been open. We've always been the place that has attracted the tired, hungry and incredibly energetic. And I think these other countries are increasingly pursuing that."[116]

The insidious "scalar narrative" of creativity has it that the bodies—or perhaps more accurately, the souls—of creative individuals have become the preeminent carriers of economic-development potential, so the pursuit of economic growth becomes neatly synonymous with the publicly-funded seduction of the Creative Class.[117] This is a uniquely mobile factor of production, a supply-side counterpart to the footloose corporation, whose locational reach is wide and therefore whose locational preferences *must* be accommodated. If the business-oriented strategies of yore involved building industrial parks and subsidizing corporate activities, this new variant of the supply-side catechism has it that creatives will only come to cities that buzz. A premium is therefore placed on the capacity of cities to make their authentic, funky neighborhoods welcoming to monied incomers, whose inherent precociousness must be rewarded with additional gifts from the public purse, like bike paths and street-level entertainment. Florida does not pull his punches when advising city leaders: "[Y]ou need to have [these amenities] because if you don't have them, then people won't come to your city," since the question that creatives are asking, itinerant hedonists that they are, is, "What kind of location offers me the full bundle of lifestyle choices with the diversity of amenities and options that I desire?"[118]

Discursively subjected, in this way, to the soft discipline of creative-capital mobility, cities must quickly figure out how to act. Fortunately, help is on hand, since there is now a well-publicized and purposefully-circulated repertoire of strategies that (may) work. The suggested package of policy interventions has been stylized and refined to the point that the diagnosis can be readily complemented with what amounts to a manual of recommended procedures. Florida's has been but the most conspicuous contribution to this burgeoning business of "manualizing" local creativity strategies. The snake oil cannot be guaranteed, of course, because the finicky creatives may decide to stay on in Austin. But the allure of Dr. Florida's prescription has been sufficient to secure robust domestic sales, and a growing international market. The sobering evidence of this lies in the sheer number of cities that have willingly entrained themselves to his course of treatment, not to mention the unmistakable zeal of its many converts. Particularly high doses of the urban-creativity medicine must be administered if the patient has been suffering from (institutional) sclerosis, or if earlier courses of (entrepreneurial) treatment have failed. Even so, some (probably delusional) patients in rustbelt regions may develop the feeling that they have been slipped another placebo. In a rare moment of reflection, Florida has pondered whether he may have "inadvertently glorified" some creative urban strategies, which may not even be sustainable in their places of origin.[119]

The contemporary cult of urban creativity has a clear genealogical history, stretching back at least as far as the entrepreneurial efforts of deindustrialized cities. The script of urban creativity reworks and augments the old methods and arguments of urban entrepreneurialism in politically-seductive ways. The emphasis on the mobilization of new regimes of local governance around the aggressive pursuit of growth-focused development agendas is a recurring theme.[120] The tonic of urban creativity is a remixed version of this cocktail: just pop the same basic ingredients into your new-urbanist blender, add a slug of Schumpeter lite for some new-economy fizz, and finish it off with a pink twist.

The flavor, though, is a distinctive one. Cities, and urban policies, remain substantially constituted by an ideologically-amplified deference to "external" competitive forces and threats, though the struggle to replace working-class jobs is partially superseded by a nouveau-bourgeois war for talent. The indiscriminate pursuit of growth is superseded by a new emphasis on rewarding, good-quality jobs, though these are reserved for the new overclass of interloping creatives. The competitively-induced overbuilding of malls and convention centers morphs into the creatively-impelled overbuilding of bike paths and artistic venues (as if this could grow the aggregate supply of creativity), the inevitable consequence of which must surely be devaluation, no doubt followed by yet more rounds of leapfrogging creative innovation. The subordination of social-welfare concerns to economic development imperatives (first, secure economic growth, then wait for the wider social benefits to percolate down) gives way to a form of creative trickle down; elite-focused creativity strategies leave only supporting roles for the two-thirds of the population languishing in the working and service classes, who get nothing apart from occasional tickets to the circus. A new generation of entrepreneurializing subjects is formed, as the disciplines of creative productionism are extended to every aspect of self and soul, to the spheres of consumption and play, as well as to those of work, while the circumstances of those outside the favored class are rationalized according to a deficit model of creativity. And the strategic emphasis shifts from a narrow focus on the sphere of production to a deeper engagement with the marketizing and commodifying spheres of consumption and reproduction, positions within which become the primary markers of distinction in the creative city.

Finally, there is a question of speed. The extraordinary rate of adoption of urban creativity strategies can in some respects be explained in terms of the enduring legacies of entrepreneurial urbanism. The rapid diffusion and ultimate exhaustion of entrepreneurial-city strategies established a massive potential market for their creatively-inflected successors, together with an elaborate infrastructure for cross-jurisdictional policy transfer.[121] *The Rise of the Creative Class,* as a knowingly-constructed "mutable mobile," entered this hypertrophied sphere of circulation at a velocity that revealed less about its intrinsic qualities than it said about, firstly, the profound policy vacuum that characterized the neoliberalized urban realm, and secondly, the now-extensive circuitry of the fast-policy regime that has been constructed around cities. Whatever else it may be, Florida's creative-city thesis is perfectly framed for this competitive landscape, across which it has traveled at alarming speed. Agents and artifacts of fast-policy circulation help realize this process, though in themselves they surely cannot constitute the *demand* for creative fixes. The market for creative policy products is propelled by the endless pursuit of creative urban *advantage,* the (generally negative) distributional consequences of which are variously denied, obfuscated, or finessed out of existence in the creativity script and its routinized practices. The creative-cities discourse is both saturated in, and superficially oblivious to, the prevailing market ideology, such that the mere suggestion that creative advantage presupposes creative disadvantage, that there must be losers in the Creative Age, borders on the "heretical."[122] In the face of the self-evident myth that every person and every place can be a creative winner, the creativity script represents a culturally-inflected re-inscription of these competitive relations. As Florida presents the new competitive imperatives,

In the creative economy, regional advantage comes to places that can quickly mobilize the talent, resources, and capabilities required to turn innovations into new business ideas and commercial products ... [T]he nexus of competitive advantage shifts to those regions that can generate, retain, and attract the best talent. This is particularly true because creative workers are extremely mobile and the distribution of talent is highly skewed.[123]

So packaged, creativity strategies were in a sense preconstituted for this fast policy market.[124] They empower, though only precariously, unstable networks of elite actors, whose strategies represent aspirant attempts to realize in concrete form the seductive "traveling truths" of the creativity script; they give license to ostensibly portable technocratic routines and replicable policy practices that are easily disembedded and deterritorialized from their centers of production—at least in a shallow, essentialized form—for all the talk of local "authenticity"; they reconstitute urban-elitist, "leadership" models of city governance, despite their ritual invocation of grassroots efforts; they foster experimental and mutually referential policy development processes, framed within the tight parameters of urban fiscal capacity, and manifest in the form of the serial reproduction of an increasingly clichéd repertoire of favored policy interventions, the value of which is eroded in the very act of their (over)construction; they legitimate new urban development models and messages, which travel with great speed through interlocal policy networks, facilitated by a sprawling complex of conferences, web sites, consultants and advocates, academic camp followers, policy intermediaries and centers of technocratic translation, the combined function of which is to establish new venues and lubricate new channels for rapid "policy learning"; and they discursively and institutionally select subnational scales, highlighting, in particular, gentrifying urban neighborhoods as the preeminent sites for both privileged forms of creative action and necessary modes of political proaction, the places that *can and must* act. As such, creativity strategies subtly canalize and constrain urban-political agency, even as their material payoffs remain extraordinarily elusive. The cult of urban creativity is therefore revealed in its true colors, as a form of soft law/lore for a hypercompetitive age.

Notes

1. Dreher, C. (2002) Be creative—or die, *Salon* June 6, accessed at <http://www.salon.com>.
2. Shea, C. (2004) The road to riches? *Boston Globe,* February 29: D1.
3. Florida, R. (2003) The new American dream, *Washington Monthly,* March: 27.
4. Malanga (2004: 36).
5. Glaeser, E. L. (2005) Review of Richard Florida's *The Rise of the Creative Class, Regional Science and Urban Economics,* 35/5: 593.
6. Dreher, C. (2002) Be creative—or die, *Salon* June 6, accessed at <http://www.salon.com>.
7. Florida (2002: x).
8. See MacGillis, A. (2010) The ruse of the creative class, *American Prospect,* January 4: 12–16.
9. Florida, R. (2004) Revenge of the squelchers, *Next American City,* 5: ii.
10. See, especially, Frank (2000) and Maliszewski (2004).
11. Marcuse, P. (2003) Review of *The Rise of the Creative Class* by Richard Florida, *Urban Land,* 62: 40.
12. See Frank (2000); Thrift, N. J. (2001) "It's the romance, not the finance, that makes the business worth pursuing": disclosing a new market culture, *Economy and Society,* 30/4: 412–432.
13. Florida (2002: 227).
14. Baris, M. (2003) Review: Richard Florida: *The Rise of the Creative Class: And how it's transforming work, leisure, community, and everyday life, The Next American City,* 1: 42.
15. Florida (2002: 229).
16. Steigerwald, B. (2004) Q&A: Florida sees a "different role" for government, *Pittsburgh Tribune-Review* April 11, accessed at <http://www.pittsburghlive.com>.
17. *Economist* (2004) The son rises, *Economist,* July 24: 39–40.
18. Michigan, Department of Labor and Economic Growth (2004) *Cool Cities.* Lansing, MI: State of Michigan, 1.
19. Creative 100 (2003) *The Memphis Manifesto.* Memphis Tomorrow and Mpact, Memphis, TN, 2.
20. Florida (2002: 21).
21. Florida (2002: ix).
22. Florida (2002: 68).
23. Florida (2002: 12, emphasis added).
24. "Creative Class people literally live in a different kind of time from the rest of the nation." (Florida, 2002: 144).
25. Florida (2002: 315, 326).
26. Florida (2002: 304).
27. Florida, R. and G. Gates (2005) Technology and tolerance. In R. Florida, *Cities and the Creative Class.* New York: Routledge, 131.

28. Florida (2002: 177); Florida, R. (2007) *Who's Your City?* New York: Basic Books.
29. Florida (2002: 151).
30. See Florida (2002: 322; 2005b).
31. Florida (2002: 316–317). Most Twentieth Century forms of progressive politics—the civil rights, women's, peace, and labor movements—are written off as relics of a defunct, preCreative era, the achievements of which apparently pale into insignificance alongside the transformative power of creativity. (Florida, 2002: 203).
32. Maliszewski (2004: 76).
33. Gertner, J. (2004) What makes a city hot, *Money,* June: 88–89.
34. Quoted in Dreher, C. (2002) Be creative—or die, *Salon* June 6, accessed at <http://www.salon.com>.
35. See Peck (2011).
36. MacGillis, A. (2010) The ruse of the creative class, *American Prospect,* January 4: 13.
37. See Hall, T. and Hubbard, P., eds. (1998) *The Entrepreneurial City.* Wiley, Chichester.
38. Memphis Talent Magnet Project and Coletta & Company (2003) *Technology, Talent, and Tolerance: Attracting the Best and Brightest to Memphis.* Memphis, TN: Coletta & Company, 8.
39. Bulick, B. *et al.* (2003) Cultural development in creative communities. *Monograph,* November, Americans for the Arts, Washington, DC.
40. Catalytix and Richard Florida Creativity Group (2003) Providence: an emerging creativity hub, *Creative Intelligence,* 1/5: 1.
41. Catalytix and Richard Florida Creativity Group (2003) Providence: an emerging creativity hub, *Creative Intelligence,* 1/5: 2.
42. Catalytix and Richard Florida Creativity Group (2003) Providence: an emerging creativity hub, *Creative Intelligence,* 1/5: 2.
43. Michigan, Office of the Governor (2003) *Michigan Cool Cities Initial Report.* Lansing, MI: State of Michigan, 3.
44. Governor Jennifer M. Granholm (2004) Our determination, our destination: a 21st Century economy, State of the state address, January 22, accessed at <http://www.michigan.gov/gov/0,1607,7-168-23442_21981-84911–,00.html>>.
45. Michigan, Department of Labor and Economic Growth (2004) *The Michigan Cool City Program Pre-bid Workshop—Questions and Answers.* Lansing, MI: Michigan Department of Labor and Economic Growth, 2.
46. Gertner, J. (2004) What makes a city hot, *Money,* June: 88.
47. Michigan Cool Cities Pilot Program, project summaries, accessed at <http://www.michigan.gov/mshda>.
48. <http://www.creativetampabay.com>.
49. Impresa and Coletta & Company (2004) *The Young and the Restless: How Tampa Bay Competes for Talent.* Portland, OR and Memphis, TN: Impresa and Coletta & Company.
50. Trigaux, R. (2003) Dr. Florida's prescription: creating a vision for cities, *St. Petersburg Times,* April 14: 1E.

51. Impresa and Coletta & Company (2004) *The Young and the Restless: How Tampa Bay Competes for Talent*. Portland, OR and Memphis, TN: Impresa and Coletta & Company, 17, 64–65.

52. Florida (2002: 294).

53. Cincinnati Tomorrow (2003) *Creative City Plan*. Cincinnati Tomorrow, Cincinnati, 8, 16.

54. Quoted in Trapp, D. (2003) A creative city. Want young professionals in Cincinnati? Lighten up! *CityBeat* 9/16: 3; Cincinnati Tomorrow (2003) *Creative City Plan*. Cincinnati Tomorrow, Cincinnati, 16.

55. National Public Radio, *Morning Edition,* September 7, 2004.

56. Florida (2002: 302–303, 305).

57. Quoted in Steigerwald, B. (2004) Q&A: Florida sees a "different role" for government, *Pittsburgh Tribune-Review* April 11, accessed at <http://www.pittsburghlive.com>.

58. Cronheim, C. C. (2004) Reviews of *Creative Destruction* by Tyler Cowen and *The Rise of the Creative Class* by Richard Florida, *Journal of Policy Analysis and Management* 23/4: 934.

59. See Glaeser, E. L. (2000) The new economics of urban and regional growth. In G. L. Clark, M. P. Feldman and M. S. Gertler, eds., *The Oxford Handbook of Economic Geography*. Oxford: Oxford University Press, 83–98.

60. Quoted in Shea, C. (2004) The road to riches? *Boston Globe,* February 29: D1; Glaeser, E. L. (2005) Review of Richard Florida's *The Rise of the Creative Class, Regional Science and Urban Economics,* 35/5: 594.

61. Malanga (2004).

62. Malanga (2004: 40, 45). To his credit, Florida has taken the argument directly to social conservatives, editorializing against the policies of the Republican Right in locations like *USA Today* and beltway publications like the *Washington Monthly* (Florida, R. (2003) Creative class war, *Washington Monthly,* January/February: 31–37; (2003) Gay-tolerant cities prosper economically, *USA Today,* April 30: A13). Though whether reactionary social policies are most effectively opposed on the grounds of their supposed economic inefficiency, rather than on human-rights or other progressive principles, remains (highly) debatable.

63. Kotkin, J. and Siegel, F. (2004: 16–18).

64. Kotkin, J. (2003) Paths to prosperity, *American Enterprise,* July/August: 34, 33.

65. Baris, M. (2003) Review: Richard Florida: *The Rise of the Creative Class, Next American City,* 1: 44.

66. See Maliszewski (2004) and Peck (2009).

67. Florida (2005a: 4–5).

68. Quoted in Dreher, C. (2002) Be creative—or die, *Salon* June 6, accessed at <http://www.salon.com>.

69. Sawicki, D. (2003) Review of *The Rise of the Creative Class* by Richard Florida, *Journal of the American Planning Association,* 69/1: 90.

70. Florida, R. (2004) Revenge of the squelchers, *Next American City*, 5: ii; Florida (2005a: 20–25).

71. Florida, R. (2004) Revenge of the squelchers, *Next American City*, 5: vi.

72. Richard Florida, quoted in Steigerwald, B. (2004) Q&A: Florida sees a "different role" for government, *Pittsburgh Tribune-Review* April 11, accessed at <http://www.pittsburghlive.com>; Florida (2005b: 245).

73. Catalytix and Richard Florida Creativity Group (2003) Inequality and the creative economy, *Creative Intelligence*, 1/6: 1–6.

74. Florida, R. (2003) The new American dream, *Washington Monthly*, March: 30.

75. Florida (2005b: 246).

76. See Bishop, B. and Florida, R. (2003) O, give me a home where the like-minded roam, *Washington Post*, March 23: B5; Bishop, B. (2008) *The Big Sort*. New York: Houghton Mifflin Harcourt.

77. Shaw, C. (2003) 40 million strong? *Newtopia Magazine*, May. <http://www.newtopiamagazine.org/issue10/features/40million.php>.

78. Florida, R. (2003) The new American dream. *Washington Monthly* March: 31.

79. Shaw, C. (2003) 40 million strong? *Newtopia Magazine*, May. <http://www.newtopiamagazine.org/issue10/features/40million.php>.

80. See Cannon, T., Nathan, M. and Westwood, A. (2003) *Welcome to the Ideolopolis*. London: The Work Foundation; Bradford, N. (2004) *Creative Cities Structured Policy Dialogue Report*. Background paper F45, Family Network. Canadian Policy Research Networks, Ottawa.

81. Florida (2002: 301).

82. Florida (2002: 115).

83. Florida (2002: 115).

84. Florida, R. (2003) The new American dream, *Washington Monthly*, March: 28–29.

85. Quoted in Steigerwald, B. (2004) Q&A: Florida sees a "different role" for government, *Pittsburgh Tribune-Review* April 11, accessed at <http://www.pittsburghlive.com>.

86. Florida (2002: 315).

87. Malanga (2004: 40).

88. Kotkin, J. and Siegel, F. (2004: 17).

89. See Kotkin (2003) and Malanga (2004).

90. Malanga (2004: 45).

91. Kotkin, J. and Siegel, F. (2004: 16).

92. Kotkin, J. and Siegel, F. (2004: 17).

93. Malanga (2004: 36). On the contagious spread of creativity policies, see Peck (2009, 2011).

94. Florida, R. (2004) Revenge of the squelchers, *Next American City*, 5: ii, v.

95. Harvey (1989).

96. Harvey (1989: 9).

97. Harvey (1989: 14).

98. Florida (2002: 166).

99. Florida (2005a: 5).

100. Smith (2002: 443).

101. See Levine, M. A. (1987) Downtown redevelopment as an urban growth strategy: a critical reappraisal of the Baltimore renaissance, *Journal of Urban Affairs,* 9/2: 103–124; Harvey (1989).

102. Tom Wilcox, President of the Baltimore Community Foundation, quoted in *Next American City* (2004) The Peabody Institute Forum. *Next American City,* 6: 21.

103. City of Baltimore, Mayor's Office of Community Investment (2004) *New Ideas for Promoting Baltimore City.* Baltimore: Mayor's Office of Community Investment.

104. Florida (2005a: 151–152).

105. Quoted in *Next American City* (2004) The Peabody Institute Forum. *Next American City,* 6: 20.

106. Florida, R. (2004) Response to Edward Glaeser's review of *The Rise of the Creative Class.* <http://www.creativeclass.com/rfcgdb/articles/ResponsetoGlaeser.pdf>, 5, original emphasis.

107. Peck (2011).

108. Cincinnati Tomorrow (2003) *Creative City Plan.* Cincinnati Tomorrow, Cincinnati, 15.

109. See Frank (2000).

110. Lehmann, C. (2003) Class acts, *Raritan* 22/4: 163–164.

111. Osborne, T. (2003) Against "creativity:" a philistine rant, *Economy and Society,* 32/4: 507.

112. Quoted in Michigan, Office of the Governor (2003) *Michigan Cool Cities Initial Report.* Lansing, MI: State of Michigan, 3.

113. Florida, R. (2004) Revenge of the squelchers, *Next American City,* 5: iii.

114. Quoted in Gertner, J. (2004) What makes a city hot, *Money,* June, 90; Dreher, C. (2002) Be creative—or die, *Salon* June 6, accessed at <http://www.salon.com>.

115. Richard Florida, quoted in Dreher, C. (2002) Be creative—or die, *Salon* June 6, accessed at <http://www.salon.com>.

116. Gertner, J. (2004) What makes a city hot, *Money,* June: 92.

117. See Peck (2002b, 2009); Swyngedouw, E. A. (1997) Neither global nor local: "glocalization" and the politics of scale. In K. Cox, ed., *Spaces of Globalization.* New York: Guilford Press, 137–166.

118. Quoted in Dreher, C. (2002) Be creative—or die, *Salon* June 6, accessed at <http://www.salon.com>.

119. Quoted in Gertner, J. (2004) What makes a city hot, *Money,* June: 90; see also MacGillis, A. (2010) The ruse of the creative class, *American Prospect,* January 4: 12–16; compare Florida, R. (2010) *The Great Reset,* Toronto: Random House.

120. See Leitner, H. (1990) Cities in pursuit of economic growth: the local state as entrepreneur, *Political Geography Quarterly,* 9/2: 146–170; Harvey (1989); and Peck (2009).

121. See Wacquant (1999); Peck (2002b, 2011).

122. Bradford, N. (2004) *Creative Cities Structured Policy Dialogue Backgrounder.* Background paper F46, Family Network. Canadian Policy Research Networks, Ottawa, 9.

123. Florida (2005a: 49–50).

124. See Peck (2002b, 2009); Peck and Theodore (2010).

6

Decoding Obamanomics

Hope and change. The election of Barack Obama coincided with, and for some epitomized, a conjunctural movement of potentially world-historical significance. An African-American president with a progressive electoral mandate and a solid congressional majority clearly offered the hope of real change, but the challenges were also practically overwhelming: two wars, a homegrown financial crisis still at the free-fall stage, and a legacy of willfully malign governmental neglect. Obama's Grant Park speech on election night duly marked the historical moment, with references to the legacies of slavery and the civil rights movement, to the New Deal and the fall of the Berlin Wall, but the understandable hysteria of the crowd was somewhat at odds with the air of somber purpose exuded by the President-elect. The moment of Obama's election would be captured in the headline "Change has come to America," the very fact of it apparently affirming that this was "a place where all things are possible," but the acceptance speech also included the caution, "The road ahead will be long. Our climb will be steep. We may not get there in one year or even one term, but...we as a people will get there."[1]

The load of responsibilities that Obama immediately assumed—through the final weeks of Bush's absentee presidency—was only matched by the weight of expectation that he also carried. Hopes for a genuinely progressive presidency, which had been sullied during the Clinton years and suppressed during the two long terms of the Bush Administration, were now being projected with unprecedented intensity onto a President-elect whose political charisma, inspirational oratory, and compelling life story many considered potentially equal to the task. No less a worldly observer than Robert Kuttner, for example, had argued that Obama was the first chief executive since Lyndon Johnson "with the potential to be a transformative progressive president." Kuttner's knowingly optimistic book,

Obama's Challenge, written in anticipation of the election victory, under-scored the fact that the challenges confronting the would-be progressive presidency were not only "external" ones. Across the Democratic Party there was an "undertow of stale thinking" which limited the scope and sapped the potential for "transformative policies." Candidate Obama, moreover, had only partly earned the progressive vote, much of it he had acquired by default. "Obama will need to be a more radical president than he was a presidential candidate," Kuttner concluded.[2]

On matters of economic policy, in particular, candidate Obama had been remarkably elusive, melding caution, calculation, and a reluctance to commit with countervailing doses of motivational rhetoric and enigmatic flair. Against the jaded theory of trickle-down economics, Obama promised an alternative, "bottom-up economics," founded on a principle central to his campaign, that of economic justice: "trade deals like NAFTA," Obama argued during the campaign, "have been signed with plenty of protections for corporations and their profits, but none for our environment or our workers."[3] In a revealing moment, in an otherwise meticulously managed election campaign, some of this talk was however shown to be duplicitous. A commitment to renegotiate the NAFTA treaty was a guaranteed applause line at blue-state campaign stops in Ohio and Michigan, but Obama's senior economic advisor, Austan Goolsbee, had privately assured Canadian consulate officials that this was merely primary politics, not policy. The leak of a consular memo to this effect caused Goolsbee, on leave from the University of Chicago, some moments of discomfort,[4] but the affair soon blew over. It was later suggested that the story was fabricated, or that misinformation had come from the Hillary Clinton campaign, but wherever the truth lies, renegotiating NAFTA is clearly not an Obama Administration policy, let alone priority.

Goolsbee would subsequently be appointed to Obama's Council of Economic Advisors. Like his University of Chicago friend, the President, Goolsbee exudes an air of post-ideological pragmatism. "It's not, here we've got a left-right divide and let's pick some spot in the middle," Goolsbee has said, "It's really more about trying to get away from that and think of some different way to view it." In an eulogy to Milton Friedman in the *New York Times*, Goolsbee had earlier explained that the Friedmanite worldview, that economics is neither "a game [nor] an academic exercise [but] a powerful tool to understand how the world works" is one that today "holds sway throughout much of the profession." By way of reciprocation, Goolsbee's Chicago colleague, Gary Becker, said of the Obama advisor during the campaign that, while he disagreed with him on some issues, he respected his work as an economist and "would be pleased to have him shaping national policy."[5]

The group of economic advisors recruited during the campaign—including Goolsbee; Robert Rubin associate and Wal-Mart defender, Jason Furman; and fellow Harvard economists and former Clinton advisors, David Cutler and Jeffrey Liebman—were generally regarded as market-friendly pragmatists of a centrist political cast, "smart and orthodox" in Robert Kuttner's words, though the *Wall Street Journal* found them, rather like Obama, difficult to pigeonhole.[6] A shrewd determination not to be classified according to existing labels may indeed have served the presidential candidate well, though by the same token it is revealing that significant differences over economic policy were a feature neither of the Democratic primaries, nor of the general election campaign. Largely bereft of new economic-policy ideas (beyond the neoliberal fixture of rolling tax cuts), senator McCain was fatally to demonstrate his detachment with the off-key remark that "the economic fundamentals are sound," delivered in the face of indisputable evidence of the deepening financial crisis.[7] Senator McCain never recovered, even as the scale of the crisis threatened to deliver votes to the candidate with "experience," rather than the neophyte Obama. So, Obama was to win the election, with his fresh message of change and renewal, even as "Obamanomics" remained more of a pundit's question than a coherent philosophy. In fact, the true nature of Obamanomics seems to have eluded critics and followers alike.

Reflecting on some of the ways in which the near-empty vessel of Obamanomics has since been filled, this chapter reconsiders the question of neoliberal hegemony in light of Obama's management of the economic crisis. It was Milton Friedman, of course, who wrote, at the beginning of Reagan's transformative presidency, that "*only* a crisis . . . produces real change,"[8] a Machiavellian injunction that Rahm Emanuel, Obama's chief of staff, is wont to reiterate.[9] But would Obamanomics successfully define and exploit the crisis, or would the crisis define and delimit the Obamanomics? Would it signal a break with those neoliberal orthodoxies that had held sway in the United States for nearly three decades, and which had been reduced to something between parody and travesty by the previous administration? Alternatively, would Obamanomics prove to be a rerun of Clintonomics, which according to Robert Pollin had "serve[d] the crucial function of defining a left boundary for the neoliberal model against which George W. Bush could retreat rightward"?[10] Obama assumed the presidency at a crossroads moment, following the overreach and effective collapse of Bush's governing ideology, the onset of a potentially game-changing global economic crisis, and with the benefit of both an open-ended mandate and a Republican rout in Congress. Having rejected the false choice "between an oppressive, government-run economy and a chaotic, unforgiving capitalism,"[11] would the new president find a new way of inhabiting the "radical center"? Would he push firmly to the left or drift to the right? Or would he end up muddling through, responding to short-term circumstances and pressures?

Making up Obamanomics

The first sightings of Obamanomics characteristically revealed as much about the onlookers as they did about the enigmatic phenomenon itself. The term may have been coined by the *Wall Street Journal* in the spring of 2007, whose early attempt to "fill in the blanks" on Obama's economic policy deduced that the Illinois senator's position, "tempered" by the experience of the Clinton years, would remain a centrist one, wary of protectionism and "class warfare."[12] A few weeks later, *The Economist* endeavored to determine who was the "real left-winger" among the Democratic candidates, positioning Obama to the left of Hillary Clinton but to the right of John Edwards. Chiding Obama for his occasional weakness for politicized economic rhetoric, this keeper of the neoliberal flame nevertheless gave the Chicagoan's team of economic advisors high marks (they "bode well for Obamanomics"), while noting that the candidate, even when playing with the fire of free-trade policy, seemed "more concerned with helping people deal with globalisation than trying to slow it down." Concluding that Obama was more of an "instinctive free-trader" than Hillary Clinton, *The Economist* stopped just short of a positive endorsement, on the grounds that it was "too early to declare Obamanomics to be sensible centrism just yet."[13] (The endorsement did, however, come later.)

Crain's Chicago Business was more suspicious, placing the local candidate firmly in the Democratic Party mainstream: "For all his rhetoric about moving beyond partisanship, [Obama's] economic policies hew closely to classic Democratic lines and differ little from those of his primary opponents," Paul Merrion argued, "Except for a few business-friendly wrinkles, he mostly caters to the party's traditional base."[14] This was also pretty much the view of Deidre McCloskey, who pigeonholed the President-elect as just another "Lakefront Liberal (as Chicagoans say)," whose administration would bring increased minimum wages, higher taxes, "and a lot of other standard-issue Democratic Party symbolic silliness in economics."[15] Her prayer that Obama would surround himself with "a bunch of Chicago School economists," however, almost came to pass, although his faculty picks would not have been exactly the same as hers.

One of these, Austan Goolsbee, had only contributed further layers of inscrutability, by portraying Obama's position as "a bit of an eclectic approach to economic policy, not an old-style liberal Democratic approach," but one distinct from the rest of the Democratic field in placing "more faith in market-based solutions and incentives than his opponents do."[16] From the left side of Chicago politics, David Moberg also pegged Obama as a centrist Democrat, albeit an idiosyncratic one, potentially open to new ideas. His "main flaw seems to be excessive caution," Moberg pointed out, noting that the general orientation of Obama's advisors suggested that, at best, "he would rely on marginal tinkering with markets and incentives to try to achieve some progressive ends, such as more equality and opportunity."[17]

At the same time, *The Economist* fretted over Obama's weakness for playing to the blue-collar gallery on the primary campaign trail, where images of a world in which "laid-off parents compete with their children for minimum-wage jobs while corporate fat-cats mis-sell dodgy mortgages and ship jobs off to Mexico," seemed to threaten a neopopulist "descent into economic miserabilism." Combing through the Chicagoan's campaign website, however, the editors found a number of "intelligently designed, reasonably centrist proposals" that were more to their tastes, especially Goolsbee's plan for simplifying the tax code ("a gem"), deciding in the end to focus their complaints more on the style than the substance:

The sad thing is that one might reasonably have expected better from Mr. Obama. He wants to improve America's international reputation yet campaigns against NAFTA. He trumpets "the audacity of hope" yet proposes more government intervention. He might have chosen to use his silver tongue to address America's problems in imaginative ways—for example, by making the case for reforming the distorting tax code. Instead, he wants to throw money at social problems and slap more taxes on the rich, and he is using his oratorical powers to prey on people's fears...Mr. Obama advertises himself as something fresh, hopeful and new. But on economic matters at least he, like Mrs. Clinton, has begun to look a rather ordinary old-style Democrat.[18]

The Economist concluded with grudging respect, however, for Obama's willingness "to approach economic questions with a keen intellect, an open mind and an aversion to radicalism," suspecting that the candidate "understands economics better than he lets on."[19]

Obama seems to have left a similar impression with David Leonhardt, economics columnist for the *New York Times*, whose in-depth interviews may have come closest to nailing down Obamanomics, if partly by a process of painstaking elimination. Leonhardt went first to putatively "environmental" influences, focusing on Obama's time in Chicago, not as a community organizer, but as a lecturer in constitutional law at the University of Chicago. Having talked to friends and colleagues, Leonhardt concluded that Obama's twelve years at the font of free-market theory had neither turned him into a doctrinaire Friedmanite, nor caused him to reject the neoliberal worldview: he had learned "to appreciate markets more," acquiring an "intellectual framework for his instincts." Obama himself seemed to confirm this analysis, but dated his appreciation for practical solutions shorn of ideological baggage to his youth, and explaining that his

core economic theory is pragmatism...figuring out what works. [My upbringing] led me to have an orientation to ask hardheaded questions. During my formative years, there was still ideological competition between a social-democratic or even socialist agenda and a free-market, Milton Friedman agenda. I think it was natural for me to ask questions of both sides and maybe try to synthesize approaches.[20]

Cass Sunstein, who often ate lunch with Obama at the Law School and who would later become the President's "regulation tsar" (after relocating to Harvard), explained to the *Wall Street Journal* that, above all, Obama is "a University of Chicago Democrat, so he's very attuned to the virtue of free markets and the risks of free-market regulation. He's not an old-style Democrat who's excited about regulations [for their own sake]."[21] Obama would, however, be interested in the kind of "positive" regulatory interventions that can otherwise incentivize, encourage, or "nudge" favored behavior, in the spirit of Sunstein's influential book on behavioral economics.[22] What is variously characterized as a neo- or post-Chicago School project, behavioral economics holds that if laissez-faire is working, then laissez-faire will do, and that smart interventions should work to shape "choice architectures," in contrast to heavy-handed regulation. Sunstein likes to point out that Obama's approach to the law is likewise "realistically based on human behavior," that as a politician he has been solutions-oriented, "someone who is independent of mind, someone who is idiosyncratic," and that as President he would surprise supporters and enemies alike: "As Nixon went to China, Obama will go to deregulation."[23]

Obama has certainly not been wary of embracing fulsomely pro-market positions, extending to positive appraisals of the Reagan legacy. In the *Audacity of Hope*, he asserted that, after the Carter administration, "the people wanted the government to change...Reagan's central insight—that the liberal welfare state had grown complacent and overly bureaucratic, with Democratic policy makers more obsessed with slicing the economic pie than with growing that pie—contained a good deal of truth."[24] As Obama told a CNBC interviewer in June, 2008: "Look, I'm a pro-growth, free-market guy; I love the market."[25] These reflect more than passing affirmations of a market commonsense, more even than some sort of Clintonesque "comfort level" with the realities of the global marketplace. At times, Obama can sound almost Hayekian in his embrace of market idealism: "The market is the best mechanism ever invented for efficiently allocating resources to maximize production," Obama told the *New York Times*, "[T]here is a connection between the freedom of the marketplace and freedom more generally."[26]

There may be echoes of Third-wayism in Obama's rhetoric and difference-splitting policy positions, but Sunstein at least insists that he is no Clintonian triangulator.[27] When David Leonhardt attempted to pin down Obama's economic philosophy, one strategy he tried involved taking the senator back to the early months of the Clinton Administration, and the struggles between the Wall Street contingent on Clinton's economic team, led by Robert Rubin, and those of a more neo-Keynesian, pro-labor persuasion, led by Robert Reich. In a now-infamous outburst, Clinton had reacted to the assertion that Wall Street interests effectively possessed a form of veto power over his economic policy, with an investment exodus and soaring interest rates likely following imprudent or interventionist moves in Washington: "You mean to tell me that the success of the [economic] program and my re-election hinges on the Federal Reserve and a bunch of fucking bond traders?"[28] The answer, according to Bob Woodward's account of these events, came in the form of silent nods; no dissent. The subsequent course of Clinton's economic policy program, as Reich's memoir recounted, reflected a near-comprehensive victory for the Rubinistas, culminating in what Bluestone and Harrison portrayed as a "Wall Street–Pennsylvania Avenue policy accord."[29] Well schooled in this history, Obama characteristically turned to both Reich and Rubin for policy advice, leading to speculation that one or both might be appointed to his cabinet. Obama reportedly explained to the two Bobs that the "world is more complicated" than the outdated caricatures of their respective positions, noting that in any case the viewpoints of the two had converged in significant respects since the early 1990s.[30] Reich now concedes that deficit reduction played an important role in securing the Clinton boom of the second half of the 1990s, while for his part, Rubin has recognized that distributional issues have since become a major concern, given the socially-unbalanced character of the boom and the regressive program subsequently pursued by Bush.

Obamanomics correspondingly blends pro-market fiscal conservatism with an ameliorative concern for the entrenched problem of inequality. As he argued in *The Audacity of Hope*, a continuation of the Bush trajectory would mean

a nation even more stratified economically and socially...one in which an increasingly prosperous knowledge class, living in exclusive enclaves, will be able to purchase whatever they want on the marketplace—private schools, private health care, private security, and private jets—while a growing number of their fellow citizens are consigned to low-paying service jobs, vulnerable to dislocation, pressed to work longer hours, depending on an underfunded, overburdened, and under-performing public sector for their health care, retirement, and their children's educations.[31]

The response to these conditions, however, tends to come in the soft-focus language of "economic justice and opportunity for all," coupled with modest redistribution through the tax code, rather than in the form of a commitment to tackle the underlying *causes* of unequal economic growth and regressive social distribution. Rolling back the Bush tax cuts for the most wealthy, coupled with modest tax breaks for the majority, represents a timid, if not simply inadequate, response to the deeply embedded problem of inequality. When pressed on the issue during the campaign, Obama's less-than-fully-persuasive response was to cite one of his economic advisors—who in this case happened also to be the world's richest man, Warren Buffett. "If you talk to Warren," Obama informed the *New York Times*, "he'll tell you his preference is not to meddle in the economy at all—let the market work, however it's going to work, and then just tax the heck out of people at the end and just redistribute it ... That way you're not impeding efficiency, and you're achieving equity on the back end."[32] Notwithstanding the political costs of "taxing the heck out" of the relatively well-off, fiddling with the tax code is unlikely to be sufficient to turn the tide of economic inequality.[33] A rhetorical emphasis on the plight of the "middle class," on the other hand, masked a rather circumscribed position on the troubles of low-waged workers.[34] While Obama eventually campaigned on a pledge to raise the minimum wage, the principles of *Obamaism*, as long-time confidant Cass Sunstein explained, suggested a rather different perspective:

Unlike most Democratic Senators, [Obama] acknowledges that large increases in the minimum wage might "discourage employers from hiring more workers," which helps explain his enthusiasm for the Earned Income Tax Credit, an anti-poverty policy with Republican roots that supplements wages but does not have disemployment effects.[35]

Instead, this resembles the kind of Third Way confection, elaborated by Clinton and Blair in the 1990s, in which the market is allowed to do its work, relatively unimpeded, complemented by modestly compensatory forms of social amelioration. Too often, elusive formulations of "equity on the back end" have proved to be empty promises, or social-liberal apologia for trickle-down.

The pattern of economic advice sought by candidate Obama and President-elect Obama unequivocally confirmed these premonitions of warmed-over centrism. The panel of advisors assembled in the summer of 2008, for example, included Warren Buffett and a like-minded group of CEOs and financiers, together with a group of Clinton-era retreads—like Lawrence Summers, Robert Rubin, Laura Tyson, and Robert Reich. With just under twenty members, however, this group included no representatives from the labor movement or from social-advocacy organizations. Following the election, with the spiraling financial crisis generating intense media scrutiny, Obama appointed his core economic team. There was no Reich, from the left flank of the previous panel of advisors, but instead the group was further tilted in favor of financial-sector interests and relatively market-friendly technocrats. The most prominent, and by all accounts senior figure was Lawrence Summers, Clinton Treasury Secretary, hardball specialist, and one of the architects of the Financial Modernization Act of 1999, which had established some of the decisive deregulatory preconditions for the crash of 2008. (As Summers explained to a reporter around the time of the 1999 legislation, while he had once railed against the "Hayek legacy," he had since come to appreciate the hidden hand of the market over the visible hand of intervention: "As for Milton Friedman, he was the devil figure in my youth. Only with time have I come to have large amounts of grudging respect. And with time, increasingly ungrudging respect."[36])

Announcing what most commentators would portray as a "market-oriented economic team," shortly after the November 2008 election, Obama underlined his determination to "do whatever is required" to stabilize the financial system.[37] In addition to Summers, the team included Timothy Geithner, president of the New York Federal Reserve, and a key figure in the negotiation of the Bush Administration's financial bailout; Peter Orszag, Rubin acolyte and healthcare spending hawk; and towards its "left" side, relatively speaking, Christina Romer, a monetary economist with neo-Keynesian sympathies, and Paul Volcker, chair of the Federal Reserve under Carter and Reagan and eponymous author of the monetarist "shock" that cured inflation in the early 1980s at the price, first, of a deep recession in the United States and, second, the Latin American debt crisis. These appointments, which triggered an approving jump in stock prices, were taken as an indication that the incoming president would pursue "aggressive, yet centrist policies" in a manner unlikely to alarm the financial markets.[38] According to one of those who conspicuously did not receive a call from the White House, Joseph Stiglitz, Obama selected this Wall Street-oriented team despite the fact that "he must have known—he certainly was advised to that effect—that it would be important to have new faces at the table who had no vested interests in the past, either in the deregulatory movement that got us into this problem or in the faltering rescues [of 2008]."[39]

The philosophical core of Obamanomics is perhaps most clearly defined by the Hamilton Project at the Brookings Institution, founded by Robert Rubin in 2006 with funding from Goldman Sachs and welcomed by the *Financial Times* for its "clear preference for market-based solutions."[40] The strategy document that launched the project, coauthored by Rubin and Orszag (the latter serving as the organization's director), called for a renewal of pragmatic centrism in economic policy, framed in the context of competitive threats:

The Hamilton Project's economic strategy reflects a judgment that long-term prosperity is best achieved by making economic growth broad-based, by enhancing individual economic security, and by embracing a role for effective government in making needed public investments. The Project's strategy . . . calls for fiscal discipline and for increased public investment in key growth-enhancing areas. The Project will put forward innovative policy ideas from leading economic thinkers throughout the United States—ideas based on experience and evidence, not ideology and doctrine [. . .] Many options for addressing the fiscal problem have been identified; the most pressing need now is not new ideas, but greater political will and a bipartisan political process [. . .] The failure to invest wisely in sound policies to promote economic growth is particularly problematic in light of the growing competition U.S. workers and firms face as the people of China, India, and other nations rapidly enter the global economy. Significant new intellectual work is needed to identify evidence- and experience-based policies to promote individual opportunity and strengthen America's economy.[41]

Obama was closely associated with the Hamilton Project from the start, commenting in a speech at its launch—where he felt at home in a room in which "most of us are strong free traders and most of us believe in markets"—how much he regretted the tendency in Washington "to cling to outdated policies and tired ideologies instead of coalescing around what actually works."[42] The Project, which would also later involve Austan Goolsbee and Jason Furman (Orszag's successor as director), was met with skepticism on the left as an initiative of "Wall Street Democrats," but maneuvered deftly in the waning years of the Bush Administration to fashion a "grand bargain" between market-friendly, fiscally-conservative Democrats and moderate Republicans. Significantly, its big tent would include Ben Bernanke (Bush's Federal Reserve chair, later reappointed by Obama), along with others concerned to consolidate a somewhat nebulous "new center" on matters of economic policy.[43]

Foreshadowing Obama's political persona, the Hamilton style sought to be "warm hearted, but cool-headed," according to Peter Orszag.[44] It similarly married shape-shifting rhetoric, with an ostensibly post-ideological commitment to experience, experimentation, evidence, and "what works." As David Brooks shrewdly observed in the *New York Times*, the "Hamilton Project [has been] churning out policy ideas that defy easy categorization [but which might] serve as a blueprint for an innovative, moderate administration"; correspondingly, the "Stalinist on-message style" of politics seemed also to have become "passé... rising young politicians like Barack Obama... never talk in that predictable party-hack way."[45] On the other hand, what has been decidedly less than nebulous about the Hamilton Project is its unwavering commitment to fiscal discipline and free trade, to market-oriented approaches, and to strategies for tackling inequality that are detached from new entitlement commitments.

Another neoliberalism?

The elusive character of Obamanomics may in fact be its defining quality. Wildly divergent interpretations of the means and ends of Obama's economic policy program are not simply a function of the partisan political climate in the United States,[46] the project itself seems to invite multiple readings, having painstakingly constructed for itself a space of ideological ambiguity. Centrist chameleons like Fareed Zakaria, editor of *Newsweek*, who can be considered broadly sympathetic to the project, see Obama-nomics as an opportunity to rejuvenate the Third Way following a damaging episode of Republican overreach. The cocktail here is based on a mixture of "pro-market, pro-trade policies aimed at promoting growth [which may] encourage government efforts in certain areas where the private sector isn't sufficient," and the result: "a new governing ideology for the West."[47] This represents a nightmare scenario for some Republican strategists, especially the few who have attempted to think beyond small-government fundamentalism and tax-cutting cure-alls. Ross Douthat and Reihan Salam—in an account that David Leonhardt found to be "one of the best summaries of [Obama's] economic policy that I have read"—had intuited, back at the beginning of Bush's second term, that a "new liberal consensus [was] taking shape."[48] A Democratic Party form of "neoliberalism," as they plainly (though perhaps somewhat innocently) named it, had been gradually shaping an alternative project, in the wake of the defeats of the 1970s and 1980s: "At their best, these neoliberals were centrists with an edge, willing to contemplate radical ideas...in the name of moderation and post-partisanship," Douthat and Salam observed. They were prepared to cut a new path,

push[ing] a liberalism that would spend more money than Carter or McGovern on the military (though not so much as Reagan); that would hold the welfare and education bureaucracies accountable (though without necessarily cutting spending); that would regard organized labor's demands for higher wages with suspicion (but without necessarily taking management's side); and that would stop coddling criminals and accept the necessity of tougher prison sentences (though not necessarily the death penalty).[49]

These positions, which would become associated with the New Democrats, with the agenda of the Democratic Leadership Council from the mid-1980s, and ultimately with the Clinton presidency, moved the party away from its traditional commitments to large-scale social programming-cum-social engineering, away from government-led redistribution, and away from tax-and-spend. In its place came a new emphasis on the aspirational values of "hard-working families" and a commitment to an "opportunity model" of social justice, based on equality of access to education, health-care, and employment. This represented, in effect, a form of supply-side social democracy, reconfigured around an ideologically ring-fenced market, in which old commitments to social rights and New Deal constituencies gradually morphed into a new embrace of individual rights and the opportunity to compete.

This realignment culminated in what Douthat and Salam characterized, from the perspective of the thinking right, as the "neoliberal moment" of the Clinton era, which was associated with a generational shift in the cultural politics of the Democratic leadership, away from the radicalism of the 1960s and early 1970s "to the half-conservative, half-libertine ideology of bourgeois bohemianism." For these sharp-eyed critics, proponents of "Sam's Club Republicanism," this revealed

the central truth of the neoliberal moment, and the Clinton administration that [the New Democrats] had created—namely, that this was very much an ideology crafted by the upper-middle class, reflecting their concerns and their prejudices in its mix of tough-on-crime posturing (they had kids now, after all!), liberal internationalism (they were a globalized elite, weren't they?), fiscal conservatism (no class warfare in the suburbs, thank you very much), and social liberalism (because the Sexual Revolution needed to be preserved).[50]

The hope in the 1990s was that "neoliberalism [could also be] something more than this," however; it was, potentially, a winning electoral formula that would inoculate the reconstituted Democrats "against conservative attacks and lure working-class voters back into the . . . fold, while [winning over] some country-club Republicans with its mix of fiscal sobriety and cultural liberalism and *also* holding the rest of the Democratic coalition (blacks, union members, feminists, and so forth) together because they had nowhere else to go."[51]

If this amounts to a canny assessment of Clinton's Third Way, viewed from the right, its preoccupation with cultural politics leaves unexamined the pact with Wall Street, which effectively shackled the project to the long-term goals of deficit reduction and fiscal restraint. Clinton may have initially bridled at the power of the unelected cabal of "fucking bond traders," but he would later establish his economic bona fides by embracing Rubinomics and balancing the budget—not to mention passing NAFTA and "reforming" welfare along the way—while making his peace with Wall Street. And although Bush was able to govern on a much looser fiscal leash (much to the dismay of deficit hawks amongst his own ranks, who also had nowhere else to go), Obama would move to preemptively pacify Wall Street, in his alignment with the Hamilton Project, well before declaring his presidential ambitions. This is a much less radical realignment than the Douthat–Salam specter of a resurgent, leftish neoliberalism, wedding "the free-market centrism of the Clinton years to a revived push for

European-style social democracy, the American Left's age-old dream." The rhetoric of Obama and other prominent Democrats may have occasionally suggested this, especially during primary campaigns, but it is surely going too far to suggest that, in practice, it would involve "vastly expanding the tax-and-spend state, with new bureaucracies, increased welfare spending, and rising public-sector employment smoothing over the anxieties of working-class life."[52]

More materialist analyses of the optics of Obama's economic-policy appointments, in contrast, tend to make more of the web of substantive connections to Wall Street. For Ismael Hossein-Zadeh, for example, this suggested continuity rather than change:

Details of Obamanomics remain to be seen when Obama arrives in the White House. There are strong indications, however, that, so far, his economic policy messages and projections fall way short of audacious or pioneering. Indeed, they seem to be designed to project policy continuity and stability, as desired by Wall Street. This is clearly reflected in the composition of his team of economic advisors who, having come from the current and previous administrations, championed most of the policies of deregulation, privatization and outsourcing that gradually led to the current market meltdown [...] Based on all the major signs and signals revealed thus far, Obamanomics portends to be an amalgam of Herbert Hoover economics, New Deal economics and Reaganomics.[53]

Change might be anticipated, Hossein-Zadeh speculated, in fields like civil liberties, environmental policy, diplomatic protocols, and race relations, but economic policy seemed much more likely to follow a well-formatted pattern. Its Hooverian face would be reflected in an extension of the bank bailouts engineered by Geithner on behalf of the Bush Administration; its New Deal face would entail some form of job-creation stimulus effort, perhaps including a major component of public works; and in its Reaganomics face, the program would be outsourced to the maximum extent possible, including the routing of funding initiatives through Wall Street institutions.

Notwithstanding the new nomenclature, the sober analysis of past "restructuring schemes," fashioned in the midst of crisis situations, revealed that their ultimate form had more to do with the configuration of immediate economic pressures and class forces than with the projection of presidential power, according to Hossein-Zadeh: "rescue plans of such troubled economies... are often shaped not so much by abstract presidential visions as they are by market or capitalist imperatives, on the one hand, and the balance of power of the conflicting socioeconomic interests on the other."[54] If this suggested a less-than-transformative presidency, at least on the crucial terrain of economic policy, then there were also those arguing against the preemptive abandonment of hope. "Never in my political lifetime," Robert Kuttner mused, "has more apprehension come bundled with more hope." Slavoj Žižek likewise acknowledged the prosaic possibility that "Obama will make only some minor improvements, turning out to be 'Bush with a human face' [in his pursuit of] the same basic policies in a more attractive way," but this would still be a terrain of political struggle, not a foregone conclusion: the real battle would begin, in this sense, after Obama's election, during which time progressive forces should not preemptively disarm themselves as "victims of cynical pragmatism."[55]

Crisis manager

Obama's inauguration, in January 2009, came at a time when few were able to predict either when the economy would bottom out, or what the bottom would look like. Characteristically, the speech soared, and with respect to economic philosophy again sought cleverly to square the post-ideological circle:

[E]verywhere we look, there is work to be done. The state of our economy calls for action: bold and swift. And we will act not only to create new jobs but to lay a new foundation for growth. We will build the roads and bridges, the electric grids and digital lines that feed our commerce and bind us together [. . .] What the cynics fail to understand is that the ground has shifted beneath them—that the stale political arguments that have consumed us for so long no longer apply. The question we ask today is not whether our government is too big or too small, but whether it works . . . Where the answer is yes, we intend to move forward. Where the answer is no, programs will end . . . Nor is the question before us whether the market is a force for good or ill. Its power to generate wealth and expand freedom is unmatched, but this crisis has reminded us that without a watchful eye, the market can spin out of control—that a nation cannot prosper long when it favors only the prosperous.[56]

Progressives took heart from the references to positive government and the need for a "watching eye" on the market. But if there were echoes of the New Deal here, they were to remain largely rhetorical. The modern echo of the "alphabet soup" of 1930s works programs would come, instead, in the form of a crop of ungainly acronyms for various "lending instruments," hastily designed by the Federal Reserve to staunch the financial hemorrhaging.[57] Paul Krugman, in an open letter to the newly-inaugurated President in *Rolling Stone*, argued that he would now have to "pull this plane out of its nose dive [himself], because the Fed has lost its mojo." This was not the time to listen to the deficit hawks, Krugman counseled, as Roosevelt had done during the "first New Deal" of 1933–1937, but to heed the lesson that FDR had learned the hard way, "to be really bold in your job-creation plans."[58]

When Obama's economic advisors had gathered, in December 2008, to draw together the Administration's strategy for managing the crisis and for steering a "postbubble" trajectory, it was Christina Romer, the specialist in depression economics, who delivered what would be known as the "holy-shit moment."[59] Even the best-case projections, Obama has since recalled, were "chilling," describing "an imminent downturn comparable in its severity to almost nothing since the 1930s," and the fiscal consequences were likewise "entirely dismal," in the words of Peter Orszag. "Having concluded that it was too late for me to request a recount," Obama joked, "I tasked my team with mapping out a plan to tackle the crisis on all fronts."[60]

Obama's stimulus package, designed to attract bipartisan support and immediately rushed through Congress, may have been bold in comparison with the Bush Administration's ham-fisted efforts, but it was hardly radical. Its largest item, at fully 37 percent of the $787 billion package, went on tax cuts, followed by state and local fiscal relief (accounting for an additional 18 percent), which in another echo of the first New Deal was negated almost immediately by even sharper spending cutbacks at those subnational scales of government. In order to broaden its bipartisan appeal, the stimulus package had been pared back in both scale and intensity (Obama's initial plan had called for over $800 billion of spending in two years; the Act provided for less than this, spread over ten years), and the balance of provisions had been dramatically altered in favor of tax cuts. In a pattern that was to be repeated, never more egregiously than in the case of the healthcare reform effort later in the year, these bipartisan overtures were spurned in any case. The American Recovery and Reinvestment Act of 2009 (ARRA) won the support of just three Republican Senators and not a single Republican member of Congress.

Most mainstream assessments concluded that the ARRA would indeed be stimulative, and that it would function in the broadly-based fashion that the Administration claimed, from school spending to green initiatives, but that it was not nearly sufficient to cope with the unprecedented scale of the economic collapse. The Congressional Budget Office estimated that the package would boost gross domestic profit (GDP) by 2.6 percent in 2009. At the time of its passage, the US economy was experiencing back-to-back quarterly losses of more than 6 percent of GDP, the most severe economic contraction recorded since the Great Depression. Christina Romer, chair of the Council of Economic Advisors, sensed that "Rooseveltian moment" might be coming on, in the weeks after the stimulus package was passed. But if such moments have been occasionally anticipated during the Obama presidency, precious few have materialized. "Acting in a Rooseveltian manner," John Cassidy countered, "involves defying orthodoxy, challenging powerful interests, and giving voice to the public's disgust at the corrupt financial establishment."[61]

And if the ARRA stimulus package was judged by most to be sub-Rooseveltian—Paul Krugman, among others, reckoned that it needed to be at least twice the size—then the accompanying bundle of timid financial reforms was positively Hooverian. Treasury Secretary Geithner has broadly maintained the softly, softly posture of the Bush Administration, moving to "stress test" the banks, but demurring from bolder steps like (temporary) nationalization, a proposal to which even Alan Greenspan warmed, after having confessed to Congress that he had "found a flaw" in the neoliberal reasoning that had guided his policies serenely into first the tech bubble and then the housing-market bubble.[62] Following massive infusions of public funds, with remarkably few strings attached, the banking system was rapidly stabilized, albeit at the cost of future moral hazards, now that the (even bigger) remaining banks had effectively been licensed as "too big to fail." Before long, Wall Street profitability was even restored, and the major banks brazenly reintroduced their bloated bonus systems, as if to demonstrate their indifference not only to public opinion but even public relations. The symbol of the Administration's policy on the banking sector was destined, for the time being at least, to remain Timothy Geithner's first prime-time press conference. Promoted by the President himself as the occasion of a significant announcement, Geithner plainly had nothing of substance to say. The pundits pounced and the stock-market slide resumed.[63] John Cassidy thought that the back-channel plan proposed by Geithner "could work," despite its unfortunate similarities with the wildly unpopular Bush–Paulson–Geithner plan that preceded it, but for the rather damning shortcomings that "it is incremental rather than definitive; it is opaque; it works with the financiers who caused the crisis; and it is based on the assumption that an economic recovery will begin [in 2010]."[64]

When Obama addressed the Business Council, an organization that had been founded as a New Deal sounding board in 1933, he invoked what he saw as a

once in a generation chance to act boldly and turn adversity into opportunity. [Faced with the Great Depression, we] adapted. We changed. We boldly defended our system of free enterprise even as we enacted policies to transform the ways that it would function. We did not give in to ideologies that dismissed or derided the role of government—nor those that denied the role of the marketplace [. . .] I'm absolutely confident that if we're smart and if we are bold, if we work together, if we're willing to cast aside some of the theories that have already failed us and we remain open to new approaches and new ideas, and we think about the problems in our economy the way you think about your business—in practical, hardheaded, clear-eyed terms unclouded by dogmas—then I'm absolutely confident that we can lead our nation through this transformative moment and come out stronger and more prosperous than ever before.[65]

The deeply pragmatic program that followed, beginning with the stimulus package and the non-reform of the financial sector, led Paul Krugman and James K. Galbraith, among others, to accuse Obama of attempting, in effect, to finesse the crisis.[66] His subsequent path would run consistently (and sometimes considerably) to the right of the position of the Economic Policy Institute, which tends to define the left flank of beltway opinion on economic policy, while only occasionally overlapping with the *Progressive Program for Economic Recovery and Financial Reconstruction*, an agenda developed by a network of progressive economists immediately following Obama's election (see Box 6.1.).

If the progressive economists' manifesto boldly promised to "close the book on the neoliberal era of macroeconomic and financial management, a set of policies and practices that has led the world to the brink of disaster,"[67] the first year of the Obama Administration can be said to have offered mixed signals at best. According to Epstein's assessment, while the new administration had "taken major steps away from the neo-liberal approach," in fields like climate change, on the critical questions of short-term bank restructuring and long-term financial-sector reform, "the Obama policy [had] utterly failed"—indeed it seemed "oddly stuck in the prior regime."[68] Odd in the sense that economic conditions clearly presented an opportunity, if not the necessity, for some kind of bold realignment, even if congressional politics had been less propitious than had been anticipated. Not only had the Democratic majorities in the House and especially the Senate been disinclined to support a radical

---

Box 6.1. PROGRESSIVE ECONOMISTS' PRINCIPLES AND GOALS FOR A PROGRAM OF ECONOMIC RECOVERY AND FINANCIAL RECONSTRUCTION

Our program consists of principles and policies to:

- Revive the economy by instituting a massive public investment program focusing on jobs, housing, state and local services, green investments, and infrastructure investments, supported by expansionary monetary policy.
- Reform the financial sector bailouts to be fairer, less costly and more effective, by broadening and strengthening the oversight of financial institutions . . .
- Reverse extreme inequality and increase the prosperity and power of families and communities.
- Re-regulate and restructure the financial sector while upgrading capabilities for effective public supervision and management.
- Reform international economic governance to make the transition to a more balanced, prosperous and just global economy . . .

We aim to:

- End the downward global economic spiral and promote economic recovery through a massive and well-targeted spending program at home.
- Promote coordinated global expansion and aid for the poor abroad.
- [Place] a moratorium on foreclosures, creating new financing mechanisms for mortgages, and increasing opportunities for renting.
- Provide jobs at decent wages for all who need them through public investment, fiscal expansion and employer of last resort programs.
- Provide financing to state and local governments so they can maintain employment and continue to provide the basic services central to the well being of families . . .
- Make available affordable, universal health insurance coverage, to help families prosper and businesses restore competitiveness.
- Provide a basic standard of living for all.
- Promote the transition to a green economy through a series of public investments, tax credits, and loan guarantee programs.
- Create a stable and efficient financial system that provides for the needs of people, communities and businesses, rather than serving as a safe harbor for gambling, fraud and abuse that enriches a few while destroying the economy.
- Restore income, economic power and security to the vast majority of people (the bottom 80%) . . .
- Rebuild the nation's infrastructure through a massive public investment program.
- Promote economic cooperation and aid to poor countries which will suffer most from this crisis and where prosperity can help restore long-run health to the global economy.

Source: Ash *et al.* (2009: 4–5).

"change agenda," Republican opposition had hardened to the point of party-line recalcitrance. (No we won't!)

This said, on economic policy matters at least, the White House had hardly been pushing the reform envelope. Lawrence Summers summarized the Administration's economic strategy as one "directed at having a somewhat different and healthier expansion than in the past, driven by a sense that the expansion is likely to be more secure and its benefits widely shared." Robert Reich, on the other hand, averred that, "Obamanomics... has been animated by a bold vision of what we need to do but has been quite cautious in practice."[69] Reich was soon revising the record somewhat, arguing in his blog that the White House would really prefer everyone to believe that Obamanomics was an inconsequential formulation, married to a set of policies "so modest as to hardly raise an eyebrow," when really the project was subtly transformative, even "revolutionary."[70] In a published excerpt in the *Wall Street Journal*, Reich drew out the distinctions between Reaganomics and Obamanomics making the case that the "animating idea" of the latter was effectively opposite to the neoliberal orthodoxy of the 1980s:

The real distinction between Obamanomics and Reaganomics involves government's role in achieving growth and broad-based prosperity. The animating idea of Reaganomics was that the economy grows best from the top down. Lower taxes on the wealthy prompts them to work harder and invest more. When they do so, everyone benefits [...] Under Reaganomics, government was the problem. It can still be a problem. But a central tenet of Obamanomics is that there are even bigger problems out there which cannot be solved without government. By building the economy from the bottom up, enhancing public investment, and instituting reasonable regulation, Obamanomics marks a reversal of the economic philosophy that has dominated America since 1981.[71]

For all this cheerleading, when Obama sat down again with David Leonhardt of the *New York Times*, to discuss the translation of his economic philosophy into practice, there was also more than a hint of defensiveness in his account of the political optics of Obamanomics. In response to the suggestion that he had surrounded himself with "Rubin protégés" and Wall Street deficit hawks, Obama conceded that he did not have a Paul Krugman or a Joseph Stiglitz among his advisors, but (or perhaps because) "what I've been constantly searching for is a ruthless pragmatism when it comes to economic policy."[72]

Bailing out

Ruthless pragmatism certainly ruled in the tumultuous bailout-cum-re-structuring of the auto industry, which had been overseen by Summers and Geithner under the leadership of "car tzar" Steven Rattner. New York financier, corporate consigliere, and Democratic Party fundraiser, Rattner struck some as a curious appointment, even as it reaffirmed the new administration's habit of turning to Wall Street fixers. Rattner explained that White House advisors had assured him "that the fact that I barely knew one car from another was less important than my 26 years advising, financing, and investing in companies [because in] their minds, this was a restructuring challenge, not a management job."[73] Under the provisions of the Troubled Asset Relief Program (TARP) inherited from the Bush Administration, Rattner and his team steered General Motors (GM) and Chrysler back from the brink of collapse. The self-styled Team Auto went to work like "a mini investment bank," firing GM's "utterly docile" chairman, Rick Wagoner, guiding both Chrysler and GM into (and out of) bankruptcy, and overseeing an unprecedented downsizing of the companies' production and dealer networks. Rattner, who had been told by the President, "I want you to be tough, and I want you to be commercial," was simply following what he liked to call the "golden rule of Wall Street: He who has the gold makes the rules."[74]

The unmistakable evidence of the bank bailout, of course, was that these rules did not apply to Wall Street itself. Reflecting on the way in which the carmakers had been taught an abrupt lesson in the logic of twenty-first century capitalism by the Obama Administration, Floyd Norris would later wonder, "what would have happened to Wall Street if the government had been willing and able to impose market discipline on the banks, so that creditors took large losses and shareholders were wiped out even as the banks kept operating and performing their economic functions"; perhaps, "if that had happened, the chances of getting real financial reform through Congress would have been a lot greater than they now appear to be."[75] Ruthless pragmatism in economic policy apparently meant very different things for Wall Street and Main Street. While the banks and their top managers were treated with kid gloves, the auto companies were forced through structural adjustment. This was evidence of a "clear double standard," according to Joseph Stiglitz: "Low-income workers who had worked all their life and done nothing wrong would have to take a wage cut, but not the million-dollar-plus financiers who had brought the world to the brink of financial ruin."[76]

Obama's campaign pledge, that "the fight for manufacturing is the fight for America's future" might have concealed an ambiguous truth, but the irony was not appreciated in the industrial regions of the Midwest, which faced devastating job losses while Wall Street was effectively feather-bedded.[77] Clearly conscious of these discrepant messages, Obama explained in the midst of the Chrysler and GM bankruptcies that,

[T]he touchstone for economic policy is, does it allow the average American to find good employment and see their incomes rise ... [W]e do want to grow the pie, but we want to make sure that prosperity is spread across the spectrum of regions and occupations and genders and races ... [E]conomic policy should focus on growing the pie, but it also has to make sure that everybody has got opportunity in that system.[78]

This commitment to socially inclusive economic growth, and to spreading opportunity, apparently need not—and indeed does not—imply active industrial or labor-market policies, freighted down as they may be with old-economy signifiers. For Obama, social justice in the "postbubble economy" has more to do with fair access to, and fairer returns on, education and job training. "I've always claimed that if a Wal-Mart associate was getting paid 25 bucks an hour like the auto-worker, then there is no reason to complain," Obama has said, even while recognizing that "the loss of manufacturing is a loss of a way of life and not just a loss of income ... I don't think those jobs should vanish [but] they will constitute a smaller percentage of the overall economy."[79]

This is strongly reminiscent of the "employability" philosophy of the 1990s, which married active government measures on the supply side with passivity on the demand side.[80] In a speech on job creation and job training in May 2009, for example, Obama affirmed his support for the soft-workfare principle that "the unemployment system should be ... not just a safety net but a stepping stone," pointing displaced workers to the administration's new program, Opportunity.gov, and to the increased availability of Federal Pell Grants, while announcing a new taskforce for the promotion of community colleges.[81] Despite his reiteration of the favorite Chicago injunction that this was "not the time for small plans," with nationwide job losses about to breach the six million mark (including two million in manufacturing), these plans seemed less than bold. And on the demand side, the auto-industry downsizing plan and some scattered initiatives for green-collar jobs hardly amounted to an industrial policy, or indeed anything approaching one. Their ad hoc nature was reflected in Lawrence Summers' characterization of this element of his economic-policy portfolio as "a number of things to support manufacturing."[82] When Obama visited GM's Lordstown assembly plant in September 2009, the man who "didn't run for President to manage auto companies," was able to strike a tone of cautious optimism—now that the production lines were moving again—while candidly leveling, "You deserve better."[83]

Back in the territory in which the presidential campaign had been fought, Obama returned to a familiar theme in promising the autoworkers that, "We know that the battle for America's future is not just going to be won in the big cities, not just on the coasts, but in towns like Elkhart, Indiana, and Pittsburgh, Pennsylvania, and Warren and Youngstown." A few days later, though, Obama was in Pittsburgh and engaged in a different kind of battle. Chairing the second G20 summit of the year, which formalized the new group's status as the "premier forum for our international economic cooperation," Obama sought to broker an international agreement on a "framework for strong, sustainable, and balanced growth."[84] There was dissent, however, both inside and outside the conference hall. On the inside, the fairly toothless accord on economic-policy coordination masked a series of disagreements on a range of issues, including financial regulation and bankers' pay (where the United States insisted, with Britain, on a cautious approach), climate change (where the US line was to lower expectations, in advance of the upcoming Copenhagen summit), and a resuscitated proposal for a "Tobin tax" on financial speculation (with support from France and Britain, but concerted opposition from the Obama team).[85] Along with a modest increase in the voting rights of developing countries, now wielding market power of their own, the meeting fashioned a shared position on an enhanced regime of policy surveillance, managed by the International Monetary Fund. On the outside, protesters were greeted with armored vehicles, sonic weaponry, and teargas. Questioned on his attitude to the protests at the closing press conference, Obama replied,

I think that many of the protests are just directed generically at capitalism. And they object to the existing global financial system. They object to free markets. One of the great things about the United States is . . . that you can speak your mind and you can protest; that's part of our tradition. But I fundamentally disagree with their view that the free market is the source of all ills [. . .] Ironically, if they had been paying attention to what was taking place inside the summit itself, what they would have heard was a strong recognition from the most diverse collection of leaders in history that it is important to make sure that the market is working for ordinary people; that government has a role in regulating the market in ways that don't cause the kinds of crises that we've just been living through; that our emphasis has to be on more balanced growth, and that includes making sure that growth is bottom up, that workers, ordinary people, are able to pay their bills, ... make a decent living [...] I would recommend those who are out there protesting ... read the communiqué that was issued.[86]

Walking the tightrope of market reform in the context of a global economic crisis, while maintaining some degree of forward momentum on vexing issues like the healthcare overhaul, climate change, and the war in Afghanistan, was proving to be a near-overwhelming challenge for the transformative president. A year after the election, he could still fire up the crowd, at a factory visit in Ohio or a town-hall meeting in New Orleans, but in many other ways, as a year-one retrospective in the *New York Times* put it, "the hope and the hubris [had] given way to the daily grind of governance."[87] Despite the dulling effect of what was clearly going to be a protracted economic recovery, and the shrill, looping soundtrack provided by Fox News and the tea-party conservatives, Obama nevertheless retained his enigmatic promise in the eyes of many. As the *Times* concluded, the President remained, "a study in dichotomy, bold yet cautious, radical yet pragmatic, all depending on whose prism you use."

This seems certainly to have been true of Obamanomics, which has been as politically illusive as it has ideologically elusive. It has been Obama's singular feat to resemble a barely-reconstructed free-marketeer when viewed from the left and a new-age socialist when viewed from the right, while never being entirely fixed as either. Grist for both mills can be recovered from Obama's political talk and to some extent from his actions too. The extraordinary measures that were enacted in the first months of 2009 were steered by a crisis-managing White House mainly distinguished from its predecessor by an increased supply of technocratic competence. The return of pragmatic effectiveness, however, seems barely to have moved the ideological needle. Playing hypotheticals, a "third Bush term" in the form of a McCain presidency (against which Obama campaigned so effectively) would certainly have meant even deeper tax cuts, with a more regressive skew, but beyond that many of the "imperative" responses to the economic crisis would have been essentially the same. In this sense, the first rounds of crisis measures—from the financial bailout to the emergency stimulus—defined the fledgling presidency more than it defined them. Obama has practically conceded as much in his acknowledgment that those "were not decisions that were popular or satisfying; [they] were decisions that were necessary."[88]

The lagging indicator

Towards the end of the first year of the Obama presidency, however, a potentially more defining cluster of economic-policy decisions began to present themselves—those relating to jobs. Weak growth had been restored, at least across the primary business indicators of GDP, corporate profitability, stock prices, and productivity, but the "lagging indicator" of unemployment had tumbled deep into the red zone. The official rate of joblessness had surpassed 10 percent in the fall of 2009, a disastrous headline that only concealed further layers of collateral damage in the form of "discouraged worker" exits from the labor market, involuntary part-time work, and depressed earnings. It was a story that even the perennially distracted media could not miss: continued pain on Main Street versus the return of plenty on Wall Street. Worse still, it was now plain for all to see that the Wall Street trough had been replenished at the public's expense. Notwithstanding the material and social consequences of the pain on Main Street, this also represented a politically-toxic combination of circumstances for the party in power as the midterm elections of 2010 drew inexorably closer.

In the space of a few weeks, what Noam Scheiber of *The New Republic* described as the Democrats' "tidy consensus" on the economy—that the stimulus package had basically worked, that growth had been restored, and that the monthly rate of job losses had at least slowed—had descended into a "pigsty" of singularly fraught choices in policy and politics.[89] In the midst of this economic-policy quagmire, a jobs summit was convened at the White House in December 2009, an event which managed to be, in turn, urgent and forlorn. As Obama confided to the diverse group of delegates, "We've got about as difficult an economic play as is possible."[90] The challenge, in what the President had taken to calling "the era of fiscal constraint,"[91] was to establish the foundations for a "postbubble economy," much less reliant on debt and unsustainable consumption, at the same time as accelerating job creation across a skittish business sector.

By self-imposed ideological necessity, "the Obama team [had become] wary of anything that smacks of bigger government," *The Economist* noted.[92] In this context, the twin challenges of job creation and deficit reduction were revealing the limits not only of governmental action—a now-familiar presidential refrain—but also of late third-way triangulation. As Vice President Biden put it, in his unvarnished way, at the opening session of the jobs summit before more than a hundred blue-chip corporate

255

leaders, economists, and union officials, "We're counting on you." Although the stimulus package had generated 1.6 million jobs, the real engines of job creation, Obama went on to explain, were located in the private sector. The government's role was to establish a supportive framework for economic growth, to listen and respond, and to respect the effective constraints imposed by the dictates of fiscal responsibility and deficit reduction. Invoking FDR's spirit of "bold, persistent experimentation," Obama informed the summiteers that he was "looking for fresh perspectives."

I am open to every demonstrably good idea, and I want to take every responsible step to accelerate job creation. We also, though, have to face the fact that our resources are limited. When we walked in, there was an enormous fiscal gap between the money that is going out and the money coming in. The recession has made that worse [. . .] So we can't make any ill-considered decisions right now, even with the best of intentions. We're going to have to be surgical and we're going to have to be creative.[93]

If the collapse of the financial system had apparently licensed an unrestrained governmental embrace of any means necessary, whatever it takes, and whatever it costs, the jobs crisis marked a return to limited government-as-usual. The watchwords again were those of prudence, responsibility targeting, and "smart and surgical" interventions. And the outcome looked decidedly like a bundle of small plans, wholly insufficient to the task. The Administration's proposal, a few days after the jobs forum, rolled together an extended package of tax cuts for small businesses; a boost in spending for infrastructure projects; incentives for consumers to weatherize their homes; and an extension of emergency measures in the Recovery Act for seniors, unemployed workers, and for the prevention of public-sector layoffs. As if to accentuate the underwhelming nature, and likely impact, of this announcement, Obama concluded the announcement by adding, "Of course, there is only so much government can do."[94]

There was much more, of course, that the government might have done. With the endorsement of the unions' peak organization, the AFL-CIO, the Economic Policy Institute (EPI) had proposed a much more aggressive employment plan, scored to create 4.6 million jobs in the first year. EPI's five-point plan would have overlapped with the Obama proposal by strengthening the safety net, shipping emergency funds to the states, and stepping up infrastructure spending, but it would have also authorized a mini-Works Progress Administration initiative for public-service jobs (focusing initially on activities like environmental cleanup and childcare, but transitioning into more training-intensive fields linked to emerging job opportunities); and a job creation tax credit (delivered at low cost across the private, public, and nonprofit economy).[95] Perhaps most significantly, these initiatives would have been funded by a financial transactions tax on the sale of stocks and other financial products, a proposal that had won the support of more than 200 prominent economists on the eve of the jobs summit.[96]

Soon after, when Obama visited the Brookings Institution to give what was billed as a major speech on job creation. The lukewarm reaction, however, focused more on the timid nature of the underlying policy proposals, not the rhetorical sales job itself. The *New York Times* headline read: "Obama offers help for small businesses," noting in passing that the newly announced policy measures were "intended to promote job creation," before moving on to discuss how they might be funded from funds left over from the unloved TARP program.[97] Later, the *Times* would editorialize that the subsequent draft of the Jobs for Main Street Act represented an "honorable effort" that was nevertheless "seriously deficient," especially in light of the scale of the unemployment crisis amongst young people, and inner city minority youth in particular, whose *employment* rates were stuck around 10 percent.[98] Across the country as a whole, broad measures of the unemployment rate, which included involuntary part-timers and discouraged workers had now reached 17 percent (or 26.5 million workers)— approaching 25 percent for black and Hispanic workers.[99] EPI's president, Lawrence Michel, issued a statement welcoming Obama's initiative—at least that component of it that had engaged with the labor movement-endorsed proposal—while questioning the "round about" logic of supporting job creation through a targeted small-business tax break and reminding the White House and Congress that "the scale of their job creation plan matters tremendously."[100] There was no mention of the financial transactions tax.

At the limits of nudge-ocracy

"There are no grand theorists in the Obama orbit, certainly no in-house ideologists," Foer and Scheiber have observed; "Obama sold himself as a green-eyeshade pragmatist...[though] there is, in fact, if not an ideology, then certainly a sensibility that reigns in Obamaland." This sympathetic account of Obama's emergent "nudge-ocracy" detects a distinctive policy rationality, constructed on some of the foundations of Clintonomics, but with strong doses of behavioral economics and postbubble pragmatism:

Obama has no intention of changing the nature of American capitalism...His program doesn't set out to reinvent whole sectors of the economy, not even our broken banking system. And, unlike postwar liberals, he has no zeal for ramping up the regulatory state [...]

Obama has a deep respect for the market and wants to minimize the state's footprint on it. He has little interest in fixing prices or rationing goods or reversing free-trade agreements. But, while he basically shares the New Democrats' instincts, he rejects their conclusions. Reacting against the overweening statism of their liberal ancestors, many New Democrats came to believe that if government largely got out of the way and let markets work properly, the natural result would be widely shared prosperity. You only need to view the extent of Obama's domestic agenda to know he doesn't agree.

Instead, Obama has set out to synthesize the New Democratic faith in the utility of markets with the Old Democratic emphasis on reducing inequality. In Obama's state, government never supplants the market or stifles its inner workings—the old forms of statism that didn't wash economically, and certainly not politically. But government does aggressively prod markets—by planting incentives, by stirring new competition—to achieve the results he prefers...Rather than force markets to conform to his wishes, he shapes their calculus so they conclude (on their own) that their interests coincide with his wishes.[101]

The result, on this sanguine reading, is an(other) amalgam of activist government and market rationality, in which smart interventions are deployed to variously nudge, steer, and harness market capacities, incrementally in the direction of a more egalitarian and sustainable trajectory. The promise is that of a competently managed capitalism, protected from its own excesses, in which the benefits of growth can be more fairly distributed at the margin. It would resemble Clinton's vision of the Third Way, with the benefit of historical lessons learned from the tech and housing bubbles, deregulatory miscalculations, and the doggedness of social inequalities. The now-more-worldly Rubinistas were to get the chance of a do-over.

The occasion was one of Lawrence Summers' rare trips outside Washington, in August 2009—a series of meetings with policymakers and business leaders in Detroit, the epicenter of the bailout economy. Summers listened patiently to an advocate of a Michigan loan program, designed to assist manufacturers transitioning to new-economy sectors, before explaining that while the struggling auto-parts suppliers had a case, it was not a special case. The White House was developing some policies for manufacturing, but theirs must be a whole-economy perspective. And an administration caught wasting money might jeopardize not only the rationale for activist government, but perhaps the progressive project itself: "I would have guessed that bailing out banks was going to be unpopular, and bailing out real companies where real people work was going to be popular," Summers reasoned, "But I was wrong. They were both unpopular. There's a lot of suspicion around. Why this business and not that business? Is this industrial policy? Is this socialism?"[102]

A favorite Obama line had come to capture the unprincipled necessity of the bailouts: "You can be sure that when I was running for office, things like saving the banks and rescuing auto companies were not on my to-do list. They weren't even on my want-to-do list."[103] What Obama had wanted to do was to finesse free-market capitalism, keeping a watchful eye, incentivizing positive behaviors here, bending cost curves and adjusting the choice architecture there, in order to rein in self-destructive tendencies and spread the benefits of growth. This would entail light-touch regulation not heavily-handed interventions, establishing—in another favorite Obama phrase— "commonsense rules of the road" for well-behaved market participants. This would mean checking some of the more egregious behavior, most conspicuously on the part of the financial sector and its lobbyists. As Obama had explained in his "Renewing the American economy" speech at Cooper Union, in the spring before the presidential election.

The future cannot be shaped by the best-connected lobbyists with the best record of raising money for campaigns. This thinking is wrong for the financial sector and it's wrong for our country. I do not believe the government should stand in the way of innovation or turn back the clock on an older era of regulation. But I do believe that government has a role to play in advancing our common prosperity, by providing stable macroeconomic and financial conditions for sustained growth, by demanding transparency and by ensuring fair competition in the marketplace.[104]

To almost no-one's surprise, however, the financial lobby did not unilaterally disarm in the face of such (often repeated) threats. And neither did the tight knots of entrenched economic power and ingrained market incentives unravel on their own, even under the pressure of an unprecedented crisis. Several decades of governmental accommodation to the structural power of finance, under the particular historical conditions of financialization,[105] have fostered a symbiotic relationship between the logics of Wall Street and Pennsylvania Avenue, which in many ways the crisis tightened. "Congress and the Obama administration [still] have plans to re-regulate the financial industry," Kevin Drum comments, "but you can't undo

30 years of intellectual capture in a few months—especially when the reform effort is mostly in the hands of former finance executives."[106]

In the post-bailout period, however, the politics of this process are proving to be especially treacherous. What may look like smart regulation to White House insiders looks more like soft peddling to many on the outside; back-stairs cajoling is easily mistaken for public capitulation. When Obama went to Federal Hall in New York City to address the financial industry, in September 2009, his pitch on financial reform was interpreted as "stern" and "tough" by pundits but, perhaps more revealingly, it was mocked by satirists. Not only did the President find it necessary to publicly reburnish his free-market credentials, on issues like free trade ("make no mistake, this administration is committed to pursuing expanded trade and new trade agreements; [which are] absolutely essential to our economic future") and fiscal responsibility ("I am absolutely committed to putting this nation on a sound and secure fiscal footing; [that is] why we're pushing to restore pay-as-you-go rules in Congress"), he was also careful to demarcate the limited scope and rationale of regulatory intervention:

I have always been a strong believer in the power of the free market. I believe that jobs are best created not by government, but by businesses and entrepreneurs willing to take a risk on a good idea. I believe that the role of the government is not to disparage wealth, but to expand its reach; not to stifle markets, but to provide the ground rules and level playing field that helps to make those markets more vibrant—and that will allow us to better tap the creative and innovative potential of our people...So I promise you, I did not run for President to bail out banks or intervene in capital markets. But it is important to note that the very absence of common-sense regulations able to keep up with a fast-paced financial sector is what created the need for that extraordinary intervention...The lack of sensible rules of the road, so often opposed by those who claim to speak for the free market, ironically led to a rescue far more intrusive than anything any of us—Democratic or Republican, progressive or conservative—would have ever proposed or predicted.[107]

Confronted with unmistakable evidence that business-as-usual had been resumed on Wall Street—including a crop of multi-billion dollar bonus packages and an unseemly scramble to repay government loans before restrictions on executive compensation could bite—Obama nevertheless meekly invited the captains of finance to "join us in a constructive effort to update the rules," based on the principles of transparency and accountability; emphasizing that "we want to work with the financial industry to achieve that end." Reminding the financiers of their responsibilities and obligations, words that were used more than twenty times in the speech,

Obama pleaded with the industry to call off its lobbyists, and, above all, "to embrace serious financial reform, not resist it."[108]

But as the legislation for the re-regulation of the financial sector lumbered through Congress, checked and diluted by the most formidable lobby of them all, many sensed that the historic opportunity for real, biting regulation had already been squandered.[109] As crisis passed to normalcy, leverage had been lost. Exhortation and second-best efforts seemed to be all that were left. To make matters worse, the banks that had been restored to rude profitability at the public expense were failing to reinvest in the still-ailing domestic economy. This was the proximate cause of Obama's uncharacteristic outburst, on national television, against the behavior of that "bunch of fat cat bankers on Wall Street"—promptly derided by the *Wall Street Journal* as a crass return to the populist playbook, "banker baiting 101."[110] If this was an attempt to use the bully pulpit, in advance of a private meeting with the major banks scheduled for the next day, it backfired. Savvy enough to avoid the use of corporate jets, and therefore repeating the public-relations gaffe committed by bailed-out auto executives earlier in the year, the heads of Goldman Sachs, Citigroup, and Morgan Stanley opted to take commercial flights on the morning of the meeting, but were delayed by fog. Other banking leaders made the White House meeting, by way of a combination of trains, automobiles, and more thoughtful planning, but the moment was again mostly lost. While Obama did his best to prod the bank bosses, with the aid of a speakerphone link to New York, to start lending again to small businesses and to stop fighting the regulations that were being formulated in Washington, the *New York Times* reported that the President had publicly "confronted the limits of his power."[111]

What was also being confronted, in these and other similar situations, was the limits of "nudge-ocracy," if this is defined in Foer and Scheiber's terms, as "a hands-off approach to markets, but a hands-on approach to the incentives and defaults that influence decisions."[112] Notwithstanding the third-way patina of such market-nudging interventions, they remain, in essence, market-complementing forms of regulation, which work around the market, stopping considerably short of restructuring and re-regulating the market. First comes the market; the government's role is reduced to shaping the rules of engagement, if not securing effective competition itself. In principle, this logic of market policing might be extended to the kinds of interventions that frontally challenge the most powerful market actors, but this rhetorical promise of Obamanomics has yet to be meaningfully realized. While clearly intrigued by what they portrayed as a distinctive approach to squaring the (de)regulatory circle, Foer and Scheiber concede that, in practice, "the lengths to which Obama goes to avoid impinging on the market are almost too great."[113]

For all the promise of "bottom up economic development," Obamanomics has so far proved to be a hollow shell. Beneath the third-way wordplay, it signals little more than a progressively flavored form of technocratic competence. In as far as Obamanomics defines a space of ideological principle, this has taken the form of a series of adaptations of the mutating neoliberal order, rather than any kind of significant break with that order. For Susan Watkins, it represents "a turn to neo-Reaganomics."[114] Market deference remains both a political and a practical necessity, shored up with warmed-over "necessitarian" homilies about fiscal discipline, global competition, level playing fields, and races to the top. Of course, this is not to say that nothing has changed. Generally cool competence, on its own, marks an improvement on the craven incompetence of the Bush Administration, for which government failure became, in effect, a self-fulfilling vocation.[115] But competence "has its limits as a source of inspiration... [And] with unemployment at around 10 percent and still on an upward trajectory, the Administration is left arguing *not* that jobs are being created but that without Obama's policies things would be worse," Ryan Lizza has observed—"not a very pithy slogan."[116] Worse still, in fact, the long-term distributive consequences of unemployment—captured in the statistic that the "real" unemployment rate is 4 percentage points above the official rate for white workers, but 15 percentage points higher for blacks and Hispanics, and higher still for young people across the board— means that broadly-based, bottom-up growth will not occur on its own. Neither are supply-side adjustments to the education system or post hoc reforms of the tax code even remotely adequate to this deepening problem, even in the medium term. Rather, a neoliberalized mode of growth has effectively institutionalized inequality, locking in excessive gains for those at the top, while rationing extraordinarily thin pickings for those at the bottom.[117] Real progress on jobs, like real progress on financial reform or environmental policy, means tackling the market, not tinkering with incentives or playing at the margins. As yet, nothing in the practice of Obamanomics suggests there is even a taste for such market-transforming interventions.

If Obamanomics represents little more than a series of rhetorical positions, then it should come as no surprise that its transformative traction has been severely limited. Transformative change, historically speaking, is more often achieved by movements, rather than mere manifestos. Obama's presidential candidacy may in some senses have been a product of social movements, even if large parts of his broad electoral coalition were primarily repelled by the alternative on offer, and have since largely deserted him. The Obama movement seems to have been overtaken by quietude, if not by various degrees of frustration and disillusionment. Its erstwhile leader has since governed in a markedly detached fashion, holding progressive constituencies at arm's length and apparently preferring to surround himself with orthodox experts and new-age "pragmacrats." As George Packer perceptively observed, just after the election, the Obama phenomenon had been a unique product of "the meeting of a man and a historical moment," with the risk that it might amount to "something less than a durable social force." And then the prediction: "With a movement behind him, Obama would have the latitude to begin to overcome the tremendous resistance to change that prevails in Washington... Without one, he will soon find himself simply cutting deals."[118]

Notes

1. Barack Obama, Grant Park speech, Chicago, November 4, 2008, accessed at <http://www.chicagotribune.com>.
2. Kuttner (2008: 1, 2, 4).
3. Quoted in Talbott (2008: 34, 30).
4. Luo, M. (2008) Memo gives Canada's account of Obama campaign's meeting on NAFTA, *New York Times*, March 4: A17.
5. Austan Goolsbee and Gary Becker, quoted in Calhoun, B. (2008) The man behind Obama's economic plan, *NPR News*, April 8; Goolsbee, A. (2006) A charismatic economist who loved to argue, *New York Times*, November 17, C1.
6. Kuttner (2008: 9); Solomon, D. (2007) Seeking clues to Obamanomics, *Wall Street Journal*, April 24, A4. If the famously Wal-Mart friendly Jason Furman was going to be representative of Obamanomics, the conservative *New York Sun* surmised, then there would be little to fear from an Obama administration economic policy (*New York Sun* (2008) Obama-nomics, *New York Sun*, June 10: 8).
7. Cooper, M. (2008) McCain laboring to hit right note on economy, *New York Times*, September 17, A1. McCain was regarded by the *Wall Street Journal* editorial team as a borderline economic illiterate. See Cassidy, J. (2008) Bailing out, *New Yorker*, September 29: 25.
8. Friedman (1982: viii, emphasis added). See also Chapter Three.
9. "Never allow a crisis to go to waste... They are opportunities to do big things" (Rahm Emanuel, quoted in Zeleny, J. (2008) Obama weighs quick undoing of Bush policy, *New York Times*, November 10, A19.
10. Pollin (2003: 174).

11. Barack Obama, Renewing the American economy, Cooper Union, New York City, March 27, 2008, accessed at <http://www.nytimes.com/2008/03/27/us/politics/27text-obama.html>.

12. Solomon, D. (2007) Seeking clues to Obamanomics, *Wall Street Journal*, April 24: A4.

13. *Economist* (2007) Who's the real left-winger? *Economist*, May 10, 34.

14. Merrion, P. (2008) Obamanomics: candidate of change follows party line on economic policy, *Crain's Chicago Business*, January 14: 1.

15. McCloskey, D. (2008) Is there any hope for this man? *Reason*, 40/6: 51.

16. Austan Goolsbee, first quoted in and then paraphrased by Merrion, P. (2008) Obamanomics: candidate of change follows party line on economic policy, *Crain's Chicago Business*, January 14: 1.

17. Moberg, D. (2008) Obamanomics, *In These Times*, March 10, 35.

18. *Economist* (2008) Hope and fear: Obamanomics, *Economist*, March 1: 15.

19. *Economist* (2008) Dr Obama's patent economic medicine: Obamanomics, *Economist*, March 1: 31–32.

20. Barack Obama, quoted in Leonhardt (2008: 30–31).

21. Cass Sunstein, quoted in Weisman, J. and Bravin, J. (2009) Obama's regulatory Czar likely to set a new tone, *Wall Street Journal*, January 8, A4.

22. See Sunstein, C. and Thaler, R. (2008) *Nudge*. New Haven, CT: Yale University Press. Thaler has since become an advisor to the British Conservative Party.

23. Cass Sunstein, quoted in Hundley, T. (2009) Ivory tower of power, *Chicago Tribune*, March 22: 10. See also Sunstein, C. (2008) The visionary minimalist, *New Republic*, January 30: 13–15.

24. Obama (2006: 157–158).

25. Barack Obama, quoted in Hundley, T. (2009) Ivory tower of power, *Chicago Tribune*, March 22: 9.

26. Quoted in Leonhardt (2008: 32).

27. Sunstein, C. R. (2008) The visionary minimalist, *New Republic*, January 30, 13–15.

28. Bill Clinton, January 1993, quoted in Woodward, B. (1994) *The Agenda: Inside the Clinton White House*. New York: Simon and Schuster, 84. Participants at the meeting explained to Woodward that this was the point where "economic realities" had begun to bite, and Clinton understood that "his fate was passing into the hands of the unelected Alan Greenspan and the bond market." On the same day, Reich was not with Rubin and the economic team with Clinton in Little Rock but was facing his Senate confirmation hearing, where he innocently declared, "The President [elect] hasn't said that deficit reduction is his number one priority" (Reich, 1997: 40).

29. Reich (1997). According to Bluestone and Harrison, the Wall Street–Pennsylvania Avenue policy accord was based on the following principles: (a) balance the federal budget/run surpluses, (b) encourage unlimited free trade, (c) maintain downward pressure on wages, (d) deregulate domestic markets, (e) encourage

employment insecurity, (f) deregulate domestic markets, and (g) deregulate global markets. See Bluestone, B. and Harrison, B. (2000) *Growing Prosperity*. Boston: Houghton Mifflin; Peck (2002a).

30. Barack Obama, quoted in Leonhardt (2008: 30).

31. Obama (2006: 148).

32. Quoted in Leonhardt (2008: 35).

33. Moberg, D. (2008) Obamanomics, *In These Times*, March 10, 34–35; Bluestone, B. and Harrison, B. (2000) *Growing Prosperity*. Boston: Houghton Mifflin; Kenworthy, L. (2004) *Egalitarian Capitalism*. New York: Russell Sage Foundation.

34. Obama's campaign positions were summarized as a "Great Society" program for the middle class (see Sanger, D. (2009) "Great Society" plan for the middle class, *New York Times*, February 28: A14).

35. Cass Sunstein on Barack Obama, quoted in Sunstein, C. R. (2008) The visionary minimalist, *The New Republic*, January 30, 15.

36. Lawrence Summers, quoted in Cassidy (2009: 84).

37. See Fletcher, M. A. (2008) A market-oriented economic team, *Washington Post*, November 25: A3; Barack Obama, quoted in Wall, T. (2008) In rough times… give thanks, *Washington Times*, November 25: A19.

38. Zeleny, J. (2008) Obama and Bush work to calm volatile market, *New York Times*, November 25: A1.

39. Stiglitz (2010: 46–47).

40. The *Financial Times* continued: the Hamilton Project "makes a strong case for the state to play a more constructive role both in improving the efficiency of America's market economy, but also in addressing the growing inequity of market outcomes," and while there might be "room for more scepticism about the group's argument that growing income inequality harms economic growth," the markets would be reassured by the emphasis on shrewd investment and fiscal discipline. (*Financial Times* (2006) Tackling America's growing inequality, *Financial Times*, April 6: 12).

41. Altman, R. C., Bordoff, J. E., Orszag, P. R., and Rubin, R. E. (2006) *An Economic Strategy to Advance Opportunity, Prosperity and Growth*. Washington, DC: Brookings Institution, 5.

42. Posted at Obama's "smoking gun": his Hamilton Project speech shows his links to Goldman, entitlement cuts (Part 2), <http://seminal.firedoglake.com/diary/17984>, December 7, 2009.

43. When Bernanke gave a speech in February 2007, bemoaning the economic costs of rising inequality, and proposing a response that married individual security with flexible markets, it was interpreted as a signal of his willingness to join the conversation about the Hamilton Project's "grand bargain" (Pearlstein, S. (2007) The grand bargainer, *Washington Post*, February 7: D1).

44. Quoted in Foer and Scheiber (2009: 23).

45. Brooks, D. (2006) Don't worry, be happy, *New York Times*, May 11: 37.

46. For a sample, ranging from the credulous to the scathing and paranoid, see Talbott (2008); Wasik, J. F. (2009) *The Audacity of Help*. New York: Bloomberg Press; Carney, T. P. (2009) *Obamanomics*. Washington, DC: Regnery Publishing; Moore, S. (2009) *How Barack Obama is Bankrupting the U.S. Economy*. New York: Encounter.

47. Zakaria, F. (2008) Obama can chart a new governing ideology for the West, *Newsweek*, November 17: 27–28.

48. Leonhardt (2008: 35).

49. Douthat and Salam (2009: 10, 83).

50. Douthat and Salam (2009: 91).

51. Douthat and Salam (2009: 91, original emphasis).

52. Douthat and Salam (2009: 10).

53. Hossein-Zadeh, I. (2008) Whose interests will shape Obama's "change"? *Counterpunch*, December 10, accessed at <http://www.counterpunch.org/zadeh12102008.html>.

54. See Foster, J. B. and McChesney, R. W. (2009) A new New Deal under Obama? *Monthly Review*, 60/9: 1–11.

55. Kuttner (2008: 200); Žižek, S. (2008) Use your illusions, *London Review of Books*, November 14, accessed at <http://www.lrb.co.uk>.

56. *Wall Street Journal* (2009) Obama's inaugural address; as delivered, *Wall Street Journal*, January 20, accessed at <http://blogs.wsj.com/washwire/2009/01/20/president-obamas-inaugural-address/>.

57. See Cassidy, J. (2008) Anatomy of a meltdown, *New Yorker*, December 1: 48–63.

58. Krugman, P. (2009) What Obama must do, *Rolling Stone*, January 22: 44–49.

59. Christina Romer, quoted in Lizza (2009: 86).

60. Remarks by the President on job creation and economic growth, December 8, 2009, accessed at <http://www.whitehouse.gov/the-press-office/remarks-president-job-creation-and-economic-growth>.

61. Cassidy, J. (2009) Harder times, *New Yorker*, March 16: 41. See also Romer, C. (2009) The case for fiscal stimulus. Speech at the University of Chicago, February 27, accessed at <http://www.whitehouse.gov/administration/eop/cea/speeches-testimony>.

62. Questioned about his defining faith in self-regulating markets in the fall of 2008, Greenspan admitted, "I have found a flaw," to which Representative Henry Waxman countered: "In other words, you found that your view of the world, your ideology, was not right; it was not working." Greenspan replied: "Absolutely, precisely" (quoted in Stiglitz, J. (2009) Capitalist fools. In Flippin, R., ed., *Best American Political Writing 2009*. New York: PublicAffairs, 115).

63. Calmes, J. (2009) For Geithner's debut, a lukewarm reception, *New York Times*, February 10: B1.

64. Cassidy, J. (2009) Harder times, *New Yorker*, March 16: 41.

65. Barack Obama, Remarks by the President to the Business Council, February 13, 2009, accessed at <http://www.whitehouse.gov/the_press_office/remarks-by-the-president-to-the-business-council/>.

66. Krugman, P. (2009) Obama's bailout. In Flippin, R., ed., *Best American Political Writing 2009*. New York: PublicAffairs, 116–126; Galbraith, J. K. (2009) No return to normal. In Flippin, R., ed., *Best American Political Writing 2009*. New York: PublicAffairs, 127–141.

67. Ash *et al.* (2009: 19).

68. Epstein, G. (2009) Obama's economic policy: achievements, problems and prospects, *Revue de la Régulation*, 5/1: 6, 11.

69. Lawrence Summers and Robert Reich, quoted in Stevenson, R. W. (2009) Capitalism after the fall, *New York Times*, April 19: S4–7.

70. Reich, R. (2009) Is Obamanomics conservative or reactionary? March 11, accessed at <http://robertreich.blogspot.com>.

71. Reich, R. B. (2009) Obamanomics isn't about big government, *Wall Street Journal*, March 28: A11.

72. Quoted in Leonhardt (2009: 41).

73. Steven Rattner, quoted in Rattner, S. and Cendrowski, S. (2009) The auto bailout: how we did it, *Fortune*, November 9: 56.

74. Barack Obama followed by Steven Rattner, quoted in Rattner, S. and Cendrowski, S. (2009) The auto bailout: how we did it, *Fortune*, November 9: 64, 68.

75. Norris, F. (2009) U.S. teaches carmakers capitalism, *New York Times*, November 20: B1.

76. Stiglitz (2010: 43).

77. See Nichols, J. (2009) The case for Kenosha, *The Nation*, June 1: 12–16.

78. Quoted in Leonhardt (2009: 41).

79. Quoted in Leonhardt (2009: 39–40).

80. See Peck and Theodore (2000).

81. Barack Obama, Remarks by the President on job creation and job training, May 8, 2009, accessed at <http://www.whitehouse.gov/the_press_office/remarks-by-the-president-to-the-business-council/>.

82. Quoted in Uchitelle, L. (2009) Help wanted, *New York Times*, July 21: B1.

83. Barack Obama, Remarks by the President to General Motors plant employees, September 15, 2009, accessed at <http://www.whitehouse.gov/the_press_office/Remarks-by-the-President-to-GM-Lordstown-Assembly-Plant-Employees-in-Ohio-9/15/2009/>.

84. G20 (2009) Leaders' statement: the Pittsburgh Summit, September 24–25, accessed at <http://www.pittsburghsummit.gov/mediacenter/>.

85. At a follow-up meeting, in Scotland, Geithner moved to take the proposal off the table altogether, flatly declaring, "That's not something we're prepared to support" (quoted in *Wall Street Journal* (2009) Gordon Brown's global tax trap, *Wall Street Journal*, 13 November: A22).

86. Remarks by President Obama at G20 closing press conference, September 25, 2009, accessed at <http://www.whitehouse.gov/the_press_office/Remarks-by-the-President-at-G20-Closing-Press-Conference/>.

87. Baker, P. (2009) No walk in the park, *New York Times*, November 4: A19.

88. Remarks by the President on job creation and economic growth, December 8, 2009, accessed at <http://www.whitehouse.gov/the-press-office/remarks-president-job-creation-and-economic-growth>.

89. Scheiber, N. (2009) Spend and save, *New Republic*, December 30: 12.

90. Quoted in Scheiber, N. (2009) Spend and save, *New Republic*, December 30: 12.

91. Remarks by the President during the meeting of the President's Economic Recovery Advisory Board, November 2, 2009, accessed at <http://www.whitehouse.gov/the-press-office/remarks-president-during-meeting-presidents-economic-recovery-advisory-board>.

92. *Economist* (2009) The jobs summit: any ideas? *Economist*, December 5: 33–34.

93. Remarks by the President and Vice President at the opening session of the Jobs and Economic Growth Forum, December 3, 2009, accessed at <http://www.whitehouse.gov/the-press-office/remarks-president-and-vice-president-opening-session-jobs-and-economic-growth-forum>.

94. Remarks by the President on job creation and economic growth, December 8, 2009, accessed at <http://www.whitehouse.gov/the-press-office/remarks-president-job-creation-and-economic-growth>.

95. Economic Policy Institute (2009) *American Jobs Plan*. Washington, DC: Economic Policy Institute.

96. Even on reduced trading volumes, the tax could raise $100 billion per year. See Baker, D. (2009) *The Benefits of a Financial Transactions Tax*. Washington, DC: Center for Economic Policy Research.

97. Calmes, J. (2009) Obama offers help for small businesses, *New York Times*, December 9: B1.

98. *New York Times* (2009) Americans without work, *New York Times*, December 23: A30.

99. See Edwards, K. (2009) Minorities, less-educated workers see staggering rates of underemployment, *Economic Snapshot*, November 18, accessed at <http://www.epi.org/economic_snapshots>.

100. EPI applauds Obama's focus on jobs, December 8, 2009, accessed at <http://www.epi.org/analysis_and_opinion>.

101. Foer and Scheiber (2009: 24, 22).

102. Lawrence Summers, quoted in Lizza (2009: 82).

103. Remarks by the President on the economy at Allentown, PA, December 4, 2009, accessed at <http://www.whitehouse.gov/the-press-office/remarks-president-economy-allentown-pa>.

104. Barack Obama, Renewing the American economy, Cooper Union, New York City, March 27, 2008, accessed at <http://www.nytimes.com/2008/03/27/us/politics/27text-obama.html>.

105. See Krippner, G. (2005) The financialization of the American economy, *Socio-Economic Review*, 3/2: 173–120.

106. Drum, K. (2010) Capital city, *Mother Jones*, January/February: 37–79.

107. Remarks by the President on financial rescue and reform, September 14, 2009, accessed at <http://www.whitehouse.gov/the-press-office/remarks-by-the-president-on-financial-rescue-and-reform-at-federal-hall/>.

108. The administration's definition of serious reform involved: (i) strengthened consumer protection, (ii) the closure of regulatory loopholes, (iii) regulatory coordination, in the form of an oversight council, and (iv) international regulatory harmonization.

109. Drum, K. (2010) Capital city, *Mother Jones*, January/February: 37–79.

110. Barack Obama on *60 Minutes*, December 14, 2009, quoted in *Wall Street Journal* (2009) Banker baiting 101, *Wall Street Journal*, December 15: A20.

111. Cooper, H. and Dash, E. (2009) Obama presses biggest banks to lend more, *New York Times*, December 15: A1.

112. Foer and Scheiber (2009: 25).

113. Foer and Scheiber (2009: 25).

114. Watkins (2010: 18).

115. See Frank, T. (2008) *The Wrecking Crew*. New York: Henry Holt.

116. Lizza (2009: 95, emphasis added).

117. See McCall, L. (2001) *Complex inequality*. New York: Routledge; Peck J. (2002a); and Pollin (2003).

118. Packer, G. (2009) The new liberalism: how the economic crisis can help Obama redefine the Democrats. In Flippin, R., ed., *Best American Political Writing 2009*. New York: PublicAffairs, 155–156.

Afterword ... the end?

Barack Obama's statement, shortly before his inauguration and at the sharp end of the financial unraveling, seemed to many to be uncontroversial: "There is no disagreement that we need action by our government, a recovery plan that will help to jumpstart the economy"—at least in light of the excesses of the Bush Administration's bailout and the precipitous declines registered on practically every economic indicator. But it was too much for the libertarian Cato Institute, which was soon at work organizing a petition of free-market economists to contest the case for a stimulus package. In an open letter later published as a full-page ad in the *Wall Street Journal* and the *New York Times* in January 2009, more than 200 economists signed on to the statement that,

Notwithstanding reports that all economists are now Keynesians and that we all support a big increase in the burden of government, we the undersigned do not believe that more government spending is a way to improve economic performance. More government spending by Hoover and Roosevelt did not pull the United States economy out of the Great Depression in the 1930s ... [It] is a triumph of hope over experience to believe that more government spending will help the U.S. today. To improve the economy, policymakers should focus on reforms that remove impediments to work, saving, investment and production. Lower tax rates and a reduction in the burden of government are the best ways of using fiscal policy to boost growth.[1]

The letter's signatories included Nobel laureates Vernon Smith, Edward Prescott, and James Buchanan, and a number of Mont Pelerin Society members, including the organization's current president, Deepak Lal, and past presidents Smith and Buchanan. Sensing the urgency of the moment, Lal had earlier enlisted the support of the Heritage Foundation to convene a special meeting of the MPS, ostensibly to discuss the globalizing financial crisis, but also to consider the imminent threat of Barack Obama making a sharp left turn down the road to serfdom.

During the fall of 2008, Lal had been watching the online political betting site, *Betfair*, which was tracking short-term movements of the odds of an Obama victory in the presidential election. Initially heartened by the fact that Sarah Palin's nomination, as John McCain's running mate, yielded an uptick in the chances of a Republican victory, Lal was soon dismayed to observe that the Lehman Brothers' bankruptcy was the more decisive turning point: "The Lehman catastrophe doomed the Republicans, and the hopes of a classical liberal resolution of the spiraling crisis." The odds suddenly shifted in favor of a Democratic victory, and "change was coming to America." Lal wanted the special meeting of the MPS to address "what went wrong" in the run-up to the crisis, "when 'our side'—as it were—were in charge," but more fundamentally to assess whether the crisis (and Obama's responses to it) might "stall or reverse the wholly benign process of globalization" that had accompanied the "seeming intellectual 'victory' of classical liberal ideas" since the 1970s.[2] In the wake of earlier sightings of the Mont Pelerians' intellectual victory, Lal recalled, there had been proposals from "distinguished members" of the Society to wind up the organization, first in 1975 and again in 1991.[3] On these previous occasions, residual fears of the Leviathan state had been sufficient to defeat the motion for self-abolition. The concerns were apparently warranted, for there was work still to be done. In the charged atmosphere of the New York meeting, in the spring of 2009, the Society's president made the case for an urgent *renewal* of its Hayekian mandate.

Predictably, the aging delegates found that they were in strong agreement about the need to stay the course, recommitting to their singular, but now palpably stale, worldview. Lal decried the Obama stimulus package— despite its being heavily tilted towards tax relief—as a "dog's breakfast," reiterating the staple plea for "a massive across-the-board tax cut accompanied by an equivalent fiscal deficit."[4] Gary Becker was similarly skeptical, insisting that government fingerprints had been all over the crisis and joining the tax-cuts chorus. Stepping out of the meeting, he informed a *Wall Street Journal* reporter that, "When the market economy is compared to the alternatives, nothing is better at raising productivity, reducing poverty, improving health and integrating the people of the world."[5] In the paper shared with MPS delegates, however, Becker conceded that the outcome of "the free market's trial by fire" would likely turn more on material circumstances, on the depth of the unfolding global economic crisis:

In my opinion, what will happen to worldwide support for competition and privatization, freer trade, and market-based economies depends greatly on how the American and other major economies fare during the next year or so […] I am confident that sizable world economic growth will resume before long under a mainly capitalist world economy. On the other hand, if I am wrong and there is a prolonged and deep worldwide depression, not simply a recession, the retreat from capitalism and globalization could be severe, as happened during the Great Depression.[6]

In other words, macroeconomic events—and political responses to those events—might conspire to bring about a reversal of what Milton and Rose Friedman once dubbed the "Hayek tide" in economic thinking.[7]

The previous summer, Becker must have experienced a momentary sense of the tide turning, or at least a flashback to the days of the campus protests against the Chicago School's alliance with Pinochet, when the University of Chicago found itself embroiled in a little crisis of its own making. With impeccably poor timing, as the credit system unraveled daily, the University had announced a plan to establish a Milton Friedman Institute, with an endowment of $200 million (to be raised mainly from private sources). The research institute would not—the founding prospectus rather less than credibly claimed—hew to any particular ideological position. It would nevertheless follow "Friedman's lead" in the design and advocacy of policies "that respect the incentives of individuals and the essential role of markets," since as "Friedman and others continually demonstrated, design of public policy without regard to market alternatives has adverse social consequences."[8] A letter of protest, signed by more than 100 Chicago faculty members was immediately sent to the University's president, Robert J. Zimmer, countering that, "The effects of the neoliberal global order that has been put in place in recent decades, strongly buttressed by the Chicago School of Economics, have by no means been unequivocally positive. Many would argue that they have been negative for much of the world's population."[9] Emeritus professor of anthropology, Marshall Sahlins, publicly accused the authorities of attempting to outsource the University to "partisan interests," claiming that the "Milton Friedman Institute would be the vanguard of an intellectual coup d'etat in the academy [comparable to] the one the Chicago Boys helped pull off in Latin America."[10]

Apparently taken aback, but undeterred, defenders of the proposal wanly countered that, "The institute will pursue the best ideas in economics without preconception, wherever they may lead."[11] They were to timidly demur, however, from nominating a debating partner for Naomi Klein, who had been invited to speak on campus, by strategically savvy students, in the thick of the controversy. Confident and self-assured—after all, the season's events were validating central elements of her *Shock Doctrine* thesis—Klein argued that it was time to accept that the "model failed":

Ideas have consequences. And when you leave the safety of academia and start actually issuing policy prescriptions . . . when you start advising heads of state, you no longer have the luxury of only being judged on how you think your ideas will affect the world. You begin having to contend with how they actually affect the world, even when that reality contradicts all of your utopian theories [. . .] The Milton Friedman Institute, in its name and essence, is about trying to recapture a moment of ideological certainty that has long passed. It has long passed because reality has intervened.[12]

Reality intervened again when the fundraising effort for the new institute reportedly had to be suspended, a few months later, due to the effects of the financial crisis.[13] By the end of 2009, though, the Milton Friedman Institute was on a more stable footing—with Lars Peter Hansen, financial econometrician and former chair of the economics department, installed as its founding director. No longer, however, was the Chicago School riding downstream on the Hayekian wave. Although they had doggedly maintained their forward momentum, at least for now, the swirling currents had evidently become much more treacherous.

If the postwar Keynesian paradigm had been constructed on the basis of the preceding, long ascendancy of Fabian thinking, only to be undone by the stagflation crisis of the 1970s, then perhaps the neoliberal orthodoxy might now be confronting its own dénouement, in an appropriately globalizing crisis of deregulated capitalism? If so, surely the true believers in Chicago and at the Mont Pelerin gatherings would be amongst the last to see it coming, in light of their dogmatic attachment to neoliberal precepts, not so much as a paradigm, but as a regime of truth.[14] In New York City, at the dawn of the Obama era, the Mont Pelerinians seemed to be ventilating the same, alternating currents of hubris and paranoia that have characterized high-church neoliberalism for decades. The mood was captured by Antonio Martino, Italian conservative politician and former MPS president,[15] in his remarks at the meeting:

Is the golden age of the market coming to an end? Are we returning to the prevalence of mercantilism, State ownership of industry, central planning, price and income policies, confiscatory taxation, monetary instability and deficit spending? Maybe, but I can't help being optimistic. Throughout human history but especially so in the last thirty years economic liberty has provided ample and sure illustration of its superiority over any other kind of social arrangement. No one, except in Burma and at Harvard University, today believes that there are better alternatives to the free market. Only unadulterated folly can make humanity move in the wrong direction. The market, one of the greatest discoveries of the human race, is here to stay, despite the politicians' attempts to kill it.[16]

One thing had changed, at least, in comparison to the time when the upstart monetarists were taking on the Keynesian establishment back in the 1970s: at the nadir of the global economic crisis, in the winter of 2008–2009, it was the emeritus class of neoliberals who were now sounding like dinosaurs.

Evidently still inclined to see hobgoblins under all the beds, as Alvin Hansen had portrayed the Hayekian psyche in 1945,[17] the Mont Pelerinians' unforgiving purity tests clearly cannot accommodate the cabal of Harvard-affiliated economists in the Obama Administration, no matter how market-friendly they appear (to others) to be. The neoliberals' monochromatic worldview still seems barely capable of distinguishing between a third- or fourth-way variant of market rule and crypto-socialism. Ironically, the free-market project—or rather, some recalibration of the free-market project—may actually be rather safer in the hands of Lawrence Summers and his White House colleagues than in those of the fundamentalists at the MPS, who apparently still do not know where to draw the line, or when to stop.[18] Maybe the Mont Pelerinians have forgotten Hayek's injunction, that the new liberalism must, perforce, be a flexible credo,[19] but the same cannot be said of the new generation of *pragmacrats* that have been steering responses to the economic crisis in Washington, DC and in economics ministries around the world. If the emergent form of Obamanomics is any guide, the combination of political timidity, calculated compromise, and technocratic management will be more than enough to maintain *some kind* of market order.

Perhaps the global economic crisis does mean the end of the most hubristic and audacious forms of neoliberal policy advocacy, portending a future of more sober managerialism (along with slower, shakier phases of economic growth). But as Susan Watkins has argued in the *New Left Review*, this hardly means that the neoliberal paradigm itself has been transcended. Instead, a neoliberal makeover in the form of "regulatory liberalism" seems to have been accomplished.

With the exception of a few lone voices calling for a free-market clear-out, establishment convergence around what might be called regulatory liberalism seems all but complete. Proponents of other "varieties of capitalism" have been muted—perhaps because they are regulatory liberals, too. [...The] present unanimity is striking in contrast to earlier crises [prior to the neoliberal ascendancy], where diagnoses and prescriptions were contested from above and below. [...] Ideologically, regulatory liberalism would seem to reflect an inflection point of the neo-liberal paradigm rather than any rupture with it. [...] That neo-liberalism's crisis should be so eerily non-agonistic, in contrast to the bitter battles over its installation, is a sobering measure of its triumph.[20]

Neoliberalism's demonstrated capacity to rise phoenix-like even from crises of its own making suggests that it has acquired a kind of flexibility in practice that it may some time ago have lost in theory. Perhaps the stick is now being bent back in favor of Ordoliberal strategies—towards more orderly, restrained forms of market rule, and away from the buccaneering deregulation of the Chicago School—but this hardly marks a paradigm-busting adjustment. Rather, it would represent another instance of neoliberal adaptation in the face of crisis.

More consequential for the prospects of a counterhegemonic challenge to the still-morphing neoliberal order is the absence of a widely circulating and aggressively pushed alternative paradigm. While the long wave of neoliberalism has spawned a diverse array of contending social movements, these have yet to articulate a coherent and broadly shared economic philosophy—either in the shape of a utopian countervision, or as a workable political compromise. There have been lots of splashes, but few signs yet of a rising post-Hayekian tide. It is notable that the most concerted challenges to neoliberal economic policies, when the Wall Street crisis was biting hardest, took the form of a makeshift retro-Keynesianism, pushed not by social forces but by tenured members of the economic commentariat. Not long afterwards, with the crisis already being discussed in the past tense, the prospects even of some form of centrist, ameliorative liberalism, married with a social and environmental conscience, seem to be eroding. In the short term, the odds may be long ones for progressive opponents of neoliberalism, but if one further lesson can be taken from history, it is that what was *made*, in the form of the long-gestating project of neoliberalism, can surely be unmade as well as remade.

Recent reports of the death of neoliberalism, however, seem to have been exaggerated. The long American Century may now be drawing towards its disorderly close, but a new matrix of global economic interests is already taking shape, as Beijing, Brasilia, New Delhi, Moscow, and other ascendant capitals begin to reshape the neoliberal regime (a.k.a. regulatory liberalism) according to their own interests. Meanwhile, the battered centers of first-wave neoliberalization, London and Washington, are preparing for a new age of public austerity and economic insecurity. (Such are the fruits of three decades of "freedom.") An especially perverse outcome of the global economic crisis might therefore be the consolidation of a more broadly embedded, *multipolar* neoliberal order, coupled with historically receding scope for meaningful action against socioeconomic inequality and environmental degradation. In this context, neoliberalism appears to have achieved a sort of default status even (or perhaps especially) in moments of crisis. It is now the option favored by worldly pragmatists, certainly not the principled, "outsider" alternative it once was. Both the ideological fervor and the intellectual bite of neoliberalism seem to have been blunted, but "domesticated" versions of the project nevertheless live on. Which is more difficult to counter, one might ask—neoliberalism in its most vanguardist and outspoken form, or the house-trained, mealy-mouthed version?

For the left, the need to confront neoliberalism in its many mongrel, shape-shifting forms represents both a practical and an analytical challenge. One of the messages of this book is that it is necessary to recognize the free-market project's adaptive (and co-optive) capacities, rather than relying on cartoon-like versions of its supposedly invariant essence, or resorting to a left-critical version of hobgoblin-spotting. Like it or not, neoliberalism is in here, not just out there, and this calls for a careful parsing of the costs and consequences of (various forms of) market rule, in the context of a wide array of cohabitative arrangements. It also calls for grounded assessments, not blanket pronouncements. Labeling something, or someone, "neoliberal"—political swearword that it has become—cannot be the end of the conversation. *How* social formations and relations are neoliberalized, and with what path-forming consequences, really makes a difference. Differences are going to matter here too: not only does the neoliberalization process yield polymorphic, uneven outcomes, its contradictions and crises are differentiated too. Analytically, this underlines the importance of a process-based understanding of neoliberalism, as an evolving pattern of regulatory restructuring, associated with a flexible repertoire of policy rationales and practices; rather than a static, regime-like conception, once totalizing but now teetering. Maybe neoliberalism will not go out with a big bang after all—in the kind of cataclysmic crisis that dialectically calls forth (and validates) ideological alternatives. Maybe it will peter out, exhausted, or find itself gradually—progressively?—transcended by various forms of post-neoliberal practice.[21] However it works out, we know that any successor to neoliberalism will have to be generated from the terrain that the market revolution has imperfectly shaped.

Even if neoliberalism is apparently all over the place, it cannot ever be all that there is—for market rule cannot survive on its own. Forced to dwell amongst its others, neoliberalism must always contend with counter-neoliberal alternatives, right in its own backyard. These contrary currents cannot simply be assessed according to whether they are "statist" or not—perhaps the laziest definition of "non-neoliberal," and one that fails to recognize that, in practice, neoliberals too are statists (just different *kinds* of statists). These alternatives should be assessed both in their own terms, and also according to how they articulate anti-neoliberal principles and interests, for example, in their preference for long-term sustainability over short-term gains; in their commitment to progressive (social and spatial) redistribution; in their utilization of socializing, rather than competitively individualizing, strategies; in their capacity for enabling new collectivities and common interests; and in their potential for *challenging and transforming*, rather than deferring and conforming to, markets and market forces. Meaningful alternatives to neoliberalism will have to be forged politically, of course, possibly on the anvil of crisis itself, but they will have to be pushed both by social *and* intellectual movements. Ideas will continue to have consequences, on all sides of the multifaceted struggle against what has become a polymorphically-resilient neoliberalism.

Striking as it did at the heart of twentieth century neoliberalism, the last Wall Street crash was sufficiently profound to have unnerved the Mont Pelerinians, just as it interrupted the Chicago School's plans for another round of self-congratulation. Unlike the Asian financial crisis a decade earlier, the politics of this "heartland" event could not be managed by parables of far-off varieties of "crony capitalism"—despite the ironic resonance of corruption narratives amid the craven behavior of the New York banks. In contrast to the crisis on the Gulf Coast, it has been rather more difficult to pin this one on its victims, though not for want of trying. If the most recent financial crisis is ultimately "localized" too—as a crisis of the Wall Street model, rather than a crisis of *and for* neoliberalism—then this could be a prelude to further rounds of distinctively twenty-first century neoliberalization. For now, we seem to be confronted with a rerun of a familiar story: ever crisis-prone, neoliberalism loses another of its nine lives, but again manages to fail-and-flail *forward*. As the world emerges shakily from the Great Recession, neoliberalism has not so much been replaced as repaired. Maybe the next crisis will be different?

The conceit that the social world can be predicted is one perhaps best left to the Chicagoans. We cannot tell, in advance, which crises might be terminal, or how some sequence of conjunctural crises might cumulatively "pile up." But if the specificities of the next crisis cannot be predicted, they can at least be prepared for. This said, something that surely *is* known is that, even if individual crises can be contained, neoliberalism's systemic proneness to crisis surely cannot. Bubbles will continue to burst and mal-regulated markets will continue to fail, while more slowly metabolizing crisis tendencies originating from social and environmental exploitation will also inevitably take their toll. How far variants of neoliberal, Ordoliberal, regulatory-liberal governance will be able to adapt in the face of such pressures remains, at this point, an open question. But adapt they no doubt will. That is, until they encounter the kinds of immovable objects and countervailing forces that cannot be accommodated, or socioecological limits that can no longer be contained. Either way, it promises to be a bumpy ride.

Notes

1. With all due respect Mr. President, that is not true, Cato Institute petition, accessed at <http://www.cato.org/special/stimulus09>.
2. Lal (2009) The Mont Pelerin Society: a mandate renewed, Paper presented at the special meeting of the Mont Pelerin Society, New York City, March 5–7, 2009: 6, 2, accessed at <http://www.montpelerin.org/nyc2k9.cfm>.
3. See Hartwell (1995). Interestingly, both moves to wind up the Society occurred under Chicago School leadership—first with Friedman and then with Becker.
4. See Lal, D. (2009) A Hayekian recession with Fisherian consequences, *Business Standard*, March 31: 9.
5. Gary Becker, quoted in O'Grady, M. A. (2009) Now's not the time to give up on markets, *Wall Street Journal*, March 21: A9.
6. Becker, G. S. (2008) The free market's trial by fire, Becker-Posner blog, October 19, circulated at the Mont Pelerin Society meeting, New York City, March 5–7, 2009, accessed at <http://www.montpelerin.org/nyc2k9.cfm>.
7. See Friedman and Friedman (1988); Hartwell (1995: 195).
8. Quoted in Cohen, P. (2008) On Chicago campus, Milton Friedman's legacy of controversy continues, *New York Times*, 12 July: A9.
9. Quoted in Goldstein, E. R. (2008) Milton Friedman's controversial legacy, *Chronicle of Higher Education*, August 1: B4.
10. Sahlins, M. (2008) Institute will give the U. of Chicago a bad name, *Chronicle of Higher Education*, August 18 (online edition), accessed at <http://www.chronicle.com>.
11. Hansen, J. M., Reny, P. J., Rosenbaum, T. F., Snyder, E. A. (2008) A new economics institute at the U. of Chicago, *Chronicle of Higher Education*, September 19: A36.
12. Naomi Klein, quoted in MacFarquar, L. (2008) Outside agitator, *New Yorker*, December 8: 61–71; and speech at the University of Chicago, October 1, 2008, accessed at <http://www.democracynow.org/2008/10/6/naomi_klein>.

13. Siddiqui, H. (2009) Canada's star left-winger, *Toronto Star*, February 15: A19.

14. Compare the incisive discussion of the crisis in the Keynesian paradigm in Hall (1993).

15. Martino, a professional economist, was a founder member of the Forza Italia party and a two-time member of Silvio Berlusconi's cabinet. He served as MPS president between 1988 and 1990.

16. Martino, A. (2009) Thirty years of economic freedom: has the free market's Golden Age come to an end? Paper presented at the special meeting of the Mont Pelerin Society, New York City, March 5–7, accessed at <http://www.montpelerin.org/nyc2k9.cfm>.

17. Hansen (1945).

18. Keynes [1944], quoted in Skidelsky (2005: 723).

19. Hayek (1944: 17).

20. Watkins (2010: 13, 20).

21. See Ferguson, J. (2010) The uses of neoliberalism. In N. Castree, P. Chatterton, N. Heynen, W. Larner, and M. W. Wright, eds., *The Point is to Change It*. Oxford: Wiley-Blackwell, 166–184; Peck *et al.* (2010).

Bibliography

Note on the arrangement of references in the bibliography and endnotes

In order to keep the bibliography to a manageable size, not all the references cited in the endnotes appear here. Bibliographical details are provided below for more substantial sources and those to which frequent reference is made. More specific citations, web site and press material, and ephemera are detailed only in the endnotes for each chapter.

All URLs to which reference is made here are correct as of June 2010.

Albert, M. (1993) *Capitalism against Capitalism*. London: Whurr.

Anderson, M. (1987) *The Power of Ideas and the Making of Economic Policy*. Palo Alto, CA: Hoover Institution.

——(1988) *Revolution*. New York: Harcourt Brace Jovanovich.

Ash, M., Balakrishnan, R., Campbell, A., Crotty, J., Dickens, E., Epstein, G., Ferguson, T., Ghilarducci, T., Greisgraber, J-M., Griffith-Jones, S., Guttmann, R., Jayadev, A., Kapadia, A., Kotz, D., Meerepol, M., Milberg, W., Moseley, F., Ocampo, J. A., Pollin, R., Sawyer, M., and Wolfson, M. (2009) *A Progressive Program for Economic Recovery and Financial Reconstruction*. New York and Amherst: Schwartz Center for Economic Policy Analysis and Political Economy Research Institute.

Auerbach, N. N. (2007) The meanings of neoliberalism. In R. K. Roy, A. T. Denzau, and T. D. Willett, eds., *Neoliberalism*. Oxford: Routledge, 26–50.

Barone, M. (2004) The urban renaissance. In B. C. Anderson, ed., *Turning Intellect into Influence*. New York: Reed Press, 47–56.

Bark, D. L. and Gress, D. R. (1989) *A History of West Germany*, volume 1. Oxford: Blackwell.

Barro, R. J. (1995) *Getting it Right*. Cambridge, MA: MIT Press.

Barry, N. P. (1989) Political and economic thought of German neo-liberals. In A. Peacock and H. Willgerodt, eds., *German Neo-liberals and the Social Market Economy*. London: Macmillan, 105–124.

Bartley, R. L. and Shlaes, A. (2004) The supply-side revolution. In B. C. Anderson, ed., *Turning Intellect into Influence*. New York: Reed Press, 29–46.

Becker, G. S. (1991) Milton Friedman. In E. Shils, ed., *Remembering the University of Chicago*. Chicago: University of Chicago Press, 138–146.

Berger, S. (1992) Reconstructing New York, *City Journal*, 2/1: 54–60.

Blumenthal, S. (1988) *The Rise of the Counter-Establishment*. New York: Harper and Row.

Blyth, M. (2002) *Great Transformations*. Cambridge: Cambridge University Press.

Boas, T. C. and Gans-Morse, J. (2009) Neoliberalism: from new liberal philosophy to anti-liberal slogan, *Studies in Comparative International Development*, 44/2: 137–161.

Bockman, J. and Eyal, G. (2002) Eastern Europe as a laboratory for economic knowledge: the transnational roots of neo-liberalism, *American Journal of Sociology*, 108/3: 310–352.

Bourdieu, P. (1998) *Acts of Resistance*. New York: New Press.

Bourdieu, P. and Wacquant, L. (2001) NewLiberalSpeak: notes on the new planetary vulgate, *Radical Philosophy*, 105: 2–5.

Breit, W. (1990) Galbraith and Friedman: two versions of economic reality, in J. C. Wood and R. N. Woods, eds., *Milton Friedman*, volume 4. London: Routledge, 1–11.

Breit, W. and Ransom, R. L. (1998), *The Academic Scribblers*. 3rd edition. Princeton, NJ: Princeton University Press.

Brenner, N. (2004) *New State Spaces*. Oxford: Oxford University Press.

Brenner, N. and Theodore, N. (2002a) Cities and the geographies of "actually existing neoliberalism." In N. Brenner and N. Theodore, eds., *Spaces of Neoliberalism*. Oxford: Blackwell, 2–32.

——, eds. (2002b) *Spaces of Neoliberalism*. Oxford: Blackwell.

Brenner, N., Peck, J., and Theodore, N. (2010) Variegated neoliberalization: geographies, modalities, pathways, *Global Networks*, 10/2: 1–41.

Bronfenbrenner, M. (1962) Observations on the "Chicago School(s)," *Journal of Political Economy*, 70/1: 72–75.

Brustein, J. (2003) Think tanks. *Gotham Gazette*, March 29, accessed at <http://www.gothamgazette.com>.

Butler, S. M., Carafano, J. J., Fraser, A. A., Lips, D., Moffit, R. M., and Utt, R. D. (2005) How to turn the President's Gulf Coast pledge into reality, *Web Memo*, No. 848, Heritage Foundation, Washington, DC.

Caldwell, B. (2004) *Hayek's Challenge*. Chicago: University of Chicago Press.

Cassidy, J. (2009) *How Markets Fail*. New York: Penguin.

Cerny, P. G. (2008) Embedding neoliberalism: the evolution of a hegemonic paradigm, *Journal of International Trade and Diplomacy*, 2/1: 1–46.

Cerny, P. G. (2009) Neoliberalisation and place: deconstructing and reconstructing borders. In B. Arts, A. Lagendijk, and H. van Houtum, eds., *The Disoriented State*. Dordrecht: Springer, 13–39.

Clarke, J. (2008) Living with/in and without neo-liberalism, *Focaal*, 51/Summer: 135–147.

Coats, A. W. (1960) The politics of political economists: comment, *Quarterly Journal of Economics*, 74/4: 666–669.

——(1963) The origins of the "Chicago School(s)"? *Journal of Political Economy*, 71 (5): 487–493.

Cockett, R. (1995) *Thinking the Unthinkable*. London: Fontana Press.

Christ, C. F. (1994) The Cowles Commission's contributions to econometrics at Chicago, 1939–1955, *Journal of Economic Literature*, 32/1: 30–59.

Davenport, J. (1946) The testament of Henry Simons, *Fortune*, 34/3: 116–119.

de Long, J. B. (1990) In defense of Henry Simons' standing as a classical liberal, *Cato Journal*, 9/3: 601–618.

Denord, F. (2009) French neoliberalism and its divisions: from the Colloque Walter Lippman to the Fifth Republic. In P. Mirowski and D. Plehwe, eds. *The Road from Mont Pèlerin*. Cambridge, MA: Harvard University Press, 45–67.

Desai, R. (1994) Second-hand dealers in ideas: think tanks and Thatcherite hegemony, *New Left Review*, 203: 27–64.

Dezalay, Y. and Garth, B. G. (2002) *The Internationalization of Palace Wars*. Chicago: University of Chicago Press.

Doherty, B. (1995) Best of both worlds, *Reason*, 27/2: 32–38.

Doussard, M., Peck, J., and Theodore, N. (2009) After deindustrialization: uneven growth and economic inequality in "postindustrial" Chicago, *Economic Geography*, 85/2: 183–207.

Douthat, R. and Salam, R. (2009) *Grand New Party*. New York: Anchor Books.

Ebenstein, A. (2003a) *Friedrich Hayek*. Chicago: University of Chicago Press.

——(2003b) *Hayek's Journey*. London: Palgrave Macmillan.

——(2007) *Milton Friedman*. New York: Palgrave.

Edwards, L. (1997) *The Power of Ideas*. Ottawa, IL: Jameson Books.

Epstein, G. (2009) Obama's economic policy: achievements, problems and prospects, *Revue de la Régulation*, 5/1: 2–14.

Eucken, W. (1950) *The Foundations of Economics*. London: William Hodge.

Feulner, E. J. (1999) *Intellectual Pilgrims*. Washington, DC: Edward J. Feulner.

Florida, R. (2002) *The Rise of the Creative Class*. New York: Basic Books.

——(2005a) *Cities and the Creative Class*. New York: Routledge.

——(2005b) *The Flight of the Creative Class*. New York: HarperBusiness.

Foer, F. and Scheiber, N. (2009) Nudge-ocracy, *The New Republic*, May 6: 22–25.

Foster, J. B. and Magdoff, F. (2009) *The Great Financial Crisis*. New York: Monthly Review Press.

Foucault, M. (1997) The birth of biopolitics. In P. Rabinow, ed., *Ethics*. New York: New Press, 73–79.

——(2008) *The Birth of Biopolitics: Lectures at the College de France, 1978–79*. Basingstoke: Palgrave.

Fourcade-Gourinchas, M. and Babb, S. L. (2002) The rebirth of the liberal creed: paths to neoliberalism in four countries, *American Journal of Sociology*, 108/3: 533–579.

Frank, T. (2000) *One Market Under God*. New York: Doubleday.

Frazer, W. (1988) *Power and Ideas*, volume 1. Ocala, FL: Gulf/Atlantic Publishing.

Friedman, M. (1951) Nyliberalismen Og Dens Muligheter [Neoliberalism and its prospects], *Farmand*, February 17: 89–93.

——(1953) *Essays in Positive Economics*. Chicago: University of Chicago Press.

——(1962) *Capitalism and Freedom*. Chicago: University of Chicago.

——(1967) The monetary theory and policy of Henry Simons, *Journal of Law and Economics*, 10: 1–13.

——(1974) Schools at Chicago. *University of Chicago Magazine*, Autumn: 11–16.

——(1980) *Free to Chose*. New York: Harcourt Brace Jovanovich.

——(1982) *Capitalism and Freedom*. Chicago: University of Chicago.

——(1983) *Bright Promises, Dismal Performance*. New York: Harcourt Brace Jovanovich.

——(2004) Milton Friedman. In W. Breit and B. T. Hirsch, eds., *Lives of the Laureates*. Cambridge, MA: MIT Press, 65–78.

Friedman, M. and Friedman, R. D. (1984) *Tyranny of the Status Quo*. New York, Harcourt Brace Jovanovich.

——(1988) The tide in the affairs of men. In A. Anderson and D. L. Bark, eds., *Thinking about America*. Stanford, CA: Hoover Institution Press, 455–468.

——(1998) *Two Lucky People*. Chicago: Chicago University Press.

Frost, G. (2002) *Antony Fisher*. London: Profile.

Galbraith, J. K. (1987) *Economics in Perspective*. Boston: Houghton Mifflin.

Gamble, A. (1994) *The Free Economy and the Strong State*. Basingstoke: Palgrave.

——(1996) *Hayek: The Iron Cage of Liberty*. Cambridge: Polity.

——(2006) Two faces of neo-liberalism. In R. Robison, ed., *The Neo-Liberal Revolution*. Basingstoke: Palgrave, 20–35.

Gelinas, N. (2005) Who's killing New Orleans? *City Journal*, 15/4: 14–27.

Gill, S. (1995) Globalisation, market civilisation and disciplinary neoliberalism, *Millennium*, 24/3: 399–423.

Goldman, M. (2005) *Imperial Nature*. New Haven, CT: Yale University Press.

Gotham, K. F. and Greenberg, M. (2008) From 9/11 to 8/29: post-disaster recovery and rebuilding in New York and New Orleans, *Social Forces*, 87/2: 1039–1062.

Graefe, P. (2006) Social economy policies as flanking for neoliberalism: transnational policy solutions, emergent contradictions, local alternatives, *Policy and Society*, 23/3: 69–86.

Graetz, M. J. and Shapiro, I. (2005) *Death by a Thousand Cuts*. Princeton, NJ: Princeton University Press.

Gramsci, A. (1971) *Selections from the Prison Notebooks*. New York: International Publishers.

Gray, J. (1998) *Hayek on Liberty*. 3rd edition. London: Routledge.

Greider, W. (1989) *Secrets of the Temple*. New York: Simon and Schuster.

Hall, P. A. (1989) Conclusion: the politics of Keynesian ideas. In P. A. Hall, ed., *The Political Power of Economic Ideas*. Princeton: Princeton University Press, 361–391.

——(1993) Policy paradigms, social learning, and the state: the case of economic policymaking in Britain, *Comparative Politics*, 25/3: 275–296.

Hall, P. A. and Soskice, D., eds. (2001) *Varieties of Capitalism*. Oxford: Oxford University Press.

Hall, S. (1988) *The Hard Road to Renewal*. London: Verso.

——(2003) New Labour's double-shuffle, *Soundings*, 24: 10–24.

Hammond, J. D. (1999) *The Legacy of Milton Friedman as Teacher*. Northampton, MA: Edward Elgar.

Hansen, A. (1945) The new crusade against planning, *New Republic*, January 1: 9–12.

Hartwell, R. M. (1995) *A History of the Mont Pelerin Society*. Indianapolis: Liberty Fund.

Harvey, D. (1989) From managerialism to entrepreneurialism: the transformation in urban governance in late capitalism, *Geografiska Annaler B*, 71(1): 13–17.

——(2005) *A Brief History of Neoliberalism*. Oxford: Oxford University Press.

Hay, C. (2001) The "crisis" of Keynesianism and the rise of neoliberalism in Britain: an ideational institutionalist approach. In J. L. Campbell and O. Pedersen, eds., *The Rise of Neoliberalism and Institutional Analysis*. Princeton: Princeton University Press, 193–218.

——(2004) The normalizing role of rationalist assumptions in the institutional embedding of neoliberalism, *Economy and Society*, 33/4: 500–527.

Hayek, F. A. (1944) *The Road to Serfdom*. Chicago: University of Chicago Press.

——(1949) The intellectuals and socialism, *University of Chicago Law Review*, 16/3: 417–433.

——(1960) *The Constitution of Liberty*. Chicago: University of Chicago Press.

——(1967) *Studies in Philosophy, Politics and Economics*. Chicago: University of Chicago Press.

——(1992 [1947]) Opening address to a conference at Mont Pelerin. In P. G. Klein, ed., *The Collected Works of F. A. Hayek*, volume iv. Chicago: University of Chicago Press, 237–248.

——(1994) Chicago–Freiburg. In S. Kresge and L. Wenar, eds., *Hayek on Hayek*. Chicago: University of Chicago Press, 125–155.

Jayasuriya, K. (2006) *Statecraft, Welfare and the Politics of Inclusion*. Basingstoke: Palgrave.

Jessop, B. (2000) The crisis of the national spatio-temporal fix and the ecological dominance of globalizing capitalism, *International Journal of Urban and Regional Research*, 24/2: 323–360.

——(2003) *The Future of the Capitalist State*. Cambridge: Polity.

Jessop, B., Bonnett, K., Bromley, S., and Ling, T. (1988) *Thatcherism*. Cambridge: Polity.

Johnson, D. (1989) Exiles and half-exiles: Wilhelm Röpke, Alexander Rüstow and Walter Eucken. In A. Peacock and H. Willgerodt, eds., *German Neo-liberals and the Social Market Economy*. London: Macmillan, 40–68.

Johnson, H. G. (1971) The Keynesian revolution and the monetarist counter-revolution, *American Economic Review*, 61/2: 91–106.

——(1977) Cambridge as an academic environment in the early 1930s: a reconstruction from the late 1940s. In D. Patinkin and J. C. Leith, eds., *Keynes, Cambridge and the General Theory*, London: Macmillan, 98–114.

Kitch, E. W. (1983) The fire of truth: a remembrance of law and economics at Chicago, 1932–1970, *Journal of Law and Economics*, 26/1: 163–234.

Klein, N. (2007) *Shock Doctrine*. New York: Metropolitan Books.

Kogut, B. and Macpherson, J. M. (2008) The decision to privatize: economists and the construction of ideas and policies. In B. A. Simmons, F. Dobbin, and G. Garrett, eds., *The Global Diffusion of Markets and Democracy*. New York: Cambridge University Press, 104–140.

Kotkin, J. and Siegel, F. (2004) Too much froth, *Blueprint*, 6: 16–18.

Kuttner, B. (2008) *Obama's Challenge*. White River Junction, VT: Chelsea Green.

Lakoff, G. (2002). *Moral Politics: How Liberals and Conservatives Think*. Chicago: University of Chicago Press.

Larner, W. (2003) Neoliberalism? *Environment and Planning D*, 21/5: 509–512.

Leeson, R. (2000) *The Eclipse of Keynesianism*. Basingstoke: Palgrave.

Lehmbruch, G. (2001) The institutional embedding of market economies: the German "model" and its impact on Japan. In W. Streeck and K. Yamamura, eds., *The Origins of Nonliberal Capitalism*. Ithaca, NY: Cornell University Press, 83–84.

Leitner, H., Peck, J., and Sheppard, E. (2007) Squaring up to neoliberalism. In H. Leitner, J. Peck, and E. S. Sheppard, eds., *Contesting Neoliberalism*. New York: Guilford, 311–327.

Lemke, T. (2001) The birth of bio-politics: Michel Foucault's lecture at the College de France on neo-liberal governmentality, *Economy and Society*, 30/2: 190–207.

Leonhardt, D. (2008) A free-market-loving, big-spending, fiscally conservative wealth redistributionist, *New York Times Magazine*, August 24: 29–54.

——(2009) After the great recession, *New York Times Magazine*, May 3: 36–87.

Lizza, R. (2009) Inside the crisis, *New Yorker*, October 12: 80–95.

London, S. (2003) Milton Friedman: the long view, *Financial Times Weekend Magazine*, June 7: 12.

Magnet, M. (2001) Solving President Bush's urban problem, *City Journal*, 11/1: 14–22.

Malabre, A. L. (1994) *Lost Prophets*. Boston: Harvard Business School Press.

Malanga, S. (2004) The curse of the creative class, *City Journal*, 14/1: 36–45.

Maliszewski, P. (2004) Flexibility and its discontents, *The Baffler*, 16: 69–79.

McCloskey, D. N. (2003) Milton, *Eastern Economic Review*, 29/1: 143–146.

McMahon, E. J. and Siegel, F. (2005) Gotham's fiscal crisis: lessons unlearned, *Public Interest*, 158: 96–110.

Meese, E., Butler, S. M., and Holmes, K. R. (2005) *From Tragedy to Triumph*. Special Report, No. 05. Washington, DC: Heritage Foundation.

Micklethwait, J. and Wooldridge, A. (2004) *The Right Nation*. London: Penguin.

Miller, H. L. (1962) On the "Chicago School of Economics," *Journal of Political Economy*, 70/1: 64–69.

Mirowski, P. (2002) *Machine Dreams*. Cambridge: Cambridge University Press.

——(2009) Postface: defining neoliberalism. In P. Mirowski and D. Plehwe, eds., *The Road from Mont Pèlerin*. Cambridge, MA: Harvard University Press, 417–456.

Mirowski, P. and Plehwe, D., eds. (2009) *The Road from Mont Pèlerin*. Cambridge, MA: Harvard University Press.

Mises, L. (1978) *Ludwig von Mises, Notes and Recollections*. South Holland, IL: Libertarian Press

Moody, K. (2007) *From Welfare State to Real Estate*. New York: New Press.

Morgan, M. S. and Rutherford, M. (1998) American economics: the character of transformation. In M. S. Morgan and M. Rutherford, eds., *From Interwar Pluralism to Postwar Neoclassicism*. Durham, NC: Duke University Press, 1–26.

Mudge, S. L. (2008) What is neoliberalism? *Socio-Economic Review*, 6/4: 703–731.

Müller-Armack, A. (1965) The principles of the social market economy, *German Economic Review*, 3/2: 89–104.

Murray, C. (1984) *Losing Ground*. New York: Basic Books.

Naím, M. (2000) Washington consensus or Washington confusion? *Foreign Policy*, 118: 87–103.

Nelson, R. H. (2001) *Economics as Religion*. University Park, PA: Pennsylvania State University Press.

Neumayr, G. (2005) The desolate city, *American Spectator*, November: 48–50.

Nicholls, A. J. (1994) *Freedom with Responsibility*. Oxford: Clarendon Press.

Obama, B. (2006) *The Audacity of Hope*. New York: Crown.

O'Connor, A. (2008) The privatized city: the Manhattan Institute, the urban crisis, and the conservative counterrevolution in New York, *Journal of Urban History*, 34/2: 333–353.

Oliver, H. M. (1960) German neoliberalism, *Quarterly Journal of Economics*, 74/1: 117–149.

Ong, A. (2006) *Neoliberalism as Exception*. Durham, NC: Duke University Press.

——(2007) Neoliberalism as a mobile technology, *Transactions of the Institute of British Geographers*, 32/1: 3–8.

Peacock, A. and Willgerodt, H. (1989) Overall view of the German liberal movement. In A. Peacock and H. Willgerodt, eds., *German Neo-liberals and the Social Market Economy*. London: Macmillan, 1–15.

Peck, J. (2001) *Workfare States*. New York: Guilford.

——(2002a) Labor, zapped/growth, restored? Three moments of neoliberal restructuring in the American labor market, *Journal of Economic Geography* 2/2: 179–220.

——(2002b) Political economies of scale: fast policy, interscalar relations, and neoliberal workfare, *Economic Geography*, 78/3: 331–360.

——(2004) Geography and public policy: constructions of neoliberalism, *Progress in Human Geography*, 28/3: 392–405.

——(2005) Economic sociologies in space, *Economic Geography*, 81/2: 129–176.

——(2009) The cult of urban creativity. In R. Keil and R. Mahon, eds., *Leviathan Undone*. Vancouver: University of British Columbia Press: 159–176.

——(2010) Zombie neoliberalism and the ambidextrous state, *Theoretical Criminology*, 14/1: 1–7.

——(2011) Creative moments: working culture . . . between municipal socialism and neoliberal urbanism. In E. McCann and K. Ward, eds., *Mobile Urbanism: Cities and Policymaking in the Global Age*. Minneapolis: University of Minnesota Press, in press.

Peck, J. and Theodore, N. (2000) Beyond "employability," *Cambridge Journal of Economics*, 24/6: 729–750.

——(2007) Variegated capitalism, *Progress in Human Geography*, 31/6: 731–772.

——(2010) Mobilizing policy: models, methods, and mutations. *Geoforum*, 41/2: 169–174.

Peck, J., Theodore, N., and Brenner, N. (2009) Neoliberal urbanism: models, moments, and mutations, *SAIS Review of International Affairs*, 29/1: 49–66.

——(2010) Postneoliberalism and its malcontents. In N. Castree, P. Chatterton, N. Heynem, W. Larner, and M. W. Wright, eds., *The Point is to Change It*. Oxford Wiley-Blackwell, 94–116.

Peck, J. and Tickell, A. (1994a) Jungle law breaks out: neoliberalism and global-local disorder, *Area*, 26/4: 317–326.

——(1994b) Searching for a new institutional fix: the *after* Fordist crisis and global-local disorder. In A. Amin, ed., *Post-Fordism*. Oxford: Blackwell, 280–316.

——(2002) Neoliberalizing space, *Antipode*, 34/3: 380–404.

——(2007) Conceptualizing neoliberalism, thinking Thatcherism. In H. Leitner, J. Peck, and E. S. Sheppard, eds., *Contesting Neoliberalism*. New York: Guilford, 26–50.

Playboy (1973) Playboy interview: Milton Friedman, *Playboy*, February: 51–68, 74.

Plehwe, D. (2009) Introduction. In P. Mirowski and D. Plehwe, eds. *The Road from Mont Pèlerin*. Cambridge, MA: Harvard University Press, 1–42.

Polanyi, K. (1944) *The Great Transformation*. Boston: Beacon.

Pollin, R. (2003) *Contours of Descent*. New York: Verso.

Prasad, M. (2005) *The Politics of Free Markets*. Chicago: University of Chicago Press.

Prashad, V. (2003) *Keeping Up with the Dow Joneses*. Cambridge, MA: South End Press.

Ptak, R. (2009) Neoliberalism in Germany: revisiting the Ordoliberal foundations of the social market economy. In P. Mirowski and D. Plehwe, eds., *The Road from Mont Pèlerin*. Cambridge, MA: Harvard University Press, 98–138.

Reder, M. W. (1982) Chicago economics: permanence and change, *Journal of Economic Literature*, 20/1: 1–38.

——(1987) Chicago School. In J. Eatwell, M. Milgate, and P. Newman, eds., *The New Palgrave*, volume 1. London: Macmillan, 413–418.

Reich, R. (1997) *Locked in the Cabinet*. New York: Alfred A. Knopf.

Röpke, W. (1969 [1931]) The intellectuals and "capitalism." In W. Röpke, *Against the Tide*. Chicago: Henry Regnery.

Rothbard, M. N. (1980) *The Essential von Mises*. Grove City, PA: Libertarian Press.

Sennholz, H. F. (1978) Postscript. In L. von Mises, *Ludwig von Mises, Notes and Recollections*. South Holland, IL: Libertarian Press.

Sheppard, E. (2005) Constructing free trade: from Manchester boosterism to global management, *Transactions of the Institute of British Geographers*, 30/2: 151–172.

Shils, E. (1991) Foreword. In E. Shils, ed., *Remembering the University of Chicago*. Chicago: University of Chicago Press, ix–xxi.

Silk, L. (1976) *The Economists*. New York: Basic Books.

Silva, P. (2006) The politics of neo-liberalism in Latin America: legitimacy, depoliticization and technocratic rule in Chile. In R. Robison, ed., *The Neo-Liberal Revolution*. Basingstoke: Palgrave, 39–57.

Silver, B. J. and Arrighi, G. (2003) Polanyi's "double movement": the belle époques of British and U.S. hegemony compared, *Politics and Society*, 31/2: 325–355.

Simons, H. C. (1934) *A Positive Program for Laissez Faire*, Public Policy Pamphlet No. 15. Chicago: University of Chicago.

Sites, W. (2003) *Remaking New York*. Minneapolis: University of Minnesota Press.

Skidelsky, R. (2005) *John Maynard Keynes, 1883–1946*. New York: Penguin.

Smith, N. (2002) New globalism, new urbanism: gentrification as global urban strategy, *Antipode*, 34/3: 434–457.

Sobel, R. (1980) *The Worldly Economists*. New York: Free Press.

Stigler, G. J. (1959) The politics of political economists, *Quarterly Journal of Economics*, 73/4: 522–532.

——(1962a) Comment, *Journal of Political Economy*, 70/1: 70–71.

——(1962b) The intellectual and the market place, *New Individualist Review*, 2/3: 3–9.

——(1969) Does economics have a useful past? *History of Political Economy*, 1/2: 217–230.

——(1975) The intellectual and his society. In R. Selden, ed., *Capitalism and Freedom*. Charlottesville, VA: University Press of Virginia, 311–321.

——(1982) *The Economist as Preacher, and Other Essays*. Chicago: University of Chicago Press.

——(1988) *Memoirs of an Unregulated Economist*. New York: Basic Books.

Stiglitz, J. (2010) *Freefall*. New York: W. W. Norton.

Talbott, J. R. (2008) *Obamanomics*. New York: Seven Stories.

Tickell, A. and Peck, J. (2003) Making global rules: globalization or neoliberalization? In J. Peck and H. Yeung, eds., *Remaking the Global Economy*. London: Sage, 163–181.

Tribe, K. (1995) *Strategies of Economic Order*. Cambridge: Cambridge University Press.

Turner, R. S. (2009) *Neo-Liberal Ideology*. Edinburgh: Edinburgh University Press.

Valdés, J. G. (1995) *Pinochet's Economists*. Cambridge: Cambridge University Press.

Van Horn, R. (2008) Reinventing monopoly and the role of corporations: the roots of Chicago Law and Economics. In P. Mirowski and D. Plehwe, eds., *The Road from Mont Pèlerin*. Cambridge, MA: Harvard University Press, 204–237.

Van Horn, R. and Mirowski, P. (2009) The rise of the Chicago School of Economics and the birth of neoliberalism. In P. Mirowski and D. Plehwe, eds., *The Road from Mont Pèlerin*. Cambridge, MA: Harvard University Press, 139–178.

Van Overtveldt, J. (2007) *The Chicago School*. Chicago: Agate.

Wacquant, L. J. D. (1999) How penal common sense comes to Europeans: notes on the transatlantic diffusion of the neoliberal *doxa, European Societies*, 1/3: 319–352.

——(2009) *Punishing the Poor*. Durham, NC: Duke University Press.

Walters, A. (1987) Milton Friedman. In J. Eatwell, M. Milgate, and P. Newman, eds., *The New Palgrave*, volume 2. London: Macmillan, 422–427.

Warsh, D. (1993) *Economic Principals*. New York: Free Press.

Watkins, S. (2010) Shifting sands, *New Left Review*, 61: 5–27.

Williamson, J. (2003) Our agenda and the Washington Consensus. In P-P. Kuczynski and J. Williamson, eds., *After the Washington Consensus*. Washington, DC: Institute for International Economics, 323–331.

Yergin, D. and Stanislaw, J. (2002) *The Commanding Heights*. New York: Touchstone.

Žižek, S. (2009) *First As Tragedy, Then As Farce*. London: Verso.

Index

Index

Index